I0031748

Center for Basque Studies
Basque Politics Series, No. 5

Expelled from the Motherland

The Government of President Jose Antonio Agirre in Exile, 1937–1960

by Xabier Irujo

Translated by

Cameron J. Watson and Jennifer Ottman

Basque Politics Series, No. 5

Center for Basque Studies
University of Nevada, Reno
Reno, Nevada

This book was published with generous financial support from the Basque government.

The book has also been financed by a Faculty Summer Research Grant stipend to assist with the author's research project "The Basque Government in Exile (1937–1960)"

Center for Basque Studies
Basque Politics Series, No. 5
Series Editor: Xabier Irujo

Center for Basque Studies
University of Nevada, Reno
Reno, Nevada 89557
http://basque.unr.edu

Library of Congress Cataloging-in-Publication Data

Irujo Ametzaga, Xabier.
Expelled from the motherland : the government of president Jose Antonio Agirre in exile, 1937-1960 / by Xabier Irujo ; translated by Cameron Watson and Jennifer Ottman.
p. cm. -- (Basque politics series ; no. 5)
Includes bibliographical references.
Summary: "Draws on archival and documentary evidence to describe the presidency and exile of Basque president Jose Antonio Agirre, who led the Basque government-in-exile following the Spanish Civil War"--Provided by publisher.
ISBN 978-1-935709-25-1 (hardcover) -- ISBN 978-1-935709-20-6 (pbk.)
1. País Vasco (Spain)--History--Autonomy and independence movements. 2. País Vasco (Spain)--Politics and government--History--20th century. 3. Spain--History--Civil War, 1936-1939--Governments in exile. 4. Aguirre y Lecube, José Antonio de, 1904-1960--Exile. 5. Nationalism--Spain--País Vasco--History. 6. Presidents--Spain--País Vasco. 7. Political refugees--Spain. I. Title.

DP302.B53I695 2012
946'.60824--dc23

2011049735

CONTENTS

I have led you forty years in the wilderness.
Your clothes have not worn out on you, and your sandals have not worn off your feet.

—Deuteronomy 29:5

Euskal herrietatik euskal herrietara gure seme alabek Euskal Herrian bizi ahal izateko berrogei urteko bidaia burutu zuten gure arbasoei

(To our ancestors who underwent a trip of forty years
from the Basque Country to the Basque Country
so our children and their grandchildren can live again in peace in our land)

List of Abbreviations

AA/AN FSAE	Abertzaletasunaren Agiria/Archivo del nacionalismo vasco de la Fundación Sabino Arana (Sabino Arana Foundation Archive of Basque Nationalism)
ACR	Acció Catalana Republicana (Catalan Republican Action)
AEF	Action Européenne Fédéraliste (European Federalist Action)
ANFD	Alianza Nacional de Fuerzas Democráticas (National Alliance of Democratic Forces)
AVASC	Asociación Vasca de Acción Social Cristiana (Basque Christian Social Action Association)
BCC	Basque Children's Committee
CAEE	Comité d'Accueil aux Enfants d'Espagne (Committee for the Aid of Spanish Children)
CAS	Consejo de Acción Social (Social Welfare Council)
CCSE	Comité Central Socialista de Euskadi (Basque Socialist Central Committee)
CECR	Congress of European Communities and Regions
CEDA	Confederación Española de Derechas Autónomas (Spanish Confederation of the Autonomous Right)
CENR	Congress of European Nations and Regions
CEVA	Confederación de Entidades Vascas de América (Confederation of Basque Organizations of the Americas)
CFEME	Consejo Federal Español del Movimiento Europeo (Spanish Federal Council of the European Movement)
CFTC	Confédération Française des Travailleurs Chrétiens (French Confederation of Christian Workers)
CGT	Confédération Générale du Travail (General Confederation of Labor)
CIA	Central Intelligence Agency

CNAB	Comité National d'Accueil aux Basques (National Committee for Aid to the Basques)
CNAE	Comité Nacional de Ayuda a España (National Committee for Aid to Spain)
CNT	Confederación Nacional del Trabajo (National Confederation of Labour)
CNVG	Confédération Nationale des Victimes de la Guerre (National Confederation of Victims of the War)
COI	Coordinator of Information
CSB	Comité de Secours aux Basques (Committee for the Assistance of the Basques)
CTARE	Comité Técnico de Ayuda a los Refugiados Españoles (Technical Committee to Aid Spanish Refugees)
CVFE	Consejo Vasco por la Federación Europea (Basque Council for the European Federation)
EA	Euzko Anaitasuna (Basque Brotherhood)
EAE-ANV	Eusko Aldedi Ekintza/Acción Nacionalista Vasca (Basque Nationalist Action)
EAJ-PNV	Euskal Alderdi Jeltzalea/Partido Nacionalista Vasco (The Basque Nationalist Party)
EBB	Euzkadi Buru Batzar (executive committee of EAJ-PNV)
EIB-OPE	Euzko Izpar Banatzea/Boletín de la Oficina de Prensa de Euskadi (Bulletin of the Euskadi Press Office)
EKA	Euskal Kulturaren Alde (Pro Basque Culture)
ELA-STV	Eusko Langileen Alkartasuna/Solidaridad de Trabajadores Vascos (Basque Workers' Solidarity)
EMEK/CVME	Europako Mugimenduaren Euskal Kontseilua/Consejo Vasco del Movimiento Europeo (Basque Council of the European Movement)
ERC	Esquerra Republicana de Catalunya (Republican Left of Catalonia)
ETA	Euskadi ta Askatasuna (Basque Homeland and Freedom)
FEVA-EABA	Federación de Entidades Vasco Argentinas/Eusko Argentinar Bazkun Alkartasuna (Argentine Federation of Basque Organizations)
FSV	Federación Socialista Vasca (Basque Socialist Federation)
IAA	Irujo Ametzaga Archive
IR	Izquierda Republicana (Republican Left)

Irargi	Euskadiko Dokumentu Ondarearen Zentroa/Centro de Patrimonio Documental de Euskadi (Center for Document Heritage of the Basque Country)
JARE	Junta de Auxilio a los Republicanos Españoles (Relief Council for Spanish Republicans)
JEL	Junta Española de Liberación (Spanish Board of Liberation)
LIAB	Liga Internacional de Amigos de los Bascos (International League of Friends of the Basques)
MFE	Movimento Federalista Europeo (European Federalist Movement)
MRP	Mouvement Républicain Populaire (Popular Republican Movement)
NAM	Non-Aligned Movement
NARA	National Archives and Records Administration
NATO	North Atlantic Treaty Organization
NEI	Nouvelles Equipes Internationales (New International Teams)
NJCSR	National Joint Committee for Spanish Relief
NM	National Movement
ODCA	Organización Demócrata Cristiana Americana (American Christian-Democratic Organization)
OSS	Office of Strategic Services
PCE	Partido Comunista de España (Spanish Communist Party)
POUM	Partido Obrero de Unificación Marxista (Workers' Party of Marxist Unification)
PRG	Partido Republicano Galego (Galician Republican Party)
PSOE	Partido Socialista Obrero Español (Spanish Socialist Workers' Party)
SERE	Servicio de Evacuación de Refugiados Españoles (Spanish Refugee Evacuation Service)
SEV	Solidaridad de Empleados Vascos (Basque Employees' Solidarity)
SI	Servicio Interior (Domestic Service)
SIEB	Société Internationale des Études Basques (International Society for Basque Studies)
SODRE	Servicio Oficial de Difusión, Radiotelevisión y Espectáculos (Official Service for Diffusion, Radio and Television, and Events)
UCPEO	Unión Cultural de los Países de la Europa Occidental (Cultural Union of the Countries of Western Europe)
UEF	Union Européenne des Fédéralistes (European Union of Federalists)
UGT	Unión General de Trabajadores (General Union of Workers)

UN	United Nations
UNE	Unión Nacional Española (Spanish National Union)
UNESCO	UN Educational, Scientific, and Cultural Organization
UR	Unión Republicana (Republican Union)

Acknowledgments

This book has been the result of a long intellectual process. The number of people to thank is exhaustive, and any listing may exclude someone, so my apologies in advance. First, I wish to thank the Irujo family, my family, whose documents provided a great deal of the primary research for this book. In addition, I wish to thank Iñaki Goiogana for providing me hundreds of documents relevant to the study of the Basque government-in-exile. I would also like to express my debt to all the persons that I have interviewed who have given me the insights of this story. I owe a debt of gratitude to the people who have helped me in the preparation and critical examination of the present book, Arantzazu Ametzaga and Pello Irujo, Iñaki Anasagasti, my old friend Alberto Irigoyen, Oscar Alvarez, and Santi de Pablo, among many others.

My thanks also to my translators, Cameron J. Watson and Jennifer Ottman; their tireless work has made this book possible. Thanks to the Editorial Board of the Center for Basque Studies who have supported my research from the outset. I also would like to thank Katherine Faydash for her careful copyediting and useful suggestions, Daniel Montero, the publications editor at the Center who has guided the book through publication, and Kimberly Daggett for her editorial assistance. I would also like to thank Mark Lucas, the head of the Document Delivery Services/Interlibrary Loan at UNR and Shannon Cisco at the Basque Library. Finally, to my wife and five children, *anitz esker.*

Preface

On July 17, 1936, a group of Spanish army officers, supported by right-wing political parties and the Spanish Catholic Church, launched a coup d'état from Morocco against the Spanish Republic. The initial coup attempt failed and led to the international "Spanish Civil War," which was a prologue to World War II. Although the military coup was planned and initially directed by Generals Mola, Sanjurjo, and Franco, two months after the uprising, on September 29, 1936, General Franco became sole "head of government," with unchecked powers over the new state.

Only two days after the military uprising, General Franco sought material assistance from the Italian and German regimes. Franco first met with Mayor Giuseppe Luccardi, military attaché at the Italian Consulate in Tangier, to discuss the possibility of purchasing planes to transport rebel troops from Africa to the Iberian Peninsula. At the same time, Rudolph Hess scheduled a meeting for Franco's emissaries with Hitler at Bayreuth. After a short meeting on July 25—following the performance of *Siegfried*, conducted by Wilhelm Furtwangler—Hitler decided to launch Operation Feuerzauber (Magic Fire) with the purpose of overthrowing the republic through support of General Franco.

On October 24, Galeazzo Ciano, Mussolini's minister of foreign affairs, met with Hitler at Obersalzberg, a mountain retreat near Berchtesgaden, in the Bavarian Alps. They agreed to reinforce their military and political presence in the Spanish state and to officially recognize the Spanish regime once the rebels took over Madrid. Approval of the protocol of mutual assistance between the Spanish and Italian regimes on November 28 prompted a sharp increase in the shipment of war matériel and troops between December 15, 1936, and February 1, 1937. As reported to British Foreign Secretary Anthony Eden in the Fisher Memorandum, fifteen thousand Italian troops and about seven thousand German troops—the Condor Legion—had been shipped during the first three weeks of January 1937 to ports in rebel-controlled areas.

After one year of war, from July 1936 to June 1937, Franco's capture of Bilbao started the Basque exile in June 1937. Children were among the first war victims, especially victims of the German bombing campaign in the Basque Country. At the beginning of the conflict children taken out of the biggest cities and schools were placed in places such as Gernika or Durango, far enough from the front lines and, consequently, out of danger. Nevertheless, due to the notion of "strategic terror" and "total warfare" developed by the rebels, a high number of children were counted among the victims of the bombings. The Basque government then started the plans for evacuating civilians en masse. Consequently, approximately 120,000 Basque citizens (26 percent of them children) were evacuated between May and October 1937 from the Basque Country, primarily to Great Britain, the French Republic, and Belgium. In total, approximately thirty-two thousand children under seventeen years of age, nearly 20 percent of the children in the area controlled by the Basque government, were evacuated from the Basque Country by ship between the end of April and June 1937.

After the Republican army was defeated in April 1939 in Catalonia, the war was over. Due to the significant support of the German regime to the Francoist forces, the Spanish Civil War is also known as "the war that Hitler won." A massive Basque exile into Western European countries started. The Basque government had to make a decision about its future: to dissolve and renounce further fighting or to act from exile and face, together with the rest of the European and American democracies, the totalitarian forces in the widely anticipated international war expected to soon start. The decision to go on fighting was somewhat preordained; the Basque government was, after all, among the first governments in Europe to fight the Nazis and the Fascists—both politically and militarily. Therefore, when World War II started in September 1939, the Basque government-in-exile in Paris made a public statement expressing their will to fight alongside the allies. However, after the German occupation of Paris in June 1940, the Basque government was forced to evacuate their office in Paris and move to London. While fleeing the Gestapo, President Jose Antonio Agirre Lekube*[1] disappeared in Dunkirk in June 1940—and remained undercover in Berlin for a year and a half, and Manuel Irujo* assumed the temporary presidency of the Basque National Council, an institution that replaced the Basque government until the reappearance of Agirre in October 1941.

The German occupation of France provoked a massive Basque exile to the Americas. Between February and September 1939 around ten ships carried Basque exiles who, departing from the ports of the Northern Basque Country, Burdeos, or Marseilles, escaped the European horrors for the Americas. The Basques escaped from German troops and the Gestapo, who were persecuting them in collaboration with the Spanish secret police and the Vichy regime's forces. Hence, it was an exile caused by the German occupation and not directly by the Spanish dictatorship. In fact, on November 30, 1940, Heinrich Müller, head of the Gestapo, ordered that "Spanish Reds" up to fifty-five years of age who had worked for the French army be sent to German concentration camps. This measure, agreed upon with the Spanish police, had already begun to be implemented in August 1940 and led to the detention, torture, and death of numerous Basque, Catalan, and Spanish exiles in concentration camps as well as in labor camps.

---

1. Names marked with an asterisk at first mention also appear alphabetically listed in the biographical appendix starting on page 227.

In less than a month the Basque National Council and the British government had made their first agreement on military collaboration. Robert J. G. Boothby, representing the British government, and Jose Ignacio Lizaso, representing the Basque National Council, signed the first agreement on July 29, 1940, which spelled out that the British government was committed to defending the independence of the Basque Country if the Spanish government went to war on the side of the Axis powers. The Basque National Council also signed cooperation agreements with the Conseil de Défense de l'Empire Français (Council of Defense of the French Empire) led by General Charles de Gaulle. As a consequence of this and other similar agreements, a Basque force, the Gernika Battalion, fought within the French army in the battle of the Médoc in April 1945, during the campaign for the liberation of the French Republic.

President Jose Antonio Agirre reappeared—after a year-and-a-half odyssey in Nazi Germany—in October 1941, in Montevideo, Uruguay. The Basque government was reinstituted, and the central offices were transferred from London to New York until the liberation of Paris in 1944. In October 1941, and, even more so after the bombing of Pearl Harbor on December 7, 1941, the Basque government initiated diplomatic and strategic negotiations with President Franklin D. Roosevelt's administration.

The two administrations agreed to initiate a partnership between their intelligence agencies, the Basque Secret Services and the Office of Strategic Services (OSS), which would continue from May 1942 until the end of 1949. The Basque-American agreement comprised four main points: (1) The Basque Secret Services would collaborate with the US Office of Strategic Services; (2) the Basque Secret Services would operate under direct Basque command; (3) the Basque Secret Services would operate in South and Central America, in Europe, and in the Philippines; and (4) the main priority was to dissolve the Nazi and Fascist spy networks in Latin America and fight Japanese occupation in the case of the Philippines.

Forty years of brutal repression of the Basque people led to the revolt of July 1936 and Franco's dictatorship (1936–1975). Beginning with the killing of thousands of prisoners of war during their period of confinement at concentration or labor fields, Basques—and also Spanish, Galicians, and Catalans—would suffer four decades of death, prison, and exile.

This work investigates the exile caused by the capture of the Southern Basque Country by the Francoist forces—including the German Condor Legion and the Italian Aviazione Legionaria—in June 1937 and the occupation of the Northern Basque Country by the German forces in June 1940.

This is a story that has not been written in English before and is rather unknown to the Basque, Spanish, and French historiography. Thus, the present manuscript is based on primary sources, archival documentation, as can be seen by the references in the footnotes and in the note on sources. In addition, the author has interviewed several Basque political exiles, members of the resistance, and former prisoners of labor camps, and has also had access to the primary bibliography generated during the years of expatriation

(1937–1975) by the key figures of the Basque political exile. These are contemporary documents written by people involved in the events that took place at that time and most of them are registered as diplomatic or political files.

Introduction—The Principal Characteristics of the 1936 Basque Exile

The exile of 1936 was not the first Basque political exile. The Basque Country has suffered widespread and bloody exile experiences from the beginning of the nineteenth century onward.

The word *erbeste* in Basque means "to be in a territory or land other than one's own," and the etymology implies being in other territories or countries. Together with this implication, from the eighteenth century on the word came to mean "a forced stay" or "time spent away from one's homeland or territory." The verb *erbestetu* has been used since 1745 or 1749 in written texts in Basque. The Basque language first used the word *erbestetasun*, to signify the suffering of being forced away to another land and the deplorable situation this implied, in 1802, just thirteen years after the French Revolution and thus at the beginning of a troublesome political period of Basque history. The word *erbestetar* (foreigner) was used in written form for the first time in 1820, after the Napoleonic Wars.[1] Following the Second Carlist War (1873–1876) and subsequent exile, specifically during and after 1885, the verb *erbesteratu* was used more widely in Basque literature. Linguist Ibon Sarasola notes this word being used for the first time in 1952, sixteen years after the Basque exile of 1936.[2]

Most dictionaries indicate that *atzerri* and *erbeste* are synonyms, and that antonyms for *atzerri* are *aberri* (homeland) and *dierri* (nation). The Basque word *atzerri* was documented in 1596 as meaning "a territory other than one's own."[3] By semantic extension, *atzerri* came to refer to a forced stay outside one's homeland or territory. Twentieth-century Basques added the words *atzerrialdi* and *erbestealdi* (or *erbestaldi*) to the noun *atzerri* and the verbs *atzerriratu* (in 1929) and *atzerritu* (in 1745) to define a forced stay or period of time abroad or in a foreign country. It is no coincidence that one clearly sees *atzerrialdi* words in Basque documents starting in 1949, following the harsh times of exile after 1937 and 1940. In 1959, the verbal noun *erbesteratze* (banishment or exile) appeared, and

1. See Xabier Irujo Ametzaga, "Euskal erbestea eta erbesteak," *Guregandik: Revista del Centro de Estudios Arturo Campion* 4 (May 2008): 66–100.

2. Ibon Sarasola, *Euskal Hiztegia* (Donostia-San Sebastián: Kutxa Gizarte eta Kultur Fundazioa, 1996).

3. Ibon Sarasola, *Hauta Lanerako Euskal Hiztegia.* Available at www.erabili.com/lantresnak/hiztegiak/euskal_hiztegia.

in the period after 1975, the new word *atzerriatze* was added to Basque to express a similar sense of anguish and suffering.

The word *diaspora*, meaning "exodus," has been used to describe the 1937 Basque exile. However, *exile* is not a synonym for *diaspora* or, for that matter, *migration*. In Basque, diaspora refers to the Basque Country outside the Basque Country; it is the "eighth province," encompassing all places Basques gather and live. From this perspective, both exile and migration form integral parts of the Basque diaspora.

There are many economic and social reasons for migration, however here I focus on the political: exile. Exile is a specific kind of migration that takes place for political reasons and as a result of violence. Exile punishes not only individuals but whole families and also entire social, political, and ethnic groups. For example, exile in the case of many Basques was a punishment received as a result of the summary process of judges impaneled on Franco's Tribunal of Political Responsibilities. And while the men and women living in the Basque centers of the Americas and the Basque government's delegations had not received death sentences or similar punishments from the Tribunal of Political Responsibilities, they remained exiles and found their whole families affected. There were people who had left their land because their husbands or fathers had received the penalty of exile, either from fear of being punished or of becoming victims of reprisal. Every one of the Basque exiles received by Basque centers in the Americas between 1937 and 1940 was there by necessity and obligation.[4] Many of the exiles would not see their birthplace, parents, siblings, or friends ever again.

Similar to the help that the various Basque Provincial Councils provided in the eighteenth century to Basque emigrants in the Americas or in different parts of Europe, exiles received help from Basque government delegations in the Americas. Following the Law of Political Responsibilities of February 9, 1936, the exiles in many cases lost their Spanish citizenship.[5] Because exiles were consequently stateless and without documentation, the help offered by Argentina, Chile, Uruguay, and Venezuela was vital; these governments welcomed the Basque immigrants and allowed them access to citizenship despite their having been stripped of identity documents by the Spanish regime.

With Basque center assistance, it was not hard for exiles to get help from democratic governments in the Americas and to establish Basque government delegations in those countries. Exiles received diplomatic protection in fleeing from Europe and in crossing the Atlantic; institutional and administrative aid from democratic countries in the Americas; and practical and moral support at the Basque centers. Basque exiles were offered Argentine, Mexican, Uruguayan, and Venezuelan citizenship, among others, without having to go through almost any administrative procedures. Basque exiles docked in Argentina, Mexico, Uruguay, Venezuela, and to some extent the Dominican Republic

4. Irujo Ametzaga, "Euskal erbestea eta erbesteak," 70–77.

5. Preface to the Ley de Responsabilidades Políticas, *Boletín Oficial del Estado* 44, February 13, 1939, 824–47.

and Cuba, without having to go through humiliating quarantine measures—the effect of the aforementioned institutional support.

The process of writing this book has led me to delve very deeply into the Basque literature and letters written by Basque exiles and this has revealed to me that, for the exiles the Americas represented democracy, and the political project and struggle in exile would help maintain their dream of returning. While welcomed into their host communities, exiles became Americans with difficulty; they wanted to continue the struggle from abroad as Basques and to promote from the Americas their political project which they hoped to implement upon their return to the homeland.

Of course, not all exiles took part in the political struggle from abroad. Moreover, many emigrants who went to the Americas both before and after 1936 willingly took part in the struggle of the exiled. This book is a history of this Basque exile, a history of the Basque government-in-exile and of all of the people who struggled against Spanish dictatorship or who arrived in the Americas escaping from the Vichy police or Gestapo. In short, it is the story of the Basque exile community and their spirit of sacrifice and single-minded determination.

1

Origins of the Basque Autonomous State and Basque Nationalist Ideology in 1936

After two years of the conservatives being in power, the Spanish leftist political parties established and signed an electoral alliance with republicans in January 1936. The resulting coalition, led by Manuel Azaña, was named the Popular Front and comprised the Spanish Socialist Workers' Party (PSOE); the Republican Left (IR); the Republican Union (UR); the Spanish Communist Party (PCE); the Workers' Party of Marxist Unification (POUM); and two labor unions, the General Union of Workers (UGT) and the National Confederation of Labor (CNT).[1] The alliance was also supported by the Catalan nationalist coalition Catalan Left (EC) and by the Galician nationalist league of the Galician Republican Party (PRG). The Basque Nationalist Party (EAJ-PNV) did not sign the agreement, but the Basque social democratic, nationalist force Basque Nationalist Action (EAE-ANV) became part of the electoral coalition.

The leftist parties handily won the elections in Spain in February 1936. Of a total of 475 seats in Congress, the left-wing parties won roughly 289 seats (60.8 percent); the center, 32 seats (6.7 percent); and the right, 151 seats (31.7 percent). Consequently, Manuel Azaña, leader of the leftist coalition, became president of the Spanish state. Meanwhile, the Spanish Fascist Nationalist Party (Falange) received only 6,800 votes (0.07 percent) and did not win any seats in the elections—this only a few years before it would become the political support behind the military uprising led by Generals Francisco Franco and Emilio Mola and, consequently, the only political party of the Spanish regime from 1939 to 1975.

Basque politics involved politics both at state level, at Congress in Madrid, and also in the Basque provinces. As regards politics in the Basque territories, the EAJ-PNV won nine seats.[2] Those nine seats corresponded to 37.5 percent of the Basque representation

---

1. Given the complexity of language issues involved in this book, I have preferred common English-language names for organizations, or translations, with their most common acronym in Spanish, Basque, Catalan, Galician, and so on—or a mixture for organizations such as the EAJ-PNV, which is well-known in Basque and Spanish (hence EAJ-PNV). Readers are encouraged to visit the List of Abbreviations (page 9) at the beginning of the book for the full names in their original languages of organizations.

2. Joxe Mari Lasarte, independent Social-Christian politician, joined the EAJ-PNV parliamentary group in Congress.

and 1.9 percent of the seats in the Spanish Congress. With nine representatives, the EAJ-PNV remained the largest political force in the Basque Country and won three of the four Basque territories: Araba, Bizkaia, and Gipuzkoa. The conservative coalition, which included Carlists, members of the Spanish Confederation of the Autonomous Right (CEDA), and independents, won eight seats to become the second political force in the Basque Country. Moreover, the coalition won about 40 percent of the vote in Nafarroa. The leftist forces won seven seats, but their strength was divided into three different blocs.

The Catalan nationalists of the EC won twenty-six seats of the fifty-four from Catalonia, or 48.14 percent of the Catalan delegation—and five more seats than the coalition had won in the elections of December 1933.[3] The Catalan regionalist party Catalan League, led by Francesc Cambó, won twelve seats, or 22.22 percent, which was far from the twenty-five seats the party earned in 1933. Catalan Republican Action (ARC), led by Lluís Nicolau d'Olwell, secured five seats, or 9.25 percent. Those forty-three seats represented 79.62 percent of the total Catalan delegation and 9 percent of the Spanish Congress. In general, Catalan nationalism maintained its political strength. The Galician nationalists within the PRG coalition won three out of forty-nine seats from Galicia, or 6.12 percent of votes in the region, thus representing 0.63 percent of the Spanish Congress. The Galician coalition lost roughly half the votes it had earned in December 1933.

On April 15, 1936, the representatives of the Basque districts of Araba, Bizkaia, and Gipuzkoa presented to Congress the draft Statute of Autonomy, which had passed in 1933. The following day, the Spanish Congress created a commission to examine the project once again. PSOE member Indalecio Prieto headed the commission, with Jose Antonio Agirre, a member of the EAJ-PNV, acting as secretary.[4] The drive toward regional autonomy in the Basque region seemed unstoppable after the success in Catalonia:

> In accordance with the announced policy of the present regime to grant autonomous rights to those regions which, like Catalonia, have a distinct racial and cultural identity and express a desire for such autonomy by a two-thirds vote in a plebiscite to be held on the question, the measure granting regional Statute to the Basque provinces is expected to be submitted to the Cortes shortly. It is recalled that a petition requesting that such a Statute be granted by the present Cortes was submitted to the president of the Chamber on April 15, signed by all of the deputies from that region with the exception of the Traditionalist deputy from Araba.[5]

---

3. With the addition of two seats from the Leftist Nationalist Republican Party, led by Joan Lluhí; one seat from the Catalan Proletarian Party, led by Pere Aznar; and two seats from the Union of Lessors and Other Field Cultivators of Catalonia, led by Josef Calver.

4. In this book, we use the Basque spelling of Agirre's name. In Spanish, his name is José Antonio Aguirre.

5. US Ambassador to the Spanish Republic Claude G. Bowers, Weekly Report No. 1156 to Secretary of State Cordell Hull, Madrid, June 6, 1936, National Archives and Records Administration, College Park, MD, US Ambassador Claude

The commission's first task was to determine the legality of the referendum that had been held on August 8, 1933. By May 12, 1936, it had favorably decided on the issue. Prieto then ordered the creation of a new, three-member commission on May 20 to redraft a more concise and understandable text of the statute. The commission finished the work in less than a week, on May 26. Three weeks later, on June 15 and 19, the Council of Ministers of the Spanish government convened to discuss the new draft. During that meeting, even though every ostensible objection to Basque autonomy seemed to have been resolved, Minister of the Economy Enrique Ramos found another objection: he claimed that the proposal would be incompatible with the economic agreement that the state had signed with the four Basque territories. Ramos also declared that granting autonomy to the Basque region would be discriminatory against other Spanish regions and detrimental to the treasury.[6] Once again, the process was suspended.

Then, on July 10, Ramos's initial objections to the Basque statute were finally resolved when the Council of Ministers decided to approve the proposal. Three conservative members of Congress, led by José Calvo Sotelo, requested a technical memorandum from the Ministry of the Economy on the question of a Basque fiscal exemption. This meant a further technical delay. Three days later, Calvo Sotelo was assassinated, and war broke out on July 17. The violence seemed to kill all hopes for Basque autonomy: the situation of the Spanish political arena was certainly not ideal for addressing delicate questions of power, such as those of Basque political aspirations. Indeed, as early as June 6, the US ambassador to the Spanish Republic, Claude G. Bowers, had warned Secretary of State Cordell Hull of the possibility of a military uprising:

> Disquieting rumors have been circulating for several days regarding conditions in the Spanish Zone of Morocco, where some of the military forces are said to be hostile to the present regime. It is recalled in this connection that colonial troops from Morocco were instrumental in suppressing the proletarian revolt in Asturias in October, 1934, and are accused of having committed numerous acts of brutality. The left-wing Socialist newspaper *Claridad* has several times referred recently to the allegedly pro-Fascist attitude of army officers in Morocco and of naval officers on several of the most important units of the Spanish fleet.[7]

On July 17, 1936, it happened: Generals Francisco Franco, Emilio Mola, and José Sanjurjo[8] led—with the support of the Spanish Catholic hierarchy—a rebellion against the Republican order in the Moroccan colonies. On July 18, the coup started a war in the Iberian Peninsula that would last until April 1, 1939.

G. Bowers Files, files 852.00/ . . . , boxes 3687–3701 (hereafter "Bowers Files"), doc. no. 852.00 P.R./451, p. 12.

6. US Ambassador to the Spanish Republic Claude G. Bowers, Weekly Report No. 1172 to Secretary of State Cordell Hull, Madrid, June 22, 1936, Bowers Files, doc. no. 852.00 P.R./453, pp. 12–13.

7. US Ambassador to the Spanish Republic Claude G. Bowers, Weekly Report No. 1156 to the Secretary of State Cordell Hull, Madrid, June 6, 1936, Bowers Files, doc. no. 852.00 P.R./451, pp. 9–10.

8. José Sanjurjo died soon after, on July 20, 1936.

The cause of Basque nationalism temporarily came to a halt. The EAJ-PNV declared itself on the side of the democratically elected Republican government, although party officials publicly reiterated statements that they would not give up their demands for autonomy or independence. Two nationalist members of parliament, Manuel Irujo and Joxe Mari Lasarte,* gave the first declaration on the radio on July 19. The coup d'état had the support of the Carlist Party in Nafarroa and Araba, so the rebels had almost complete control of those two Basque territories from the first day of the uprising.

Immediately after the outbreak of the revolt, Irujo promoted the idea of a Basque provisional government to stop the quick advance from Nafarroa of rebel troops, led by Colonel José Solchaga, against Gipuzkoa and Bizkaia. Stunningly, after five years of delays and excuses from Madrid, the Republican government decided to hasten the administrative process that had until then blocked Basque autonomy, and the Spanish Congress finally passed the Statute of Autonomy for a Basque autonomous state on October 1, 1936. On October 5, the Basque government called for elections in the Basque territories. Because of the wartime conditions, general elections were impossible, so the city councilors were given authority to elect the first president, or *lehendakari*, of the Basque government. After an agreement struck among the Republican, leftist, and nationalist political forces, Jose Antonio Agirre, member of the EAJ-PNV, was elected by 291,471 votes, or 99.96 percent. One week later, on October 7, the autonomous Basque state was created, and on October 8 the first Basque government was formed:

> Today an autonomous Basque government takes office. As night fell yesterday amidst a silence broken only by the rustle of autumn leaves, the first President elect of the Basque people, Don Jose Antonio Aguirre, stood under the ancient oak tree at Guernica and in the presence of representatives of the people took the oath that is as old as the tree. First in Basque, then in Spanish, he said, "Humbly before God, but erect on Basque soil, beneath the Oak of Biscay, on the memory of my ancestors I swear to fulfill my duties faithfully." The Governor of Biscay then conferred office on the new President in the name of the central Government and called upon him to make known his Cabinet. This is composed of eleven members.[9]

President Agirre organized a government, with representation from the EAJ-PNV, the PSOE, the IR, the EAE-ANV, the UR, and the PCE. The ministers of the new government were the following: president and minister of defense, Jose Antonio Agirre Lekube (EAJ-PNV); vice president as well as minister of justice and culture, Jesús María Leizaola* (EAJ-PNV);[10] interior (home office) and public safety, Telesforo Monzon* (EAJ-PNV); economy, Eliodoro de la Torre* (EAJ-PNV); agriculture, Gonzalo Nardiz* (EAE-ANV); social assistance, Juan Gracia* (PSOE); labor and communications, Juan

9. US Ambassador to the Spanish Republic Claude G. Bowers, Report on Basque Autonomy No. 1223 to the Secretary of State Cordell Hull, Donibane Lohitzune, October 12, 1936, Bowers Files, doc. no. 852.00/3553, pp. 1–2.

10. Jesús Maria Leizaola became president upon the death of Jose Antonio Aguirre in 1960.

de los Toyos* (PSOE); industry, Santiago Aznar* (PSOE); supplies and commerce, Ramón María Aldasoro* (IR); health, Alfredo Espinosa (UR); and public works, Juan Domingo Astigarrabia (PCE).

However, in some respects, the statute was approved too late, after the rebel army had already captured large zones of Araba and Gipuzkoa, in the absence of any opposing forces. The rebels quickly gained control of Nafarroa, which had gained nothing from the statute. It is worth remembering that, only five years before the uprising, the Spanish Congress had passed the Constitution of 1931, which stated in its article 6 that the Spanish state "renounces war as an instrument of national policy."

The leaders of the National Movement initially believed that the EAJ-PNV, being Christian democrat and conservative, would provide support for the military uprising. This calculation was based on four basic facts about both political forces: (1) they were mainly conservative; (2) they were Catholic; (3) they were opposed to the government of the Spanish Republic; and (4) the Carlist Party and the Basque nationalist streams had their roots in the same nineteenth-century historical process and consequently shared some ideological principles, such as the restoration of the ancient Basque laws that had been abolished in 1876.[11] However, that support was not to be. Although the two forces shared some similarities, they also had many, and extreme, differences.

The pastoral letter by Marcelino Olaechea, bishop of Iruñea (Pamplona), and Mateo Mújica,* bishop of Gasteiz (Vitoria), written on September 1, 1936, is one of the first documented examples of the ecclesiastical hierarchy's attempts to attract the Basque nationalists to the military effort against the Republican order.[12] Also, on September 8, 1936, an official call for the Basque nationalists to join the uprising was transmitted by radio:

> You cannot in any way contribute, neither much nor little, nor directly nor indirectly, to the fissure of the Spanish Army and the corps of non-combatant officers and employees of the military, "Requetés," members of the Falange and the civil militia, that in raising the authentic two-colored Spanish flag, fight heroically for Religion and the Fatherland. Oh! If the Marxists prevail, once the docks of Religion, moral and decency are broken, the sweeping wave would sink all of us in its furious impetus. There would not be salvation for the Catholics, and the Marxists would at all costs try to erase the last vestige of God! What a difference in what happened in the provinces that resolutely joined the Rescuing Movement of the Spanish Army! . . . The Crucifix has been restituted to its position of honor in the schools, the venerated image of the Sacred Heart has returned to the throne that previously occupied the city councils and regional governments. The rights of the Sacred Church are respected. Priests, monks and nuns are respected, supported, loved. . . . Stop fighting the victorious Spanish

11. Xabier Irujo Ametzaga, *On Basque Politics* (Brussels: EURI, 2009), 89–90.

12. Ibid., 90.

> Army, support it, cooperate with it, save the life of all so that we all, forgetting hatreds and resentments, can live in peace and sacred freedom.[13]

Despite these appeals, the Basque nationalists quickly demonstrated that they would back the democratically elected Republican government. In fact, as already mentioned, on July 19, 1936, parliamentary members Manuel Irujo and Joxe Mari Lasarte, after hearing mass in the Church of the Capuchins in Donostia, transmitted a wireless message describing the EAJ-PNV's support for the democratic forces and demanding that the civil governor of Gipuzkoa, Jesús Artola, do the same.[14] Furthermore, on July 21, the EAJ-PNV published an official notice in two newspapers, *Euzkadi* and *La Gaceta del Norte*, emphasizing its opposition to the military coup d'état:

> Faced with the events happening in the Spanish state that may have a direct and painful repercussion on the Basque Country and its destiny, the EAJ-PNV declares—without renouncing its ideology, that today solemnly ratifies [i.e., the fight for independence]—that, the fight having begun between the the citizenry and Fascism, between the Republic and the Monarchy, its principles irrevocably cause the party to fall on the side of the citizenry and the Republic, keeping ourselves with the democratic and republican regime which was characteristic of our people during centuries of freedom.[15]

The ideological and doctrinal differences between Christian-Democrat Basque nationalism and Generalissimo Franco's National Movement were many and deep. In principle, both forces opposed the Republican government; however, the causes of the confrontation were completely different.

The National Movement objected to the Popular Front, a coalition of leftist political forces, for four fundamental reasons: (1) the National Movement opposed the process of political decentralization carried out by the Popular Front; (2) it opposed the leftist conception of a lay state; (3) it opposed the agrarian reforms promoted by the left; and (4) the National Movement's doctrine opposed that of the socialist, communist, and anarchist currents associated with the Popular Front.

Conservatives, the majority of the Bishops of the Spanish Catholic Church, and the military establishment considered the Republican government's policy of decentralization an assault on the unity of the state and an attempt to dismantle the country. That assault was one of the main causes that led to the political union of conservative political forces, the ecclesiastical hierarchy, and the army. Pressed by the Basque and Catalan nationalist forces, the first Republican government held a plebiscite to statutorily grant autonomy to Catalonia. Nearly 90 percent of the population voted for the statute (592,961 votes in favor versus 3,276 against), which took effect in 1932. Consequently,

---

13. Bernardino M. Hernando, *Delirios de cruzada* (Madrid: Ediciones 99, 1977), 107. Unless otherwise noted, all translations are by the translators and are translated solely for this book.

14. Irujo Ametzaga, *On Basque Politics*, 90–91.

15. *La Gaceta del Norte* (Bilbao), July 21, 1936.

the Generalitat, the Catalan autonomous government, was formed, and the Catalan language was declared an official language of Catalonia along with Castilian. Five years later, in October 1936, the Basque people also voted for autonomy, and the Basque government, under the presidency of Jose Antonio Agirre, was created. The creation of the two autonomous governments led by nationalist political forces, as well as the announcement of a possible third government in Galicia, provoked lively and divergent reactions among the different factions of the nationalist right.

The National Movement considered the secularization of political life and the rise to power of a predominantly liberal regime that advocated freedom from creed and a lay education system a political disease.[16] After the first draft of the Constitution of 1931 declared the strict separation of church and state in article 26, Manuel Azaña, the minister of war and future president of the Spanish Republic, declared on October 13, 1931, "Spain is no longer Catholic." Pope Pius XI expressed his strong opposition to the separation of church and state in his encyclical *Dilectissima nobis* on June 3, 1933.[17] The Holy See also criticized the Popular Front's reforms of the education system, which limited intervention by the church, which had previously administered the system through its various religious communities.

Landowners viewed the agrarian reforms promoted by the leftist parties as an aggressive attack on their interests. The "Ley de Bases de la Reforma Agraria" of September 9, 1932, known as National Economic Reform, which outlined the legal framework for agrarian reform, was based on the principle that private property must have a social benefit. In virtue of the referenced law, private property depended on the exploitation of the soil; therefore, the law gave the government authority to expropriate uncultivated lands and to offer parcels to laborers who worked on land that did not belong to them. At the same time, the law prohibited government evictions of farmers who invaded uncultivated lands. It also provided for the loss of ownership if land went uncultivated for ten years. In those cases, the state could expropriate the land and give it to farmers who did not own any land. A group of some of Spain's largest landowners organized an alliance called the Patriotic Association to oppose the law; the group included the Catholic Church, one of the state's biggest landholders. Indeed, Pope Pius XI addressed the issue in *Dilectissima nobis*.[18]

The predominantly conservative ecclesiastical and military hierarchies viewed socialism, communism, and anarchism with distrust. One of the Popular Front's first measures under the presidency of Manuel Azaña was to grant amnesty to all prisoners who had participated in the 1934 labor riot and other leftist strikes between 1931 and 1936.

---

16. Irujo Ametzaga, *On Basque Politics*, 93.

17. Pope Pius XI, *Dilectissima nobis*, Rome, June 3, 1933.

18. Irujo Ametzaga, *On Basque Politics*, 96.

The Basque nationalists, by contrast, opposed each of the Republican governments, whether right wing or left wing, for the main political aspiration of Basque nationalism was the creation of an independent Basque state. The diverse Basque nationalist forces demanded from the central government the right to self-determination so that the Basque population could decide on its own political future. The various Republican governments' distrust of Basque nationalism delayed approval of a statute of autonomy for the Basque Country and the formation of the Basque government until October 1936. The nationalists, without renouncing the right to self-determination, accepted the statute as a first step toward political autonomy. So, while conservative forces viewed the policy of decentralization as an unacceptable concession, the Basque nationalists saw it as a timid step toward an independent Basque Federal Republic.

Even if the EAJ-PNV, a Christian-Democrat political force, never supported the economic reforms of the Spanish Popular Front, it was not completely opposed to necessary social reforms. In 1936, the EAJ-PNV, the main political force in the Basque Country, formed a coalition government with the Socialist Party and other leftist forces such as the IU, the UR, the PCE, and the EAE-ANV. The EAE-ANV, a Basque nationalist and leftist political force, did not oppose the social policies of the National Front, although certain differences of opinion sometimes led to political disputes among the parties. However, the main objection of the Basque nationalists to the Republican regime was not centered on social policies.

There were more extreme divergences between the National Movement and the Basque nationalists. The leaders of the National Movement and the main instigators of the military coup idealized a centralized, hierarchic, and authoritarian government. Although the National Movement encompassed groups with diverse beliefs (national Catholic, monarchist, Carlist monarchist, fascist, Nazi, ultraconservative), all its constitutive political forces backed the concept of the organic state, a government whose institutions derive from and depend on the power of a supreme chief of state, in other words, a dictatorship. The Spanish organic state was a dictatorship for three primary reasons.

First, it was a totalitarian government backed by the military and ecclesiastical hierarchies. The parliament was to become an advisory body, and the political parties were to be outlawed, with the exception of the Falange, an extreme-right pseudofascist force. Human rights were to be suppressed, including the rights to free association, free thought, opinion, and creed. The government would also suppress habeas corpus and most other procedural rights in court cases where the police or military forces considered doing so opportune. The right of citizenship was to be revoked from "all those who do not deserve to continue being Spanish," which resulted in the statelessness, or lack of citizenship, of exiled Republicans: "the economic sanctions will be supplemented with others of different nature, such as the incapacity to hold certain public positions or the prohibition of living close to the previous places of residence. In certain cases of significant gravity the sanctions could mean the loss of citizenship for those who do not deserve to continue being Spanish."[19] The penal code was to be redesigned, capital punishment was to be fully employed, and concentration and labor camps for prisoners were to be created.

Second, the dictatorship featured the union of church and state in the form of a Catholic confessional state in which the church would maintain significant authority over the educational system and civil matters (mostly with regard to marriage and, by extension, family and women).[20] Bishop Enrique Pla i Deniel proclaimed at the end of the war, "The war, a Crusade for Christian civilization, whose victory we are celebrating, has been a second conquest of Spain. The first began under the protection of the Virgin of Covadonga. . . . The second has begun under the protection of the Virgin of Africa, invoked by the Caudillo [Generalissimo Franco] in order to expel the Communists and their allies throughout the Pyrenees."[21] As US Ambassador Claude G. Bowers stated, "The difference between the Basque Catholic and the Carlist [Basque monarchists, or traditionalists] is that the latter want Church domination of the State and the Basques do not."[22]

Third, the dictatorship was a unified central government. The autonomous governments were overturned. The Basque, Catalan, and Galician languages were to be completely expelled from the legal system and their use prohibited in all other scopes of public life. Castilian became the only language allowed in the education system and at all levels of administration.[23]

By contrast, the Basque nationalist forces preferred a completely different model of state. The EAJ-PNV and EAE-ANV supported the idea of a federal republic, a decentralized democratic state, based on a parliamentary system of political parties as guarantors of human rights. Although the Basque nationalists promoted the right to self-determination as a path toward political independence, the two parties viewed the Basque state as becoming part of a pan-European republic, along with other European nations. Membership in the community of European nations with economic and political openness in the international sphere, as opposed to the National Movement's closed-off autarky, was one of the main ideals—and still is—of the Basque nationalists.[24] Manuel Irujo defended the formation of a European commonwealth, a community of nations sustained by the right to self-determination that confronted totalitarian regimes during times of war and military threats and despotism during times of peace:

---

19. Ley de Responsabilidad Política, *Heraldo de Aragón*, February 28, 1939; Fernando Díaz-Plaja, *La guerra de España en sus documentos* (Barcelona: Plaza & Janés, 1975), 596.

20. The role of the church in state matters was years later delineated in the concordat signed between the Vatican and the government of Generalissimo Franco in 1953.

21. Hernando, *Delirios de cruzada*, 684.

22. US Ambassador Claude G. Bowers, Report to the US Secretary of State, May 5, 1937, Bowers Files, doc. no. 852.00/5427.

23. Irujo Ametzaga, *On Basque Politics*, 96–98.

24. Ibid., 98.

> If that solution is the best, we should not try to oppose it for another one that we could describe as good, on the assumption—probable—that it is not possible to try it while it is unavoidable to subjugate Germany and Italy; we will happily join the Western Confederation, located between the Rhine and Gibraltar, formed by the present states of Holland, Luxembourg, Belgium, France, Spain and Portugal, and perhaps German Rhenania. This confederation brings together 100 million inhabitants. 150 million if we include their colonial empires. There would be 250 million human beings under a great confederal law. This enormous super-state would include from the Rhine, the central Atlantic river in Europe, to the Congo, the central Atlantic river in Africa. The conception is difficult, wonderful, splendid. Important problems will be solved: The Galician-Portuguese, the Basque on both sides of the Pyrenees, the Walonian, the unity of Morocco, the affective, spiritual incorporation of all the Latin American Republics to a state organization without the fear of a new Spanish imperialism. The colonial problems of Portugal and Holland, so many times discussed, would be solved also. Catalonia and Andalusia would be the privileged countries of the Confederation, due to their possibilities in Africa and their geographic proximity to Africa, antecedent of their historical and racial kinship. The Iberian Peninsula would fulfill the geopolitical objective of being a bridge between two continents and a barrier between two seas, a reality that has always been denied.[25]

Later, after the outbreak of World War II, Irujo foresaw the evolution of the European Community and its advantages:[26]

> The most interesting inter-ally phenomenon is the common nexus of England and France, that already constitute a super-state. The currency continues to be called "pound" and "franc" but the value of the currency is the same, the credit is distributed the same, the loss and the rise of the two are the same, the instruments of change have been unified in fact. Just like the currency, all the remaining services are coordinated every day, not only the military, but those of propaganda, information, economy, foreign trade, etc. France and England are today, already, in fact, the United States of Western Europe. The English and the French people support this work with decision and without any doubt. It will be very difficult to find the party or the man who faces the responsibility of stopping it. The English and French sovereignty is yielding every day its position to the ally in facets really separated from the course of the war. The managers of this work have not been the socialist parties, but the democrats. But the socialists are behind it, they support it with decision and they sustain it. Follow this subject with attention. The Allied triumph is the triumph of the Allied federation. The doctrine of Federal Europe has had only General ideological adhesions, but without advancing in the field of politics. Simultaneously, England and France, without invoking doctrines but realities, federate, bind and unite in fact, with ties that never before

---

25. Manuel Irujo to Francisco Belaustegigoitia, London, September 16, 1941, Irujo-Ametzaga Agiritegia-Irujo Ametzaga Archive (IAA), GT-Irujo.M.1941.

26. Irujo Ametzaga, *On Basque Politics*, 99.

were achieved between any other sovereign and independent countries. Today England and France are less independent of each other than our Basque countries and the Crown of Castile were historically.[27]

The EAJ-PNV was a Christian-Democrat political force, and the National Movement was a coalition of conservative forces that soon gained the full support of the Roman Catholic Church; however, the National Movement and the Christian-Democrat Basque nationalists also maintained radically different views of the Catholic faith.

The Spanish ecclesiastical hierarchy promoted a Catholic faith marked by a hierarchic, dogmatic militarism with strains of fanaticism. From this perspective, the internal organization of the Catholic Church resembled a hierarchical military order, with severe penalties for interfering in its structure. In addition, Franco's Catholicism was strongly saturated with militarism. The writings of Cardinal Isidro Gomá, primate of the church in Spain, and the bishop of Salamanca Pla i Deniel, among other Spanish Catholic priests who supported the military coup, are characterized by the glorification of the military and the prolific use of military terms. Religious and military images even commingled in public ceremonies; for example, after the end of the war in June 1939, an official decree granted military honors to the Virgin of Covadonga, whose image was in the Spanish embassy of Paris. The image of the Virgin was led in a military procession from Paris to the Sanctuary of Covadonga, where General Pablo Martín Alonso, head of the joint staff (*casa militar*) of Franco, and General Juan Vigón, minister of the air travel, deposited it.[28]

Cardinal Gomá and other members of the ecclesiastical hierarchy turned the aspiration for political unity into Catholic dogma, which permeated ecclesiastical speeches and sermons. As a consequence, to desire or to promote Basque, Catalan, or Galician nationalism—or even to be a Basque, Catalan, or Galician nationalist—was considered a sin. Religion understood in this way was also tied to the idea of the Spanish race and the Spanish state. Race, Spanishness, and Catholicism were lumped together into a single idea within the ideological framework of Spanish national Catholicism. For Gomá, the Spanish Catholic creed was defined by its religiosity and racial superiority, for example, in its transformation of Native American societies during Spanish colonial conquests by means of racial mingling. In a speech delivered in Buenos Aires on October 12, 1934, the cardinal outlined his theory of the generosity and redemption that the injection of Spanish blood offered the Americas:

> Blood fusion, because Spain did with the native Americans what no nation in the world did with the conquered peoples: to prevent the boarding of unmarried women so that the Spanish men married indigenous women, giving birth therefore to the Creole race, in which, like in Garcilaso de la Vega, a representative of the new people

---

27. Manuel Irujo to Juan Ajuriagerra, London, April 12, 1940, IAA, GT-Irujo.M.1940.

28. Irujo Ametzaga, *On Basque Politics*, 100.

> arose in these virgin lands, the robustness of the Spanish soul raised to its current level the weak Indian race. And the Spanish, who in his own lot denied Jews and Arabs the purple shining of his blood, did not have shyness to knead it with Indian blood, so that the new life of America was, with all the force of the word, Hispano-American life. You see the distance that separates Spain from the Saxons, and the Indians of South America from the Native Americans. . . . America is our work; this work is essentially made of Catholicism. Therefore, there is indeed a relation of equality between race or Spanishness and Catholicism.[29]

Religion in general and Catholicism in particular was studied, taught, and understood mostly in terms of dogmas by the promoters of the coup. Catechism was valued for indoctrination, whereas reading and studying the Bible on one's own was discouraged. Dogmatism and fanaticism would even drive Spain's Catholic hierarchy to accept collaboration with the Axis powers, Nazi Germany and fascist Italy, in the war against the Republican forces and during World War II.

A logical axiom of the National Movement was the unity of church and state, or the creation of a confessional state. The exclusivity of the Catholic religion within the state was one of the most important features of the dictatorship. After the coup, tens of thousands of teachers and professors were demoted and dismissed. The rest were forced to swear allegiance to the ideological principles of the regime and to the Catholic creed in particular, in the form of article 2 of the Law of Education, which specified that teachers must instruct their students in the fascist principles of the Falange and in the Catholic dogma. In a literal interpretation of the motto of General Millán Astray "¡Viva la muerte! ¡Muera la cultura!" ("Long live death! Death to culture!"), approximately six thousand teachers were shot, another seven thousand imprisoned, and more than forty thousand fired.

The Catholicism espoused by the EAJ-PNV, as a Christian-Democrat political party with a Christian agenda, was diametrically opposed to such a conception of Christianity. Inspired by the Christian humanism of Jacques Maritain, a member of the International League of Friends of the Basques (LIAB), the vast majority of Basque clergy positioned themselves on the side of the republic, democracy, and human rights. It should be noted that the EAJ-PNV was one of the first Christian-Democrat political forces in Europe, which is why the militants of the party openly accepted Christian humanism and the social doctrine of the church. Politics, understood from the perspective of the EAJ-PNV, were to be based on two basic principles. First was a lay social state. From the Christian socialist perspective, the state was created for the benefit of its citizens, not the reverse. In the words of Maritain, man does not exist for the state; but the state for man.[30] Thus, the EAJ-PNV and the EAE-ANV advocated the separation of church and state and for a

---

29. Isidro Gomá, speech given at the Teatro Colón of Buenos Aires to commemorate the Day of the Spanish Race, October 12, 1934, in Isidro Gomá, "Apología de la hispanidad," *Acción Española*, November 1, 1934, 193–230.

30. Jacques Maritain, *L'Homme et l'Etat* (Paris: PUF, 1965), 47.

lay education system. The Basque Christian democracy also encouraged the creation of Christian labor unions to improve the situation of underprivileged workers.

Second was a democratic state. The Basque nationalist forces believed that the fascist, Nazi, and Falange ideologies were explicitly opposed to the Christian faith and Christian humanism. The only suitable political system from a Christian point of view was a state founded on democracy and representative government, a republic standing for the preservation of freedom, equality, and respect for all human rights. In the words of Maritain, "During twenty centuries, preaching the Gospel to the nations and facing the different powers to defend the freedom of the spirit, the Church has taught the freedom of man. No matter how miserable the present times can be, those who love the Church and freedom have reasons to be glad due to the clarity of the historical situation that we are confronted with. The great drama of the present days is the confrontation of man and the totalitarian state, which is nothing but the old spurious God of the Empire, without submission to the law, that bends everything to its adoration."[31]

As a consequence of the clash between these two divergent ways of understanding religion, the Basque clergy faced many forms of persecution, including sanctions, arrests, and exile, not to mention executions, after the National Movement's occupation of the country.[32] In 1936, sixteen Basque priests were executed by firing squad in the Basque Country because of their nationalist ideology, which diverged from the new political and ecclesiastical order.[33] As Cardinal Gomá expressed, "The war goes against those who fight in favor of Marxist materialism, corrosive of all the pieces of the magnificent monument of western civilization, and against those who fight the Christian creed and the spirit of the Fatherland, made of hierarchy and respect, without which Europe and Spain would go backwards twenty centuries in their history."[34] As US Ambassador Claude G. Bowers reported, "Apropos of the killing of priests, which from the press one could conclude has been confined to the loyalists, we now have the statement given by Don Alberto de Onaindia y Zuluaga, the Canon of Valladolid, long before the war one of the foremost Catholic propagandists of the Basque Country. He gives a list of Basque priests, supporters of the Government, who have been shot by the Franco forces in Pamplona [Iruñea] and Vitoria [Gasteiz]. These include: Fr. Adarraga, aged sixty-four; Fr.

---

31. Jacques Maritain, *El hombre y el estado* (Madrid: Fundación Humanismo y Democracia, 2002), 191.

32. *Le clergé basque: Rapports présentés par des prêtes basques aux autorités ecclésiastiques* (Paris: H. G. Peyre, 1938), #.

33. The following priests were killed by the Spanish army in the Basque Country: Martín Lekuona and Gervasio Albizu, vicars of the parish of Rentería, assassinated on October 8, 1936; Jose "Aitzol" Ariztimuño, Alexander Mendikute, and Jose Adarraga, shot on October 17, 1936, in Hernani; Jose Arin, archpriest of Mondragón, shot on October 24, 1936, in the cemetery of Oihartzun; Jose Peñagarikano, vicar of Markina, shot on October 27, 1936; Zelestino Onaindia, vicar of Elgoibar, shot on October 28, 1936 (prosecutors did not find his brother, Alberto, canon of Valladolid, so Zelestino was shot instead); Jose Iturri, parish priest of Marín; Aniceto Eguren, Jose Markiegi, Leonardo Guridi, and Jose Sagarna, priests, shot on October 24, 1936; in October 1936 Fathers Lupo, Otano, and Roman were also shot, the latter a superior at the convent of the Carmelite of Amorebieta. See Iñaki Anasagasti, "Santidad, ¿Y los curas vascos?," Galeuzca-ren Biltzarra, 2006.

34. Isidro Gomá, *El caso de España: Instrucción a sus diocesanos y respuesta a unas consultas sobre la guerra actual* (Iruñea: n.p., 1936).

Iturri-Castillo, aged twenty-nine; Fr. Onaindia, aged thirty-eight, brother of the Canon; Fr. Peñagaricano, aged sixty-five; Fr. Arin, aged sixty-five; Fr. Mendikute, aged forty-two; Fr. Guridi, aged thirty-nine; Fr. Markiegi, aged thirty; Fr. Lekuona, aged twenty-nine; Fr. Albisu, aged sixty-two; Fr. Sagarna, aged twenty-nine; Fr. Otano, aged forty; Fr. Aristimuño, aged forty."[35]

Finally, the political strategy itself (war as a means to attain political goals) differed between Spanish and Basque nationalists. The two political forces favored very different strategies for countering the Republican government. The National Movement embraced a strategy that viewed war as a crusade and considered it necessary to impose political ideas and religious beliefs on citizens. The military regime continually violated human rights during the war and in the thirty-eight years of dictatorship that followed. The Basque nationalist forces aimed for a peaceful political solution based on respect for human rights; they therefore could not support a military rebellion against a legitimately elected government. From this point of view, it was not ideologically tolerable, or Christian, to support the National Movement or the Nazi and fascist parties on the international level. This viewpoint, more than any other, inspired the opposition of the Basque nationalist bloc to the National Movement.

The confrontation was therefore inevitable and also expected. Bowers wrote on July 18, 1936, to Cordell Hull expressing that a coup was expected at noon: "Wendelin in Madrid telephones by special permission coup d'état planned for noon today. Telegraphic and telephonic communication closed. Will wire when information more definite."[36] And this is what occurred.

As the revolt spread, the territories of Bizkaia and Gipuzkoa, where Basque nationalism was the major political force, remained loyal to the Republican government. In the case in Nafarroa and Araba, as has already been mentioned, the National Movement rebels quickly prevailed. The military assistance of the German Luftwaffe and Italian motorized infantry units made the rebel command believe that they would capture Bilbao within three weeks in the summer of 1936. However, the war in the Basque Country lasted for more than a year, until Bilbao was taken on June 19, 1937. After the war, rebels established a brutally repressive regime. An estimated two thousand people were executed in Nafarroa during the first year of war (June 1936 to June 1937), most of them members of the political opposition. From the summer of 1936 to the spring of 1939 more than three thousand people were killed in Nafarroa.[37] The regime's execution of prisoners of war on the battlefield, in prisons, and in concentration camps must be added to that total. In addition, the persecution of Basque political leaders or others accused of even being involved in politics did not end in June 1937.

---

35. US Ambassador to the Spanish Republic Claude G. Bowers, "The Religious Phase," report to the Secretary of State Cordell Hull, Donibane Lohitzune, February 24, 1937, Bowers Files, doc. no. 852.00/4889, p. 5.

36. US Ambassador to the Spanish Republic Claude G. Bowers, telegram to the US State Department, Donostia-San Sebastián, July 18, 1936, Bowers Files, doc. no. 852.00/2174, p. 1.

37. Altaffaylla Kultur Taldea, *Navarra 1936: De la esperanza al terror* (Lizarra: Altaffaylla Kultur Taldea, 2003).

Thus started the Basque political exile. Most Basques first escaped to the Northern Basque Country or to Catalonia. However, after the Nazis gained control of France in 1940, German and French authorities cooperating closely with the Spanish police arrested or killed many Basque refugees. That prompted a second exile, to London and the Americas, which lasted until the death of the Spanish dictator in November 1975.

2

The Summer of 1936: The First Basque Exile

All too often we hear that the Basque exile began in 1937—it really began on July 18, 1936. In July 1936, while many people were killed or sent to jail in conquered territories in Nafarroa and Araba, those Basques who could escape went into exile, some via the Baztan Valley to Iparralde (the Northern Basque Country) and others to Gipuzkoa and Bizkaia.[1] In the fall of 1936 and especially during the spring of 1937 many refugees from Araba, Gipuzkoa, and the occupied towns and valleys of Bizkaia fled to Bilbao. Indeed, the first Basque exile lasted from July 1936 through June 1937.

With the coming of war, thousands of people were forced to flee from one country to another. According to a report of the Basque government of March 1939, approximately forty thousand Basque citizens crossed the French border while escaping from the Spanish Nationalists, after the capture of Irun on September 12, 1936, and two thousand more people would cross the border from Gipuzkoa or Nafarroa between September 1936 and May 1937. According to the figures of William E. Chapman, the US consul in Bilbao, before the bombardment of Gernika, there were between eighty thousand and one hundred thousand refugees in the city.[2] Of course, in the aftermath of the bombing campaign, which the Nationalists had started in the spring of 1937, thousands more refugees would quickly make their way to Bilbao. Indeed, according to Chapman, by the end of March 1937, the population of the city had doubled, and there were approximately two hundred thousand refugees in the city. Moreover, in April 1937, the Spanish navy had begun a blockade of Bilbao, thus increasing the scarcity of food and medicine. Thereafter, one of the Basque government's principal policies became maintaining health services and finding shelter and food for civilians.

---

1. Nafarroa in Basque, Navarra in Spanish, and Navarre in French and English. Araba is spelled Álava in Spanish; it is one of the seven Basque historic states. Iparralde means "Northern Basque Country" in Basque; it refers to the three historical Basque states now within the French Republic, namely, Nafarroa Beherea (Lower Navarre), Lapurdi, and Zuberoa. Gipuzkoa is spelled Guipúzcoa in Spanish. Bizkaia is spelled Vizcaya in Spanish and occasionally Biscay in English, as in the Bay of Biscay. Here for consistency's sake I refer to all territories by their names in Basque.

2. William E. Chapman, "Notes on Political Affairs in the Consular District of Bilbao," report to US Ambassador Claude G. Bowers, Donibane Lohitzune, March 30, 1937, National Archives and Records Administration, College Park, MD, Bilbao Consulate General Records (1936–1946; hereafter "Bilbao Consulate General Records"), box 3 (1937), 2.

Among the refugees were many children younger than sixteen years of age. Wishing to attend swiftly and decisively to serious problems affecting those children, the Basque government began a children's evacuation operation in Bilbao in March 1937. In the words of Jesús María Leizaola, vice president and minister of justice and culture of the Basque government, the government acted to evacuate the children abroad to remove them from the potentially dangerous situation of bombardment.[3] On April 29, three days after the bombing of Gernika, to move people to safety away from the war, the Basque government began to explore the possibility of evacuating three hundred thousand people: "the civilian population would be evacuated 'en masse' to the West."[4] The Basque government quickly reached agreement with the British National Joint Committee for Spanish Relief to take between two and four thousand Basque children to England. Before the end of April, Yvon Delbos, the minister for foreign affairs of the French Republic, told the US ambassador William C. Bullit that, in regard to the Basque government's request, France was willing to take one hundred thousand Basque children.[5]

These evacuated children were among the first exiles to leave the Basque Country. Moreover, this was the first large-scale evacuation of children in contemporary history, and the Basque government faced major challenges, including the sea blockade. However, between May and October 1937, the authorities managed to move 120,000 refugees, 26 percent of whom were children, to safety: around 26,000 civilians from Bilbao were evacuated by sea; 30,974 from Santander; and 62,199 from Asturias.[6] Between April and June, around thirty-two thousand children younger than seventeen, or 20 percent of all children living in the Basque government–controlled area, were evacuated by sea. According to US Consul Chapman's data, fifteen thousand children had been evacuated from Bilbao by May 26, and thirty thousand refugees left Bilbao by ship on June 14.[7] Most of them never returned to their homeland, and many never saw their parents again.

On June 19, Bilbao fell under the control of the pro-Franco international coalition. Leaving aside the ebb and flow of the military campaign, the Nationalists conquered all of Bizkaia and, without any other option, the Basque army, Eusko Gudarostea, decided to sign an armistice with the Italians in October 1937. However, breaking the agreement, Franco ordered the incarceration of the *gudariak* (Basque soldiers) on October 27, just as

3. Jesús María Leizaola to Arantzazu Ametzaga, Paris, February 15, 1979, IAA, GT-Leizaola.JM.1979.

4. George L. Steer, *The Tree of Gernika: A Field Study of Modern War* (London: Hodder and Stoughton, 1938).

5. US Ambassador to the French Republic William C. Bullit to the US State Department, Paris, April 30, 1937, National Archives and Records Administration, College Park, MD, US Ambassador Claude G. Bowers Files, files 852.48/ . . . (hereafter "Bowers Files"), doc. no. 852.48/71.

6. Tony Kushner and Katharine Knox, *Refugees in an Age of Genocide: Global, National and Local Perspectives during the Twentieth Century* (London: Routledge, 1999), 105. See also Dorothy Legarreta, *The Guernica Generation: Basque Refugee Children in the Spanish Civil War* (Reno: University of Nevada Press, 1984), 50.

7. William E. Chapman, memorandum for the Ambassador by US Consul in Bilbao, to US Ambassador Claude G. Bowers, Donibane Lohitzune, June 14, 1937, Bilbao Consulate General Records, box 4 (1937), p. 2.

they were preparing to leave from the port of Santoña (Cantabria). The events of Santoña led to a crisis in relations between the Basque government and the government of the Spanish Republic, with the latter, led by Juan Negrín, viewing Eusko Gudarostea's surrender as treachery. In fact, the Ministry of Justice of the Spanish Republic decided to prosecute Lehendakari Jose Antonio Agirre on the charge of "initiating a process to renounce responsibility for the loss of the loyal northern territories." In response, the Basque government wrote up a report in his defense titled *President Agirre's Report to the Government of the Republic regarding the Events That Influenced the Fall of the Northern Front.*[8] Here, Basque government authorities argued that war had not been lost in Santoña but much earlier, beginning in October 1936, as a result of not having planes to combat the Nazi air force.

Together with the refugees, the Basque government also took responsibility for the relatives of prisoners in Spanish jails and those killed during the war. The repression was harsh. In the summer of 1936, there were 1,757 executions in Nafarroa, and more than 3,000 by the spring of 1939.[9] Between the summer of 1936 and 1937, there were 157 executions in Araba, 65 percent of which occurred without any prior trial.[10] Meanwhile, in Gipuzkoa, two hundred bodies were found in the cemetery of Hernani.[11] In total, and with research still incomplete, different authors have calculated that there were between five hundred and eight hundred deaths in Gipuzkoa.[12] Between 1936 and 1945, 639 people received the death penalty, 485 of whom (75.9 percent) were executed.[13] With studies on the topic still ongoing, the latest figures available suggest that the Nationalists executed around nine hundred people in Bizkaia between 1937 and 1939.[14] To these, one should add the Basques executed outside the Basque Country, as well as those who were murdered without legal proceedings.

In this atmosphere, the Basque authorities had to decide what to do: to continue fighting in Catalonia or to give up and go into exile. They chose the first option. Ideologically, it was not even an option: they had to fight totalitarianism. Strategically, surrender was not a real option. The Basque prisoners in Spanish concentration camps and the thousands of refugees in Catalonia and in the French Republic needed urgent

---

8. José Antonio Aguirre, *El informe del Presidente Aguirre al gobierno de la República: Sobre los hechos que determinaron el derrumbamiento del frente del norte (1937)* (Bilbao: La Gran Enciclopedia Vasca, 1978).

9. Altaffaylla Kultur Taldea, *Navarra 1936: De la esperanza al terror* (Lizarra: Altaffaylla Kultur Taldea, 2003).

10. Javier Ugarte, "Represión como instrumento de acción política del 'nuevo Estado': Álava, 1936-1939," *Euskal Herriaren Historiari buruzko Biltzarra* 7 (Vitoria-Gasteiz: Eusko Jaurlaritzaren Argitalpen Zerbitzu Nagusia, 1988), 275–304; José Luis de la Granja, ed., *La Guerra Civil en el País Vasco: Un balance histórico* (Bilbao: Euskal Herriko Unibertsitateko Argitalpen Zerbitzua, 2007), 666.

11. Mikel Aizpuru, ed., *El otoño de 1936 en Gipuzkoa: Los fusilamientos de Hernani* (Irun: Alberdania, 2007).

12. Jean Pelletier, *Seis meses en las prisiones de Franco: Crónica de hechos vividos* (Madrid: Ediciones Españolas, 1937).

13. Pedro Barruso, "La represión en las zonas republicana y franquista del País Vasco durante la Guerra Civil," *Historia Contemporánea* 35 (2007): 653–82.

14. Ibid.

assistance, and the exiled children throughout Europe required support and daily care. Peace and neutrality in these circumstances were no longer possible.

In terms of politics, there was no reason to capitulate. World War II was about to break out, and there was a chance that the Catalonia front might officially become an international war. In that event, the strong network of Basque delegations in the Americas would become very active, as well as interesting in a geopolitical sense for the American and British administrations. In the context of the Pan-American Conferences, the Franklin D. Roosevelt administration was stressing neutrality as an alternative to intervention in favor of thc Axis, an option clearly tempting for several Latin American dictatorships. In these circumstances, the Basque political and social lobby—especially the influence of the Basque societies in the South American Catholic Church—was an essential diplomatic tool for the future Allies.

On December 21, 1936, the governments of the American states held the Inter-American Conference for the Maintenance of Peace at Buenos Aires, and declared the principles of inter-American solidarity and cooperation and, on December 23, 1936, the Protocol of Nonintervention. In 1938, the eighth International Conference of American States met in Lima, and the twenty-one member states passed on December 24 the Inter-American Declaration known as the Declaration of Lima: "The peoples of America have achieved spiritual unity through the similarity of their republican institutions, their unshakable will for peace, their profound sentiment of humanity and tolerance, and through their absolute adherence to the principles of international law, of the equal sovereignty of states and of individual liberty without religious or racial prejudices."[15] That statement was an obvious ideological refusal of the Nazi or fascist doctrines. Furthermore, the conference attendees agreed to reaffirm continental solidarity and, in clear reference to the future Axis powers, the decision to defend the Americas against all foreign intervention or activity that may threaten it, by coordinating their respective sovereign wills by means of the procedure of consultation, established by conventions in force and by declarations of the inter-American conferences, using the measures that in each case the circumstances deemed advisable.

After 1938, it was clear that the South American states, led by the United States, would both ideologically and militarily support the British and French governments in their struggle with the Axis powers. As a consequence, during the first consultation meeting of ministers of foreign affairs, at the eighth International Conference of American States from September 23 to October 3, 1939, the ministers, aware that the international situation might disrupt the peace of the Americas, underlined their neutrality with respect to the conflict and passed the Declaration of Neutrality and the Joint Dec-

15. *Peace and War: United States Foreign Policy, 1931–1941* (Washington, D.C.: US Government Printing Office, 1943), 438–39.

laration of Continental Solidarity.[16] Both declarations ensured that no American state would openly support the Axis powers, for most of them, and the most influential ones, were positioned with the Allies. Indeed, only two days after the Japanese bombed Pearl Harbor, the third consultation meeting of ministers of foreign affairs was called; they met in Rio de Janeiro in January 1942.[17] Consistent with the doctrine of the Uruguayan foreign minister Alberto Guani, the member states decided to break diplomatic relations with the Axis powers and to promote the production of strategic materials to supply the Allies.

16. "Consultative Meeting of Foreign Ministers of the American Republics," *American Journal of International Law* 34, no. 1, suppl. (January 1940): 1–20.

17. "Second Meeting of Ministers of Foreign Affairs of the American Republics: Habana July 21–30, 1940," *American Journal of International Law* 35, no. 1, suppl. (January 1941): 1–32.

3

The Exodus of Thirty-Two Thousand Basque Children

As William E. Chapman, US consul in Bilbao, wrote, a steady stream of Gernika residents fled to Bilbao, adding thousands to refugees already in the city and generating a precarious food situation. By the end of March 1937, there were enough women and children in Bilbao to equal the entire population of the city before the war started in July 1936. Consequently, after the blockade of Bilbao at the beginning of the Spring Offensive in late March 1937, the Basque administration faced a shortage of food and medicine. According to Chapman's reports, food was a serious concern, as thousands were suffering from hunger since the Basque authorities had reduced considerably the rations of the troops, even to those on the front lines, and had halved the rations of civilians, which consisted almost exclusively of rice and beans.[1]

As the secretary of the Foreign Office, Anthony Eden, told the House of Commons on April 9, 1937, the military governor of Irun, acting on Franco's instructions, informed the British ambassador to the Spanish Republic, Sir Henry Chilton, that rebel warships would resist the entry of four British ships to Bilbao.[2] The information was received in London on April 10, but it was not taken to the British House of Commons until nine days later. Sir Archibald H. M. Sinclair complained about the delay. The information had reached the United States much faster, so that C. H. Jordan, chair of the American Society for Technical Aid to Spanish Democracy, became one of the first voices abroad to protest the blockade on April 15:

> By refusing to ship aid to the beleaguered people of Bilbao, by recognizing and refusing to go through the blockade of the rebels, enemies of their democratically elected government, by ceasing free shipment to the Spanish government—recognized by Britain,

---

1. US Consul in Bilbao William E. Chapman, "Notes on Political Affairs in the Consular District of Bilbao," Report to US Ambassador Claude G. Bowers, Donibane Lohitzune, March 30, 1937, National Archives and Records Administration, College Park, MD, Bilbao Consulate General Records (1936–1946; hereafter "Bilbao Consulate General Records"), box 3, 1937, p. 2.

2. *Parliamentary Debates*, 5th ser., vol. 322, House of Commons, Official Report, 2nd sess., 37th Parliament of the United Kingdom of Great Britain and Northern Ireland, 6th vol., sess. 1936–1937, His Majesty's Stationery Office, London, 1937, col. 1410.

> with whom Britain is supposedly on friendly terms—the government of Great Britain is, in effect:
>
> Assisting the enemies of democratic Spain; recognizing fascists whom she officially condemns; cooperating with the enemies of the people of Spain; violating the spirit of neutrality and free shipping which she has ostensibly taken; and acting in a way incompatible with the ideals of the democratic peace-loving people of her own country and of the world.
>
> Therefore: be it resolved, that we respectfully request that the British Consulate officially register our protest with his government against the action taken by this government in recognizing the fascist blockade of Bilbao.[3]

In the United States, the North American Committee to Aid Spanish Democracy, the United Youth Committee to Aid Spanish Democracy, the Motion Picture Artists' Committee for Defense of Spanish Democracy, and the American League against War and Fascism all backed the protest.

In Great Britain, too, the blockade stirred public opinion. On April 14, Labour Party member Clement R. Attlee promoted a censure motion against Prime Minister Stanley Baldwin in the House of Commons for his failure to protect British vessels at the Bay of Biscay. The Labour Party forced Eden to promise that the British navy would escort British merchant vessels to Bilbao. Sir John A. Simon, First Viscount Simon and British home secretary, noted that General Franco had been told directly that the British government could not concede to him belligerent rights or tolerate any interference with British ships at sea. Simon added that Franco had been warned that any warning given to British shipping would not affect his responsibility for damage to British vessels and, in reply to an intervening question from Lloyd George asking whether the navy would act to protect any British ships attacked by Franco's warships, Simon replied that the British government would not tolerate any such attack and that British warships would protect them.[4]

On April 20, William H. Roberts, captain of the *Seven Seas Spray*, put out to sea in an effort to maneuver around the blockade, and he slipped easily into the city. Roberts told reporters, "I didn't see a single damn rebel warship or a single mine."[5] The blockade was over. In the following days, the steamships *MacGregor*, *Hamsterly*, and *Stanbrook* reached Bilbao on April 23, and the merchant ships *Thurson* and *Stesso* on April 25.[6] At

---

3. American Society for Technical Aid to Spanish Democracy to the US State Department, Los Angeles, April 15, 1937, National Archives and Records Administration, College Park, MD, US Ambassador Claude G. Bowers Files, files 852.48/ . . . (hereafter "Bowers Files"), doc. no. 852.48/70.

4. US Ambassador Claude G. Bowers, "The Situation at Bilbao," Report to the US Secretary of State. Donibane Lohitzune, April 16, 1937, Bowers Files, doc. no. 852.00/5235.

5. "Foreign News: Welsh Basques," *Time*, May 3, 1937.

6. *Parliamentary Debates*, 5th ser., vol. 323, House of Commons, Official Report, 2nd sess., 37th Parliament of the United Kingdom of Great Britain and Northern Ireland, 7th vol., sess. 1936–1937, His Majesty's Stationery Office, London, 1937, col. 11.

the beginning of May, former British prime minister David Lloyd George hurried to Immingham Dock, Humber River, in the north of England, where the *Backworth* had loaded ten thousand dollars worth of sugar, flour, fruit, and dried and salted fish for the starving Basque population in Bilbao. At the dock, Lloyd George loudly declared to the press, "I too am a Basque! . . . Marshal Foch was a Basque! The Welsh and the Basques are the same race."[7] The former prime minister paid for more than a tenth of the cargo.

However, the shortage of food and medicine was not the primary challenge confronting the Basque government. After the bombing of Gernika on April 26, "many of the civilian survivors took the long trek from Guernica to Bilbao in antique solid-wheeled Basque farm carts drawn by oxen. Carts piled high with such household possessions as could be saved from the conflagration clogged the roads all night. Other survivors were evacuated in government lorries, but many were forced to remain round the burning town lying on mattresses or looking for lost relatives and children, while units of the fire brigades and the Basque motorized police under the personal direction of the Minister of the Interior, Señor Monzon, and his wife continued rescue work till dawn."[8]

One of the most tragic consequences of the bombing of open cities was the death of numerous children. When the Basque government created *ikastolak* (public Basque-language schools) at the beginning of the war, it placed them in towns that, like Durango and Gernika, were far from the front and lacked military interest:

> In the weeks preceding the appointment [of Bingen Ametzaga* as director of primary education for the Basque government], German aviation, in assistance of Franco's uprising, had bombarded Bilbao and Las Arenas, and as a result of such indiscriminate bombings, as were the ones mentioned, 96 persons were killed, including 18 women and children. Ametzaga, acting as Director of Primary Education, had, as I did, only one major concern: that the schools and school-age children did not fall under the bombs of the enemy's aircrafts. I can assure you that the author of the following pages [Ametzaga] toured Bizkaia up and down in search of potential places of refuge for the children and their teachers. He has also elected places where Mayors understood this first and fundamental concern and collaborated accordingly. He did not make a single mistake in any of their choices and, if there were children who became victims of the air strike, they were never killed while in schools.[9]

The rebels' strategy of terror warfare left no safe place for children in the Basque Country during the war. As a result of the bombings and machine-gunning and the deaths of many children, the Basque government began planning a huge evacuation operation.

---

7. "Welsh Basques," *Time*, May 3, 1937.

8. George Steer, "Guernica," *London Times*, April 27, 1937.

9. Jesús María Leizaola to Arantzazu Ametzaga, Paris, February 15, 1979, IAA, GT-Leizaola.JM.1979.

As early as April 29, three days after the attack, the Basque government began discussing the possibility of sending up to three hundred thousand women, children, and elderly people to other parts of Europe, far from the dangers of war: "The civilian population would be evacuated 'en masse' to the west."[10] The Basque authorities and the British National Joint Committee for Spanish Relief soon reached an agreement that would allow between two thousand and four thousand children to be transferred by ship to different parts of England, where they would be hosted in temporary homes. At the end of April, the French foreign minister Yvon Delbos told William C. Bullit, US ambassador to the French Republic, that the French government could receive approximately one hundred thousand Basque women and children.[11] As Eden said in the House of Commons on May 3, the Basque government had approached the British government, stating its desire to evacuate from Bilbao women, children, and elderly people threatened by the approach of the war zone to the city and requesting the protection of His Majesty's ships for the purpose of the evacuation. In reply, the British government asked whether the government intended that the evacuation apply to persons of all political creeds and whether the Basque government would consent that His Majesty's consul in Bilbao be kept in close touch with the arrangements so that he might be in a position to ensure that the Basque government was strictly observing impartiality in spirit and letter. The Basque government sent assurances on these points, and the British government accordingly agreed to instruct its ships to afford all possible protection on the high seas to any ships leaving Bilbao with noncombatant refugees on board.[12]

The British navy would escort the ships involved in the evacuation, but Delbos and the British Foreign Office decided that a truce with the rebels was needed before evacuating the first group of fifteen thousand noncombatants from Bilbao.[13] Regarding the escort, Joseph M. Kenworthy, Baron Strabolgi, told the House of Lords on April 29:

> The Basques are a very pious, ancient, courageous and altogether an admirable people. Not even the noble Lord, Lord Newton, could accuse them of being Bolsheviks. Therefore that excuse for lack of interest in their welfare and lives cannot be put forward. They helped us when we needed help in the Great War. They were very friendly to us when much of Spain was hostile, and they have helped us in the past. We have never had occasion to complain about them in recent years, and I think they

---

10. George L. Steer, *The Tree of Gernika: A Field Study of Modern War* (London: Hodder and Stoughton, 1938), 324.

11. US Ambassador to the French Republic William C. Bullit to the US State Department, Paris, April 30, 1937, Bowers Files, doc. no. 852.48/71.

12. *Parliamentary Debates*, 5th ser., vol. 323, House of Commons, Official Report, 2nd sess., 37th Parliament of the United Kingdom of Great Britain and Northern Ireland, 7th vol., sess. 1936–1937, His Majesty's Stationery Office, London, 1937, col. 771.

13. "Britain, France to Evacuate 300,000 Women, Children in Bilbao," *Oakland Tribune* (California), April 29, 1937.

are deserving of what assistance we can give them, of course within the four corners of the Non-Intervention Agreement.[14]

On April 30, Chilton informed Franco that the British government was instructing ships to assist and to give all possible protection on the high seas to any vessel that had left Bilbao with noncombatant refugees. Not wishing to lose time, the British government communicated the details of this arrangement to the Spanish regime as an act of courtesy, advising the rebel authorities not only not to set up any obstacles but also, on the contrary, "to accept them [British decisions to evacuate refugees] with the same wishes that inspire His Majesty's government to mitigate suffering."[15]

On May 1, Franco responded that it was unacceptable that President Agirre, whom he described as the head of a region responsible for countless crimes, address a foreign state to request protection against Franco's own sovereign government. Franco also noted that it was impossible to guarantee the safety of operations because of the possibility of aerial attacks on port traffic and factories of military interest. He also pointed out that the region stretching from Bilbao to Santander was far from the front and controlled by the "reds," thus making it unnecessary to evacuate abroad. Finally, Franco said he was willing to admit anybody into rebel territory without regard to creed, with the exception of those guilty of crimes. The communication ended with the expression that "the evacuation of women, children and old people is not a voluntary act of the people, but a command from Russia, which today dominates Bilbao; which wants to sacrifice the wealth and goods and art of this nation, bring war to cities and towns and to set them on fire when they are evacuated, as were Irun, Eibar, Guernica and even Madrid, for which operations the civil population is an obstacle. Acquiescence with this evacuation would mean cooperation in the future destruction of Bilbao."[16]

The British embassy responded on May 5 that it would proceed with the evacuation (carried out by Spanish vessels operating between Bilbao and French ports) and that the ships would be identified by the flag of St. George, a red cross on a white background. Every precaution was taken to return to Bilbao in ballast, and representatives of the British embassy at Hendaia were present at French ports where refugees from Bilbao were discharged. The evacuation would continue for almost four months, and the British government protected the ships on both their outward and return voyages.[17]

---

14. *The Parliamentary Debates*, 5th ser., vol. 115, House of Lords, Official Report, 2nd sess., 37th Parliament of the United Kingdom of Great Britain and Northern Ireland, 2nd vol., sess. 1936–1937, His Majesty's Stationery Office, London, 1937, col. 90.

15. Charles A. Bay, US consul in Seville, "Communication Exchange by the British Government and General Franco concerning the Evacuation of Women and Children from Bilbao," Report to the US State Department, Seville, May 11, 1937, Bowers Files, doc. no. 852.48/100, p. 2.

16. Ibid., 3–5.

17. British Ambassador Sir Henry Chilton, "Notes to General Franco," Hendaia, May 5, 1937, Bilbao Consulate General Records, box 4 (1937), 1.

Franco responded again and protested the impending violation of the blockade at Bilbao and the intervention of the British navy contrary to international law. He described the British plan as "an act of insolence," unprecedented in the history of maritime blockades.[18]

The refugees were taken, mostly by sea, to big ports like Pauillac or La Pallice. Indeed, according to a report from the Basque government in Paris on March 18, 1939, the refugees arrived in France via five main ports: Pauillac (84,111), La Pallice (21,635), St. Nazaire (9,000), Nantes (1,650), and Verdon (350), for a total of 116,746 refugees.[19] But the evacuation trips were not always easy. Rebel planes tried to stop the British warships by attacking them on several occasions. On May 1, the British destroyer *Faulkner* was attacked, though not severely damaged.

Contrary to the rebel authorities' claims, evacuation of children was strictly voluntary, and in the case of children sent to the Soviet Union, special permits signed by their parents or guardians were required. However, Cardinal Gomá, in a letter to the Catholic Church's hierarchy in Belgium, Great Britain, Mexico, France, and elsewhere, expressed that the Marxists were stealing the children and that most of the children evacuated by "the Red Government of Spain belonged to right winged families whose parents have been killed or were orphaned cared by religious associations that have been exterminated. Since these children were in charge of the State, the Government has preferred to get rid of them who were members of rightist families."[20] This was a claim he knew to be untrue.

The recruitment of teachers for the refugee children was also voluntary. The Basque government's minister of culture, Jesús María Leizaola, publicized the opportunity in the press. Volunteers to teach the refugee children abroad could register with the Ministry of Culture in Bilbao. Bingen Ametzaga, director of primary education at the Ministry of Culture, made the final appointments, matching groups of children to each teacher.[21] As one parent who decided to evacuate his children wrote:

> By the spring of 1937, medicine, as well as food, was very scarce. My poor wife's tuberculosis became much worse, and I brought her to the sanitarium in Plencia, on the seacoast. Each day, I took my boys to my mother's house in La Peña where I had been born and reared. By April, they were spending all day in the air raid shelter. One day, rumor reached them that a bomb had destroyed the building where I worked, and my

18. US Ambassador to the Spanish Republic Claude G. Bowers, "Note to the US State Department," Donibane Lohitzune, May 4, 1937, Bowers Files, doc. no. 852.00/5317.

19. Jesús J. Carballés Alonso, *1937: Los niños vascos evacuados a Francia y Bélgica; Historia de una memoria de un éxodo infantil*, (Bilbao: Elkartea, 1998), 486.

20. *El Diario Vasco*, May 8, 1937. See also *Boletín Oficial del Obispado de Vitoria*, November 15, 1937; Jesús J. Carballés Alonso, *1937: Los niños vascos evacuados a Francia y Bélgica: Historia de una memoria de un éxodo infantil* (Bilbao: Atzerriraturiko Haurren Elkartea, Asociación de Niños Evacuados el 37, 1998), 134.

21. Arantxa Beti Saez, "El exilio vasco: Educación-universidad," in *La cultura del exilio vasco*, eds. J. A. Ascunce and María Luisa San Miguel (Donostia-San Sebastián: J. A. Ascunce, 1994), vol. 2, 211.

> ten year old ran to me, three kilometers away, saying he wanted to die with me. They were all three getting more and more anxious. My youngest, then eight, asked me why we didn't change the Lord's Prayer from "Give us this day our daily bread" to a more truthful "Give us this day our daily bombs," since bread could be found rarely, but raids were now every day. They became afraid to be away from me, and began to rise with me at 5:00 a.m., and stay in the air raid shelter in the basement of my workplace all day. A friend who brought milk from a nearby farm to sell gave me rice cooked with milk to feed my boys each day. My superior soon worried about their lack of maternal care and food, and sent me to Social Assistance. They enrolled my boys in a model orphanage for children whose fathers had been killed in battle, in a building close to my job. They got regular food, and even saved me some. Soon, the director decided to evacuate the entire orphanage. By then, I knew it was the only salvation. Days later, my boys were given their identity tags, with their number on the expedition list. My youngest exclaimed happily, "Look, Papa, what they have given us," while my middle son, always very sensitive, cried, "No, they have put labels on us, the same as sacks of garbanzos." I gave my oldest a notebook, where I wrote the family addresses, some words of counsel, and put a few family photos. This upset him, and he begged me to keep a copy of these photos, so that if he came back to older, changed parents, we could be sure he would not be given to some other family.[22]

After the first trip of 450 refugee children at the end of March 1937, 22,400 more Basque refugee children arrived in France through October 1937.[23] Indeed, the organization of the evacuation of about 150,000 noncombatants, mostly women and children, from Bilbao started by March but it was not until the end of April as the rebels approached the iron ring surrounding Bilbao, that thousands of civilians started to be evacuated.

After the children spent a night on the steamer *Habana*, the first massive evacuation of children started on May 6. The *Habana* carried 2,300 children to France. They said good-bye to their families, and many people gathered at the dock, while teachers, doctors, and nursing staff embarked with them. "They slept on board and departed for France at dawn. On board the children were given cakes, biscuits, and sweets. The food on board will consist of milk and other basic nutrients. The shipment has been a model of organization. Along with this expedition approximately one thousand more persons, including women and elderly people, who will survive on their own in France and England, are also facing this trip. The children will go to Oleron and the rest to Biarritz."[24]

---

22. Yvonne Cloud (born Yvonne Kapp) and Richard Ellis, *The Basque Children in England: An Account of Their Life at North Stoneham Camp* (London: Victor Gollancz, 1937). See also Dorothy Legarreta, *The Guernica Generation: Basque Refugee Children in the Spanish Civil War* (Reno: University of Nevada Press, 1984), 44–45.

23. *Parliamentary Debates*, 5th ser., vol. 326, House of Commons, Official Report, 2nd sess. of the 37th Parliament of the United Kingdom of Great Britain and Northern Ireland, 10th vol., sess. 1936–1937, His Majesty's Stationery Office, London, 1937, col. 8.

24. *Euzko Deya* (Paris), May 9, 1937.

The French cubist painter Amadée Ozenfant said in 1937 at the Catalan café of the Spanish pavilion in Paris that "their parents were all they had had in the world . . . and suffering has made their expressions as profound as those of grown men."[25]

Also on May 6, 319 more evacuees left aboard the *Goizeko Izarra.* Both vessels departed at 6:30 a.m. and were escorted by the Republican destroyer *Ciscar* and the Basque navy warships *Gipuzkoa* and *Bizkaia.*[26] The boats accompanied the *Habana* and the *Goizeko Izarra* to the limit of Basque territorial waters, where a British destroyer picked up the escort. About fifteen miles from the coast, the rebel warships *Cervera* and *Velasco* tried to block the vessels, without success. Thus, the long process of evacuation had begun. On May 9, another two thousand evacuees departed on the French vessels *Château Margaux, Palmer,* and *Carimare.* Between May 18 and May 22, three thousand new refugees and one thousand passengers left Bilbao on the ships *Zurriola, Luchana, Galea, Cape Crown,* and *Goizeko Izarra.*[27] On May 16, the steamship *Habana* again left Bilbao for France, with approximately 3,869 refugees, among them 2,185 children. On May 21, the vessel *Habana* left Bilbao once again with approximately 3,800 refugee children and 120 teachers on the way to Southampton, United Kingdom. Also on May 21, the steamship *Goizeko Izarra* departed for Baiona with 120 refugees onboard.[28] On June 1, the *Habana* began another journey with 4,205 refugees, among them 2,318 children; on June 6, 4,251 more refugees (2,337 of them children) were transported on the *Habana* to French ports. The *Goizeko Izarra* transported the children interned at the Gorlitz hospital in two trips on June 10 (139 children) and June 13 (131 children). The last big trip before the capture of Bilbao was by the steamship *Habana,* which transported 4,500 children to Pauillac, France, on Sunday, June 13. On May 15, the small steamship *Alice Marie* also left for La Pallice, France, with 593 more refugees.

Even though the rebel government said it would not accept such a blow to the prestige of its navy, more than one hundred thousand Basque citizens were evacuated between May and October 1937. Some 26,000 went into exile from Bilbao, 30,974 from Santander, and 62,199 from Asturias,[29] 26 percent of whom were children. Approximately thirty-two thousand children younger than seventeen years old, or nearly 20 percent of the children in the area controlled by the Basque government, were evacuated from the Basque Country by ship between the end of April and June 1937. According to data provided by the US consul at Bilbao, William E. Chapman, fifteen thousand children had been evacuated from Bilbao by May 26. By June 14, the total noncombatants

---

25. Judi Freeman, *Picasso and the Weeping Women: The Years of Marie-Thérèse Walter and Dora Maar* (Los Angeles: Los Angeles County Museum of Art, 1994), 115.

26. The *Habana* had 2,273 children on board and the *Goizeko Izarra,* 163.

27. *La Lucha de Clases,* LXII, 1.960, May 18, 1937.

28. *Euzko Deya* (Paris), May 23, 1937.

29. Katharine Knox and Tony Kushner, *Refugees in an Age of Genocide: Global, National and Local Perspectives during the Twentieth Century* (London: Routledge, 1999), 105. See also Legarreta, *The Guernica Generation,* 50.

evacuated numbered nearly thirty thousand.[30] According to Alonso Carballés, 20,854 of them (65 percent) were evacuated from Bilbao between May 5 and June 19, 1937. The other 11,000 children (35 percent) were evacuated between the end of June and the end of October 1937 from Santander or Gijón.[31] About 50 percent of the children were evacuated alone, for they had lost both parents or their fathers were in prison; many never returned to their families or lost track of them during the war. As table 3.1 shows, the French state cared for most of the children.

Table 3.1. Destination countries of exiled Basque children

Destination Country*	Number of Children	Percent
France	22,800	71.5%
Great Britain	3,861	12%
Belgium	3,278	10.3%
Soviet Union	1,610	5%
Switzerland	250	0.8%
Denmark	100	0.3%

* Some Basque children were evacuated to Mexico in 1936 and early 1937 from Mediterranean ports. The exact number is unknown, but it seems to be less than 100.

In the days before the capture of Bilbao on June 19, the rebel air force intensified its raids on the city, especially in the harbor area. As a result, refugee evacuations moved to the port of Santander, about sixty-eight miles from Bilbao. Evacuations also occurred by bus, and one of the last groups of children to evacuate Bilbao fled by bus only hours before the rebels took the city, in the middle of the night, and machine-gunned the road between Bilbao and Santander. As Mari Carmen Hendaia, one of the children evacuated that day, recalled, "We were required to stay on the floor of the bus for the whole trip; I was sixteen years old and was taking care of my youngest sister who was so scared."[32] After a brief stay at the Hotel Real in Santander, the children left for Bordeaux in the Ploubazlanec. When they arrived in Donibane Garazi in the Northern Basque Country, the residents closed their windows and doors while chiding them in Basque, "*Gorriak, gorriak*!" ("Reds, reds!"). The fascist propaganda had arrived in the city before them. As Bingen Ametzaga, director of the camp at La Citadelle, an eighteenth-century castle with no heat or running water, recalled, "After two months we had made clear that we were Catholic, prosecuted, and innocent of the crimes we had been charged of."[33]

---

30. US Consul in Bilbao William E. Chapman, Memorandum for the US Ambassador Claude G. Bowers, Donibane Lohitzune, June 14, 1937, Bilbao Consulate General Records, box 4 (1937), p. 2.

31. Carballés Alonso, *1937: Los niños vascos evacuados a Francia y Bélgica,* 152–53.

32. Interview with Mari Carmen Hendaia, Boise, ID, March 15, 2006.

33. Mercedes Iribarren Gorostegi, voice recording, 1970. Mercedes Iribarren was married to Bingen Ametzaga on June 14, 1937, at 3 a.m. in the bombed church of Areeta, before facing exile.

Most of the children were taken to France. In November 1937, the General Confederation of Labor (CGT) sponsored the Committee for the Aid of Spanish Children (CAEE), which, under the presidency of Léon Jouhaux and Victor Basch, aimed to evacuate as many children as necessary. Nearly twenty thousand people attended a rally organized by the CAEE in Paris in May 1937 to raise money for the evacuation effort. Unlike Great Britain and other European states, the French Republic and the CGT funded the evacuation campaign with 3.5 million francs in 1937, although the Basque government spent the most toward the effort: 14 billion francs. Adoptive parents mostly covered the costs of the CAEE settlements, as they paid twelve francs per week for each child's expenses.[34]

The prefects of the Gironde and Charente-Interieure received the children and gave them food, supplies, clothing, and anything else they might need. Each child had to undergo medical testing. Most of the children were healthy, though poorly clothed and malnourished. They were then sent by train to their temporary homes, where they would live with a family, aided by the Quartermaster Corps and Sanitary Services of the army if necessary.[35]

The CGT, in coordination with the French government, rehabilitated several sites, such as orphanages, schools, castles, retirement homes, and summer resorts, to house the children. The CAEE boarded approximately 1,650 children with Basque families in the Basses-Pyrénées, Loire, and Gironde regions, as close as possible to the Basque Country, in 1937. The group also appointed fifty inspectors to make regular visits to the families and to write reports on the children's health conditions, school progress, and general adjustment.

By the end of 1937, the CAEE reported that it was caring for about 9,000 Basque refugee children; of those, about 3,600 were housed in one of the fifty camps, and more than 5,000 were living in adoptive homes. The rest of the children, about eleven thousand, were under the protection of the Basque government. According to a December 1937 tally by the Basque government titled *Censo de Vascos Refugiados en Francia*, approximately twenty-four thousand Basques were living in France, most of them children in adoptive homes (seven thousand) or families on their own (six thousand; for a further breakdown, see table 3.2).

On April 10, 1938, Édouard Daladier became president of the Council of the French Republic and minister of national defense and war. Unlike his predecessors, Augustin Paul-Boncour and Édouard Hérriot, Daladier tried to block spending on the Basque refugee children. Consequently, the Basque government completed a third census in Baiona in the spring of 1938, which counted about 5,700 Basque children living either in the camps or in adoptive homes. One year later, at the end of the war in 1939, thousands

34. Legarreta, *The Guernica Generation,* 56–59.

35. William C. Bullitt, US ambassador to the French Republic, Dispatch to the US State Department, Paris, May 5, 1937, Bowers Files, doc. no. 852.48/79, pp. 2–3.

Table 3.2. Destination of exiled Basque childen.

Destination	Number
In CAEE adoptive homes	7,000
Living on their own	6,000
In fifteen camps sponsored by the Basque government	3,940
In families sponsored by the Basque government	1,800
In families sponsored by the PNV	1,500
In French refugee camps	1,500
In charge of artistic groups (Eresoinka, Elai Alai)	1,000
In Basque children camps	816
In three residences of the PNV	440
In Spanish refugee camps	400

Source: *Censo. Vascos Refugiados en Francia,* December 1937. In Dorothy Legarreta, *The Guernica Generation: Basque Refugee Children in the Spanish Civil War*, University of Nevada Press, Reno, 1984, p. 359.

of Basque refugee children were still in adoptive homes or in camps sponsored by the CAEE or other organizations, and 645 children remained in camps maintained by the Basque government.

The Basque government also took care of the wounded and sick refugees. The British vessel *Bobie* sailed from Santander to Baiona on August 27, 1937, carrying four hundred ill people. The government had set up La Roseraie hospital in Bidart, the Osasuna sanatorium in Kanbo, and the Berck-Plage sanatorium for 350 children who had come from the sanatorium of Gorlitz in Bizkaia. After the assassination of the thirty-four-year-old Basque minister Alfredo Espinosa on June 24, 1937, Eliodoro de la Torre, former minister of economy, was named minister of health in charge of the Basque hospitals and wounded refugees in France. La Roseraie hospital was inaugurated on August 25, 1937, under the directorship of Gonzalo Aranguren. A total of seventy people worked at the hospital from 1937 to 1940. During that time, 726 *gudaris* (Basque soldiers) and 823 Basque refugees were interned in La Roseraie. Between August 1937 and mid-1939, approximately 7,500 consultations and 2,400 operations took place. The first sons of exile were born at La Roseraie, a total of 143 children (50 in 1938, 64 in 1939, and 29 in 1940), including my own father.[36] Only three children died during childbirth (0.4 percent of all registered births in the hospital), and three died during operation. In early 1939, there were still about 255 war-wounded people in La Roseraie.

With respect to children evacuated to the United Kingdom, the National Joint Committee for Spanish Relief (NJCSR) had begun arranging for evacuations as early as February 1937. In early April 1937, the British consul at Bilbao proposed to Foreign

36. Jean-Claude Larronde, *"La Roseraie"ko ospitalea (1937-1940)* (Milafranga: Bidasoa, 2002), 20.

Secretary Eden a large-scale evacuation. On April 30, 1937, four days after the bombing of Gernika, the British Home Office was pressed to accept Basque refugee children into Great Britain and to escort vessels carrying refugees to other places in Europe. The Home Office imposed several conditions, including the following:

- The British government would not pay for the maintenance of the refugee children.
- A special committee of the NJCSR would have to take responsibility for the entire operation and for coordinating with the Home Office.
- The evacuation would be available to people of all political affiliations, and the British consul in Bilbao would be allowed to supervise the arrangements.
- Before the children's arrival, an ad hoc committee would decide how to accommodate the children and maintain them in institutions and private homes.
- The Basque refugee children's stay was understood to be temporary.

By May 15, the Basque Children's Committee (BCC) had been created. James R. McNamara and Wilfrid H. W. Roberts, joint secretaries of the BCC, as well as Leah Manning, of Spanish Medical Aid, and Edith Pye, of the Society of Friends, were appointed to travel to Bilbao in April 1937 to arrange the evacuation to the United Kingdom of nearly four thousand Basque children. Before any of the children could be evacuated, doctors Audrey Russell and Richard Ellis would examine them.[37] They would be examined again upon their arrival in Great Britain for any contagious or infectious diseases. However, the children were healthy, and only two cases of contagious disease, such as trachoma, were detected.

Leah Manning arrived in Bilbao on April 24. On April 26, she met with minister Juan Gracia at the offices of the Ministry of Social Assistance in Bilbao to discuss the general guidelines for the evacuation.[38] According to the US consul at Bilbao, William E. Chapman, nearly 3,800 children left Bilbao, with 120 Basque nurses, teachers, and priests, on board the *Habana* at 6 a.m. on May 20, 1937. They arrived in Southampton, on Sunday, May 23. As Chapman wrote, "When the *Habana* got out upon the high seas away from the danger from shore batteries, insurgent warships led by the *Canarias* came up. The *Canarias* is said to have located itself in front of the *Habana* and to have failed to obey the instructions of the British battleship *Royal Oak* to move away until the latter took position and trained its guns for action. Then the *Canarias* did obey without delay."[39]

---

37. *The Parliamentary Debates*, 5th ser., vol. 115, House of Lords, Official Report, 2nd sess. of the 37th Parliament of the United Kingdom of Great Britain and Northern Ireland, 2nd vol., sess. 1936–1937, His Majesty's Stationery Office, London, 1937, col. 229.

38. Ray Atherton, Counselor of the US embassy at London, "Note to the US State Department," London, May 5, 1937, Bowers Files, doc. no. 852.48/113. See also Leah Manning, *A Life for Education* (London: Victor Gollancz, 1970).

39. US Consul in Bilbao William E. Chapman, Memorandum for the US Ambassador Claude G. Bowers, Donibane Lohitzune, May 26, 1937, Bilbao Consulate General Records, box 4 (1937), p. 5.

The press described the arrival of the ship:

> In this great British port we were very warmly received. The children were distributed sweets. The members of the health service climbed aboard and arranged for the following day, Sunday, the medical examinations. The health services finished all examinations by Monday at noon and all 4,000 children landed. In the camp there were 450 tents, each one large enough for nine children, made of waterproof cloth, with plenty of running water and a full installation of showers, kitchens, etc. All children were required to have a bath and were supplied with clothing, shoes, raincoats, rubber shoes, and so on. There were also a few stalls, similar to those of the rural pilgrimages, with books and magazines for children, clothing and snacks. We all were, in short, very warmly welcomed, with a sort of seriousness not lacking much sincere cordiality. The "Habana" was supplied coal in Southampton and later in Portland, facing its return trip escorted by the same British destroyer that had escorted us in our way to Southampton.[40]

Before leaving Bilbao, Manning told the press, "What I am sorry for is that I am not able to take all the children in Bilbao with me."[41] The mayor of Southampton ordered decorations to remain in the streets so that the children could see them and think that they had been placed in their honor. Thousands of people gathered in the streets, blowing kisses and waving handkerchiefs, while the children boarded buses to Stoneham Camp. All the children who felt ill were taken to the camp's hospital. The littlest ones were transported to a smaller camp, overseen by young Girl Scouts, with a capacity of 250 children. A teacher and an assistant were assigned to each of the children's tents. The next morning, after a brief commotion, the staff devised a system to feed such a great number of children, Manning recalled. It helped that few of the children were sick. Soon, a group of four hundred children were transported to a camp in Clapton, and other groups would soon follow. Stoneham camp was empty within a month and a half.[42]

On May 25, Basil S. H. Temple-Blackwood, Fourth Marquess of Dufferin and Ava, addressed the political ideology of the refugee children on behalf of the Home Office before the House of Lords. The conservative press and Thomas W. Legh, Second Baron Newton, had expressed concern about the communist danger inherent in the evacuation and who in the public press raised the question of the danger of the four thousand non-English-speaking children inculcating revolutionary doctrine. Temple-Blackwood said that all the arrangements for bringing the Basque refugee children to Great Britain were not made by the government but by the NJCSR, which was a purely voluntary body, and that the committee accepted all financial responsibility of the children. It was,

---

40. *La Lucha de Clases*, 62, 1.968, May 31, 1937.

41. *Euzkadi*, 25, 7.613, May 21, 1937.

42. *La Lucha de Clases*, 67, 1.969, June 1, 1937.

furthermore, accepted that the children to be evacuated from Bilbao were selected without any reference to class or their parents' political beliefs. Temple-Blackwood finished by expressing "the opinion of His Majesty's Government that at any rate for the moment these children are unlikely to influence the electoral results in the next five years."[43]

The NJCSR took responsibility for the care and maintenance of the children while they were in the country, with no recourse to public funds. By May 23, most of the children had secured lasting shelter, and plans were in place for the rest. After brief stays at the Southampton camp, most children were taken to larger camps throughout the country, where they were taught by Basque priests, nuns, and schoolmasters who had to promise not to spread propaganda about the Spanish conflict while the children were in Great Britain.

As Cyril Forster Garbett, bishop of Winchester, noted in the House of Lords on July 8, 1937, the children's health soon improved, and they began to forget the horrors of war: "I saw these children when they first came. They were overstrained, terrified and nerve-stricken, and the change in them has been quite remarkable during the months they have been in the camp."[44] Members of the Conservative Party even started to press for the refugees' return to the Basque Country. On July 8, Lord Newton, noting that Bilbao was quiet and calm, proposed that the children be sent back to the Basque Country, even without the consent of their families. George Harley Hay, Fourteenth Earl of Kinnoull, replied:

> It seemed to me that the noble Lord was doing some excellent propaganda for Generalissimo Franco. He asked about sending these children back to Bilbao, and said Bilbao is now very quiet. It probably is very quiet. Has the noble Lord seen some of the photographs which I have seen of Bilbao when the dust is laid after aerial bombing? It usually is very quiet then. I would like to know, if some of these poor little children are going to be repatriated, whether their fathers and mothers are there. From what I have read and know personally a good many of these mothers and fathers have been killed by General Franco's aerial bombers. . . . The noble Lord went on to say that these children are being used for anti-Fascist propaganda. There can be no anti-Fascist or anti-anything propaganda in the case of children who would probably have been maimed or killed by aerial bombs had we not evacuated them. . . . With regard to the contributions which go to keep these children, I may say that thousands of letters have been received from men and women throughout the country who are willing to take one or two children into their own homes and keep them for the duration of the war, but the Home Office—possibly owing to a scare regarding various diseases—have seen

43. *The Parliamentary Debates*, 5th ser., vol. 115, House of Lords, Official Report, 2nd sess. of the 37th Parliament of the United Kingdom of Great Britain and Northern Ireland, 2nd vol., sess. 1936–1937, His Majesty's Stationery Office, London, 1937, col. 229.

44. *The Parliamentary Debates*, 5th ser., vol. 115, House of Lords, Official Report, 2nd sess. of the 37th Parliament of the United Kingdom of Great Britain and Northern Ireland, 2nd vol., sess. 1936–1937, His Majesty's Stationery Office, London, 1937, col. 229.

> fit to refuse to allow the children to be adopted in this way by people who are willing to take them into their homes. It is nonsense for the noble Lord to suggest that these children would be simply thrown on to the British Government. There are people sufficiently nice-minded in this country who are only too willing to look after these children, and if they cannot take them into their homes, they are prepared to subscribe sufficient money to see that they are kept properly until this dreadful war is over. The arguments of the noble Lord are, it seems to me, on a par with the suggestion that Abyssinian children might be repatriated to Addis Ababa under Mussolini's rule, when probably their parents have been killed or tortured. I sincerely hope we shall hear from the Government that there is no suggestion to repatriate these children.[45]

Everyone agreed that the children had come to Great Britain only temporarily, even if there remained a certain danger for them in Spain. About ninety camps had been opened in Great Britain in 1937, yet by the end of that summer, there were only forty left; only five remained active by the end of the war in 1939. But because of repression in the Basque Country and the general economic situation there, only 265 children had been returned to their homes by the end of 1937. Donations to the NJCSR had also fallen off significantly after the capture of Bilbao. By September 1939, when Great Britain declared war on Germany, there were still nearly 600 Basque refugee children in the country, but "for the [following] six years the world had no time to worry about the fate of the Basques."[46] By the end of World War II in 1945, 410 Basque children were living in Great Britain, where most of them remained for the rest of their lives.

Children also had been evacuated to other countries, such as Belgium, the Soviet Union, Switzerland, and Denmark. Paul-Henri Charles Spaak, the minister of foreign affairs of Belgium, pledged his country's help by hosting the refugees in camps and private homes. As in Great Britain and France, the ad hoc Committee to Aid the Children of Spain was created to coordinate the evacuation and supervision of the children in Belgium. Immediately, hundreds of children in France were sent to Belgium. The first group of 230 children arrived in late May 1937 in Brussels. They were hosted first in camps at Ostend, Newport, and Heyst. Overall, from 1937 to 1939, 3,278 children were sheltered in Belgium, until the beginning of World War II. As in France, a group of Catholic officials in Belgium, including Cardinal Jozef-Ernest van Roey, helped with the evacuation plans.

On June 1, the Basque Ministry of Social Assistance headed by the Socialist Juan Gracia called for the transportation of nearly 1,500 children to the Soviet Union. Their parents had to present themselves at the ministry's offices on May 28, 29, and 31 to

---

45. *The Parliamentary Debates*, 5th ser., vol. 115, House of Lords, Official Report, 2nd sess. of the 37th Parliament of the United Kingdom of Great Britain and Northern Ireland, 2nd vol., sess. 1936–1937, His Majesty's Stationery Office, London, 1937, col. 227.

46. Bradford has been a sanctuary for many different groups of refugees in the twentieth century; in the 1990s, Kosovars and Bosnians fleeing Serbian ethnic cleansing sought asylum in the same city.

learn the details. Those who did not attend would lose their evacuation tickets.[47] All the children were sons and daughters of members of the communist, anarchist, and socialist parties. Gracia listed five conditions under which children would go to the Soviet Union:

1. Their parents must voluntarily give permission in writing.
2. The Soviet government would care for all the children's needs in Russia, placing them in colonies or with families.
3. The children would be educated by Spanish teachers that the Republican government had already sent to the Soviet Union.
4. The Ministry of Social Assistance was to correspond continuously with the children and to keep the parents informed, using a file on each child in triplicate.
5. The children would be repatriated when their parents wished.[48]

The first group of 1,610 Basque children taken to the Soviet Union departed for Leningrad on June 11, 1937. Most of them were soon transferred to camps near Odessa, at Artak, in Crimea. In late September, two more steamships from Gijón arrived in Leningrad, transporting 1,061 more children, most of them Asturian, but also some of them Basque. Ultimately, there were five children's houses—in Moscow, Krasnovidov, Numovski, Pravda, and Petrovska. Other children were cared for in Leningrad, Crimea, and other parts of Ukraine.[49]

There also had been plans to take some children to Norway and Sweden, where the ad hoc Swedish Relief Committee was created.[50] Five hundred children were expected to arrive in Sweden on or about July 10 and to remain until conditions become less dangerous in their homeland. However, the British vessel on which they were going to sail from Santander was chartered for another purpose at the last moment.[51]

It was highly unsuitable for the Spanish regime to have thousands of children evacuated from the Basque Country. After his ordination as archbishop of Synnada (Phrygia), Ildebrando Antoniutti was appointed papal envoy to the Spanish state by Pius XI on July 25, 1936. His official mission was to promote the exchange of prisoners and to provide assistance to priests and nuns in areas controlled by government forces, mainly to those in prison or those sentenced to death or exile. Antoniutti was named charge d'affaires before Generalissimo Franco on September 21, a step toward the Holy See's official recognition of the military government. On July 31, 1937, Antoniutti met with

47. *La Lucha de Clases*, 62, 1.968, May 31, 1937.

48. Legarreta, *The Guernica Generation*, 160.

49. Legarreta reports that 1,745 children were evacuated to the Soviet Union. See ibid., 166.

50. US Ambassador to the Spanish Republic Claude G. Bowers, "Note to the US State Department," Donibane Lohitzune, July 15, 1937, Bowers Files, doc. no. 852.48/149.

51. US Ambassador to the Spanish Republic Claude G. Bowers, "Note to the US State Department," Donibane Lohitzune, July 15, 1937, Bowers Files, doc. no. 852.48/150.

Franco, who alerted him to threats from the Basque clergy and assured him that some of the Basque and Catalan priests had to be severely punished:

> The General told me that he would also avoid any repressive measure against Basque priests, but said that some of these priests who were dangerous for the maintenance of the public order were to be expelled for at least some time. In the case that more serious measures against these priests were to be taken, he assured me that the ecclesiastical authorities would be promptly notified.[52]

As Antoniutti reported to Cardinal Pacelli on August 17, 1937, there were eighty-one Basque priests in prison in Bilbao who had been charged with acquiescence with the Basque nationalists, and four of them had been sentenced to death. Nineteen had been already shot under the same charge, and another sixty-six had been forced into exile.[53] After the surrender of the Basque army at Santoña in August 26, 1937, another thirty-six Basque priests were imprisoned.

From the capture of Bilbao on June 19, 1937 through July 1938, one of Antoniutti's main tasks was to return the Basque children to their homeland. Pope Pius XI sent Father Roca Gabana three hundred thousand Italian lira to assist with the repatriation process, and he appointed a new bishop in Gasteiz, Francisco Javier Lauzurica y Torralba, to replace Mateo Mugica, who had been exiled. Soon after being named bishop, Lauzurica created Section Five: Repatriation of Children Abroad, a special committee for the "protection" of minors. Lauzurica wrote and published a pastoral letter in October 1937 calling for parents to immediately request the repatriation of all their children, who "for vicious reasons [were] dragged violently from their homes by an unjust order, and taken in foreign ships far from their parents by these enemies of God and country. The presence of the refugee children serves to provoke general compassion towards the Basques."[54] Antoniutti and Lauzurica pressed Catholic Church officials all over Europe to push for repatriation.

The bishop never took into consideration the health and welfare of the children. There is no mention of the situation of the parents or of the nutritional problems that the children would face in the Basque Country. Indeed, the Basque people faced rationing of the most basic foods, such as bread, oil, and sugar, until 1955.

The task assigned to Antoniutti was not easy. He confronted an overwhelming refusal by most parents to bring their children home, in addition to the fact that foreign administrations did not trust Section Five officials because of the proliferation of falsified documents in the last months of 1937. In addition, Section Five did not receive a complete list of refugee children abroad until October 1937.

---

52. Ildebrando Antoniutti to Cardinal Eugenio Pacelli. Salamanca, August 1, 1937, in Santiago Martínez Sánchez, "Monseñor Antoniutti y el clero nacionalista vasco (julio-octubre 1937)," *Sancho el Sabio* 27 (2007): 44.

53. Ildebrando Antoniutti, report to Cardinal Eugenio Pacelli, Bilbao, August 17, 1937, in ibid., 49–70.

54. Legarreta, *The Guernica Generation,* 160.

Once Section Five obtained the list, it used whatever means necessary to repatriate the children, including blackmailing families to make them lure their children home, which was particularly easy with families who had relatives in prison sentenced to death. As the neutral commission appointed by the BCC to coordinate the process of repatriating the children discovered, many parents did not want their children to return but were afraid of the consequences of not urging them to come home. During one of the BCC's meetings in Great Britain, committee members found that some of the applications had been written under pressure by Spanish authorities:

> One of the boys received a letter from his parents, saying that everything in Bilbao was now normal, and food was plentiful, and he must come back and join the Black Arrow Regiment. The child became highly excited upon reading the letter, and said he knew his father would never wish him to join the Black Arrows. He pointed to a small tear at the corner of the letter which he said was a pre-arranged signal from his father that nothing in a letter with a torn corner was to be believed. Mrs. Manning submitted that pressure was being brought on Bilbao parents to write such letters by Bilbao authorities.[55]

Antoniutti sent Father Gabana to Great Britain in September 1937 with a list of parents who reportedly had requested the repatriation of their children. However, the list was full of inaccuracies, and most of the letters were typed rather than handwritten, which was highly suspicious, as few families had typewriters at home. The truth was that most of the children did not want to return to Bilbao at that time, and, in the context of a postwar depression, neither could their parents properly look after them. As the Basque consul Miguel Uranga wrote in a letter to the minister Juan Gracia, he had word from the teachers of a Catholic colony that Gabana had visited. The envoy told the children that he came in the name of Catholic Spain to apprise them of General Franco's desire that they return to Bilbao. Upon hearing the word *Catholic*, the girls especially, all Basque Nationalists, made a general uproar. The envoy, Gabana, not content with this response, then spoke of Gernika, saying that the communists had burned it. The indignation of the children was such that the envoy had to leave the colony hurriedly.[56]

Moreover, the Basque government compiled letters from forty-three parents who did not want their children to appear on Gabana's lists. Some of the letters Gabana carried had clearly been signed by parents under coercion, and others were not even written by the parents. As Lydia Gee found out in November 1937 when the first group of Basque refugee children returned home, many parents told her that they had wanted their children to remain in the British camps. Some of the fraudulent letters had even been signed in Bilbao, when the parents were, in fact, in exile. When those children

55. Ibid., 213.

56. Correspondence maintained in the years 1937 and 1938 by Juan Gracia, Minister of Social Assistance, with Miguel Uranga and the Basque Children's Committee. Includes reports and dossiers of the Basque Children's Committee. Archivo del Nacionalismo Vasco. "Asistencia social a los refugiados: Secretaria particular." GE,K.00034, C.3.

were repatriated, some of them had to be hosted in houses of close relatives, as their parents were abroad.

However, the press in Bilbao, completely censored and government controlled, continued to publish articles pressing parents to request that their children be returned and launched a strident campaign over the refugee situation. The press manipulated the slightest incident; for instance, when the children at Southampton cried out after learning that Bilbao had been captured, the pro-Franco press in Spain and Great Britain quickly published news on "the wild Basque children terrifying Southampton" as an "undisciplined mob of anarchists":

> I never saw anything like it; can you imagine four thousand Basque children and senoritas crying right through the night? It was an extra-ordinary experience. There was complete hysteria. The PNV [Basque Nationalist Party] kids from middle-class families were completely prostrated. Gone was the last hope. Their parents were being butchered as well. This was a crisis point, too, because some 300 of the older boys reacted differently too—they didn't lie down and weep about it—they marched down to Southampton with the intention of getting a boat back to help their parents. Now this played right into the hands of the pro-Franco press and from that moment, they had a handle on destroying the sympathy. They said, "These red anarchists and communists are "marching" on Southampton they're likely to do a lot of destruction," that kind of propaganda, and immediately, donations began to drop off. People who were politically neutral stopped helping us. Our funds then depended entirely on those sympathetic to the Republican cause; a turning point. That was when the BCC got cold feet and brought in 13 army officers to run the camp, playing right up to the publicity. "This undisciplined mob of anarchists, we've got to hold them down." A gross injustice, as one Basque boy told me: "It's all right. You bring us here and feed us, but you don't give our parents weapons. You make us orphans."[57]

Section Five tried to generate pressure in the various countries that hosted the children. In Great Britain, the Duke of Alba, unofficial representative of the Spanish regime to Great Britain, called for the creation of a repatriation committee, which was finally formed under the directorship of Sir Arnold T. Wilson, an ardent pro-Franco conservative member of Parliament. In Denmark, which did not recognize the Spanish regime and where Spain lacked any representatives, the Nazi ambassador took charge of pressuring the conservative politicians in the country, emphasizing "the profound ignorance concerning Nationalist Spain that reigns here, creating the impression that returning the children would expose them to terror."[58]

The Belgian government decided to follow Sweden and Norway in sponsoring colonies in France and in providing funds to transport and maintain the children abroad. By the end of September 1938, the children were cared for in a castle near Paris. President

57. Ibid., 115.

58. Ibid., 209.

Agirre formally protested the activities of Section Five in a letter to the Spanish Republican ambassador to the French Republic, Ángel Ossorio y Gallardo, on September 3, 1937.[59]

The Basque government compiled 650 letters signed by Basque parents living in exile in France, Great Britain, and Belgium stating that their children were not to be repatriated. In response to Antoniutti's demand to the French Catholic hierarchy that the children in the Donibane Garazi camp be sent back home, the Basque government replied that at least 156 of the children (nearly one third of the total) had parents in exile outside of the Basque Country. The Basque government prepared a dossier that documented that many of the requests for repatriation were fallacious or signed under pressure, that the parents who refused to ask their children to return would be persecuted, and that the children repatriated would be driven to paramilitary camps.

The repatriation procedure was supposed to be initiated by request from the parents or legal custodians of a child. The child was then awarded a visa and, after a review of the accuracy of the information in the documents, repatriated. In Great Britain, after the Basque Children's Committee received the first requests for repatriation, the members sent a representative to Bilbao to verify the authenticity of the requests and to act according to the will of the parents. The BCC also appointed a commission of three observers to accompany the first 163 children back home. Also, three attorneys were hired to advise the BCC on the repatriation process. The attorneys examined 387 repatriation requests for approximately 800 children in October 1937 and considered that all the applications were genuine, and thus that the children should be sent back home. Thus it was done. The children arrived in Hendaia on November 12 accompanied by Lydia Gee of the BCC. When they reached the international boundary, they were lined up before the regime's dignitaries, including Antoniutti, and lectured for hours. Gee wrote: "The parents were waiting behind a barrier and all were harangued for hours, as though they were bandits. The children were finally given black bread and ersatz coffee, while we, as visitors, were given white bread. We only had a four-day safe-conduct, and if we overstayed we would be imprisoned. The children went to Irun to a dinner, and we went on to Bilbao."[60]

Once back, the children were sent to special schools, where they were reeducated in the principles of the National Movement. As in Nazi Germany, the Spanish press published weekly articles on the importance of physical education. The articles included pictures of fascist youth groups in uniform working hard for God and the caudillo. The situation was even worse for children who returned from the Soviet Union in 1956, as they were suspected of being communists and were constantly under surveillance by the regime's agents. Some were eventually forced to return to the Soviet Union.

---

59. Ibid.

60. Ibid., 237.

Despite the pressure, parents in exile strongly resisted repatriation, as did many who were still living in the Basque Country in France. Only ninety-five children were repatriated from France in 1937 and forty-three in 1938. A total of 265 children were repatriated from Great Britain in 1937. By 1939, 2,726 children had been repatriated (70 percent), whereas 1,155 (30 percent) remained in Great Britain.[61] By the end of 1939, there were still about seven hundred children in Belgium (21 percent). Most of the children sent to the Soviet Union were not repatriated until 1956, despite efforts by the Basque government to bring them back. On March 22, 1949, the Spanish government–controlled press wrote that seventeen thousand children had been returned, or about 53 percent of the Basque refugee children abroad.[62] That does not mean that only 53 percent of the children had rejoined their families, but that 53 percent of them had returned to their families in the Basque Country, as many others were with their families in exile in Europe or in America. Some of the children died in exile. Luis Cernuda, an Andalusian poet and a key figure of the Generation of 1927, dedicated a poem in his book *La realidad y el deseo* (*Reality and Desire*) to one of those Basque children who had died in England, and whom Cernuda had met as a volunteer at the North Stoneham camp. As James Valender wrote in his book *Luis Cernuda*, the poet immersed himself in volunteer work with complete dedication; indeed he was forced to quit because he identified so strongly with the plight of the children. What sparked the crisis was the death of one of them, who was ill with leukemia. In his last moments, the boy asked Cernuda to read a poem to him. When Cernuda finished, the child announced that he was going to die and turned toward the wall. Cernuda later wrote "Elegía a un niño vasco muerto en Inglaterra" (Elegy to a Basque Child Who Died in England) informed by this terrible event.[63]

61. *Repatriated* meaning being sent back with their parents, wherever they were. In many cases, parents were in exile in France or in the Americas.

62. "Los niños repatriados," *Euzko Izpar Banatzea* EIB-OPE (Paris), March 24, 1949, 4.

63. In Bernardo Atxaga, *De Gernika a Guernica* (Barcelona: Ediciones de la Central, 2007), 19.

4

Barcelona: June 1937–Spring 1939

Some have pointed to Catalonia as the location of the first Basque exile in 1937. However, as I have mentioned, thousands of Basques had been expelled from their homes by the end of 1936. Catalonia was, however, a central destination of Basques who wanted to continue the fight against Franco following the fall of Bilbao. The Basque government established a central office in Barcelona, and through the end of the war in April 1939, it fought politically and militarily against Franco and the pro-Franco international coalition. Apart from Barcelona, the Basque government also had delegations in Baiona (delegate, Javier Gortazar), Madrid, Valencia, Bordeaux, and Paris (delegate, Rafael Pikabea*).

When Manuel Irujo was appointed minister without portfolio of the Spanish republic in September 1936, he had to move to Barcelona. There was no delegation of the Basque government in the Catalan capital city; therefore, on November 5, 1936, Irujo created the first delegation of the Basque government in Catalonia. The main goals of the delegation were "to provide an adequate representation of the Basque government and to develop its policy, to assist Basque residents in Catalonia, to protect their interests and to serve as a nexus of union between Catalonia and Euskadi."[1] After Irujo, Luis Areitioaurtena was elected delegate of the Basque government in Catalonia, and from January 1938, Julio Jauregi* would be the Basque government's representative in Barcelona.[2] The Basque delegation published the weekly magazine *Euzkadi en Catalunya* from December 12, 1936, to December 25, 1937; a total of fifty-five weekly issues were published.

The Basque government-in-exile had two major concerns at the end of 1937: organizing the supervision, protection, and guardianship of the refugees and prisoners in Spanish jails or concentration camps and explaining to the world the tragedy that the Basque people were undergoing in their struggle against the totalitarian forces. Unlike in 1937, in this second phase of the Basque exile, the Basque government took all necessary

1. *Estatuto de constitución de la Delegación General de Euzkadi en Cataluña*, Irargi (Euskadiko Dokumentu Ondarearen Zentroa - Centro de Patrimonio Documental de Euskadi), *leg.* 304, doc. 2, reprinted in Gregorio Arrien and Iñaki Goiogana, *El primer exilio de los vascos: Cataluña, 1936–1939* (Barcelona: Fundación Trías Fargas and Fundación Sabino Arana, 2002), 617–18.

2. Arrien and Goiogana, *El primer exilio*, have thoroughly examined this part of the Basque exile.

measures to guarantee that the Basque refugees were assisted in the French ports at their arrival, by providing medical assistance to the wounded and sick, by distributing food and milk, and by trying to legalize their stay in foreign countries.

Because of the excellent systems put in place by the delegation and the foreign relations of the Basque government, the Basque case soon became international, drawing attention from the press and international diplomatic circles. The specific case of the Basque Catholic Church and the scrupulous respect for the freedom of creed and human rights in the area controlled by the Basque government—as well as the fact that the EAJ-PNV was a Christian-Democrat political force and that several Basque priests had been shot by Francoist forces in the Basque Country—soon awakened the interest of the international public. Furthermore, the repressive regime that the Francoist authorities established in the Basque Country after the coup d'état in 1936 and the Luftwaffe's bombing campaign in the spring of 1937 led the international public, initially openly pro-Franco, to start doubting the real nature of the war. This helped the Basque government-in-exile fight, with some success, the pro-Francoist campaign and the idea of the so-called holy crusade, which some of the ultraconservative parties in the French republic supported, such as the Catholic Action Française, an organization that encompassed some of the most significant future collaborators of the Vichy regime during World War II, including Pierre Laval, Louis Bertrand, Henry Bordeaux, Claude Farrère, and Charles Maurras.[3]

The slaughter at Badajoz and later the bombing of Durango and Gernika caused a shift in the positions of many key French Christian-Democrat figures, who judged as shameful the official position of the Catholic Church and of ultra-Catholic thinkers. The group of Christian-Democrat intellectuals openly denounced the Gernika massacre and the attitude of the French government. After the bombing of Gernika, the group, led by François Mauriac, chair of the French Academy, wrote a manifesto published in *L'Aube* on May 8, 1937, two weeks after the massacre, titled "Pour le peuple basque":

> The Spanish Civil War has just taken in the Basque country a particularly atrocious character. Yesterday it was the aerial bombardment of Durango. Today, by the same process, it is the almost complete destruction of Gernica, defenseless city and sanctuary of Basque traditions. Hundreds of noncombatants, women and children, have died in Durango, Gernica and elsewhere. Bilbao, where there are large numbers of refugees, is threatened with the same fate. For some opinions that we have on the quality of the parties that compete in Spain, it is beyond dispute that the Basque people are a Catholic people, that public worship has never been interrupted in the Basque

3. Laval became an active Nazi collaborator during World War II; captured and sentenced for high treason, he was executed in 1945. Bertrand was a member of the Académie Française. Bordeaux, an active Nazi collaborator and admirer, was included on the *d'épuration* list of the Comité National des Écrivains after World War II. Farrère categorically denied the bombing of Gernika, indicating that Basque anarchists had set the city on fire and destroyed it. Maurras, an active Nazi collaborator, was sentenced for association with the enemy. He claimed his sentence was the result of a Semitic conspiracy.

> country. In these circumstances, Catholics, regardless of the party they belong to, should raise their voice and denounce to the world the merciless killing of a Christian people. Nothing justifies, nothing condones the bombing of open cities like Gernica. We call, anguished, to all people of heart, in all countries, to immediately stop the killing of noncombatants.[4]

Sixty French Catholic intellectuals and twenty-nine students of the École Normale Supérieure signed the manifesto. Among the signatories were Jacques Maritain, a noted Catholic thinker and one of the main theorists of Christian democracy; the Catholic prelate and exiled Italian thinker Luigi Sturzo, considered one of the fathers of European Christian democracy;[5] Paul Vignaux, philosopher and historian; Francisque Gay and George Bidault, reporters at *L'Aube*; Emmanuel Mounier, philosopher and founder and editor of the magazine *Esprit*; and Pierre-Henri Simon, poet and literary critic. In addition, two groups signed the document: the French Avant-Garde and the English People and Freedom. The manifesto was also published in Toulouse's *La Dépêche* on May 7, in *La Croix* on May 8, in *Le Petit Parisien* on May 10, in *Sept* on May 14, in *La Vie Catholique* on May 15, and in *Le Figaro* on June 17. Maritain, along with Mauriac and Simon, had also published the article "Le martyre de Guernica" in *L'Aube* on April 30, 1937.[6]

Some of the signatories of the manifesto had already signed another open letter in February 1937 that called for an end to the war, noting that as Christians they had to raise their most firm protest against all inexcusable crimes, whatever their origin. Despite its intended impartiality, the open letter was addressed primarily to the military rebels. The document was signed by, among others, Yves R. Simon, Marc Sangnier, Louis Martin Chauffier, Germaine Malaterre-Sellier, Emmanuel Mounier, and Paul Vignaux.

Soon after May 1937, some of the signatories created the Comité pour la Paix Civile en Espagne (Committee for Civil Peace in Spain) and the Comité Français pour la Paix Civile et Religieuse en Espagne (French Committee for Civil and Religious Peace in Spain) in February and March 1937, respectively.[7] Francois Mauriac, who had previously denounced the massacre inside the bullring in Badajoz by the troops under the command of General Juan Yagüe,[8] published on June 17, 1937, two days before the capture of Bilbao, the emotional article "Pour le peuple basque," (For the Basque People) in which he defended the position of the Basque church, the Basque government, and, in general, the Basque people in favor of the Republic: "If they were wrong, this is not the

4. Jacques Maritain and Raissa Maritain, *Oeuvres completes* (Fribourg: Éditions Universitaires, 1984), 4:1130–31. This work was done in collaboration with Mauriac, but appears in Maritain and Maritain's complete works.

5. Sturzo published the article "Il significato di Guernica" (The Meaning of Gernika), on June 2, 1937, in *L'Aube*.

6. Paul Claudel (1868–1955), who had dedicated his poem "To the Martyrs of Spain" to the rebels, wrote in his diary on May 4, 1937, that Jackes Madaule and Francois Mauriac had signed a manifesto by Maritain in favor of the Basque traitors and added, "I will write to this idiot what I think of him."

7. Jacques Maritain, "Comité Français pour la Paix Civile et Religieuse en Espagne," in Jacques Maritain and Raissa Maritain, *Oeuvres completes*, 4:1122–29.

8. *Le Figaro*, August 18, 1936.

place to consider here. But if they have been guilty of the inexpiable fault of refusing to export to Germany the iron ore of Bilbao, the French, at least, should be lenient. One day perhaps we will understand that poor people suffer and die for us. May God allow that we do not find their dead at the point where we will have to bury ours."[9]

In August 1937, Mauriac published "Le peuple basque"[10] and, in January 1939, two months before the end of the war, he published "La victoire des basques" (The Victory of the Basques) in which he made reference to the French government's hypocritical position on the war in the Basque country: "Much has been spoken about the Basques for some time. Nevertheless, the problem of the Basque people still has no answer, and remains open today, as Spain has not found peace. Today, we can say that in the Catholic world, primarily in France, the Basques have won the battle of public opinion."[11]

Pierre Dumas also wrote several articles published in *La Petite Gironde* between August and September 1938, as well as eight essays, grouped under the title *Le tragique destin d'Euskadi* (The Tragic Destiny of the Basque Country), in which he described the attitude of the Basques regarding the war and the efforts of their government-in-exile.[12] Appointed press delegate of the LIAB, Dumas wrote numerous articles for the press, some of which were subsequently published in the book *Euskadi: Les Basques devant la guerre d'Espagne* (The Basque Country: The Basques at War in Spain).[13]

As we have already mentioned, Luigi Sturzo wrote an article entitled "Il significato di Guernica" (The Meaning of Gernika) that was published on June 2 in *L'Aube.* Jauma Ruiz, who believed that the "reds" had set Gernika on fire, answered with a bitter reply. On June 17, Sturzo responded to Ruiz, using a Christian perspective to attack the so-called holy crusade of Generalissimo Franco as unlawful. He argued that war and the violence were never permissible and that massacres plainly went against Christian beliefs. He did assert that the rebels' defense of priests and nuns and the preservation of churches and temples was lawful; but he maintained that war was one of the greatest evils, and so it was always necessary to avoid hostilities and, moreover, from a Christian standpoint crucial to prevent them.[14]

Sturzo argued that the Basques were defending their traditional independence; furthermore, they had no legal duty to back Franco and every right to oppose his illegitimate and criminal regime, especially in light of the election results of 1936. With respect to the bombing, Sturzo disputed the Francoist version that the town had been destroyed by the retreating Basques and compared the Basques with the Armenians, who had suffered similar atrocities at the hands of the Turks from 1915 to 1919. Sturzo firmly

---

9. Francois Mauriac, "Pour le peuple basque," *Le Figaro,* June 17, 1937.

10. Manuel Irujo, *Un vasco en el Ministerio de Justicia: Memorias* (Buenos Aires: Ekin, 1979), 2:200–201.

11. "La victoire des Basques," *Paris-Soir,* January 1939.

12. Pierre Dumas, *La Petite Gironde,* August 25–September 2, 1938.

13. Pierre Dumas, *Euskadi: Les Basques devant la guerre d'Espagne* (Paris: Éditions de l'Aube, 1938).

14. Luigi Sturzo to Jaume Ruiz Manent, June 17, 1937, in Luigi Sturzo, *Sritti inediti* (Rome: F. Rizzi, 1976), 2:457–59.

believed that the Basques had not burned Gernika and Durango, and he emphasized his faith in the British Foreign correspondent George Steer's reports and in testimony from witnesses like Father Alberto Onaindia* and other Basque priests who had made a report to Pope Pius XI in Rome. Sturzo also mentioned Mrs. Beer, an English Catholic who was present during the bombardment of Durango, with whom he had spoken personally.

Sturzo defended the right of the Basques to maintain their own traditions, language, and culture, all of which were threatened by the new political totalitarianism on the rise in Western Europe. He lambasted the Catholic Church for openly supporting from the start the undemocratic National Movement. However, he acknowledged that only a small group of Christian democrats were opposing the church and other Catholic organizations in Europe and the Americas. He concluded by saying that the church should not curse its persecutors but pray for them, not kill them but cure their wounds, not arm itself or others but preach peace for all.[15]

Apart from the previously mentioned writers, journalists such as Ernest Pezet and the conservative Claude Bourdet, who two years later became a leader of the French Resistance, declared that fascism, Nazism, national Catholicism, and any other form of totalitarianism were not Christian. Maurice Dignac, too, stated, "The Basque refugees in France will not be able to arrive at the feet of the Holy Father, as the Spanish refugees in Italy may. These thousands of Basque Catholics pursued by the rebels, plundered by the Crusaders, without homes or property, will not be able to reach the Father of Christianity: the Government of the fascist will stop them at the border."[16]

Members of Christian labor unions, such as Marcel Paimboeuf, chair of the French Confederation of Christian Workers (CFTC), protested against the massacre and requested help for the Basque refugee children in the French republic. Some prominent members of the Catholic Church helped the Basque government-in-exile and the refugee children, including Cardinal Jean Verdier, archbishop of Paris; Feltin Maurice, archbishop of Bordeaux and later archbishop of Paris; and Joseph Clément Mathieu, bishop of Aire and Dax.

In 1937, Monsignore Hyacinthe-Jean Chassagnon, bishop of Autun, Châlon, and Mâcon, declared "Christian charity cannot remain indifferent before this great misfortune. We urge all parish priests who have refugees in the territory of their parish to assist them, both materially and spiritually, to the extent they can. And we recommend paying special attention to the religious needs of the children."[17] Cardinal Achille Liénart, bishop of Lille, wrote similarly, "Basques are desolate; Christian charity asks us to assist

15. "La Chiesa non maledice i suoi persecutori, ma prega per essi; non li uccide, ma cura le loro piaghe, non si arma e non arma gli altri; ma predica la pace per tutti; là solamente è la Chiesa," in Luigi Sturzo to Jaume Ruiz Manent, June 17, 1937, in Sturzo, *Sritti inediti*, 2:457–59.

16. *Euzko Deya* (Paris), October 10, 1937.

17. *Euzko Deya* (Paris), September 26, 1937.

them. Most of them are our brothers in faith: this is one more reason to help them."[18] Monsignor Virgile-Joseph Béguin, archbishop of Auch, emphasized that no ideology should come before the suffering of orphan children: "The misery of the Basque people, driven from their country by the bombings and now refugees in France, is particularly distressing. . . . Our Very Dear Brothers, before these great miseries, Christian charity makes us intervene to the extent of our means, without asking anything of these sorrowful victims, under what flag their husbands, their brothers or their sons fought."[19]

Several prominent members of the Anglican Church also rose in protest against the massacre. William Temple, archbishop of York, wrote, "Surely the whole civilized world should unite to express its abhorrence of such methods of warfare. The moral judgment of mankind is in the long run, a potent force, but only exerts its influence when it is expressed. Let us, then, in the name of humanity itself, unite in condemnation of such methods as those employed in the destruction of Guernica."[20] Peter Green, canon of Manchester, stated, "If a European war comes, as seems all too likely, the scenes in Guernica will be repeated in every big town in Europe," and added, "I may live to see all central Manchester in flames."[21] Finally, Cyril F. Garbett, bishop of Winchester, declared that the bombing had been a deliberate act against the Ten Commandments and civilization: "The crime was a cruel and cowardly act of terrorism, which the conscience of humanity should brand as a crime in such a way that no man will ever again order such a hideous and appalling deed to be committed."[22]

Manuel Intxausti,* a Gipuzkoa-born Philippine industrialist, thought up the idea of creating an organization of people from politics, the Catholic Church, and culture, to offer aid to the Basque government in different countries in the same way as the Comité d'Accueil aux Basques (Basque Aid Committee) had done. After the capture of Bilbao on June 19, 1937, Intxausti met with Monsignor Clément Mathieu and the Jesuit Jean Dieuzayde to work to help the Basque refugees in the French republic. Mathieu convened a meeting in the Basses-Pyrénées, which led to the creation of the National Committee for Aid to the Basques (CNAB) under the honorary presidency of Cardinal Jean Verdier, archbishop of Paris. The committee directed a huge effort on behalf of the Basque refugees, and later it expanded its activities to Catalan and Spanish territories under the name of *Secours Catholique* (Catholic Relief), which led eventually to the creation of the International League of Friends of the Basques.

On April 27, 1938 (the first anniversary of the destruction of Gernika), Intxausti submitted to the National Board of the EAJ-PNV a draft statute on behalf of the international league. On May 5, the group released "Memorandum on a Proposal for the

18. Ibid.

19. *Euzko Deya* (Paris), October 10, 1937.

20. *Manchester Guardian*, April 30, 1937.

21. Ibid.

22. *Manchester Guardian*, May 3, 1937.

Organization of an International League of Friends of the Basques," explaining the reasons for the project, "an instrument to somewhat alleviate the sufferings of this noble people, not only through material aid but especially through the support of collective expression of sympathy in their tragedy."[23] The Basque government announced its plans for the new organization, the International League of Friends of the Basques (LIAB).[24] On December 16, 1938, Intxausti gathered a series of French political and Catholic leaders to head the project. The meeting was attended by Cardinal Jean Verdier, archbishop of Paris; Monsignor Clément Mathieu, bishop of Aire and Dax; Georges Rivollet, former minister of the French government and secretary-general of the National Confederation of Victims of the War (CNVG); François Mauriac, a member of the French Academy; a canon named Courbe, secretary of the CNAB; a person surnamed Charron, secretary of the CNVG; Claude Bourdet, secretary of the CNAB, Jesús María Leizaola, minister of justice and culture for the Basque government; Francisco Javier Landaburu;* Eugène Goyheneche; and Intxausti himself (the latter three members of the EAJ-PNV).

The French Section of the LIAB integrated two committees, chaired by Mathieu and Mauriac. The Committee for the Assistance of the Basques (CSB) included Cardinal Verdier, Édouard Hérriot, Auguste Champetier de Ribes, Georges Rivollet, Monsignor Maurice Feltin, and Louis Gillet (Honorary Committee); it was chaired by Bishop Clément Mathieu, with Bishop Rene Fontenelle and Jacques Maritain serving as vice presidents and Claude Bourdet as treasurer. The Committee Generaux d'Intérêts Euzkadi (General Committee for the Interest of the Basque Country) included Francois Mauriac as chair; Raymond Laurent as vice president; Georges Hoog and Eugène Goyheneche as treasurers; and Louis Gillet, Philippe Serres, and Pierre Dumas (members). Ernest Pezet, vice chair of the Committee on Foreign Affairs of the French Parliament, was named general secretary of both committees. Javier Landaburu was appointed the Basque government's representative and secretary of the LIAB, and Pierre Dumas was appointed delegate for propaganda.[25]

The LIAB would be the Basque government's arm working with Basques in the French Republic, and it counted among its members main figures of the French political and cultural arena: François Mauriac, Jacques Maritain, Francisque Gay, Georges Bidault, Enmanuel Mounier, Claude Bourdet, Jacques Maudale, Maurice Merleau-Ponty, Stanislas Foumet, and many others.[26] The LIAB sought to improve conditions for Basque refugees, to free Basque soldiers and civilians held in concentration camps,

---

23. Gregorio Arrien and Iñaki Goiogana, *El primer exilio de los vascos: Cataluña 1936-1939* (Barcelona: Fundación Ramón Trías and Fundación Sabino Arana, 2002), 484.

24. On LIAB, see Jean Claude Larronde, *Exilio y solidaridad: La Liga Internacional de Amigos de los Vascos* (Villafranque: Bidasoa, 1998).

25. After some success, Intxausti tried to expand LIAB to other countries in Europe and America, though "without much success." See Ligue Internationale des Amis des Basques: Section Française, *Mémoire (1940–1945)* (Paris: n.p., 1947).

26. LIAB correspondence (1945–1963), AA/AN FSAE (AA/AN FSAE), LIAB-0003-01.

to improve conditions of the Basque children's refugee collective in the French state, to regularize the administrative status of the Basque refugees, to make administrative arrangements or find employment for exiled Basque citizens with the French administration or for those hidden in Hegoalde,[27] to organize conferences at which French intellectuals would provide information on the political situation of the Basque Country to foreign media, to organize protests from exile against the Spanish dictatorship, and to contribute to a resolution of the Basque government's most serious problems through its influence with the French government (both directly and through the press).[28]

At the same time, the Basque government created, and the LIAB promoted, the choir Eresoinka, the children's music and dance group Elai-alai, and the Euskadi soccer team, cultural ambassadors for the Basque Country. In the words of the *lehendakari*:

> One can lose a war, one can lose a government, but the people retain the last word, music, dance, culture; we had lost the war in our own land, but just because of that not our spirit for the rest of the world. We wanted to demonstrate abroad just how much that Basque soul, that had been sacrificed on the altars of totalitarianism threatening to invade humanity, pulsated and we organized newspapers, journals and theater performances. . . . The chorus, called Eresoinka, sang in the main cities of France, Belgium, Holland and England, spreading our art at the same time that it changed opinion. It was propaganda, yes; but it was propaganda for liberty because, with singing, only spiritual seeds can be sown. And, singing, the Basques announced to the world that the same brutal force that had exiled those beautiful songs from the Basque Country was capable of closing the lips of other people who believed themselves more secure. Further, our artists' message was heard but not understood by many of those who would be victims of the same invaders.[29]

Led by Gabriel Olaizola, the Eresoinka choir had 110 members at its first rehearsal in Paris on December 18, 1937. Thereafter, Eresoinka undertook a two-year tour, performing in throughout the Netherlands and Belgium, as well as in Paris and London. Normally, the performances opened with an *aurreskua* (a Basque dance of honor and greeting) and ended with the acclamation, "Gora Euskadi askatuta!" ("Long live the free Basque Country!"). Eresoinka disbanded in December 1939.[30]

Along with Eresoinka, the group Elai-alai was also created. Organized and trained by Segundo Olaeta in 1926, Elai-alai consisted of about forty-five twelve- to sixteen-year-olds, most of them from Gernika. The group left Santander and went into exile in

---

27. *Hegoalde* means "Southern Basque Country" in Basque, namely, the four territories within Spain. Gasteiz (Vitoria in Spanish) is the capital of Araba; Bilbao or Bilbo of Bizkaia; Donostia (San Sebastián in Spanish) of Gipuzkoa; and Iruñea (Pamplona in Spanish), of Nafarroa.

28. Manuel Intxausti to Jorge Agirre, New York, November 25, 1940; see also Manuel Irujo to Jose Antonio Aguirre, Barcelona, June 22, 1938, AA/AN FSAE, 1-294-3.

29. Jose Antonio Agirre Lekube, *De Guernica a Nueva York pasando por Berlín* (Madrid: Foca, 2004), 73–74.

30. On the choir, see José Antonio Arana Martija, *Eresoinka* (Vitoria-Gasteiz: Servicio Central de Publicaciones del Gobierno Vasco, 1986).

Bordeaux, and from there, by train to the children's camp of Donibane Garazi. Later, they were transported again to a residence in Bry-sur-Marne. The children pursued their studies while performing in several cities in northern France and Belgium. In late 1938, Elai-alai had nearly twenty-five performances. Cardinal Achille Liénart, the archbishop of Lille, attended many performances, and the group of children was received at the bishop's residence. In 1938, Nemesio M. Sobrevilla, a well-known Basque director, directed the documentary *Elai Alai*, which featured the children's group. Elai-alai also participated in the Exposition for Social Progress, which took place in Lille in July 1939, in addition to presenting various performances in Paris. The group participated with Eresoinka in LIAB-organized events at the Salle Pleyel and the Palais de Chaillot in 1939.

Likewise, in October 1937, the Basque national soccer team left the port of Le Havre for the Americas. Its aim was twofold: it would raise money for Basque refugees and raise awareness about the Basque Country and its political conflict throughout the world. The team visited New York, Havana, Veracruz, and Mexico City. The team played ten games in Mexico—and won all of them. The team also played against River Plate, Boca Juniors, and San Lorenzo de Almargo of the Argentine league, although it was prevented from joining the league. After playing in Valparaíso, Chile, in 1938, the team went to Cuba, where it played against the team from Havana's Galician Center and against the Cuban national team, winning both games. Finally, the team competed in the Mexican professional league during the 1938–1939 season, finishing in second place.[31] After two successful years, the team disbanded in the spring of 1939 after the fall of Catalonia, mainly because of economic issues.

In addition to these efforts to promote the Basque Country, among the key initiatives of the Basque government in Barcelona was aid for Basque prisoners in Francoist jails and concentration camps and assistance to the refugees in Catalonia and France.

Prime Minister Francisco Largo Caballero had formed a new Spanish Republican government on September 5, 1936, and appointed Irujo minister without portfolio on September 25. On May 18, 1937, in the new government of Prime Minister Juan Negrín, Irujo became minister of justice, a position he held until his resignation in December 1937, when he was reappointed minister without portfolio, a position he held until August 17, 1938.

Irujo took the post reluctantly, pressured by lobbying from leaders of the EAJ-PNV. As he said, "I was the price for the statute"; his entry into the Republican government brought confirmation of the statute granting autonomy to the Basque state, on October 1, 1938. The appointment of a Basque Catholic minister allowed the Spanish republican government to present to the world the image of a democratic Spanish Republic, along with its role as protector of human rights and freedom of worship; however, thus counteracting the Francoist propaganda, based largely on the false accusation that the Spanish

31. Enrique Terratchet, *El Euskadi* (Bilbao: La Gran Enciclopedia Vasca, 1976), 65–85.

Republican government had systematically organized the assassination of hundreds of Catholic priests. Irujo had three main concerns as minister of justice of the Republic: ending *paseos*, extrajudiciary executions of priests or civilians without previous trial and reorganizing the judiciary; seeking agreements with the International Red Cross to protect and exchange POWs; and adopting legal measures to protect the human rights and freedom of religion of the most vulnerable human groups.

With respect to freedom of religion, Irujo always acted according to traditional Basque humanism, legality, and democracy, and not in defense of the privileges of the Catholic Church, which caused him numerous problems with the ecclesiastical hierarchy. Indeed, Irujo went up against the Vatican and especially José Torrent, vicar general of Barcelona, not against the Socialist Republican government, on everything related to restoring public worship in Catalonia. On January 7, 1937, Irujo presented to the Council of Ministers his Report on the Religious Situation; on July 30, he presented the draft Law on Religious Freedom, which was passed on August 17 as the Decree on the Freedom of Religion. Moreover, Irujo undertook all necessary legal and executive measures to cease religious persecution. Under his guidance, the Basque chapel was opened in Barcelona, and it continued as a worship space until the Francoist forces captured Barcelona. After the war, the Catholic Church and the Spanish state would not recognize the validity of any sacraments celebrated at the chapel—all judicial and registry paperwork written in Catalan or in Basque had been declared legally nonexistent and null.

Irujo also was deeply involved in reorganizing the judiciary according to the principles of law. Between 1936 and 1938, Irujo dedicated his time as minister to overseeing the judicial system, dismantling popular trials, abolishing summary trials, reducing the number of death sentences, working with the Red Cross, and guaranteeing the exchange of prisoners. Irujo made it clear that, as minister of justice, he would ensure that courts and judges applied the laws without illegitimate pressures and would make efforts "to humanize the war, to ensure assistance for the wounded and to save each prisoner's life, treating the prisoners with pity and not with revenge."[32] In fact, Irujo's first action as minister of justice was to visit prisons and cemeteries to bring to an end to indiscriminate acts of violence: "I went to the front lines, hospitals, prisons and barracks. My first visit was to the morgue, where I spent four hours watching one by one, all the bodies. I was terrified of the monstrous rancor hidden somehow in the peoples and the endless brutality that the war allowed to come out, staining with innocent blood the exploits of republican democracy and creating difficulties for the war effort."[33]

Irujo made sure that all the presidents of the people's courts were professional judges, he ordered the release of all imprisoned priests, and he signed as many indults as possible. Together with the Ministry of the Interior, Irujo established a system whereby political prisoners could be released to visit relatives in the hospital; no escape was ever

32. Manuel Irujo Ollo, *Manuel de Irujo, un vasco en el ministerio de justicia: Memorias I* (Buenos Aires: Ekin, 1976, 6).

33. Ibid.

registered under this system. Irujo opened the Republican prisons to the inspectors of the International Red Cross and promoted exchanges, for which he was popularly called "minister of the exchanges." Moreover, Irujo continuously criticized the treatment of prisoners in the Nationalist-controlled area, as the prisoners were subject to torture and mistreatment in concentration camps and forced labor camps, execrable conditions in jails and war hospitals, and indiscriminate executions by firing squads. In December 1937, in the Nationalist jails, there were 7,935 prisoners in Bizkaia alone; 2,136 in Larrinaga; 1,211 in El Carmelo; 532 in Escolapios; 616 in women's jails; and 532 on the *Upo Mendi* prison ship.[34] By April 1938, 724 prisoners in Bizkaia had received the death penalty.

Among those killed was Alfredo Espinosa, minister of health of the Basque government. Espinosa was the president of the UR and had worked in the Ministry of Health to improve the living conditions for patients and to provide social assistance to refugees. After the establishment of the Basque Red Cross, the ministry worked particularly in the area of the health of prisoners. Espinosa also collaborated in the creation of specialized homes for sick and injured children, a rest home for soldiers, nursing homes, a maternity home for refugees, a rest home for the elderly, and charitable foundations. In June 1937, Espinosa flew from Toulouse to Santander, where the remaining troops of the Basque army were concentrated; however, in agreement with the Nationalists, the pilot José Yanguas landed on the beach of Zarautz, where Espinosa was captured. He was executed, together with Captain Agirre, on July 24, 1937.

Indeed, the Francoist regime would create about 180 concentration camps under the supervision of the Militarized Penitentiary Colonies Service and the Department of Concentration Camps and Soldier-Workers.[35] With Executive Order 258, of July 5, 1937, the secretary of war of the Spanish government appointed Colonel Luis Martín de Pinillos to establish a commission for the creation of concentration camps.[36] Starting in November 1936, the commission collaborated with German officers, coordinated by Wilhelm Faupel, first ambassador of the German regime to the Nationalist government. The monitoring of the concentration camps was the responsibility of *Konzentrationslagerkommando* (concentration camp commandant) Paul Winzer, a member of the Gestapo, appointed by Heinrich Himmler as police attaché at the German embassy, a position he would hold until 1944. According to the Reports and Bulletin of the Depart-

34. Pedro Barruso, "La represión en las zonas republicana y franquista del País Vasco durante la Guerra Civil," *Historia Contemporánea* 35 (2007): 669.

35. The construction of concentration camps or prisons for prisoners of war is not a war crime per se. However, the violation of the principles that should govern those penitentiary institutions, such as the implementation of measures to worsen the living conditions of detainees, primarily reduced food rations, poor health measures, and the lack of bedsheets and other elements constitutes a war crime and a crime against humanity. Negligence in attaining these ends, if followed by a breach of minimum acceptable conditions, can have legal consequences.

36. *Boletín Oficial del Estado*, 258, July 5, 1937, in Conxita Mir, *La represión bajo el franquismo* (Madrid: Asociación de Historia Contemporánea, 2002), 167.

ment of Prisons of January 1940, there were 270,719 inmates in the Spanish state.[37] After four pardons in 1940 and amnesties in 1941 and 1943, by April 1943, the prison population had dropped to 114,958 inmates, 22,481 of whom were common criminals and 92,477 of whom were prisoners of war. In June 1945, 33,267 political prisoners remained in Spanish prisons.

According to the Act for the Redemption of Sentences through Work, prisoners of war could choose to work in labor camps, and by doing so, they could reduce their sentences by one day for every two days they worked—an arrangement that was in flagrant violation of the provisions of the Geneva conventions.[38] From 1939 to 1942, the prisoners of war were grouped into labor battalions under the jurisdiction of the Department of Concentration Camps and Soldier-Workers, under the Ministry of War. Several of these worker battalions were in the Basque Country: Disciplinary Battalion No. 30, in Sondika; No. 92, in Gasteiz; No. 105, in Etxalar; and No. 196, in Bilbao. By order of General Mola in January 1937, several concentration camps were created in the Basque Country; by virtue of the executive order of July 5, 1937, one was established in Burgos at Miranda de Ebro, where large numbers of Basque prisoners of war were transported. The camp, which would remain operational until 1947, was created in the image of the existing camps in Germany; during the war (1936–1939), it was directed with the assistance of units of the Gestapo and the SS, led by Winzer, and Heinrich Himmler visited the camp in October 1940. According to the Military Archives of Ávila, in April 1938 there were 715 prisoners of war in the concentration camp of Lizarra-Estella (at the Salesian school and the monastery of Iratxe) and 1,716 prisoners in Iruñea.[39] In addition, there were other concentration camps in Irun, Deusto, Saturraran (Deba), and Nanclares de Oca. Many Basque prisoners of war were taken to prisons in El Dueso in Santoña, to Logroño, or to El Puerto de Santa María (near Cádiz).

As minister of justice of the Republic, Irujo also adapted the child custody legislation to wartime conditions. Irujo issued a decree on September 7, 1937, implementing the Hague Convention of June 12, 1902, indicating that the competence for protecting the thousands of children who had been evacuated, within Europe or overseas, belonged to the government that had organized the evacuations, which made it possible to provide guardianship and legal custody to the children in exile.

Irujo resigned in August 1938 over his deep disagreement with measures of the Republican government, including the so-called police courts to prosecute crimes

---

37. *Breve resumen de la obra del Ministerio de Justicia por la pacificación espiritual de España* (Madrid: Ministerio de Justicia, 1946).

38. Glicerio Sánchez, *Los empresarios de Franco: Política y economía en España, 1936–1957* (Alicante: Publicaciones Universidad de Alicante, 2003), 160.

39. Archivo Militar de Ávila, A.1, *leg.* 58, cp. 10, ff. 4–5, box 2330, in Fernando Mendiola and Edurne Beaumont, "'Vinieron un montón de prisioneros': Los batallones de soldados trabajadores vistos y recordados por la población de la montaña navarra (Vidángoz e Igal: 1939–1941)," in *Els camps de concentració durant la guerra civil i el franquisme* (Barcelona: CEFID and Museu d'Història de Catalunya, 2002), 83, available at http://www.cefid.uab.es/files/C%C3%B2pia%20comunII-1.pdf.

summarily and the militarization of cases of high treason and espionage. In Irujo's opinion, summary trials by military tribunals for espionage or other crimes did not offer the necessary guarantees for the defense of the accused and resulted in unnecessary, and a significant number of, death penalties. Irujo also resigned in solidarity with the Catalan government. The Spanish central government's transfer to Barcelona had severely limited Catalan autonomy (e.g., all war industries created and managed by the Generalitat were confiscated), which increased friction between the Catalan and Spanish governments and affected the direction of the war.

As already mentioned, refugee assistance was among the most urgent tasks of the Basque government in Catalonia. At least six of the ministers of the Basque government-in-exile were fully involved in tasks related to the refugees or to Basque prisoners: Minister of Economy Eliodoro de la Torre, Minister of the Interior Telesforo Monzon, Minister of Social Assistance Juan Gracia, Minister of Health Alfredo Espinosa, Minister of Justice and Culture Jesús María Leizaola, and Minister of Labor Juan de los Toyos. According to a Basque government report of March 1939, between May and October 1937, 103,115 Basque citizens and 13,631 Spanish citizens escaped from the Basque Country to France on boats chartered by the Basque government. Moreover, the report indicates that five thousand more people departed from Asturian or Cantabrian ports in vessels chartered by Republican institutions. According to Gregorio Arrien and Iñaki Goiogana, by the end of 1937, there were about 150,000 Basque refugees living to the north of the Pyrenees.[40]

In Catalonia, at the end of 1936, there were around sixteen thousand Basque refugees who were more or less directly assisted by the Social Welfare Department of the Basque government. In early 1937, a few thousand more refugees came to Catalonia; after the fall of Bilbao, this figure increased significantly through 1938. In mid-January 1937, the Basque government delegation in Barcelona created the Social Welfare Council (CAS), and Irujo asked the Generalitat of Catalonia to incorporate a member of the Central Committee of Social Welfare of Catalonia into the CAS, to coordinate the work of refugee assistance with the Catalan government. The CAS provided money, supplies, and assistance to maintain the various colonies of refugee children in the Northern Basque Country.

With the increasing number of refugees, in spring 1937, the Official Committee for Aid to Euskadi and the Committee for Aid to Euskadi and the North were established, with the main task of assisting Basque refugees in Catalonia. In 1937, the Basque government tried to locate all Basque refugees in a single region and agreed to appoint a person responsible for each shelter. During July 1937, the Basque social welfare agencies provided a total of 495 services—130 injections, 125 minor surgeries, 53 home visits, 90 doctor's consultations, 95 typhoid vaccines, 2 physicals—and distributed 170 free

40. Arrien and Goiogana, *El primer exilio de los vascos*, 78.

medicines to refugees. Apart from these cases the Basque social welfare services offered another twenty-eight services in other hospitals.

At first the French government opened its doors to the refugees and invested a considerable sum of money to assist them: seven francs for each parent, four francs per woman, four francs for each child older than sixteen years, and five and a half francs for each child younger than sixteen. Moreover, from the spring of 1937 on, assistance from international private aid agencies increased considerably. Together with the existing Comité d'Ajout d'Enfants Espagnols and CNAB, the Comité Vasco de Ayuda a los Refugiados, and the Comité Sueco en favor de los Niños de España were established in the summer of 1937.[41]

However, in view of the influx of refugees, in August 1937, the French government officially declared that it would receive no more refugees. On September 27, 1937, a circular from the Ministry of the Interior ordered the forcible return of all refugees who had no financial means to sustain themselves. Prime minister Juan Negrín knew of the measure, but Basque authorities had not been notified; consequently, the Basque government did not have much time to react. Monsignor Clément Mathieu, bishop of Aire and Dax, and members of the CNAB intensified their efforts to access financial assistance to support the shelters for Basque refugee children. By the end of October, they had managed to place several hundred children in various colonies and to resettle 2,357 children in Belgium and 50 more in Switzerland. On November 4, 1937, seventeen mayors of Basque coastal cities sent a complaint to France's Ministry of the Interior, asking the government to suspend repatriation.

According to the report "Emigración Vasca" (Basque Emigration), written in Paris and published on March 12, 1939, French authorities had deported about one hundred thousand Basque refugees during the last months of 1937, of whom sixty-three thousand were driven to Catalonia and thirty-six thousand were taken to Hegoalde through Hendaia. An estimated nineteen thousand Basque refugees remained in France. In addition, approximately one hundred thousand Basque refugees entered Catalonia. That is, in early 1938 the Basque government had to provide assistance for some 160,000 Basque refugees in Catalonia and 19,000 in France.[42] As Walter C. Thurston of the US consulate in Barcelona reported at the end of February 1938, the violence of the passions aroused by the war made the lot of the civilian population a tragic one, since the occupation of new territory by the rebel armed forces was in many instances followed by drastic action against noncombatants on the grounds of their past political activities or presumed affiliations or sympathies. Occurrences of this nature produced the phenomena of wholesale exoduses—spontaneous or forced—in the face of advancing troops. To meet the situation

41. Organizations listed in this sentence are: Committee for the Aid of Basque Children, National Committee for Aid to the Basques (CNAB), Basque Refugee Aid Committee, and Swedish Committee for the Aid of Basque Children.

42. "Emigración Vasca", Paris, March 29, 1939, IAA, GT-Docs.EV.1939. See also, AA/AN FSAE, Correspondencia general / 1945–1954 / Rezola, kdp.00130, C.1. And, Irargi, Correspondencia M-P / 1942–1958 / GE-0180-01.

created by the resultant shifting of population the Republican government created the Department of Evacuation and Refugees that, at the end of the war in Catalonia, had supervision over 1,800,000 refugees and 1,200,000 evacuated persons.[43]

The situation worsened in 1938. Following a request from the French government, the Spanish Republican government created the National Committee for Aid to Spain (CNAE), an official evacuation service. Between the winter of 1938 and the spring of 1939, the CNAE helped thousands of refugees cross over into France. In the fall of 1938 there had been an exodus of five hundred thousand Catalans, Spaniards, and Basques into the French republic. Thereafter, realizing the fall of the Catalonian front was imminent, the British and French governments recognized the Francoist Spanish government in February 1939.

In this atmosphere, just as the pro-Franco international coalition was about to take the town of Igualada, the last hurdle before sweeping into Barcelona, Justice Minister Jesús María Leizaola approved several measures:

- To give priority for Basque government aid to those with direct military responsibilities or connections, who were therefore potentially subject to receiving the death penalty or a prison sentence, as well as to give priority for evacuation to France of children, women, and the sick.
- To rent buses, cars, trains, and two ships (*Danubio* and *Storm*) to mobilize evacuees.
- To guarantee rations for everyone, and to rent hotel rooms in Northern Catalonia (inside France) for people.
- To remove without delay Basque soldiers from the concentration camps organized by French authorities in Northern Catalonia.
- To organize material and spiritual aid for imprisoned soldiers (e.g., barracks, infirmaries, toilets, showers).
- To negotiate with the French administration, together with LIAB, for the acquisition of work, entry, and travel permits for Basques living abroad.

After Basque Minister of Health Alfredo Espinosa was executed, the organization of health services for Basques in exile passed on to Eliodoro de la Torre. As can be deduced from the Report of the Department of Health of December 31, 1937, a large network of hospitals and nursing homes was established abroad throughout the spring of 1937. Among them, La Roseraie hospital in Bidarte and the heliotherapy sanatorium of Berck-Plage were two of the most important. Of the total 230,846 francs spent, 96,950 were invested in La Roseraie, 96,516 francs in Berck-Plage, and the rest in other services.

---

43. "The Spanish Civil War; Movement of Population", Report by Walter C. Thurston to the US Secretary of State. Barcelona, February 26, 1938. NARA, College Park, US Ambassador Claude G. Bowers Files (Files 852.00/..., Box 6416), Document 852.00/7525. Pp. 1–2.

During the last months of the war in the Basque Country, about 250 or 300 sick children were transferred to the resort of Saint-Christau in Gorliz. In August 1937, some 108 sick children were repatriated, and the remaining 140 were transferred to Berck-Plage, a relatively distant sanatorium for sick children in Berck-sur-Mer in the Pas-de-Calais department. The children sent to Berck-Plage were treated at the Bouttilier and Vincent sanatoriums, where they were attended by eight Basque nurses, a chaplain, and a doctor, plus the French staff. The total monthly budget was about ninety-five thousand francs. The children were attended by the best specialists—mainly they suffered from pulmonary infections or problems related to malnutrition—and most completely recovered.

The sanatoriums Osasuna and Assantza in Kanbo and the clinics of Saint-Étienne and Paris also opened their gates to Basque refugees who needed health care. Moreover, the Basque government organized small health centers and infirmaries in shelters and hotels in Baiona, Cadaujac, Getari, Uztaritze (Jatxou), Orthez, Saint-Christau, Soulac, and Vouzeron. Among the largest was at the eighteenth-century citadel of Donibane Garazi. The French authorities negotiated the transfer of the citadel to the Basque government under two conditions: Basque authorities had to make necessary repairs to the citadel (it lacked water, electricity, and toilets), and no political demonstrations would be organized there. The five hundred children of the citadel were among the last to leave Bilbao.

Within a few weeks, two kitchens, an infirmary, dormitories for girls and boys, thirteen classrooms, a chapel, and a system of latrines had been established. There were twenty-five teachers, three chaplains, a doctor, a cook and assistant cooks, two nurses, and an administrator to take care of the five hundred children. At first, no one was paid. Classes were taught similarly to the *ikastolas* in the Basque Country. Religion was a compulsory subject, and the Basque government appointed several inspectors to report regularly on the situation of each school. Each student attended classes in his or her mother tongue: 60 percent learned in Basque and 40 percent in Castilian. Although the French government granted five francs daily per child, that was not sufficient. Classes were short on supplies, such as books and writing materials. And even when there was food for everyone, it did not vary, consisting mainly of rice, potatoes, and vegetables.

In December 1937, Leizaola called Bingen Ametzaga to Barcelona, Luis Arbeloa succeeded him as director of the Donibane Garazi colony. Like many other colonies, the threat of occupation by the Germans or other troops forced their closure. After two years in operation, the French government ordered the citadel at Donibane Garazi to close. The approximately three hundred children remaining at the colony were driven to Cagnotte (boys) and Poyanne (girls). Indeed, in the midst of World War II, the number of children in the colonies decreased from about 500 in March 1939 to 378 in September 1939. After the beginning of the war, most children returned to their families. By January 1937, only forty-three children were awaiting return to their families or guardians.

In total, during the period of the Basque exile in Catalonia, from 1937 to 1939, the Basque government had six colonies under supervision of the Department of Culture, fourteen rest homes and sanatoriums under supervision of the Department of Social Welfare, and three hospitals under supervision of the Department of Health. The number of people whom the Department of Health assisted decreased during 1939 from nearly 900 patients in March to 392 in November. Likewise, the Department of Social Welfare had approximately 1,400 refugees under its care in January 1939 and 303 in March 1940.[44]

In addition to all the above, Basque Brotherhood (EA), a private humanitarian association for the assistance of Basque refugees, linked to EAJ-PNV, EAE-ANV, and other Basque nationalist organizations, began to assist refugees in mid-1938. The brotherhood provided subsidies and maintained residences for refugees run by the refugees in exile. In the homes, EA organized classes on general education and Euskara for children, choirs, and folk dance groups. In addition to the daily work of running the residences and gardening—to counteract the food shortage—the refugees engaged in work such marquetry, espadrille making, and even logging. Moreover, the Basque government helped many refugees find jobs so that they could afford their own expenses while in exile. In total, EA came to organize about a dozen residences, among them L'Orée, Mary-Jeanne, Mayou, St. Joseph, Soleilhet, and Ustekabea in Capbreton; Itxasu, in Itsaso; Villa Lanne, in Ziburu; Magescq, in Arion; Maurrin, in Granade-sur-Adour; and other residences in Coquelicot, Escource, La Grive, Litte et Misse, Morcenx, Onesse, Pissos, Saubion, Solferino, and St. Paul. Also, EA organized a school in Getaria with the help of the Basque Department of Culture. In 1939, EA offered assistance to approximately two thousand people with its average monthly budget of 180,000 francs.

At the same time, the French authorities resolved in February 1939 to create a series of concentration camps, called *centres d'accueil*, for republican refugees (former soldiers). Consequently, approximately seven thousand Basque former soldiers were imprisoned in different concentration camps. Among them there were nearly eight hundred refugees at Argelès-sur-Mer, nineteen miles north of the border with Catalonia. As José Elizalde, a prisoner at Argelès-sur-Mer, stated, "Living conditions were poor, we had not much to eat, [it was] cold, the health conditions were not appropriate. Moreover, being so close to the border we were uncertain about the intentions of the French authorities and lived day after day without having any other aid and information but that granted by our government-in-exile."[45] Minister Telesforo Monzon, responsible for the Basque prisoners at French camps, sent food, clothing, medicines, tents, and tools to Basques who had been placed in the camps. As part of this aid program, a number of wooden barracks, a 150-bed infirmary, toilets, kitchens, laundries, and showers were built for the

44. Arrien and Goiogana, *El primer exilio de los vascos*, 449–77.

45. Interview with Jose Elizalde Arzua (1914–2006), soldier at Gernika Berri, in Altzuza (Nafarroa), February 2, 2000.

eight hundred Basque refugees at Argelès-sur-Mer. This new "neighborhood" within the concentration camp was named Gernika Berri, or New Gernika. Yet the aid was clearly not enough: cases of diseases caused by malnutrition or cold were frequent. "However, we were lucky, for we built barracks with a capacity for 1,500 men; had toilets, kitchen, and showers; and ate moderately well—meanwhile the rest of the republican prisoners, Spanish or Catalan, had to sleep outdoors, for their governments seemed not to care about them, and the French authorities did not grant much assistance. We organized ourselves according to our grades in companies and the Nafarroan Martín Soler was appointed commander of the camp and Father Iñaki Azpiazu was our chaplain. We had certain duties to keep us occupied during the day, organized a chorus, and celebrated a daily mass."[46]

After releasing the prisoners from concentration camps, in March 1939 the Basque government created the Oficina de Empleo (Employment Bureau) to find work for the refugees so that they could fend for themselves in exile and thus obtain the necessary permits from the French authorities to remain within France and avoid expatriation and subsequent jail time. The Basque Employment Bureau's mission was to create lists of Basque workers, employed and unemployed, and to make the necessary arrangements with the French authorities and with private employers to provide work for the refugees. José María Iturrate, the former chief of staff of the Euskalduna shipyards in Bilbao, was named head of the bureau. The offices were installed in Baiona, where most of the Basque refugees were; as a consequence, the bureau was attached to the Ministry of the Interior and not the Ministry of Labor, which was led by the socialist Juan de los Toyos.

However, much before the Bureau was created the Basque government's authorities had facilitated, with the help of the LIAB, hundreds of contracts. In the summer of 1938, Elias Etxebarria, a member of the EA and the Euzkadi Buru Batzar (EBB, executive committee of EAJ-PNV), together with Francisco Gorritxo, made an inspection trip to the workplaces in the Landes region, where Basque refugees had been employed as loggers; they compiled a list of more than seven hundred names. Of those, three hundred were *gudaris* (former Basque soldiers) who had taken part in the war on Basque battalions, two hundred and thirty were exiles of military age and had escaped after the capture of Irun and Donostia, and Etxebarria and Gorritxo could not determine the origin of the others. Months earlier, in April 1938, Julián Estévez and Ceferino Jemein had recorded two thousand Basque exiles working as loggers in the Landes and had reported that, moreover, there were hundreds of Basques working in construction or at quarries, and that many *emakume* (Basque nationalist women) were also working as maids or nursemaids in private homes or in shops and in the textile industry.[47]

---

46. Interview with Jose Elizalde Arzua, February 2, 2000.

47. Julián Estevez and Ceferino Jemein, *Report to the EBB*, April 1938, AA/AN FSAE, DP-15-3.

In a report dated July 21, 1939, the Employment Bureau listed 554 Basque exiles who had found employment. Of those, 266 were working for farmers or ranchers scattered throughout different parts of France.[48] The war led to a significant increase in the need for labor, especially for skilled workers. As of October 1, 1939, 870 Basque refugees were employed in the French war industry, 700 of whom worked in the arsenal of Tarbes.[49] In late 1939, the number of refugees registered with the Basque Employment Bureau was 2,196, of whom the vast majority were from the southern departments of the republic (Pyrénées-Atlantiques, 1,334; Les Landes, 327; Tarn-et-Garonne, 210; and Hérault, 207).[50] In the area of Tarbes, where the greatest number of Basque workers was concentrated, in January 1940 there were 818 Basque exiles employed in the three most important industrial centers of the area, namely, the arsenal of Tarbes (406 employees), the factory at Bazet (62), as well as working in construction of the new arsenal at Lannemezan (350). On January 29, 1940, Juan de los Toyos sent a report to the *lehendakari* on the achievements of the Ponencia Interdepartmental (Interdepartmental Committee), controlled by the Basque Ministry of Labor. According to De los Toyos, 346 Basque refugees had been employed near and in the Paris area in better economic conditions than those of Landes.[51]

The Basque government also organized other services to help the refugees. The Ministry of the Economy, to help workers settle in the industrial areas of Tarbes, Bazet, and Lannemezan, sent inspector Luis Sagarminaga, who, after examining the situation of the Basque workers and their families, established an aid of up to one thousand francs to bring the households of the workers to their localities. Iturrate also organized workshops at the hospital of La Roseraie. The workshops were conceived of as vocational colleges that would train the exiles to help them find better jobs in French industry. The workshops were also designed to train disabled soldiers, or those maimed or injured in war, to work under their new circumstances. The proposed sections of the vocational college included lathe operating, forging, welding, electrical work, and wood carving. One of the most successful initiatives was the manufacture of *espartinak* (sandals); the venture was so successful that the sandal producers in the area protested to the French government. In the end, the legal difficulties regarding the sale of sandals and the lack of funding forced the closure of the college in August 1939.

Under pressure from the socialist members of the Basque government, who, led by de los Toyos, watched with suspicion the achievements of the Employment Bureau, on December 30, 1939, the Basque Council of Ministers agreed to add delegates from

---

48. *Summary of the Basque Professionals Employed in the French Republic through the Employment Office of the Basque Government until July 21,1939*, AA/AN FSAE, GE-257-4.

49. Telesforo Monzon to Jose Antonio Agirre, November 2, 1939, AA/AN FSAE, 1-159-12.

50. *Report on the Employment of Laborers of the Employment Office*, December 27, 1939, AA/AN FSAE, AN-GE-114-2.

51. Juan de los Toyos, *Report on the Employment of Workers in the Paris Area*, January 29, 1940, AA/AN FSAE, S-6923.

the UGT and the Basque Workers' Solidarity (ELA-STV)[52] labor unions to the bureau. This decision led to many protests. Telesforo Monzon submitted his resignation on the grounds that the inclusion of labor union representatives was inadmissible. Iturrate, head of the bureau, also disagreed, expressing that all de los Toyos wanted was control over the bureau because of the success it had achieved. As a result, ELA-STV also protested and refused to be part of the bureau, stating that the measure was completely unnecessary as the bureau had done an excellent job in finding employment for four fifths of the refugees. In addition, the ELA-STV did not understand why it was necessary to change an institution that had achieved such good results, into a system of work "that has obtained such poor results with their famous 'responsible comrades' and 'labor union controls.'"[53]

Despite this crisis, the bureau continued to carry out its duties, and it worked closely with the LIAB until the German occupation in May 1940. In late January 1940, there were 4,127 refugees employed through the bureau; by mid-April, that number had risen to 5,881.[54]

After the fall of Catalonia in March 1939, the management and assistance of the refugees was an operation involving hundreds of thousands of people, and as a result, the Basque government needed financial support from the Spanish republican government. The Spanish Refugee Evacuation Service (SERE), the organism in charge of assisting refugees of the Republic, was created far too late, in February 1939, under the directorship of Pablo Azcarate, former ambassador of the Republic in London.

There were several disagreements between the Basque government and SERE concerning the organization and administration of aid for the refugees in exile. Although from the spring of 1939, SERE promoted sending all refugees to the Americas, especially to Mexico, the Basque government was never in favor of this solution, except when the German occupation in 1940 made it the only option. In fact, although the first official requests for the shipment of Basque immigrants from South American governments, including Venezuela, to the Basque government dated to 1938, the Basque administration's policy until 1940 was to keep refugees, including children, in Europe and to encourage their prompt repatriation to the Basque Country. Consistent with this idea, the National Council of the EAJ-PNV, with the Basque nationalist government ministers present, on September 26, 1939, formally adopted full military and political support for France in its struggle against Axis forces and, therefore, resolved not to pro-

52. Basque Workers' Solidarity. Eusko Langileen Alkartasuna (ELA) in Basque and Solidaridad de Trabajadores Vascos (STV) in Spanish.

53. Pedro Ormaetxea to the secretary of the Ponencia Interdepartamental, January 13, 1940, AA/AN FSAE, GE-258.9.

54. LIAB, *List of Basques Working in the French Republic*, February 1940, AA/AN FSAE, GE-257-1. See also *Report and Calculation of the Basques Who We Believe Are Working in the French Republic*, March 7, 1940, AA/AN FSAE, 1-158-3; *List of the Basque Citizens Who Are Working in the French Republic*, April 15, 1940, AA/AN FSAE, 1-158-3.

mote or organize the migration of Basques to the Americas. "The Basque government, of course, does not organize or support evacuations."[55]

The plight of the approximately two hundred thousand Basque refugees had moved the Basque administration in 1937 to organize a system of social assistance for the Basque refugees in Iparralde, France, and Catalonia. And likewise, the Basque government did not disregard its responsibility for the thousands of children who had been evacuated in 1937 and were in 1939 dispersed across six different countries. This fact caused considerable differences in the care of refugees abroad. Although Basque refugees benefited from social welfare services and a complex network of shelters, residences, hospitals, clinics, schools, training workshops, and an employment office, Spanish Republican exiles generally had little recourse other than escape to the Americas. Similarly, when in 1939 the French authorities confined refugees in concentration camps, the Basque government-in-exile was able to negotiate with the French authorities, with LIAB as an intermediary, for the release of most of them. This saved many Basques from being transported to German death camps; despite their efforts, it is still estimated that hundreds of Christian Basques and thousands of Jewish Basques died in those camps.[56]

These differences raised suspicions within the Republican government, and even the possibility of suspending the Basque government. To the surprise of Justice Minister Manuel Irujo, both Minister of the Interior Julian Zugazagoitia (PSOE) and Minister of National Defense Indalecio Prieto (PSOE) proposed dissolving "the Basque government that has no reason to be," so that all Republicans in exile—whether Basque, Catalan, or Spanish—would suffer the same fate. Irujo responded that a responsible government should do precisely the opposite, that is, following the Basque example, procure and manage the proper care of all exiles.[57]

In the spring of 1937, before the capture of Bilbao, the Basque Treasury Department transferred all its capital from the Bank of Spain in Santander to the bank's office in Valencia. However, this again generated problems with the Republican government. On August 25, a day after the last Basque refugees had departed from Santander into exile, Gonzalo Zabala (manager of the Bank of Spain in Baiona) and Pedro Lecuona (consul of the Spanish republic in Baiona), demanded on behalf of Prime Minister Negrín the transfer of all Basque government funds to the Republican government. Basque authorities refused, as doing so would leave refugees unattended and without care.

However, the funds that the Basque government had deposited at the Bank of Spain in Valencia were not enough to cover the expenses of the social welfare network that the Basque government had organized in exile. Because the Republican government refused to provide any capital, the Basque government was required to take out a credit of 7

55. Record of the EBB, September 26, 1939, AA/AN FSAE, DP-16-4.

56. Iosu Chueca, *Gurs: El campo vasco* (Tafalla: Txalaparta Argitaletxea, 2007), 111–12. See also, Ruth L. David, *Child of Our Time: A Young Girl's Flight from the Holocaust* (New York: Tauris & Co., Ltd., 2003), 119–25.

57. Manuel Irujo to Eliodoro de la Torre, n.d., AA/AN FSAE, AN-GE-K.00389.C5.

million pesetas from the Banco de Bilbao and the Banco de Vizcaya in Barcelona, despite Prime Minister Negrín's rejection.[58] In 1939, the total expenditures of the Basque government amounted to more than 2 million francs per month. The evacuation of Basques from Catalonia alone is estimated to have cost the Treasury Department 1,458,246 francs.[59] As Gregorio Arrien and Iñaki Goiogana note, between June 1938 and March 1939, the Basque government spent 22,530,544 francs and took in only 14.75 million francs.[60] As Minister of the Economy Eliodoro de la Torre predicted, in April 1939, the Basque government had 8,504,872.37 francs available—at a spending rate of about 2.5 million francs per month, the government would go bankrupt within three months.

On March 23, 1939, *Lehendakari* Agirre asked Prime Minister Negrín for the amount of money that the Republican government owed to the Basque government, and on March 24, Minister of Finance Eliodoro de la Torre met with Spanish Minister of the Economy Méndez Aspe to reach an agreement on fiscal matters between the two governments. Yet after the first meeting, Aspe refused to receive de la Torre. In addition, Negrín demanded from Agirre a report on the income of the Basque government since the beginning of the war in 1936 through 1939, as he believed that those revenues corresponded to the government of the republic.

Given the critical financial situation and the refusal of the Spanish government to open doors for any sort of dialogue, the General Council of the EAJ-PNV named Julio Jauregi as the delegate to restart negotiations with SERE. Jauregi visited Pablo Azcarate, president of SERE, who also expressed that all the welfare and refugee assistance institutions that the Basque government and its agencies managed in exile should be integrated into and administered by SERE. Agirre then contacted Tomas Bilbao, a member of EAE-ANV, former minister under Negrín, who would be responsible for negotiating with Jauregi an agreement satisfactory to both governments.

On April 26, an agreement was reached under which SERE would provide funds to the Basque government but only to cover social assistance for refugees and not other services (e.g., schools, hospitals); a SERE agent would audit the use of the funds as well. Because the republic had been unable to organize shelters and residences for refugees, Basque-managed shelters would become available to refugees through SERE, and the Basque government was to immediately cede two shelters to SERE. Finally, the Basque government would advise SERE and facilitate organization of the shelters that SERE needed abroad.[61]

---

58. Eliodoro de la Torre, Report on the financial situation of the Basque government to Doroteo Ziaurritz, AA/AN FSAE, AN-GE-258-4.

59. Eliodoro de la Torre to Jose Antonio Agirre, April 4, 1939, AA/AN FSAE, AN-GE-258-1. See also *Expenses Incurred by the Evacuation of Basques from Catalonia*, March 8, 1939, AA/AN FSAE, AN-GE-1-156-4.

60. Arrien and Goiogana, *El primer exilio de los vascos*, 495.

61. *Base for the Maintenance of the Shelters Set Up by the Government of Euskadi*, April 26, 1939, AA/AN FSAE, AN-GE-206-9.

Despite the agreement, SERE imposed many bureaucratic obstacles to the money transfers, and the manager of SERE's Purchasing Commission embezzled funds, thus delaying or completely obstructing some of the transfers.[62] Moreover, on March 3, 1939, before the war was officially over, President Manuel Azaña resigned; thereafter, tension increased among Spanish Republicans, mainly between Juan Negrín (a left-wing socialist, or neocommunist) and Indalecio Prieto (a moderate socialist).

In this context, in March 1939, Negrín sent the funds SERE required to Mexico on the yacht *Vita*, and he tasked Marino Ganboa, a Philippines-born US citizen of Basque descendance to take care of the money.[63] The funds were to be received by José Puche Álvarez, director of the Technical Committee to Aid Spanish Refugees (CTARE), which represented SERE in Mexico and was to receive funds, provide aid, and accommodate Spanish refugees in Mexico. However, when Prieto learned of the yacht's arrival in Veracruz on March 28, 1939, wielding the authority of the Republican parliament in exile, he took control of the funds to found the Board for the Relief of Spanish Republicans (JARE), with Lluís Nicolau D'Olwer as chair and Prieto as vice president. The result was that JARE became an alternative to SERE, and it would primarily be used as a political tool against Negrín in the confrontation between the two leaders-in-exile.

In view of the impediments and difficulties that SERE created for the Basque government, Indalecio Prieto nominated Manuel Irujo as secretary of JARE, in order to gain the support of EAJ-PNV and the Basque government in his cause against Negrín. However, because the leaders of the Basque government and the EAJ-PNV considered this a total lack of responsibility and administrative efficiency with respect to managing aid for refugees, the EAJ-PNV rejected Prieto's proposal. Irujo responded to Prieto that the JARE had been created in the context of a struggle to replace an organization that had mismanaged social assistance for refugees.[64] Doroteo Ziaurritz,* chair of the EBB, urged President Agirre to continue in his efforts to ensure the recovery of monies owed to the Basque government for refugee assistance, to undertake any necessary efforts to reduce expenditures as much as possible, and to seek sources of funding independent of the Spanish government.[65] According to a report by Eliodoro de la Torre to the *lehendakari* on September 13, 1939, the Basque government had funds amounting to 4.5 million francs, which would cover two months of its activities in exile.

The economic situation was desperate, but the Basque authorities received about 280,000 francs from the League of Invalids to lease the residence for disabled soldiers in Souston. It also received some funds from the sale of its shares in the Great Britain–based

---

62. Julio Jauregi, *Report to the EBB on the Economic Agreement with the SERE*, January 3, 1940, AA/AN FSAE, AN-PNV-107-6.

63. The boat had belonged to Alfonso XIII under the name of *Giralda*.

64. Manuel Irujo to Indalecio Prieto, August 9, 1939, AA/AN FSAE, AN-GE-258-2.

65. Doroteo Ziaurritz to Jose Antonio Agirre, July 9, 1939, AA/AN FSAE, AN-GE-261-13.

shipping company Mid-Atlantic.[66] After these infusions, the only other viable solution was for the government to become a JARE member. With strong internal dissent, on January 24, 1940, the EBB appointed Jose Aretxabaleta the EAJ-PNV representative at JARE. The EBB also instructed Jauregi, who had previously refused, to submit the proposal to join JARE. Finally, on February 19, 1940, in a meeting held of the standing joint committee (Diputación Permanente) of the Cortes, EAJ-PNV joined JARE.

As a result of the economic agreement with SERE, the Basque government received 13,674,368 francs between May and December 1939; expenditure on social assistance in the same period amounted to 14,442,666 francs. That is, the Basque government was forced to cover costs with nearly 1 million francs from its own funds.

Joining JARE did not solve the financial problems of the Basque government, as SERE and the republican government still refused to cover the costs for refugee assistance. This fact forced the Basque authorities to seek alternative financing.

With the war lost and Catalonia captured in the spring of 1939, the internationalization of the Basque case in the context of World War II was the only chance to overthrow Franco and restore democracy in the Basque Country, Catalonia, and Spain; in other words, according to President Agirre the defeat of the Axis would lead to the end of Oliveira Salazar's and Franco's regimes. Agirre, confident and optimistic, outlined the way in a letter to Joxe Mari Lasarte: the world's moral force is against totalitarianism, Franco is not going to be able to defend himself against the fall of the German and Italian totalitarian systems, and the triumph of the democracies would bring triumph or, at least, would create the immediate path to triumph of democracy in the Basque Country and in Catalonia, and also in Spain.[67]

In this context, the Basque government took direct responsibility and control for organizing aid for Basque refugees, as they considered that CNAE and other Republican organizations such as SERE were not organized enough. After the fall of Barcelona, the Basque government had two possible courses of action: to give in and abolish its government or, with the war in the Basque Country and Catalonia lost, to continue the struggle from exile in Paris. The first was not a real option, at least until the refugee question was settled. Consequently, Agirre arrived in Paris. Amid terrible circumstances—the war lost, financial instability, facing World War II, and exile—the Basque government began the third phase of the Basque exile.

66. Antonio Gamarra, *Report to the EBB*, n.d., AA/AN FSAE, AN-PNV-107-6.

67. Jose Antonio Agirre to Joxe Mari Lasarte, Paris, September 11, 1939, IAA, GT-Agirre.JA.1939.

5

Paris: April 1939–May 1940

In October 1936, the *lehendakari* had appointed Rafael Picabea as representative for the delegation of the Basque government in Paris. Between 1936 and 1939, Picabea's main responsibilities had pertained to information and diplomacy: conducting interviews and producing articles, short books, journals, and so forth. In November 1936, the periodical *Euzko Deya—La Voz de los Vascos* was published in Paris for the first time, in French, Basque, and Spanish, edited by Felipe Urkola, the former editor of the newspaper *El Pueblo Vasco*. *Euzko Deya* published 204 issues in Paris between November 29, 1936 and the German occupation of Western Europe in June 1940.[1] The Basque government's information services had two goals: first, to provide information about what was happening in the Basque Country and to clarify that, with the pretext of defending Christianity, the Spanish Nationalist government was violating human rights and was no more than a dictatorship; second, to underscore the Catholic (Christian-Democratic) nature of Basques and their desire for freedom.

Believing that it would have to deal with only a short-term exile, the aim of the first Basque government-in-exile was to pursue the political program that had been suspended as a result of the Falangist victory in the Basque Country in June 1937. During the war in 1936, the Basque government demanded and negotiated for broader powers from the Spanish Republican government. Despite the internal problems and tensions in the Spanish government, as well as the drive to win the war and a lack of structure and coordination, the *lehendakari* expanded his autonomous, and constitutional, authority.[2] In the economic sphere, the Basque government began receiving financial support from Basque centers in the Americas in 1938, mainly to help purchase the headquarters of the Basque government-in-exile at 11 Avenue Marceau in Paris.[3] As time would demonstrate, this was the only reliable source of financing for the Basque government-in-exile.

---

1. *Euzko Deya* (The voice of the Basques), being one of the most important organs of the Basque government-in-exile, was published in various important cities throughout the Basque exile, especially in Paris (1939–1975): other editions cited in this book are from Buenos Aires (1939–1975) and Mexico City (1943–1973).

2. Jose Antonio Agirre to the Comité Central Socialista de Euskadi (Central Socialist Committee of the Basque Country), Paris, May 1939. IAA, GT-Agirre.JA.1939.

3. Doroteo Ziaurritz to Paulino Gómez Beltrán, May 1939. IAA, GT-Ziaurritz.D.1939.

Facing the instability of the Spanish republican government and the Basque government's administrative and financial independence, in the spring of 1939, Jose Antonio Agirre established four foundations on which to base the work of the Basque government: (1) undertaking policies with effects in the Basque Country and bringing democracy back to the Basque Country as soon as possible; (2) guaranteeing consensus among the different political forces within the Basque government; (3) making the Basque political conflict known at the level of international institutions; and in order to fight for human rights, (4) defending the democratic project for European unity, which various European nations had drawn up, to guarantee peace in international politics. In this context, in the spring of 1940, as Manuel Irujo had promised, the Basque government established a program to maintain the Basque national idea, even from exile:

1. The government of Euzkadi was established in Gernika, under the Basque Statute [in October 1936].
2. Its original legitimacy stems from its president having been elected by Basque city halls, its cabinet being drawn up by him in full exercise of his powers, and its administration being exercised by the government, within its own jurisdiction and territory of Euskadi.[4]
3. The stipulated program among the political parties, connected by concurrence and bases, both in terms of electing the president and the forming and substance of government, was that he swore on oath to defend this and that the ministers promised their support. Basque Nationalists, Republicans, Socialists, and Communists established their solidarity regarding the formulation of joint political action, implied by that coalition government. The only voluntary withdrawals from the government team were the Communists.[5]
4. Regarding principles, that program had been fulfilled. According to Lehendakari Agirre, its development, interpretation, and adaptation, as a work of government and as regards the fact that the Basque thesis affected each political moment, were entrusted at all times to the criteria of the members of the government. That part of the program that was not carried out was the result of a reality that was beyond its control.[6]

---

4. *Euskadi* and *Euskal Herria* mean "Basque Country" in Basque.

5. As a consequence of the Ribbentrop-Molotov Pact, a nonaggression treaty endorsed by the Third Reich and the Soviet Union in August 1939, Agirre decided to expel the communist member of the Basque government. However, the Spanish Communist Party had already expelled Minister Juan Astigarrabia from the Communist Party (and thus from the Basque government) in 1937 because of his ideological approach to Basque nationalism: he appeared to be in favor of conceding autonomy to the Basque Country and defended the historical rights of the Basques. He was also charged with being responsible for the fall of Bilbao. The postwar geopolitical framework and the agreements with the Roosevelt administration (1942–1949) maintained the Communist Party members of the Basque government-in-exile. After being expelled from the party, Astigarrabia went into exile in Panama and Cuba.

6. Manuel Irujo to Antonio Gamarra, London, April 11, 1940. IAA, GT-Irujo.M.1940.

The Socialists in the Basque government were reticent about the idea of Basque national politics. In October 1936, the PSOE in Madrid formed the Basque Socialist Federation (FSV). The federation was a meeting point for socialists in Bizkaia and Gipuzkoa[7] but dependent on Madrid. Under the leadership of Paulino Gómez Beltrán,* the Basque Socialist Central Committee (CCSE) became the effective working committee of the FSV.

In any event, several important figures attended a meeting in Paris on February 14, 1939: Jose Antonio Agirre and Telesforo Monzon (EAJ-PNV); Minister Gonzalo Nardiz (EAE-ANV); CCSE members in Paris, including Miguel Amilibia; and Santiago Aznar, Juan Gracia, and Juan de los Toyos, Socialist ministers in the Basque government. As already noted, the Socialists were opposed to Agirre's idea of Basque nationhood, although the group was divided.[8] Indeed, the Basque minister and PSOE member Santiago Aznar appeared to favor the Basque government's autonomy in a note to the CCSE, and Juan Gracia also appeared to be in favor of Basque autonomy.[9] On March 10, Paulino Gómez Beltrán and Ángel Jiménez of the CCSE again opposed Aznar's ideas in a letter sent to Agirre, but the Basque government's new organization and action program was passed on May 8. The new program featured three main elements:

1. The Basque government, based on the authority stemming from the wishes expressed democratically by Basque citizens in elections, was the only legitimate government of the Basque Country.
2. The *Lehendakari* was the Basque government's effective head of authority. Together with the Basque government, the Consejo Nacional Vasco (Basque National Council) consultative body was formed. The Consejo Nacional Vasco was the legislative authority representing the will of the Basque citizens in exile. Its members would be all the ministers in the Basque government and Basque members of the Cortes [the Spanish parliament], former Basque members of the Cortes, and the former mayors of the four Basque capitals in Hegoalde.
3. Lastly, abroad, the Basque government would pursue the Basque national idea, that is, it would function as an independent government until democracy was restored in the Basque Country. The Basque government, together with the Spanish Republican government, would, after overthrowing Franco, create the Spanish state's new constitution, according to the four following agreed upon principles: (1) Recognition of the Basque national character and as a result the right associated with this to choose freely the system that best safeguards this character. (2) Certain truly democratic principles that should govern the politi-

7. In Bizkaia and Gipuzkoa (industrialized territories), socialism was a stronger political force than in Araba and Nafarroa.

8. Miguel Amilibia to the CCSE, Paris, February 17, 1940. IAA, GT-Amilibia.M.1940.

9. Document by Santiago Aznar, Paris, March 2, 1940, in Koldo San Sebastián, *Crónicas de postguerra* (Bilbao: Idatz-ekintza, 1981), 195–99.

> cal body, which should be extended without impairment from any democratic disputes that might occur in the future. (3) Certain principles of true social justice expressed by clear rules and applicable to the reality of Basque social life. (4) The clear and firm support for the democratic powers in their fight against totalitarianism.[10]

These policies were maintained throughout the Basque exile until 1975. Four points underpinned the Basque national idea, namely, the will to return, military and political interventionism in the context of World War II, the fight for human rights at national and international levels, and, finally, financial aid and relief for the Basque refugees abroad.

The first element of the Basque national idea was return, which would be the government-in-exile's drive for thirty-nine years. In May 1940, nobody imagined that the exile would last so long. Therefore, return was not considered in terms of the 1931 Spanish constitution. For Agirre, return called for a "new thirty-one"; it required a new political situation and a different legal framework as a solution to all the incongruities, faults, and mistakes of the various Spanish Republican governments between 1931 and 1936. According to Agirre and most of the members of the Basque government-in-exile, in the post-Francoist political framework, the Basque citizens had to have the right of self-determination and so be entitled to decide if they wanted to be part of a Spanish and French state or not, and the Basque language had to be co-official with Spanish and French.

The second point was interventionism. The Basque national idea called for the Basque government's active participation in World War II. The Basque government would take part politically and militarily in the war, without consulting or being under the control of the Spanish Republican government. When Great Britain and France declared war on Germany in September 1939, the Basque government made a public statement via LIAB: the Basque government, in its capacity as representative of the Basque people, had fought against the pro-Franco international coalition between 1936 and 1937 and had expressed its willingness to continue the fight; indeed, before the September 1939 declaration of war, the Basques had been fighting Nazis and fascists in the Basque Country from 1936 to 1937.

Such military intervention required an army, yet the Basque government had no means of sustaining armed forces in France or anywhere else in Europe. The only possibility, in terms of economics, politics, and administration, was to establish a secret service. There were multiple advantages to doing so: it was more economical than maintaining an army, and it allowed for placing agents in France, Great Britain, and other places in Europe and the Americas. Moreover, the Allies needed intelligence services and would be likely to sign an agreement on military collaboration in exchange for

---

10. Jose Antonio Agirre to Jose Ignacio Lizaso and Manuel Irujo, Paris, November 22, 1939. IAA, GT-Irujo.M.1939.

a political covenant on the political status of the Basque Country; and finally under Franco's dictatorship all basic rights were suspended and the only way of action of a democratic government was to act under cover (resistance), so the secret service was the only means of operating inside the Basque Country. Consequently, the Basque secret service was set up between 1937 and 1939—although it was most active between 1942 and 1950. It carried out operations under the orders of the Basque government throughout World War II.

Political intervention demanded involvement in international politics. The Basque political conflict would no longer be resolved within Spain and France. For the first time, New York and London had also heard that the Basque conflict was an international issue. This international diplomatic activity maintained direct and close relations with the secret service. Indeed, the Basque delegation placed great importance on having direct influence and a specific presence in high-level European and US politics. In this political context, the Basque government had five guiding principles.

The first principle was to defend democratic values and human rights against the Axis powers in Europe and Asia. This was to be done by developing military, political, diplomatic activities through the Basque secret service agents, starting in the Philippines and throughout Latin America and Europe.

The second principle was the right of self-determination (i.e., of a nation to become a politically independent state). Taking into account President Wilson's fourteen points after World War I, it was necessary to defend the right of self-determination for the Basque Country and other stateless nations in the post–World War II scenario.

The third principle was pro-European unity and federalism. The Basque government repeatedly supported the European Union of Nations political project. In Irujo's words, in looking at France and Great Britain, World War II had already created the European Union. Indeed, the union was considered the only way to avoid World War III, as well as the only way for Europe to be politically and economically autonomous and competitive after the war.

The fourth principle was Christian-social policy. The Axis propaganda in South America was based on the idea that most of the countries of the Axis and its satellites were Christian Catholic, such as Italy, Spain, and Austria; meanwhile most of the allied countries were non-Catholic, such as the United Kingdom and the United States. To answer to the Spanish government's propaganda throughout the Americas and Europe, the secret service and the Basque delegation underscored that the EAJ-PNV was a Christian-Democratic political force. Between 1936 and 1975, the Basque government's information services emphasized that the war was neither a civil conflict nor a struggle between Christians and atheists. This was for the Allies one of the most interesting arguments of the Basque secret services in the Americas.

The fifth principle was cultural activity. Believing that return was near in 1939, between 1938 and 1940, a working group in the Basque Department of Culture in Paris established all kinds of programs to promote the Basque language and culture in the Basque Country. Among the main objectives abroad were to establish Basque cultural centers or ministries of culture, to set up a publishing house specializing in Basque themes, and to create chairs of Basque language and culture in universities in Europe and the Americas.

Yet the Basque government's main concern after 1936 was refugees. The conditions of thousands of Basque prisoners of war was a pressing concern for the Basque government, as were the conditions of refugees and children living in colonies in Iparralde and throughout Europe.

In the summer of 1936, the EAJ-PNV established the Basque Information and Publicity Service under the direction of Joxe Mari Lasarte. Once Bilbao fell and the Basque government moved to Barcelona, the service was restructured as the Domestic Service (SI), headed by Luis Álava. As both Juan Ajuriagerra* and Lucio Artetxe were in jail at the time, they were appointed the heads of SI within the Basque Country. The main goal of the SI was to collaborate with the International Red Cross to improve conditions for Basque prisoners (e.g., food, medicine), to halt death sentences and death by firing squad, and to negotiate prisoner exchanges. Many SI agents were women—including Maritxu Aranzadi, Delia Lauroba, Maria Teresa Verdes, Itziar Múgica, and Bittori Etxeberria, because it was easier for them to gain admission to prisons to bring in food, medicine, and clothing.[11] They passed on information from various prisons (El Dueso, Larrinaga, Prisión de Pamplona, Prisión de San Cristobal, Burgos, and Penal de Puerto de Santa María) to the Basque government's secret service agents at headquarters in Baiona, and they transmitted information to the prisoners.[12] According to Iñaki Barriola, "Lauroba collected together all the information, [including the things that] María Teresa Verdes attained, and passed it on to Itziar Múgica (Donostia), who handed it in to Bittori Echeverria (Elizondo), who was in charge of passing it on to those who were waiting in the Northern Basque Country."[13] The women saved hundreds of prisoners from the death penalty. However, hundreds of prisoners were still executed, and many more died of poor health either in the prisons or in the prison hospitals.

In 1939, the competition between the two Socialist leaders did not help the refugees' situation. Following the fall of the Aragón front in March 1938, Indalecio Prieto resigned from the Spanish government over differences with Negrín. Until that point, the SERE, controlled by Negrín's government, was the main institution in charge of organizing refugee evacuation. However, on March 23, the *Vita* arrived at the Mexican port of Veracruz carrying a passenger in charge of Spanish government money. After some wrangling, Prieto, who was in Mexico at the time, managed to gain control of the money. In fact, on July 28, 1939, the Spanish Parliament's permanent councils created a committee to administer the funds that Negrín's government did not control and that

11. Iñaki Barriola, *19 condenados a muerte* (Donostia-San Sebastián: Ediciones Vascas, 1978), 15–17.

12. Interview with Maritxu Aranzadi, Iruñea, December 27, 1994.

13. Barriola, *19 condenados a muerte*, 15.

were on the *Vita*; two days later, JARE was established. On August 1, Lluís Nicolau d'Olwer was appointed director of JARE, with Prieto as one of six committee heads. Republican leaders disbanded JARE in April 1940.

The Basque government protested repeatedly at the evident lack of responsibility of Republican leaders. As a result of SERE's increasing problems, Eliodoro de la Torre, the Basque minister of economy, met with d'Olwer in December 1939 to guarantee aid money for Basque refugees. The Basque JARE representative would be José Aretxabaleta, the former director of Bank of Bizkaia and the Basque Chamber of Commerce in Catalonia.[14] However, a shortage of capital forced the Basque government to take special measures. To continue living abroad, those people without a particular political role or who had not received the death sentence or been sent to prison would have two options: to enlist in the French army or to leave France. According to the report "Rules for the Classification of People in Charge," refugees would be put into three categories for financial aid purposes: they would receive a daily allowance of 25, 15, or 7.5 francs; those who were responsible for a family would receive a specific monthly amount.[15] In the summer of 1939, financial aid was restricted to a specific period of time.

To obtain financial aid and relief, the government needed the correct documentation for the refugees and needed to sign an agreement with the French authorities to regulate the legal status of the refugees. As already mentioned, the Basque government, through the efforts of Eliodoro de la Torre, had set up the Employment Bureau for refugees in France.

The refugees who began going to the Americas by ship in 1938 and 1939 often did so with the help of the CNAE. On February 28, 1939, the *Vita* departed for Veracruz. The *Sinaia* transported 1,500 republican refugees to Mexico on May 26, helped by the British Committee for Refugee Aid; 1,000 more arrived on the *Ipanema* on June 12, aided by the Confederated Hispanic Societies. The first group to arrive in Venezuela, about sixty-five men, women, and children, left the port of Le Havre on June 25 aboard the SS *Cuba* and reached La Guaira on July 9. The *Habana* and the *Flandre* left for Caracas on June 25 and July 28, respectively, arriving in August. A group of eighty-six Basque refugees left on the *Bretagne* on August 11 for Caracas. A further 2,100 refugees arrived in Chile on August 4 on the *Winnipeg*, with the help of the Federation of Pro-Spanish Refugee Argentine Organizations. Once again, Mexico received refugees from two trips of the *Mexique*—200 and 2,100 refugees, respectively. On August 6, the *Donibane* and *Bigarrena*—two small fishing boats that the Basque Ministry of Economy rebuilt—departed for Caracas on August 9 and arrived on September 8. Moreover, SERE arranged for the transportation of around 1,500 exiles on the *La Salle*, *Flandre*, and *De Gras*. Thousands of refugees arrived in American ports from 1939 to 1942.

14. Eliodoro de la Torre to Doroteo Ziaurritz, Paris, December 15, 1939. IAA, GT-Ziaurritz.D.1939.

15. Jose Antonio Agirre to Juan Nadal, Paris, August 14, 1939. IAA, GT-Agirre.JA.1939.

At this point, the Germans were invading Western Europe. The blitzkrieg began on May 10, 1940, and shocking everyone, Hitler's troops took Paris on June 14—the armistice was signed on June 22. As Bingen Ametzaga, one of the last members of the Basque government's Department of Justice and Culture, pointed out on abandoning Paris, the Nazis took Bordeaux when they arrived and, before they arrived in Biarritz by train, the town was already theirs. In the words of Ametzaga, one of the biggest problems for the Nazis was the speed with which the French army retreated. Barely a month and a half later, German soldiers were in Hendaia, exchanging cigarettes with Franco's Civil Guards on the Bidasoa Bridge.[16]

Meanwhile, Jose Antonio Agirre had disappeared. After forging the Basque government's new program, the Basque national idea, with the Basque Socialists and Republicans, Agirre appeared in Belgium. World War II surprised him at the small Flemish town of De Panne, fourteen miles east of the beach at Dunkirk. As was the Catalonian president, Luis Companys, Agirre was in danger of being arrested by the Gestapo and handed over to the Spanish government. The Nazis captured Companys and extradited him in September 1940. On October 14, he was executed in Montjuic Castle. As Agirre recalls in his remarkable book *De Gernika a Nueva York pasando por Berlín* (*Escape via Berlin*),[17] to escape from Nazi hands, Agirre fled to Berlin. But his disappearance left the Basque government without a leader in the worst of times.

On May 8, 1940, Agirre and his family left Paris for De Panne, where they were to meet his wife's parents. On May 10, the German troops began their offensive, bombing the fuel tanks at Dunkirk. Two weeks later, the battle to control Dunkirk occurred (May 24–June 4). Having permission to board a British ship, the Agirres, along with other Basque refugees, attempted to cross the nineteen miles that separated them from the British lines at Dunkirk. On May 22, after advancing sixteen miles toward Dunkirk, they reached Bergen, where they slept outdoors in houses that German bombs had destroyed. They were unable to cross the last six miles to the British zone, and so they returned to De Panne. There, during a German bombing raid, Cesáreo Asporosa and Encarna Agirre Lekube, the *lehendakari*'s sister, were killed and another of his sisters and his sister-in-law were injured. Finally, with no contact with other members of the Basque government, the family fled to Brussels, arriving by car on June 2.

In Brussels, Agirre, accompanied by the Jesuit father Luis Chabauld Errazkin, was welcomed by the Jesuits at the Convent of San Francisco Xavier. Agirre grew a mustache and began to use nonprescription glasses to hide his identity—he knew the Gestapo was pursuing him at the request of the Spanish police officers operating in Paris, including Comisario Pedro Urraca, Juan Macías, and Antonio Fernández. For safety reasons,

16. Mercedes Iribarren Gorostegi, voice recording, 1970.

17. José Antonio Aguirre [Agirre], *De Gernika a Nueva York pasando por Berlín* (Buenos Aires: Ekin, 1944. Reprint, Madrid: Foca, 2004). Translated as *Escape via Berlin: Eluding Franco in Hitler's Europe*, trans. Robert P. Clark (Reno: University of Nevada Press, 1991).

Agirre and Chabauld moved to Antwerp, twenty-nine miles north of Brussels, where they stayed in Asporosa's house while his family moved to Leuven, nineteen miles east of Brussels. From the contacts he had previously established through the Basque government office in Antwerp, Agirre contacted Germán Guardia Jaén, consul of the Republic of Panama, who gave him a false identity and a new passport under the name José Andrés Álvarez Lastra.[18] Agirre remained hidden in Antwerp and left the city only for a trip at Christmas to Louvain, to meet with his wife, Mari Zabala, and his two children, two-year-old Aintzane and five-year-old Joseba.

The Gestapo arrested Agirre's brother Juan Mari Agirre Lekube and held him incommunicado for fifteen days. Interrogated and tortured, Juan Mari had no information on the whereabouts of the *lehendakari*. Unable to flee from Europe to the south or across the English Channel, at the end of 1940, Agirre opted to leave his family in Belgium and go to Germany to obtain passage to the Americas through Sweden for the whole family. On January 7, Agirre went by train to Hamburg, accompanied by a German officer who volunteered, without knowing Agirre's identity, to serve as an interpreter for him during the trip. There he met Guardia Jaén. On January 12, Agirre arrived by train in Berlin, accompanied by Guardia Jaén, under the cover of being a member of the Panamanian consulate.

During his stay in Berlin, Agirre visited the Foreign Ministry, the imperial palaces and various delegations, consulates, and embassies. He met with the consul of the Spanish government in Berlin, one Mr. Navarro, and with Jacinto Miquelarena, a reporter for the fascist newspaper *ABC*—no one recognized him. On March 14, "stung by curiosity," he attended the funeral mass for the Spanish king Alfonso XIII, organized by the Spanish Embassy in Berlin with the acquiescence of the German authorities.[19] Agirre even attended, on March 27, a rally addressed by Hitler, who was accompanied by Hermann Goering and Joachim von Ribbentrop, as well as by the Japanese foreign minister Matsuoka Yosuke and General Hiroshi Oshima, the Japanese ambassador to Nazi Germany during World War II.[20] "I was at about 50 meters. I have seen under cover the famous exit to the balcony of the Chancellery. I had in my hand a Nazi and Japanese flag that some members of the SS have 'so gently' given to us."[21]

Once they found passage to Sweden in May 1941, the rest of Agirre's family traveled to Berlin under false names, embarking on May 23 to Gothenburg, where they managed to board the merchant ship *Vasaholm* to Rio de Janeiro on July 31, together with a group of Polish Jews fleeing from the Nazi horror. They arrived in Rio on August 27. Agirre remained under false identity in Brazil until October 9, 1941, and he was in

18. The initials of the false name are the same as the ones of his real name, Jose Antonio Agirre Lekube.

19. Alfonso XIII, head of Spain during the fascist dictatorship (1923–1931), died in exile in Rome in 1941, after the Spanish Parliament found him guilty in 1931 of usurping popular sovereignty and being complicit in the coup d'état.

20. Interestingly, Oshima was one of the key informants for the Allies during the war.

21. Iñaki Goiogana, ed., *José Antonio Agirre Lekube: Diario 1941–1942* (Bilbao: Fundación Sabino Arana/Sabino Arana Kultur Elkargoa, 2010), 44.

constant contact with the authorities of the US embassy. Finally, having the necessary permits, Agirre crossed into Uruguay with his family, where he was received with the full honors due to a head of government. In Montevideo, he announced that he was alive and made political declarations during a special session organized by the country's administration at the Uruguayan House of Representatives.

6

London: May 1940–October 1941

Once Paris had fallen to the Nazis and an armistice had been signed, Andrés Irujo,* Miguel José Garmendia, and Julio Jauregi met with Jesús María Leizaola (the acting *lehendakari*) in Baiona. It was a precarious time; nobody knew whether Agirre was alive, and after the Nazi invasion, everyone knew that their lives were in danger. With the passing of time, the situation did not improve, and Leizaola could not run the Basque government from occupied Baiona. For that reason, the London delegate José Ignacio Lizaso suggested creating a Basque National Council: "The creation of a central institution in Basque life that would carry on with the work of the government led by you and its title of 'Basque National Council' was accepted unanimously, at my suggestion. Its automatic composition was Manuel's suggestion. The presidency could not go to anyone else who fulfilled the same conditions, qualifications and prestige but Irujo. The provisional status of the body was unanimous. Thus the Basque National Council was born."[1]

Under the leadership of Manuel Irujo, the new political initiative was made public on July 10, 1940, and it came into effect the following day (nineteen days after the armistice had been signed). The council comprised ten people: Manuel Irujo (*lehendakaria*); Ramón María Aldasoro (vice *lehendakaria*); Ixaka Lopez Mendizabal, Santiago Cunchillos, Pablo Archanco, Juan Olazabal, Francisco Belaustegigoitia, Manu Sota,* and José Ignacio Lizaso (council members); and Ángel Gondra (secretary).

The beginning of World War II and the Nazis' victory in France markedly transformed the political goals of the first exile within a few short months. Unlike 1938, the Basque National Council in London demanded the historical right of self-determination for the Basque Country in discussions with the British and French governments. Before 1943, with the prospect of return closer and the issue of self-determination central to any negotiation, the key point underpinning the second Basque government-in-exile's political program was achieving sovereignty in the Basque Country itself. With that goal in mind, the government's chief concerns were to develop diplomatic ties with the democratic governments of Europe and the Americas and to aid military action against the Axis forces.

1. José Ignacio Lizaso to Jose Antonio Agirre, London, October 24, 1942, AA/AN FSAE, AN-GE-466-1.

Indeed, although the Conservative British governments led by Prime Ministers Stanley Baldwin and Neville Chamberlain sided with the Non-Intervention Committee[2] throughout the war until 1939, from 1940 on, members of the Basque National Council thought that there would be a profound change in the Conservative government's foreign policy, even though Winston Churchill's government clearly demonstrated a similar policy toward the Spanish regime. By contrast, throughout the war, the position of Clement Atlee's opposition Labour Party and offer of help to the Basque government was quite different. The Basque National Council, in contact with the Foreign Office, drafted the Plan for the Invasion of the Iberian Peninsula on July 18, 1940, in the event that General Franco would join the Axis powers.[3] At the same time, the Basque government's institutional dealings with the US government from the winter of 1941 on raised some hopes of direct Allied intervention. On November 7, 1942, after the Allies landed in Morocco and Algeria, Franco declared a partial mobilization in the Spanish colonies of northern Africa. However, this did not lead to the hoped-for confrontation between the Allies and Franco. The landings at Normandy on June 6, 1944, completely destroyed any hopes for direct intervention. Ignoring Franco, the Allies swept through Italy and France toward Berlin.

While Agirre was still missing, the Basque National Council had four objectives: to take on the duties of the Basque government and return to work; to respond as soon as possible to the plight of the refugees in Europe; to take part actively in World War II, both politically and militarily; and to reach a political agreement that would ensure independence for the Basque Country after World War II. As for the first objective, the Basque National Council would work to maintain the Basque national idea. Indeed, more than just continuing with the idea, Irujo would give it shape. The strategy agreed on at the Meudon meetings in 1939 was put into practice in London; according to Lizaso: "The Council was not born with a new policy. It is a continuation of what President Agirre and his ministers always laid out for those of us abroad who enjoyed his trust in order to work closely with the democracies, collaborating with them to the benefit of universal interests and the specific [interest] of freedom for our homeland."[4]

As noted, the most pressing issue was that of evacuating refugees. Facing a completely chaotic situation, on February 23, 1939, the French Council of Ministers instructed General Henri Ménard to take the necessary steps to resolve the refugee problem in Northern Catalonia. And so was born the idea of creating a series of camps

---

2. Fifteen days after the insurrection started in July 17, the French government appealed to the British, Italian, and German administrations to create a system of nonintervention and by early August the French received the assent of them all. The resulting strategy was named "the Non-Intervention Agreement" even though it was not an agreement (since no document was signed) and it did not intend to stop foreign intervention (but to cover up intervention and avoid an open international conflict). The agreement affected equally trade of war materiel with any of the parties at war, republicans or rebels. Xabier Irujo, *On Basque Politics: Conversations with Pete Cenarrusa* (Brussels: EURI, 2009), 130–31.

3. *Memorandum of C. H. A. Wills: Plan de invasion de la Penísula Ibérica*, London, July 18, 1940, AA/AN FSAE, AN-GE-464-1.

4. José Ignacio Lizaso to Ramón Sota, London, March 11, 1941, AA/AN FSAE, AN-GE-464-2.

of refugees, called *centres d'accueil.* Among the camps was one in Gurs for eighteen thousand Basque, Catalan, and Spanish inmates, whose work began on March 15 and ended on April 25, 1939. As Iosu Txueka has mentioned, Jean Ybarnegaray reported to the French Parliament in March 1939, before the German invasion, that 226,000 Republican veterans were interned as refugees in five concentration camps in France: 77,000 in Argelès-sur-Mer, 90,000 in Saint-Cyprien, 13,000 in Barcarés, and 46,000 in Arles-sur-Tech and Prats de Molló.[5]

Many of these refugees, especially the Basques, were transferred to Gurs. Between April 5 and 19, 1939, there were 5,089 people registered as Basques, most of them former Eusko Gudarostea soldiers, who were moved to the A, B, C, and D sections of the camp at Gurs. Between April 19 and 23, there were 9,934 more refugees interned who were classified as *aviateurs, internacionaux,* and *espagnols.* In April 1939, in total there were 15,023 refugees at Gurs; in August 1939, 6,555 of those were Basque refugees.[6]

Before the Nazis occupied Western Europe, on March 21, 1940, Paul Reynaud was appointed prime minister of France. On May 10, Jean Ybarnegaray was designated minister of state. By that the time, the situation of the Basque refugees had worsened considerably. When in May 1940 the blitzkrieg began, 2,293 refugees remained in the camp, 1,839 of them who were members of various Spanish brigades. The Basque government-in-exile had managed to liberate almost all the Basques held there. After the Nazis took Paris, with help from LIAB the Basque government managed to get the last *gudaris* out of Gurs on June 23.

Following the May 1940 offensive, in Belgium, the Netherlands, and France (all under Nazi control), there were around sixty thousand Basque refugees and children's colonies for whom the Basque government was responsible. The Spanish authorities had sentenced many of the refugees to death. José Félix Lequerica had been the Spanish representative in Paris since 1939, and the French police and the Gestapo had started collaborating with representatives of the Spanish embassy. Meanwhile, following the armistice, Marshall Philippe Pétain was at the head of the collaborationist Vichy government, and the state police began arresting Basque refugees.

On August 2, 1940, the Spanish government's chief of security contacted the Vichy government to exchange information on the Basque exile. On August 27, Lequerica, under the orders of Spanish Interior Minister Ramón Serrano Suñer, passed on a list (drawn up by the Spanish police) of 636 refugees to the Vichy government's minister for foreign affairs, Robert de la Baume. That same day, French police handed over Lluís Companys from the Santé prison to the Spanish embassy police chief, Pedro Urraca. Lequerica maintained this policy of turning over refugees to the Spanish government until the last ones left by ship from Marseilles; on November 14, he handed over another list, this time with three thousand names, to the Vichy government. In addition

5. Iosu Chueca, *Gurs: El campo vasco* (Tafalla: Txalaparta, 2007), 25.

6. Ibid., 59.

to arresting Companys, the French, Spanish, and Nazi police and secret services arrested Max Aub; Federica Montseny; Francisco Cruz (the head of JARE's press office); and the Spanish Republic's former ministers of industry Joan Peiró and Julián Zugazagoitia.[7] The Spanish authorities executed both Peiró and Zugazagoitia. Those in charge of the Spanish embassy in France were especially interested in seizing both Spanish and Basque properties, public companies, and interests that had belonged to refugees. Doing so was the primary task of the so-called Commission for Collecting Possessions.

This new 1940 Basque exile has to be placed within the context of World War II. Now Basques in Iparralde (Northern Basque Country) and Western Europe were on the run not just from Spanish justice but also from falling into the hands of the Gestapo and Vichy police. This period of Basque exile was much more complex than the previous one. The refugees were fleeing from countries under Nazi or Axis control; for the first time, the Americas now offered Basque refugees their only escape since most of Western Europe was now occupied by the Germans or controlled by satellite governments such as Spain and Portugal. However, the Basque National Council in London had to secure ships to sail to the Americas, and the ships needed international permissions to both cross the Atlantic and dock in American ports. To all this had to be added the critical economic situation and the hostile new regime in Spain after 1939.

In addition to refugees living under German control, the Basque government had to concern itself with others in Spanish state prisons, concentration camps, and forced-labor battalions. After the German occupation of Iparralde, the Basque secret services lost their former bases in Lapurdi, Behe Nafarroa, and Zuberoa, as well as in Landes and Béarn. As a result of the coordinated efforts of Lequerica with the Spanish embassy and the Gestapo, the Spanish secret services discovered the Red Álava, a list of Basque secret agents, and a cache of 1,242 documents: bulletins, journals, censored press, letters between prisoners and family members, sentencing information, data on deaths by firing squad, military information, and so on. Twenty-eight people were arrested and tortured; twenty-one were sent to trial, including four women: Luis Álava, Agustín Ariztia, Julián Arregi, Iñaki Barriola, Luis Cánovas, Antonio Causo, Bittori Etxeberria, Esteban Etxeberria, José Etxeberria, Félix Ezkurdia, Rafael Gómez Jáuregui, Víctor González, Rafael Goñi, Patxi Lasa, Delia Lauroba, Itziar Mujika, Celestino Olaizaola, Felipe Oñatebia, Inocencio Tolaretxipi, Modesto Urbiola, and Teresa Verdes. The trial began on July 3, 1941. The defendants were charged with supporting rebellion and espionage. The prosecution asked for the death penalty in nineteen cases; only one person, Luis Álava, was executed, in 1943.[8] According to the indictment, by 1943, the Red Álava had established seventy-one secret trails to cross the Pyrenean border.[9]

---

7. Andrés Irujo, "Breve impresión de las causas que determinaron la detención de Luis Companys y Zugazagoitia," *Euzko Deya* (Buenos Aires), November 10, 1940.

8. Juan Carlos Jiménez de Aberasturi, *De la derrota a la esperanza: Políticas vascas durante la IIª Guerra Mundial (1937–1947)* (Bilbao: Instituto Vasco de Administración Pública, 1999), 141–73.

9. Barriola, *19 condenados a muerte*, 15.

Although the Red Álava had been dissolved, the Basque government's secret services did not cease operations. From 1940, Celso Lorda (the Vichy government consul in Iruñea), Gabriel Biurrun (the Uruguayan consul in Iruñea), and Matías Anoz (owner of the famous Casa Marceliano restaurant in the city) created a network in Iruñea to help Allied soldiers escape from the Spanish police.[10] After World War II, the British embassy conferred a medal on Biurrun for his work to save the lives of so many people, among them many British and American soldiers who were escaping from occupied Europe. Biurrun went to Uruguay as a delegate of the Napar Buru Batzar (the Nafarroan Executive Council of the EAJ-PNV) and worked there from 1943 to 1945 with Bingen Ametzaga, the Basque government representative in the country and the head of Basque secret services in Uruguay.[11]

Elsewhere, the problem was what to do with refugees in areas that were free but under Nazi control. From May 1940 on, moving refugees to the Americas was among the few goals, but doing so had many challenges. Eventually, with the help of Basque centers and support from several American governments, doors were gradually opened. On the occasion of renewing the Havana Convention on Asylum, an agreement signed on February 20, 1928, at the seventh International Congress of the Americas, Latin American countries signed a new convention on political asylum on December 26, 1933. Seven years later and in accordance with the convention, on August 21, 1940, Mexico signed an agreement with the Vichy government to protect refugees from the Spanish Republic and help convey them safely to the Americas. In the same vein, decrees approved by Argentina's President Roberto M. Ortiz in January and July 1940 facilitated and encouraged the migration of Basque refugees to Argentina.[12] Most other Latin American states declared themselves on the side of the Allies at the eighth Pan-American Conference in 1938 and in subsequent meetings in 1939, 1940, and 1941.

Of course, together with all the already-mentioned problems, exiled Basques in the period 1937–1940 followed a two-centuries-old Basque migration pattern. Friends and family in Basque centers abroad greeted the exiled Basques who arrived by ship in American ports with *aurreskuak* and open arms. The diaspora that resulted from the war during 1936–1939 received help and support from compatriots, which was the main reason people fled to the Americas.

As we have seen, the refugees began going to the Americas by ship in 1938 and especially 1939. However, leaving Europe became considerably more difficult after the Nazi victory. From June 1940, the only port from which one could leave for the Americas was Marseilles. And the journey was neither safe nor easy. In 1939, France had the world's fourth-largest navy, so the Nazi victory in May 1940 left Great Britain alone

---

10. Interview with Gabriel Biurrun Altadil, Iruñea, October 15, 2001.

11. Bingen Ametzaga to Joxe Mari Lasarte, Montevideo, December 18, 1943, IAA, GT-Lasarte.JM.1943.

12. *Euzko Deya* (Buenos Aires), January 30, 1940. The decree by President Ortiz was published in the *Official Journal of the Republic of Argentina* on February 12, 1940.

against Germany and Italy to control the waters of the Atlantic and Mediterranean. Moreover, German U-boats were employing *Wolfsrudel*, or "wolf pack," submarine tactics and sinking ships. Indeed, the period 1939–1942 was, in the words of Admiral Karl Dönitz, "die Glückliche Zeit" (the happy war), because the Allies had no effective means of detecting and attacking the submarines. In 1939, the Nazis sank 95 Allied ships, followed by 511 in 1940, 568 in 1941, and 590 in 1942.

To close off the coastline of the Americas to Axis ships, the Allies began asking all ships wishing to cross the Atlantic for a Navy Certificate, or Navicert. A consequence of this was to close off the Atlantic to Vichy government ships leaving Marseilles; thereafter, refugees had to board Portuguese or other neutral-state ships to leave for the Americas. Another consequence was to make things much more difficult for the Basque National Council in London, which had to ask for the required permissions from the British Admiralty. Moreover, despite the agreement between Mexico and the Vichy government, on January 21, 1941, the Mexican government refused to renew the decree and limited the number of refugees allowed to enter the country. The Vichy government also reneged on the agreement; on March 20, 1941, it extended the ban on Spanish Republican refugees between eighteen and forty-eight years of age leaving its territory.

In response, the Basque government created the Basque Relief Committee and the Committee for General Interests of Euzkadi. This reveals one of the many practical problems of the Basque national idea: with the Spanish Republican government relying less and less on sources of income and without having achieved any practical results, the Basque government had to take control of all efforts on behalf of refugees. On August 30, 1939, the Basque government delegation in Buenos Aires established the Pro-Basque Immigration Committee. Through this committee, Basque refugees managed to persuade Argentina's President Ortiz to sign immigration decrees on January 20 and July 18, 1940; Vice President Ramón S. Castillo signed another decree on August 12.[13] According to the decrees, all Basque refugees—without distinction, including those without documents—could enter Argentina without undergoing quarantine, which was obligatory for all other immigrants, and after two weeks they would obtain full Argentine citizenship.[14] There was only one condition: the committee had to verify that the refugees were Basques.[15] In a letter from February 24, 1940, Ramón María Aldasaro, delegate of the Basque government in Buenos Aires, reported that there were 170 pending files that affected five hundred people; on April 13, there were already 300 records affecting about seven hundred Basque refugees seeking permission to migrate to

---

13. However, the dictator Juan Perón refused to approve the decrees. See "Sobre la situación de los extranjeros en Argentina," EIB-OPE, April 8, 1949; "La emigración vasca a la Argentina," EIB-OPE, February 6, 1950, 4; and "La emigración vasca a la Argentina," EIB-OPE, March 28, 1950, 4.

14. *Euzko Deya* (Buenos Aires), January 30, 1940. The decree by President Ortiz was published in the *Official Journal of the Republic of Argentina* on February 12, 1940.

15. Xabier Irujo Ametzaga and Alberto Irigoyen Artetxe, *La hora vasca del Uruguay: Génesis y desarrollo del nacionalismo vasco en el Uruguay (1825–1960)* (Montevideo: Sociedad de Confraternidad Vasca "Euskal Erria," 2006), 267.

Argentina under the conditions granted by the decrees. In July 1940, Julio Jauregi, the Basque government's director of emigration services, arrived in Marseilles to aid Basque refugees onto ships with the help of the Argentine consulate delegates and Vichy government representatives. According to *Euzko Deya*, in July 1940, there were around one thousand Basque refugees in Argentina, and more than two thousand by 1943. This is especially remarkable considering that the second meeting of ministers of foreign affairs of the Eighth International Conference of American States held in Havana, on July 21–30, 1940, resolved to recommend that American governments adopt precautionary measures in issuing passports and uniform punitive measures for the use of counterfeit or altered passports or of passports from more than one country.[16]

The Argentine example was not unique. The Chilean government did not have any special decree to facilitate the entry of Basque refugees, but it complied with the wishes of the Basque exiles. As Santiago Zarranz* clarified, "Both the instructions of President Aguirre Cerdá, firstly (and of those that followed him in the same mandate), as well as those of the functionaries in the ministry of foreign relations department, Carlos Errazuriz and Luis Castellón, in charge of awarding permissions, contained precise instructions to acknowledge all Basque requests."[17] In Venezuela, likewise, exiles created a pressure group to work with the Basque government to facilitate the entry of Basques into the country. Distinguished Venezuelans such as Andrés Eloy Blanco, Rafael Pizzani, Miguel Otero, Jovito Villalba, José Tomás Jiménez Arráiz, and Gonzalo Salas were among the members of this group.[18] The Basque exile Luis Aranguren lobbied Alberto Smith Zárraga, the Venezuelan ambassador to Cuba, to convince Venezuela's President Eleazar López Contreras to recognize Basque refugees. On May 14, 1938, Simón Gonzalo Salas presented the report "Basque Immigration for Venezuela," and in the spring of 1939, Gonzalo Salas was elected vice director and Arturo Uslar Pietri director of the Venezuela Technical Institute of Immigration and Colonization. In the early summer of 1939, the negotiations between Venezuelan and Basque government representatives began to open doors to Basque refugees in Venezuela. To facilitate the Venezuelan option, Jose Antonio Agirre appointed Eusebio Irujo as the Basque government delegate and Jesús Galíndez* as secretary in Santo Domingo, Dominican Republic. Hundreds of Basque refugees, as well as many Spaniards and Catalans, could now enter Venezuela. Finally, from 1943 onward, Bingen Ametzaga managed to persuade Juan José Carbajal Victorica and Dardo Regules, the interior ministers of Uruguay, to recognize the entry of all Basque refugees into the country.[19]

---

16. "Second Meeting of Ministers of Foreign Affairs of the American Republics: Habana July 21–30, 1940," *American Journal of International Law* 35, no. 1 (1941, suppl.): 1–32.

17. Santiago Zarranz, "Presencia vasca en Chile," *Euzko Deya*, special ed., Buenos Aires, November 1983, 19.

18. Simón Gonzalo Salas, *Inmigración vasca para Venezuela* (Caracas: Impresores Unidos, 1938), 5.

19. Bingen Ametzaga to Joxe Mari Lasarte, Montevideo, August 3, 1945, IAA, GT-Lasarte.JM.1945.

On July 26, 1940, the *St. Dominique* departed from Bordeaux to Mexico. On January 15, 1941, the *Alsina* departed from Marseilles to Dakar, but, lacking a permit to cross the Atlantic Ocean, the vessel had to go back from Dakar to Casablanca. On November 4, the Basque, Spanish, and Jewish refugees of the *Alsina* embarked on the *Quanza* and departed from Casablanca to Veracruz and from there to Caracas and Havana. On March 12, 1942, the *Río de la Plata* transported Basque refugees from Havana to Argentina; on the way, a German U-boat stopped it off the coast of Brazil and delayed its arrival for hours. The Portuguese ship *Nyassa* departed from Marseilles on May 22, 1942, to the Americas. The flight of the refugees is an epic diaspora story, especially the Atlantic journeys between August and September 1939 of the fourteen-meter-long boats *Donibane* and *Bigarrena*, the 441-day odyssey of the *Alsina* between January 1941 and April 1942, and Jose Antonio Agirre's adventure that would last from May 1940 through October 1941.[20]

As mentioned, the Basque National Council in London shaped the Basque national idea.[21] As did any other National Councils in London, the Basque National Council maintained political contact with the French Empire Defense Council, led by Charles de Gaulle; the Foreign Office; and the Admiralty's secret services. In fact, British authorities closely monitored the Spanish state's positions; and there were a number of serious diplomatic problems regarding the role of the Spanish regime in World War II. In addition to the German and Italian military assistantship Franco received between 1936 and 1939, there was the Anti-Comintern Pact signed by Francisco Gómez Jordana, the Spanish foreign minister, on March 17, 1939,[22] against the Communist Party. On March 31, 1939, the Spanish and German authorities signed the Hispano-German Friendship Treaty, and Spain withdrew from the League of Nations. After Ramón Serrano Suñer was appointed foreign minister, the Consejo de la Hispanidad (Hispanic Council) was established on October 13, 1939, the Día de la Hispanidad. The Hispanic Council's task was to attract Latin American states to the Axis side through Spanish state bodies. In the context of World War II, in June 1940, Spain changed from "neutral" to "nonbelligerent," and from October 20–24, the head of the SS and the Gestapo, Heinrich Himmler, met with Franco in Madrid. Some days later, on October 23, Franco and Hitler met in Hendaia. In February 1941, Franco met with Mussolini in Bordighera and later with Philippe Pétain in Montpellier. There was no doubt that Spain would enter World War II on the Axis side. Only a strong diplomatic action on the part of Great Britain could stop Franco from taking an active role in the war.

Before the occupation, the Spanish section of the British secret services, under the direction of Laughton Higman, was located in Toulouse. Once the Basque National

---

20. Interview with Maria Teresa Agirre Lekube, sister of Agirre who went into exile to the Americas on board the *Alsina*, Algorta, October 7, 2000.

21. Manuel Irujo to Antonio Gamarra, London, April 11, 1940, AA/AN FSAE, AN-GE-499-1.

22. The Anti-Comintern Pact was concluded between Nazi Germany and the Empire of Japan on November 25, 1936 and was later signed by several other totalitarian governments, among them the Spanish government.

Council was established in London, in early July 1940 contact was made straightaway with Churchill's cabinet, via Baron Robert John Graham Boothby, parliamentary private secretary to Churchill from 1926 to 1929 and parliamentary secretary to the Ministry of Food in 1940 and 1941. From the outset, the Basque National Council's proposition was clear: the Basque secret services would collaborate with the British secret services against the Axis powers, so long as they would sign an agreement on independence for the Basque Country.[23] The proposition featured eight general points:

1. The Basque secret services would collaborate militarily with British Intelligence in the war effort.
2. Collaboration would be based on a political agreement guaranteeing an independent Basque republic after the war.
3. The thousands of Basque refugees in Europe and the Americas would receive aid via the British embassies.[24]
4. Great Britain would finance the operations.
5. Basque agents would operate under the orders of the Basque authorities.
6. Basque would be the official language of the Basque secret services.
7. The Basque secret services would work in Europe, the Americas, and the Philippines.
8. The objective was to obtain information from the fascist, Falangist, and Nazi spy network and to neutralize the work of pseudofascist organizations like the Hispanic Council in South America.

The British agreed to the proposal but had doubts on the second point: namely, that any such political agreement could push Spain over to the Axis side. Indeed, from a practical point of view, if Spain were to join the Axis powers, victory in Europe would be more difficult for the Allies. Franco's neutrality was, both militarily and economically, much cheaper to buy than undertaking a military campaign in the Iberian Peninsula. For that reason, while the Foreign Office maintained contact with the Basque National Council it was also trying to negotiate a peace deal with Franco through embassy agents in Madrid.

At the same time, facing Irujo's and Lizaso's firm stance and realizing that there was no contact between Irujo and Leizaola, Higman attempted to bypass the second point of the agreement. To do so, without Irujo's or Lizaso's knowledge, he contacted Luis Ortuzar, former Inspector of Public Order of the Basque Government (1937), to suggest that, together with Leizaola, they take a Royal Air Force plane to Paris to meet and sign an agreement with the Basques. Ortuzar agreed, and they met with Leizaola in Paris.

23. Manuel Irujo to Francisco Belaustegigoitia, London, September 16, 1941, AA/AN FSAE, AN-GE-465-1.

24. After the Japanese occupation of the Philippines many Basques suffered the consequences of the Japanese repression. As a consequence, after December 1941, Basque agents in the Philippines would also collaborate with the Allies.

Leizaola, in his capacity as vice president, signed a cooperation agreement, without any political content, between the Basque secret services and British Intelligence.[25] Higman achieved many objectives at that meeting: he tarnished the authority of Irujo and Lizaso in London. He destroyed the indispensable nature of a political agreement. Without a written agreement, Higman was free to place Basque agents under the authority of British officials, because no strategic settlement had been reached. Unbeknown to Leizaola and Ortuzar, Higman knew that Joxe Mari Lasarte—the head of the Basque secret services in the occupied zone—would not accept cooperation without a political agreement.[26] Therefore, he asked Leizaola to appoint another mediator (not Lasarte) to head up negotiations between the Basque secret services and British Intelligence. As a result, Leizaola appointed Jose Lekaroz, a Basque secret agent, to this role. Meanwhile, for the same reason, Higman asked Leizaola to appoint Ortuzar as the main contact in London with British Intelligence, and Leizaola did so.

In mid-July, Ortuzar called a meeting of members of the EBB, the Basque secret services, and Irujo and Lizaso. At the meeting, Irujo and Lizaso stated that the Paris agreement went against the orders of both President Agirre and Lasarte, as well as the authority of the Basque National Council, and Ortuzar backed down. On July 15, the Basque National Council made clear in a letter to British Intelligence and the Foreign Office that Higman's conduct demonstrated a lack of trust and betrayal. Boothby replied acknowledging this and assuring them that it wouldn't happen again. On July 30, Irujo, Lizaso, Boothby, and Robert Cary (parliamentary private secretary to the civil lords of the Admiralty) met to put the finishing touches on the agreement. The final text read as follows:

Most Secret Formula

1. His Majesty's Government sympathizes with the cause of the Basque people in their struggle for freedom and independence.
2. In the event of hostilities breaking out between the Spanish and British governments, His Majesty's Government will immediately recognize the Basque National Council as the provisional government of the Basque Country.
3. In the event that Great Britain should win the war, His Majesty's Government will do everything in its powers to assure the establishment and guarantee the safety of a Basque state.
4. The issue of drawing up borders will be addressed later.[27]

---

25. Jose Ignacio Lizaso to Manu Sota, London, July 9, 1941, AA/AN FSAE, AN-GE-504-1.

26. Jose Antonio Agirre and Joxe Mari Lasarte developed this idea before the occupation with Higman's agents in Toulouse. Jose Ignacio Lizaso to Manu Sota, London, July 9, 1941, AA/AN FSAE, AN-GE-504-1.

27. Letters between José Ignacio Lizaso and P. Carey, London, July 30, 1940, AA/AN FSAE, AN-GE-464-1.

On August 13, 1940, there was another meeting, this time with Lizaso, Boothby, and Sir Alexander G. M. Cadogan, permanent undersecretary for foreign affairs.[28] At the meeting, Lizaso was informed that the third point of the agreement would have to be modified. Instead of stating that the British government would do "everything in its powers to assure the establishment and guarantee the safety of a Basque state," it "would consider sympathetically Basque aspirations." It was clear that, between July 30 and August 13, the prospect of Spain deciding to join World War II had alarmed the British.

However, the British still wanted some kind of agreement with the Basque secret services, and because of Irujo's and Lizaso's position, they again ordered Higman to come to an accord through Ortuzar.[29] Ortuzar and Higman met in the luxurious Dorchester Hotel in London, with the latter offering the former money. A few days later, the Basque agents, ignoring Ortuzar, asked Higman for a salary of two thousand pounds per month. Irujo and Lizaso regarded the behavior of both Ortuzar and the agents involved as betrayal. On August 26, the EBB sent an order to London to cease any agreements between Higman and Ortuzar, to place the guarantee of Basque independence on the signing of any political deal, and to immediately remove anyone who did not agree with those orders. All the agents agreed to follow the Basque National Council's orders, and there were no further problems.[30] While this was going on, the British made contact with the Basque delegate in New York, Manu Sota. Like Ortuzar, Sota favored working with British spy networks in the Americas. However, following the events in London, Sota did not take it on himself to develop joint activity with the Allies.

Likewise, the French Empire Defense Council contacted the Basque National Council.[31] On November 15, it sent a letter to the Basque National Council proposing a Franco-Basque cooperation pact. After five months of negotiations, on May 17, 1941, the French council's permanent secretary, René Samuel Cassin, together with Elena de la Souchère and Maurice Dejean, as well Jose Ignacio Lizaso and Ángel Gondra, signed the cooperation agreement.[32]

Noticeably, the accord resembles that reached with the British government. In short, in exchange for the help of the Basque secret services, the French authorities agreed to ensure that aid arrived to Basque refugees in Nazi-occupied areas and to offer French citizenship to any Basques serving in the French army or in the French Resistance and to any Basques proposed by the Basque National Council, and asylum to any Basques fleeing from Spain. Members of the Basque National Council and the French Empire

28. José Ignacio Lizaso to Manu Sota, London, July 9, 1941, AA/AN FSAE, AN-GE-504-1.

29. Manuel Irujo to José Antonio Aguirre, London, January 28, 1942, AA/AN FSAE, AN-GE-465-2.

30. Elías Etxeberria to Laughton Higman, Redhill, June 10, 1941, AA/AN FSAE, AN-GE-465-1.

31. José Ignacio Lizaso to José Antonio Aguirre, London, October 24, 1941, AA/AN FSAE, AN-GE-465-1.

32. *Acuerdo entre el Consejo de Defensa del Imperio Francés y el Consejo Nacional de Euzkadi* (Agreement between the French Empire Defense Council and the Basque National Council), London, May 17, 1941, AA/AN FSAE, AN-GE-465-1.

Defense Council would establish a recruitment commission to organize the entry of Basques into the Free French Forces.[33] The French authorities would recognize the passports or border-crossing papers issued by the Basque government. The Basque National Council recognized all citizens in the Basque Country to be Basque. Finally, the French government would help all commercial companies developed by the Basque government, opening up its colonial ports and offering other similar benefits.

Within the Franco-Basque cooperation pact, the project titled "The Cultural Union of the Countries of Western Europe" was especially interesting. In addition to the economic and commercial arrangement of May 17, Irujo suggested a political project for a European confederation in postwar Europe to de Gaulle: "De Gaulle accepted the idea resolutely. The idea of making Paris the capital of Europe excited him. We never acted behind the backs of Britain or the United States. Both governments knew about our movements. We informed them ourselves in correlative notes."[34] Even though exiled Spanish republicans in London believed the idea utopian and criticized it, the Basque National Council informed both the French Empire Defense Council and British and US government representatives of the project. More than just a means of negotiating, the project was a means of driving the Basque government and the Basque Country into postwar political negotiations: "It was for us a tactic and a rationale. More the first than the second. We were looking to get out from south of the Pyrenees so as not to necessarily fall back into Spain. If, beyond this, a firm political position could be achieved, then so much the better."[35]

Like the British, de Gaulle also agreed to create an independent Basque state that would be part of the West European Confederation:

> It was a question of Euzkadi being part of the Western Confederation, free from the fear of living under the threat of a military uprising in Madrid led by the general on duty; of a great federal capital in Paris; of there being little substantial difference between Negrín and Franco, etc. He knows about the willingness of Catalans, Galicians and Basques, and the Castilian as well as Portuguese position. He made very accurate appraisals of the specific situation of the theoretical members of the confederation, understanding the difficulties of the project. It is necessary—he said—to know how to conceive of the future, without risking collapse faced with the realities of war, taking into account the need to not create problems for [Great Britain]. He spoke about Basque unity, about Guinea, about a Greater Western European State, about the democratic French-Basque propaganda organized for Latin America, etc. He offered

33. *Notes on the Agreement between the French Empire Defense Council and the Basque National Council*, London, [July] 1941, AA/AN FSAE, AN-GE-465-1.

34. Manuel Irujo to Jesús María Leizaola, London, November 29, 1944, AA/AN FSAE, AN-GE-468-1.

35. Manuel Irujo to Jesús María Leizaola, London, December 28, 1944, AA/AN FSAE, AN-GE-468-1.

> to wire his general representative in Mexico, Mr. Soustelle—a friend of ours and our people there—so that he pays his respects to you, later coming to London.[36]

With the Cultural Union of the Countries of Western Europe as a first step, the representative of a European stateless nation met de Gaulle in the French Institute of London: "We dealt with General de Gaulle. Once he agreed, we proposed the idea to the British and American governments in separate notes. At the time the idea didn't catch on in the Foreign Office. We went public, making the most of the French intellectual organization involved, who were living off British funding."[37] The fruit of these negotiations was the founding of the Cultural Union of Western Europe on September 10, 1942.

Indeed, even after Jose Antonio Agirre reappeared, de Gaulle and Irujo continued to meet to develop the Franco-Basque Pact and to discuss the terms of the Cultural Union of Western Europe. Although it took twenty more years to come about, this politico-economic project was one of the foundations of Robert Schuman's ideas to build a united Europe:[38]

> A few days ago, José Ignacio paid his respects in your name and representation to General de Gaulle. He had a very friendly hour-and-a-half long conversation with him. The general was very interested in you and in the methods used for your escape, which he celebrated with repeated demonstrations of warmth. We don't think it wise to give all the details of everything discussed. There was a frank and perceptive discussion about the European political problem and the Anglo-Saxons [British and Americans]. He displayed a great awareness and sharp perception of the peninsular problems [concerning the Basque case]. He was very interested in the idea of a Western Confederation. He remarked, so that it might be passed on to you, that as soon as the circumstances change, as regards what you state he would be willing to reach wider and more efficient formulas than those contained in the May 17 pact and in line with our position, regarding the reservations you state in your letter.[39]

Ever since the Basque government had been formed in 1936, the idea of setting up a delegation to organize aid from Basques in the Americas had been raised. The delegation would also maintain relations with Basques in Europe, Australia, and the Philippines during the period 1936–1937. However, although the idea of delegations in these countries was to strengthen commercial ties, from 1938 onward, their main task was to facilitate the influx of refugees and to supervise their legal status once there. Once the pro-Franco international coalition had taken Bilbao, the Barcelona delegation became

---

36. Manuel Irujo to Jose Antonio Agirre, London, January 28, 1942, AA/AN FSAE, AN-GE-465-2.

37. Manuel Irujo to Jesús María Leizaola, London, November 29, 1944, AA/AN FSAE, AN-GE-468-1.

38. Robert Schuman, a Christian Democrat politician, was Minister of Finance, Foreign Minister and, twice Prime Minister of the French republic. Schuman was instrumental in building post-war Europe and is regarded as one of the founding fathers of the European Union.

39. Manuel Irujo to Jose Antonio Agirre, London, January 28, 1942, AA/AN FSAE, AN-GE-465-2.

the Basque government's central office. After Barcelona fell in April 1939, the headquarters moved to Paris. Thereafter, in chronological order, the Basque government headquarters was located in London (1940–1941), New York (1942–1945), and again Paris (1946–1975). The delegations, easily moving beyond their original raison d'être, were the cradle of diaspora politics.

As relations between the delegations strengthened, alignments emerged. In 1937, the Barcelona-Paris alignment formed the administrative core of Basque diaspora politics, and during the Nazi occupation of Europe, London, Buenos Aires, and New York aligned on the administrative tasks of the Basque National Council. From 1955 on, in virtue of the vigorous economic development of the Basque colony in Venezuela, Paris and Caracas aligned for Basque diaspora politics. Indeed, the very nature of diaspora politics was founded on the network of North American and Latin American and European delegations and representatives established by the Basque government; the very existence of the Basque government-in-exile would have been impossible without this network. From 1938, and especially 1940, American delegations assumed far greater importance, for the Americas was the principal destination of Basque political refugees. In addition, from 1949, the Basque government came to depend for financing on donations from delegations in the Americas, especially Caracas.

In April 1940, just after he proposed the Basque government's plan at Meudon for an independent program of government, Jose Antonio Agirre foresaw greater political, economic, and administrative scope for the delegations:

> The current circumstances suggest reinforcing the political significance of the government, organizing administration jointly. One can point to three kinds of functions or activities:
>
> a. Domestic and foreign political relations, the delegations in different countries, information and propaganda.
>
> b. The treasury of Euskadi.
>
> c. The general supervision of Basque emigration, its institutions, and the needs of all kinds of people in exile.[40]

When the Basque National Council was created in London to establish the Basque government's proposed network of delegations, it was essential to put into practice the April 1940 program of government. After the Nazis took Paris, Agirre's proposed Paris-London alignment was replaced by the new administrative alignment of London, Buenos Aires, and New York. Irujo divided the Basque government delegations into general delegations and special delegations. The special delegations were grouped together and coordinated within specific geopolitical areas:

---

40. Jose Antonio Agirre, *Proyecto de programa para el Gobierno de Euskadi*, Paris, April 12, 1940, AA/AN FSAE, AN-CR-44-4.

We consider the general delegations to be those of Buenos Aires, Caracas, Mexico City, New York and London.

- That of Buenos Aires is responsible for Chile, Uruguay, Paraguay, Bolivia, Peru and Brazil.
- That of Caracas is concerned with Ecuador, Colombia and continental Central America.
- That of New York with the West Indies, the Antilles and the Caribbean.
- That of London with all the problems of Europe and the Mediterranean.[41]

Thereafter, under Ramón María Aldasoro's leadership, the Buenos Aires delegation became headquarters for the Basque National Council's vice president, and London became the head office for the Basque National Council. Because Buenos Aires gained importance among the Latin American delegations and because of the importance of the immigration decrees passed by Argentina's government, it was designated the head office of the Latin American delegations:

> Regarding the internal relations, organization, functioning, activities in the Americas, Basque propaganda, the running of the delegations, etc. it is sensible to locate such supervision in Buenos Aires and to be carried out by Mr. Aldasoro. Everyone knows the reasons. On the other hand, everything concerning war matters, activities related to its events, cooperation with the democracies and its consequences, should be thoroughly monitored from London, with the full authority that each case itself might require, understood by those of us here, who should gladly commit to a cause that is everyone's and that is entrusted for the care of everybody.[42]

Besides their administrative and financial tasks, the delegations would have two main duties. First, they were concerned with facilitating refugees' settlement in different American cities and towns and, once there, they cooperated closely and directly with the Basque centers. All this was to help the refugees gain legal status as soon as possible and to find work to aid their financial situation. For example, the last refugees to arrive in Buenos Aires on the *Río de la Plata*, on April 15, 1942, were received by the Laurak Bat Basque center choir, which greeted them at the port.[43] Around two hundred people received them, including members of the Buenos Aires Basque center and representatives of the city and federal government, singing "Agur Jauna" and performing the *aurreskua* on the *txistu* (Basque flute). All arrivals who needed it received a hotel room, free of charge, for a month in a Buenos Aires, and all received full Argentine citizenship and a passport within two weeks. The next day a dinner was held in their honor in the Basque center. Among the arrivals were Bingen Ametzaga and Mercedes

---

41. *Programa del Consejo Nacional de Euzkadi*, London, July 15, 1940, in Manuel Irujo to Manu Sota, London, July 15, 1940, AA/AN FSAE, AN-GE-504-1.

42. Ibid.

43. Manuel Irujo to Jose Antonio Agirre, London, February 20, 1942, AA/AN FSAE, AN-GE-465-2.

Iribarren, the author's grandparents. Most refugees found work within a month thanks to the Basque network. As "Tellagori" (Jose Olivares Larrondo*) would write, kicked out of Europe, leaving behind in their homeland parents, brothers, sisters, and friends they would never see again, with the death penalty hanging over them and moving from port to port in search of a friendly door, this reception "made them believe that in some way they were still people and that someone somewhere in the world, therefore, was concerned for them."[44]

During World War II and principally from 1940 on, the other main task of the American delegations would be to strengthen the London delegation's political activity and diplomatic image and to improve relations with the political leaders of many countries and with political parties and figures from the world of culture. Later, supervising the secret services would fall under this diplomatic goal, as spying on Nazi and fascist elements in Argentina, Chile, Uruguay, Venezuela, and Brazil became one of the most important duties of the Basque delegates. Because of this, usually each country's main delegate was also the director and coordinator of the secret services.

In short, the Basque government delegations took on all the duties of an official embassy. For example, in Uruguay, the delegate met each year with the presidents of the republic from 1943 to 1955 and each month with Uruguayan government ministers.

Finally, another task of the Basque National Council in London, via the help of Galeuzca, the acronym for Galicia, Euskadi, and Catalunya (the institution that would coordinate the work of the Basque, Catalan, and Galician governments-in-exile, and clashing with the Spanish Republican government, was to propose a government—once Franco was overthrown—that would be a basic confederation of nations with the right to self-determination. Irujo clearly set out his ideas in the 1945 book *Comunidad Ibérica de Naciones* (Iberian Community of Nations).[45] In the book, in interviews, the Portuguese Armando Cortesão, the Basque nationalist Manuel Irujo, the Catalan nationalist Carles Pi i Sunyer, and the Spanish socialist Luis Araquistain speak about the state model that might emerge after the dictatorship. Cortesão had come to favor entering an Iberian confederation of nations, so long as the confederation's constitution recognized the right of each nation to self-determination. The Basque, Catalan, Galician, Portuguese, and Spanish nations would constitute the confederation. Araquistain did not acknowledge the right to self-determination. In Irujo's opinion, if such a state were to split up because of the request, adoption, and application of the right of self-determination, it would be because of the peoples' will; consequently, to maintain a state such as the Spanish one against the will of the Basque, Catalan, and Galician peoples that constituted it was democratic nonsense. Moreover, under the motto "Una, grande, libre" ("One, great and

---

44. Jose Olivares Larrondo, pseud. "Tellagorri," to Bingen Ametzaga, Buenos Aires, July 18, 1942, IAA, GT-Tellagorri, 1942.

45. Armando Cortesão, Luis Araquistain, Manuel Irujo, and Carles Pi i Sunyer, *La comunidad ibérica de naciones* (Buenos Aires: Ekin, 1945).

free"), to contravene the civil, political, and cultural rights of Basques, Catalans, and Galicians was a pillar of the Francoist Spanish state.

The creation of the National Council of Catalonia and the Galician National Council was a necessary step toward establishing Galeuzca. Manuel Irujo set this in motion, beginning in the spring of 1940.[46] Indeed, the Catalan National Council in London operated from the headquarters of the Basque National Council. The Catalan council's Galician counterpart faced more problems. After the Basque National Council in London had tried to intervene, Agirre wrote from New York, after meeting Alfonso R. Castelao, the main leader of the Galician political exile:[47]

> In this matter I wanted the need for Galeuzca to be a demand felt by Catalans and Galicians. When I was in Buenos Aires I recommended, in extensive interviews, extolling Castelao, the creation of a Galician council. Castelao has always kept in touch with our representatives there, but it has been a slow process. However, I think they've made a lot of ground . . . and I calculate that the moment has come for Galicia to have a foreign representative body. If [Carles] Pi [i Sunyer] is lucky and bold enough to carry on, without hesitating, the course on which I understand he's on, Galeuzca might be a political construction bigger in both prestige and power than any other in the peninsula and, although Spanish democracy is firmly against it, our force will be enough to compel respect and, when the time is right, the pact, once the greater and common advantages are obvious.[48]

On January 18, 1941, the Basque National Council and the National Council of Catalonia signed a joint political declaration in London. Because Galeuzca had disbanded in 1937, this was the first time that the Catalan and Basque political authorities had appeared in exile to demonstrate their willingness to reestablish it. Four months later, on May 9, Galeuzca was formally established in Buenos Aires.[49] According to the agreement signed, the signatories did not need to establish any special agreement with the republican government:

> Galeuzca states that none of the three oppressed nations has to accept, separately, an autonomous system granted by the Spanish state, since only through a total and rational transformation of the political structure of Spain may our peoples find a guarantee of their own freedom. If circumstances dictate accepting autonomy, it should be equal and simultaneous for the nations making up the Spanish state.[50]

---

46. Manuel Irujo to Alfonso R. Castelao, London, January 18, 1940, AA/AN FSAE, AN-GE-498-2.

47. Alfonso R. Castelao (1886–1950), member of the Galician Royal Academy since 1933, after the military uprising went into exile in the Americas, where he became the main promoter of the Galeuzca Pact and the Galician National Council, created in 1944 in Montevideo. He was appointed council chair and held that post until his death in 1950.

48. Jose Antonio Agirre to Jose Ignacio Lizaso, New York, March 3, 1944, AA/AN FSAE, AN-GE-467-2.

49. *Declaración de la Delegación de Londres del Gobierno de Euzkadi* (Declaration of the Delegation of the Basque Government in London), in José Ignacio Lizaso to J. MacDonald, London, March 7, 1941, AA/AN FSAE, AN-GE-464-2.

50. *Convenio de acuerdo de Galeuzca*, Montevideo, May 9, 1941, AA/AN FSAE, AN-GE-465-1.

The newly reestablished Galeuzca was based on four main points:

1. Supporting the struggle for human rights, Galeuzca was a pro-Allied association in the context of World War II, and against any like-minded totalitarianism, whether in Europe or the Americas. In this situation, Galeuzca was created with the aim of fighting against the Spanish dictatorship, as well as against all forces and parties collaborating or siding with the Axis powers in favor of Nazi or Fascist ideologies.
2. Galeuzca supported the republican political creed, that is, it was opposed to any kind of monarchy. A new Iberian state, fully respecting human rights, needed to be based on a confederation:

   A representative democratic regime with direct universal suffrage, freedom of conscience and belief, freedom of thought and the press, popular justice, guarantees of citizens' rights, work and legitimately acquired property, freedom of profession, residence, contracting, and the regulation of resources according to the particular laws of each state that, on no account, should deplete, reduce or blemish the common minimum established in federal or confederal pacts.[51]
3. In the same way as this last point, the new Iberian state would have to avoid making past mistakes. The historical, cultural, social, economic and political rights of Catalonia, Galicia and the Basque Country demanded a state guaranteeing the right of self-determination to every nation that comprised it. That implied that a confederation of Iberian nations would require a new state within an open European Union, "to which transnational powers would be delegated, such as the coordination of services and forces, common and especially social legislation, collective security, the elaboration and application of international law, and the diffusion and circulation of the democratic principles of law and justice."[52] In fact, this last point was a condition included at the insistence of the Catalans and especially the Galicians, even though both Bingen Ametzaga, the Galeuzca president in Uruguay, and Manuel Irujo publicly supported Basque independence on several occasions.
4. Galeuzca supported the creation of another international organization to replace the League of Nations that would prevent disagreements between nations from turning into wars: "a politics of cooperation and good will, developing international relations on all fronts and supporting the creation of trans-state bodies that, considering peace eternal, have the authority and the necessary means to maintain it, to sanction the offender, and assure the free existence of institutions and peoples."[53]

51. Ibid.
52. Ibid.
53. Ibid.

In short, as Manuel Irujo wrote in the Declaration of Principles for Democracy in the Peninsula,[54] there were fourteen basic points in the Basque national idea drawn up by the Basque National Council in London:

1. A democratic affirmation, in a universal and caring sense, for men and for peoples.
2. Support for Great Britain, Russia, China and their allies in the current war.[55]
3. Acceptance of the Atlantic Declaration.
4. Agreement with setting up a federal system in Europe, based on coexistence and staggered sovereignty, with procedures for economic rapprochement, military defense, and the goals of a just and lasting peace.
5. Studying the Western Confederation, as a viable means for the European federation, and to indicate our "Western" character.
6. Franco does not represent the country. To demand for the citizenry the power to grant that representation.
7. To denounce the system of oppression that the citizenry is subjected to. There are more prisoners in Spain than in any other country in Europe, outside R[ussia] and G[ermany].
8. Protest against the executions of hostages by Germany.
9. Highlight organized Francoist activity to definitively hand over peninsular and colonial territory to Germany as a military base.
10. Reveal the maneuvering against Portugal. We democrats will not take any advantage of the force that they are involved in. We seek a Community of Nations in which Portugal, in an absolutely free way, participates, occupying its rightful place.
11. To denounce also the major maneuvering that, by means of the Hispanic Council, shrouds Nazi propaganda in the Americas, with imperial aspirations that we feel and whose lure we should not be attracted by in any way.
12. The Declaration should remain open, so that as many as possible may adhere to its content: Nothing about exclusiveness or monopolies.
13. The right of self-determination for the peninsular peoples, in a specific way for Catalonia and the Basque Country.
14. To put on record as a basic sentiment that our common democratic foundations will give us the means to overcome our differences, reaching an agreement that establishes a common judicial system based on the motto of Saint Louis: "All human freedoms are shared."

54. *Declaración de principios para la democracia peninsular*, London, November 24, 1941, AA/AN FSAE, AN-GE-465-2.

55. The United States was not at war in 1940.

7

New York: October 1941–Spring 1945

After going missing on May 8, 1940, Jose Antonio Agirre reappeared on October 9, 1941, in Montevideo:

> We caught the train for the border at six in the morning. A typical, sparsely inhabited landscape. We arrived at the border. On the last stretch of the Brazilian journey, my compatriot, Father [Domingo] Irizar, arrived.[1] We knew each other by the *ikurriña* [Basque flag] he wore on his lapel. I was taken by the arm and led to the other side without any other preamble, no inspection or stamps. A really bold stroke. These good Uruguayans didn't want to tolerate even a minute's delay. We met up with the father, [Ramón María] Aldasoro, etc. Emotion, tears, enthusiasm. We carried on. I had previously shaved off my moustache, an inseparable companion throughout so many adventures. I did so in the hotel in Rio Branco, the first town in Uruguay. Everyone, consuls, border authorities, was so friendly. In "Thirty-Three," as the people refer to it, a lot of people, flowers, speeches. In Montevideo, many compatriots, microphones, handshakes. I was sweating when I arrived at the hotel. A commission of public figures was waiting for me. Rest. To sleep dazed.[2]

On October 10—after a request by representative Julio Iturbide—the Uruguayan Parliament welcomed Agirre in a special session. In his speech, Agirre detailed the main points of the program he aimed to follow in the Americas, namely, to carry on fighting against the dictatorships of World War II via Christian democracy, to promote cooperation among democratic parties in the Americas and in Europe to encourage democracy there, and to fight to regain a legitimate government in the Basque Country.[3] The *lehendakari* met with Alfredo Baldomir, the Uruguayan president; representatives of the majority political parties; and the archbishop of Montevideo, Antonio María Barbieri,

1. Domingo Irizar, a Dominican minister, was parish priest of a church in Montevideo and one of the most active elements of the Basque exile in Uruguay. Domingo Irizar to Bingen Ametzaga, Montevideo, June 29, 1951. IAA, GT-Irizar.D.1951.

2. Iñaki Goiogana, ed., *José Antonio Agirre Lekube: Diario 1941-1942* (Bilbao: Fundación Sabino Arana/Sabino Arana Kultur Elkargoa, 2010), 139–48.

3. *Euzko Deya* (Buenos Aires), May 10, 1942.

later an active collaborator of the Basque secret services in the country.[4] Various figures from the cultural and scientific world welcomed Agirre, who participated in dozens of interviews for both the press and the radio in the few days he spent in Uruguay. Alberto Guani, the foreign minister of Uruguay and a main promoter of the sinking of the German pocket battleship *Admiral Graf Spee*, was among those who most warmly welcomed him.[5] In the context of the Pan-American Conferences and the struggle against the Nazis, Falangists, and fascists, the official welcome Agirre received in Montevideo was a symbol of Uruguay's decision to support the Allies in the Americas. From Uruguay, the *lehendakari* traveled to Buenos Aires, where he met with Argentine President Roberto M. Ortiz and a number of the country's other political figures. Finally, after passing through Santo Domingo, Dominican Republic, on November 6, 1941, the *lehendakari* arrived in New York, and it was there that the new headquarters of the Basque government was established.

The Basque government focused its international political program on the worldwide isolation of fascist regimes. Between 1941 and 1949 this meant activity in five main areas: stepping up resistance within the Basque Country; coordinating political and diplomatic activity within the Basque centers in the Americas; setting up a Basque government press and information service (establishing the Basque Press Office in 1947); maintaining institutional cooperation with the Spanish Republican government; and, finally, proceeding toward active participation at the international level within the United Nations (UN) and the European Communities.[6]

Through 1940 and 1941, under the leadership of Irujo, the Basque National Council's efforts remained Eurocentric. However, shortly before the attack on Pearl Harbor, and mainly due to the obstacles that Anthony Eden, foreign minister in Churchill's Conservative cabinet, placed in the way of meetings between de Gaulle's French National Committee and the Basque National Council, in November 1941, the Basque government turned its efforts from Great Britain to the United States. Indeed, within a month of Jose Antonio Agirre's arrival in the United States, the political situation changed totally after December 7, 1941 and the US entry into the European war. Naturally, Roosevelt's Democratic government, as well as the president himself, greatly influenced both the official US position in relation to the Franco regime and the development of political relations and cooperation with the Basque government. However, Secretary of State

---

4. Andoni Astigarraga, "De Álvarez Lastra a José Antonio de Aguirre," *Euzkadi*, July 24, 1980, 22–23. See also *Euzko Deya* (Buenos Aires), October 25, 1941.

5. Bingen Ametzaga to Jose Antonio Agirre, Montevideo, April 3, 1944, IAA, GT-Agirre.JA.1944.

6. With the exception of the general strikes of 1947 and 1951, I do not examine in more detail here the relations established with the resistance or Basque government activity in the Basque Country because my focus is on political activity in the diaspora.

Cordell Hull was strongly in favor of nonintervention and US public opinion before Pearl Harbor was openly against intervention.[7]

Following the 1939 Meudon meetings, at which the Basque national strategic line was approved, the first steps in developing cooperation between the US and Basque governments were taken in 1941, without the involvement of the Spanish Republican government. On November 20, 1941, the *lehendakari* met William S. Stephenson, head of the British Security Council, at the British embassy in New York. The following day, he met with several secret service agents from the American Office of the Coordinator of Information (COI) to advance institutional cooperation.[8] Roosevelt had created the COI at the suggestion of Stephenson and John H. Godfrey, director of British Naval Intelligence, as a means of coordinating the tasks of the different US intelligence services, on July 11, 1941. On December 23, 1941, Agirre met once more with British Intelligence. On January 8, 1942, Frederick P. Keppel, president of the Carnegie Corporation, wrote to William Joseph Donovan, head of the COI, in favor of using Basque agents in the Americas and in the Philippines. At the same time, Cordell Hull, US secretary of state, and Carlton Hayes, the US ambassador in Madrid, were against any such cooperation. Whatever the case, after the final round of meetings in May 1942, as well as the creation of the Office of Strategic Services (OSS) and the Office of War Information within the COI in June, the Basque government and the US intelligence services began cooperating. With Jerome Doyle at their head and based out of the British Secret Intelligence Service offices in New York, British agents took an active role in facilitating the cooperation process. Indeed, according to the future head of the Basque government's secret services, Anton Irala,* it was the British who put the Basque government in contact with the US organizations. This is not surprising when one considers the efforts of the Basque National Council during the previous two years in London. In fact, the Foreign Office contacted Manu Sota in London in 1940 and 1941 to reach an agreement without any political pledge, in contrast to the views of Manuel Irujo and José Ignacio Lizaso.

Initially, this cooperation directed by the Basque government and the OSS (which later became the CIA in 1947) began following the May 1942 meetings. The new agreement resembled that of the Basque National Council with the British Foreign Office in July 1940:

1. The Basque secret services would cooperate militarily with the OSS with respect to World War II.

---

7. Report 6.895 by Colonel Stephen O. Fuqua. Valencia, October 18, 1937. NARA, RG 165. Records of the Military Intelligence Division Relating to Conditions in Spain (1918–1941). Microfilm Publication MI.1445, R. 12. See also, Biddle, Anthony J. D., *Poland and the Coming of the Second World War: The Diplomatic Papers of A. J. Drexel Biddle, Jr., United States Ambassador to Poland, 1937–1939* (Columbus: Ohio State University, 1976), 12.

8. Iñaki Goiogana, ed., *José Antonio Agirre Lekube: Diario 1941-1942* (Bilbao: Fundación Sabino Arana/Sabino Arana Kultur Elkargoa, 2010), 161–164.

2. The thousands of Basque refugees in Europe, the Philippines, and the Americas would receive aid from the Allies.
3. The US intelligence services would finance the operations.
4. The Basque government would be in command of the Basque agents. In other words, information collected by Basque agents was sent to the headquarters of the Basque government. After being processed there, it was sent to the US intelligence services.
5. The Basque secret services would work in Europe, the Philippines, and especially Latin America.
6. The objective would be to obtain information about the fascist, Falangist, and Nazi spy networks and to neutralize the underground work of institutions like the Hispanic Council in Latin America.

It clearly was the same agreement, point for point, with one exception: there was no mention of any kind of political agreement, and no notion of an independent postwar Basque republic. This provoked a heated debate between Irujo and Agirre.[9] Irujo presented three reasons to demand a political agreement. First, according to the 1939 Meudon meetings and the EAJ-PNV's August 20, 1940, course of action, the main objective of the Basque national idea was the administrative and political independence of the Basque Country. Second, support for regaining democracy and independence for the Basque Country had been one of the Basque National Council's and the EAJ-PNV's main objectives since 1940 and 1942, respectively. The Basque government had prioritized support for the security and political, economic, social, and cultural rights for Basque citizens. For Irujo, thereafter, if the US or British administrations did not sign a political agreement, any cooperation was as hazardous as it was meaningless. Finally, in light of this situation, it had to be made clear to Basque agents whose lives were at risk that they were fighting a war against totalitarianism, in the defense of democracy and human rights, but they were also fighting for Basque independence; in Irujo's own words, "we cannot knowingly offer up our best people to the Gestapo, without some kind of national guarantee to compensate for the potential sacrifice that certain operations require."[10]

Of course, some members of the Basque government opposed these ideas, including Jesús María Leizaola, Manu Sota, and Ramón María Aldasoro. Indeed, on September 9, 1940, Sota told Irujo and Lizaso that he was ready to cooperate with British Intelligence in the Americas: "Valeur, one of the directors of the Office of Allied Information, called the other day to ask for my help because he remembered me from before for the pro-

9. José Antonio Agirre to José Ignacio Lizaso and Manuel Irujo, New York, December 3, 1941, AA/AN FSAE, AN-GE-465-2. See also Manuel Irujo to José Antonio Agirre, London, February 12, 1942, AA/AN FSAE, AN-GE-465-2.

10. Manuel Irujo to Jose Antonio Agirre, London, February 12, 1942, AA/AN FSAE, AN-GE-465-2.

Allied work I did. He asked for my help in working for the same cause. As one might expect, I offered to do so openhandedly."[11] Once established in the New York delegation, the *lehendakari*'s course of action would be the following:

> Our duty is to always support, with all our effort, the Allied cause, without asking for anything, without demanding anything, because it is our cause. The time will come when everyone sees what a British diplomat wrote just recently: "There is no kinder or more loyal race to the Allied cause." Here we are getting right behind it. I hope that we do so even more and more efficiently. Little by little everything else will come. But we must be bold, because we are Basques, democrats and patriots who are working for the freedom of the Basque homeland. We should say this to everyone, every day. Our concern with freedom is the same one that Britain and America are fighting for. . . . Give everything generously, because the time will come when we can harvest the fruit. Pay attention to me.[12]

What Higman had sought and achieved in London in 1940, Jerome Doyle had likewise accomplished in New York two years later.

This cooperation between the intelligence services was extremely important to the Allies for a number of reasons. Unlike in Northern Europe, the Catholic Church was very influential in Latin America. However, because neither the British nor the Americans were Catholics, they did not enjoy the influence they wanted within Catholic circles. Indeed, the church was a key focus of Nazi propaganda in Latin America because, unlike in the Allied case, the Germans' allies were Italian and Spanish Catholics. At Franco's behest, the Hispanic Council's mission in Latin America was to spread this message of supposed Catholic unity, whereas that of the Basque secret services was to invalidate the propaganda campaign.[13] As a result, many members of scattered Basque centers in several countries and many Basque and non-Basque bishops, cardinals, and priests throughout Latin America were willing to work with or for the Basque government. After this three-year counterpropaganda offensive, by 1944, the position of the church in Latin America toward Spanish and international politics had changed.

For the Basque government, the intelligence agreement was of exceptional value as a means of isolating Franco in the arena of international politics, and it was the only way to cut off Franco in the postwar era. Meanwhile, the Basque government aimed to strengthen the Latin American and European Christian-Democratic network and, ultimately, to help overcome the government's serious financial difficulties.

To carry out intelligence work, the Basque government had at its disposal something that other organizations did not: hundreds of people either working in or willing

---

11. Manu Sota to Manuel Irujo, New York, September 9 and August 31, 1940, AA/AN FSAE, AN-GE-494-6.

12. Jose Antonio Agirre to Jose Ignacio Lizaso and Manuel Irujo, New York, December 3, 1941, AA/AN FSAE, AN-GE-465-2.

13. "Lo que representa la hispanidad," *ABC*, Madrid, October 13, 1940; "Vocación imperial," *Pueblo*, Madrid, October 12, 1940.

to work for Basque delegations, drawn from a network of Basque centers and associations. This complex network had to be set up, which was the main reason for the *lehendakari*'s journey through Latin America that began on August 15, 1942 (barely three months after signing the agreement). Between August and October 1942, Jose Antonio Agirre gave twenty-three speeches and assisted more than one hundred events in ten different places: Mexico, Panama, Peru, Chile, Uruguay, Argentina, Venezuela, Puerto Rico, the Dominican Republic, and Cuba.[14] Agirre had suggested traveling through Latin America to the other members of the EBB as early as the spring of 1942.[15]

In addition to the international efforts to bring down Franco through external diplomacy, Basque exiles in the Americas carried out major endeavors to do the same within the Basque centers themselves. Agirre's trips helped maintain solidarity and comradeship around one objective, and eased the Basque government's challenges in uniting the exiled Basque community.

Similarly, the Basque centers supported Basque cultural events to encourage unity. Cultural events increased dramatically among the exiled Basque community in 1942, first in Argentina and then in Uruguay, Mexico, and Venezuela. As agreed to in Paris in 1938, the Basque exiles created various cultural organizations. For example, Buenos Aires saw the founding of the American Institute of Basque Studies, headed by Monsignor Nicolás Esandi, and the Ekin publishing house, founded by Ixaka López Mendizabal* and Andrés Irujo, with Sebastián Amorrortu's financial help. Between 1942 and 1977, Ekin would publish more than one hundred books on the Basque exile in the Americas. At the close of 1942, the Basque Culture Commission, with Telesforo Monzon as its president, was established in Mexico. The Basque Cultural Association was established in 1943 in Santiago de Chile, and for many years, Bernardo Estornés Lasa directed the cultural section of Chile's newspaper *Euzkadi*. Also in 1943, the Department of Basque Studies, headed by Bingen Ametzaga, was created at the Universidad de la República del Uruguay, in Montevideo; two courses were offered: Basque language and Basque culture. Joxe Migel Barandiaran* established Ikuska, the Basque Research Institute, and from 1947, Jon Bilbao* and Barandiaran, through the Gernika Institute, began publishing the journal *Gernika-Euskal Jakintza*. In 1948, the Gernika Institute became the International Basque Studies Society, counting among its members figures from the Basque exile community in the Americas such as Telesforo Monzon, Manuel Intxausti, Joxe Mari Lasarte, Manu Sota, and Jon Bilbao.

The principal focal points of Basque cultural activity in exile were to disseminate Basque history and culture; to publish books, essays, and academic research on Basque culture; to promote a Basque-language policy with the aim of finding strategies for the

14. Andrés Irujo published with Ekin five of the key conferences that Agirre gave on his trip to the Americas: José Antonio Aguirre, *Cinco conferencias pronunciadas en un viaje por América* (Buenos Aires: Ekin, 1944).

15. Jose Antonio Agirre to the EBB, New York, April 7, 1942, AA/AN FSAE, AN-GE-505-2.

survival of the language and its standardization; and to facilitate Basque music, dance, and cultural expression in the Americas.

For the diffusion of Basque culture, it was essential to create cultural organizations from country to country, and as a means of coordinating all this work, to organize international cultural meetings, such as those which took place in Iparralde in 1948 and 1954. Also, the Euskal Jakin Billerak conferences were organized by the Gernika Institute in Mexico, Venezuela, and Uruguay. The conferences brought together experts interested in Basque culture so that they would produce related written work or cultural events in the Americas or, via the Gernika Institute, in Iparralde and Hegoalde.

The second focus of Basque exiles' cultural endeavors was to establish Basque studies departments in universities in Latin America and North America, such as the Department of Basque Studies in Montevideo and the classes in Basque history given by Jose Antonio Agirre at Columbia University. With respect to publications on Basque topics, the Ekin publishing house in Buenos Aires stands out, as well as other publishers in Mexico, Uruguay, and Venezuela. Although it is difficult to calculate the exact number of books published in exile, it is at least in the hundreds, not including various journals and articles in magazines and newspapers. Basque exiles wrote a great deal. Indeed, many members of the Basque government and people who worked closely with them published at least three and in some cases five books each, including Jose Antonio Agirre, Francisco Abrisketa,* Bingen Ametzaga, Joxe Migel Barandiaran, Pedro Basaldua,* Jon Bilbao, Jesús Galíndez, Justo Garate,* Gabino Garriga,[16] Ildefonso Gurrutxaga, Andima Ibinagabeitia,* the Irujo brothers (Andrés, Manuel, and Pellomari), Ceferino Jemein, Pierre Lafitte, Javier Landaburu, Jesús María Leizaola, Ixaka López Mendizabal, Telesforo Monzon, Alberto Onaindia, Orixe (Nikolas Ormaetxea*), Tellagorri (José Olivares Larrondo), and Jokin Zaitegi.* At the same time, they also participated in radio broadcasts and programs. As in Montevideo in 1943, Radio Euskadi stations were created in both Iparralde and Caracas.

The Basque government's Paris headquarters was the main center involved in efforts to shape a specific Basque language policy. Although the diffusion and linguistic normalization of Basque had been banned in Hegoalde, the exiled community helped promote the language. As a result, the Basque government's linguistic policy was aimed to encourage works written in and about Euskara, the Basque language.

Basque-language classes were organized in Basque centers, schools, and universities. In 1944, a professorship of Basque was established at the Universidad de la República in Uruguay. Bingen Ametzaga held the post until 1955, when he left for Venezuela; Jose

---

16. Gabino Garriga (1885–1969), Basque nationalist Claretian missionary, collaborated in the magazine *Nación Vasca* (Basque Nation) under the pseudonym "Bidasoa." In 1937, under the pseudonym "Jose de Aralar," he published "La rebelión militar española y el pueblo vasco" (The Spanish Military Rebellion and the Basque People), which was publised in Buenos Aires by Sebastián de Amorrortu. The publisher Ekin brought out many of his works under the same pseudonym: *El conde de Peñaflorida y los Caballeritos de Azcoitia* (1942), *Los adversarios de la libertad vasca* (1944) and *La victoria de Munguía y la reconciliación de Oñazinos y Gamboínos* (1949). He also wrote articles for several newspapers and magazines of the Basque exile such as *Euzko Deya* and *Alderdi.*

Mendiola replaced him and gave classes there until 1962. In total, between 1944 and 1962, more than fifty students enrolled in the Basque-language classes every semester. Without any direct connection to the Basque government's efforts, René Lafon organized the second university-level Basque-language class in exile, at the University of Bordeaux in 1948; Laurent Labart developed another at Keio University in Japan. Meanwhile, Gotzon Gondra began teaching Basque at the London Basque center in 1945, and most Basque centers throughout the Americas and Europe copied the this example.[17] These classes were not a new idea; the Laurac Bat Basque center in Montevideo was the first to offer Basque-language classes, in 1883. At the same time, the Basque Country School was created in Montevideo in 1925 to teach children in Euskara, and the Euzkadi Ikastola was created in Caracas in 1962 (where I studied for three years). A link with this tradition exists to this day in the shape of the Boise Ikastola in Idaho, where my children were enrolled in 2005–2006.

Different book clubs, such as the Basque Book Club and Friends of the Basque Language (Euskaltzaleak) were also formed. The Euskaltzaleak association was established in the 1940s, and though there were differences from country to country, in general members undertook to buy and read any books that were published in Basque. Moreover, the association organized events in Basque and about Basque culture. For example, the Montevideo Euskaltzaleak group organized Basque Language Day starting in 1949 and presented two works translated into Basque by Bingen Ametzaga: Shakespeare's *Hamlet* and *Platero y yo* (*Platero eta biok*), by the Andalusian poet Juan Ramón Jiménez, published in 1952 and 1953, respectively.

When it came to normalizing written Basque, the exile community encouraged many translations, of which the journal *Euzko Gogoa*, published under the guidance of Jokin Zaitegi in Guatemala between 1949 and 1956, was especially noteworthy. Between 1957 and 1959, the journal was published in Miarritze (Biarritz). Zaitegi, a follower of Resurrección María Azkue's form of standard Gipuzkoan (a variety of the Basque language), helped extend the use of literary Basque, which was necessary to develop the unified Basque used in *Euzko Gogoa*. With significant variations among Basque dialects, the writers that used Resurrección María Azkue's unified Basque were the main contributors to *Euzko Gogoa*: mainly, Orixe (Nikolas Ormaetxea), Andima Ibinagabeitia, Bingen Ametzaga, Jon Mirande, Juan San Martín, and Nemesio Etxaniz, among many others. Exceptions to these were Gabriel Aresti and Federico Krutwig, who also contributed to *Euzko Gogoa*.

Translations of works from English, Spanish, German, Russian, Latin, and so on fulfilled two goals for Basque exiles: they promoted the normalization of the Basque language by refining, diffusing, and laying down specific linguistic conventions and, as opposed to Miguel de Unamuno's political theory of the languages (that minority languages like Basque were languages for domestic use and thus were sentenced to cultural death), they provided Basque-language versions of classics of universal literature.

---

17. Bingen Ametzaga to René Lafon, Montevideo, July 4, 1950, IAA, GT-Lafon.R.1950.

This demonstrated that any discourse, no matter how complex, could be expressed in Basque. Many literary classics acquired a special importance among the Basque exile community: Aeschylus, Ovid, Dante, Shakespeare, Goethe, Tolstoy, and so forth.

Closely linked to preserving the language, the Basque government and Basque cultural groups worked to raise awareness about repression of Basque and to condemn its prohibition, as had happened in Hegoalde. At the 1956 World Basque Congress, a whole session was dedicated to discussing the situation of the Basque language. Toward the same goal, from 1949, an annual Basque Language Day had been held in the Americas on St. Francis Xabier's feast day (December 3); Xabier was a Basque saint who died on December 3, 1552, on Shangchuan Island (China).[18] The Basque Language Day was the initiative of a working group in Iparralde that had been created by people close to Manuel Intxausti and Manu Sota to raise funds for the *ikastolak* (Basque schools) and pro-Basque-language events and to denounce the situation of the Basque language on the international political stage. Today Basque Language Day is still celebrated in Basque societies in the Americas and Europe.

Another initiative was the resolute support for the creation of radio stations broadcasting on a variety of political and cultural topics. Among these, the most important were stations in Venezuela (Radio Euzkadi) and, even earlier, Basque programs on Montevideo radio stations, which started in 1943. Facing various technical problems and administrative complications concerning time uses, the weekly radio program schedule was adjusted to the same schedule thanks to Valentín Herrero from 1947 to 1949 in Montevideo.[19]

Finally, the Basque exile community also encouraged Basque music, dance, and other cultural expressions. This was straightforward because most Basque centers had dance and musical groups. A prime example of such activities was Montevideo's Basque Cultural Week, promoted by the Buenos Aires delegation and organized by the Uruguayan delegation and Basque centers in Montevideo in October 1943. The delegations also programmed and promoted cultural committees and festivals within the Basque centers. According to Bingen Ametzaga:

> You'll know by now that we managed to win the vote in the battle for the executive committee of Euskal Erria. Now it's a question of making the most of the victory. I've been appointed president of the festival, art and culture committee, and I've already begun to do everything I can to achieve a series of talks and concerts together with creating dance groups and a choir that will be handy this spring and summer in our excursions inland where there aren't so many Basques and we have work to do.[20]

Generally speaking, the delegations reinforced the celebrations of traditional and historically important dates that the Basque centers already observed, such as the feast

18. Manuel Intxausti to Bingen Ametzaga, Uztaritze, June 7, 1949, IAA, GT-Intxausti.M.1949.

19. Bingen Ametzaga to Joxe Mari Lasarte, Montevideo, February 4, 1948, IAA, GT-Lasarte.JM.1948.

20. Bingen Ametzaga to Jose Antonio Agirre, Montevideo, July 31, 1944, IAA, GT-Agirre.JA.1944.

days of St. Francis Xabier (December 3), St. Ignatius of Loyola (July 31), and St. Fermin of Amiens (July 7); the Loss of the Fueros (ancient Basque code of laws) in 1839 (October 25); and bombardment of Gernika (April 26). In short, the Basque government's cultural activity in exile was extraordinary.

Political Developments

In the political field, as noted earlier, the Basque government's intelligence services began operating in 1936 in both Hegoalde and Iparralde, which was paralleled by the rise of Nazi repression: hundreds of people were rounded up and sent to forced labor camps (e.g., organized into work battalions to build the Atlantic Wall, the fortifications built around Nazi-controlled Europe). Through 1944, the Nazis hung forty-four alleged terrorists in the occupied Basque Country. In 1943, the Spanish National Union (UNE) began looking for terms on which it could work with the Basque government by forming a resistance battalion of Basques. Toward the end of 1943, Eliodoro de la Torre took over the leadership of Kepa Ordoki's battalion, which had fought in 1936 and 1937 in the Basque Country against the Germans. On August 24, 1944, there was an uprising in Zuberoa that resulted in the liberation of the province and the taking of 207 German soldiers as prisoners. A day later, resistance groups also liberated Hendaia and Baiona (there is no specific data, but it is believed that up to fifteen thousand men were involved).[21]

In late 1942 the New York delegation of the Basque government helped the Belgian Office for Latin America to fight fascism in South America by publishing two journals: The Belgian Journal in 1944 (La Revista Belga) and Both Worlds in 1945–46 (Ambos Mundos). The Belgian government in exile tried to counter the influence of totalitarian ideologies in the South American Catholic church. From 1944 the Basques were responsible for the Latin American edition of the Belgian Journal. Luis Navascués was named director and Jon Bilbao deputy director. The Catalan exile Jaume Miravitlles and the Belgians P. E. de Rooy and the Francis Goffart also helped in the project. The Belgian Journal that was distributed through the Catholic network Pro Deo, was one of the starting points of the current Christian Democracy in Latin America and proved to be a strong anti-Nazi propaganda tool. At the end of World War II the Basques surrendered the management of the Belgian Journal, launching a new publishing project: Both Worlds (Ambos Mundos). For their work in both journals, at the end of World War II Jon Bilbao was decorated as Knight of the Order of the Belgian Crown.

Following the Basque National Council's agreement with de Gaulle's French Empire Defense Council, a Basque battalion became part of the French army between the summer and winter of 1944.[22] In the spring of 1944, Ordoki had told the men in the

---

21. Interview with Jose Elizalde Arzua (1914–2006), former soldier of the Gernika Battalion, Altzuza (Nafarroa), February 2, 2000.

22. José Ignacio Lizaso to José Antonio Agirre, London, October 24, 1941, AA/AN FSAE, AN-GE-465-2.

battalion that this would be a possibility—seven of the two hundred soldiers left the battalion.[23] After the French government gave permission to establish the Basque Military Unit, on December 28, 1944, the Spanish-Basque Volunteer Battalion was inaugurated in Bordeaux with 180 men. The Basque government appointed Juan Manuel Epalza political representative for the battalion on January 10, 1945, and on January 29, Vice President Leizaola publicly announced its creation in Paris, which was followed by a further announcement by the Basque government in New York on March 2, 1945.

Through March 4, 1945, the Nazis, led by Colonel Walter Sonntag and later Colonel Oberst Prahl, had slightly more than 25,000 soldiers, 461 cannon, 528 bunkers, and nearly 800,000 mines on the Médoc front in the southwest region of the French state. De Gaulle had appointed General Edgard de Larminat commander of the French Western Forces in October 1944, and Larminat ordered Jean de Milleret (known by the nom de guerre "Carnot"), head of the Carnot Brigade, to attack Nazi positions in Pointe-de-Grave. In the attack, Gardoki's Gernika Battalion fought in the Mixed Moroccan and Foreign Regiment, led by a Polish officer with the surname of Chodzko. The regiment comprised three battalions: Gernika, led by Ordoki, and Libertad, led by a man surnamed Santos; the Moroccan Battalion; and the Mixed Battalion.

On April 14, 1945, fighting broke out in Pointe-de-Grave, on the northernmost tip of the Médoc Peninsula, at the mouth of the Gironde Estuary. It lasted for seven days. The Gernika Battalion, striking from the south, liberated the towns of Lesparre, Saint-Vivien, and Soulac, on its march northward. In total, four hundred men in the Carnot Brigade were killed and around a thousand wounded. There were 680 German casualties and 3,320 prisoners taken by the Allies, including 80 officers. The Gernika Battalion lost four men: Antonio Mugika (from Donostia); Félix Iglesias Mina (from Atarrabia); Juan José Sasia Jausoro (from Alonsotegi), and Antonio Lizarralde Garamendi (from Durango). Following the liberation of the Isle of Oléron as part of Operation Jupiter, together with the liberation of La Rochelle, La Pallice, and the Isle of Ré, the attack ended. On April 22, 1945, de Gaulle honored the battalion: "Commandant, France will never forget the efforts and sacrifices made by the Basques for the liberation of our land." On August 29, 1945, the new French authorities ordered a general demobilization. Ernest Pezet, a LIAB member, in response to a request by the Basque government, asked French authorities to delay the demobilization: "We would like to retain a small core of military forces, in order to create around this a body responsible for protecting public safety and maintaining order in our country in the event of a change in the current regime and the taking of power by democratic forces." On September 24, 1945, Leizaola wrote de Gaulle but to no effect; the Gernika Battalion was disbanded in early summer of 1945.

With World War II over and the Axis powers defeated, the time came to speak about the postwar political redrawing of Europe and an international organization to

23. Interview with Jose Elizalde Arzua, Wednesday, February 2, 2000.

replace the League of Nations capable of leading international politics. As a result of the Atlantic Charter, agreed on at the meetings at Placentia Bay, Newfoundland, in August 1941, it was clear to all that the case of Spain would provoke a heated debate. On the one hand, because it had fought for and with the Allies, the Basque government expected support from the US government; on the other hand, together with the Spanish Republican government-in-exile, the different Republican forces needed a united policy against Franco in international politics. It was, then, a complex panorama: the Basque exile community defended sovereignty for the Basque Country, at the UN and before the Spanish Republican government. As noted previously, unity among the exiled Basque, Catalan, and Galician nationalists who formed Galeuzca was absolutely vital to function politically in the postwar era.

Besides working with the Spanish Republican government, there was an even more important agreement to reach with Galeuzca. On January 18, 1941, the national councils of the Basque Country and Catalonia signed a two-way agreement in London—the first step to developing Galeuzca in exile. In Argentina on May 9, 1941, delegates of the Basque, Catalan, and Galician centers in Buenos Aires signed a three-party agreement.[24] In addition to maintaining the spirit and objectives of the Galeuzca organization, the signatories also came out in support of sovereignty for the three nations, the right of self-determination, and the Allied cause during World War II. This was an unprecedented convergence of Galician, Catalan, and Basque leaders in exile, and until that time, there had never been such common purpose abroad among the exile community.

In a letter to Castelao on March 2, 1944, Agirre outlined the work of the Basque National Council in the wake of the agreement:

> It is vital to agree on the principles:
>
> 1. [Defense] of the national reality of each of our peoples, their right of self-determination and the right to security and stability in peace.
> 2. As a common goal in the peninsular context, one might highlight the pact leading to a voluntary federation or confederation in order to create an Iberian balance, leaving the door open to the future inclusion of Portugal.
> 3. In terms of the policy in a wider context, the special friendship of the Iberian confederation with the South American peoples and agreement on major projects fostering peace, culture, freedom and democracy.
> 4. Regarding Europe, integration in its civilization and its proposals for a mainly Western federation which will bind us to the Western democratic world, the British Empire and the United States.
> 5. Friendly relations with the USSR.
> 6. Improvement of mutual understanding in peace and liberty. It is, moreover, necessary to set down the desire for peace and religious tolerance in law, together

24. *Convenio de acuerdo de Galeuzca*, Montevideo, May 9, 1941, AA/AN FSAE, AN-GE-465-1.

with intelligent diplomatic activity with the Vatican, that should not overlook the Christian and Catholic roots of the traditional society that distinguishes our peoples.

7. Our adherence to an advanced social order is essential.
8. Finally, the declaration of our belligerency in the current world struggle on the side of the UN in the fight for the freedom of all peoples.[25]

On October 24, 1944, Galeuzca Uruguay was formed under the leadership of Bingen Ametzaga.[26] On December 22, delegates from the Basque, Galician, and Catalan exile communities signed a statement in the Hotel Majestic in Mexico City in favor of carrying on with the 1941 agreement. However, despite the fact that Galeuzca held a high regard for and repeatedly defended human rights, the Spanish republican government remained suspicious of Galeuzca and opposed to any debate on the question of self-determination.[27] For Irujo, placing the principle of state unity above human rights was a political strategy not so far removed from that of Franco's National Movement. Castelao agreed with Irujo:

> The Spanish republicans don't want to consider the potential energy Galicia has. The reactionaries are more instinctively alert to this, and therefore any activity on our part frightens them. Hence, Primo de Rivera speeded up the coup d'état—he said so himself—because of the separatist demonstrations of the "Triple Alliance" (today "Galeuzca") in Barcelona, and the military rose up when Galicia presented its [autonomy] statute to the Cortes [Spanish Parliament]. It's not that we provoked the revolts; but we did contribute to the crazy indignation of those jingoists. And because "Galeuzca" is of undoubted use to the Republic, republicans fight against it without passion and think of it frostily.[28]

In November 1942, several exiled socialist groups in France created the Spanish National Union and in November 1943 the Spanish Board of Liberation (JEL) was formed in Mexico. The two groups had a similar goal, namely, before forming a Spanish government-in-exile after World War II, accumulating the forces and uniting the ideas of different groups and powers in the Socialist Party. In this context, there were a number of possibilities to consider within the boundaries of the 1931 constitution, though not the right of self-determination or alternative proposals for either a federal or a confederal state—a genuinely democratic state—in line with the principles of the Atlantic Charter. Throughout November 1943, Prieto's faction of the PSOE, the IR, the UR, the Republican Left of Catalonia (ERC), Catalan Republican Action (ACR), and the EAJ-PNV held meetings in Mexico. The EAJ-PNV delegates, Julio Jauregi and Telesforo Monzon,

25. Jose Antonio Agirre to Alfonso R. Castelao, New York, March 2, 1944, AA/AN FSAE, AN-GE-467-2.

26. "Bases de GALEUZCA," *Galeuzca* 1, no. 1 (August 1945): 32.

27. Bingen Ametzaga to Jose Antonio Agirre, Montevideo, December 24, 1943, IAA, GT-Agirre.JA.1943.

28. Alfonso R. Castelao to Jose Antonio Agirre, Buenos Aires, November 29, 1943, AA/AN FSAE, AN-GE-467-1.

left the meetings on November 23 because the right of self-determination or a referendum on independence was not considered in negotiations. In Jauregi's own words:

> Duly invited, Monzon and I, representing the PNV, went to the preliminary meeting, and because Prieto suggested the greatest respect for the principles of the 1931 constitution as a plan of action for the council, Monzon, who was admirable in every form and manner, declared that, for the PNV, the plan could only involve:
>
> 1. Fighting Franco.
> 2. Popular opposition to the restoration of the monarchy.
> 3. Respect for the freely expressed popular will of the Basque people by virtue of the right of self-determination.
>
> Because they did not accept our points of view, the meeting was suspended without any outcome, and the same people met again without us and alluded to Junta Española de Liberación.
>
> This body will be a kind of political JARE because the same people who supported that support the Junta and the same ones against are just as opposed to the new bodies. Those against are Negrín's socialists, those in Fernández Clérigo's Izquierda Republicana, Rodríguez Vega's UGT, and the Communists because they weren't invited, yet if they had been [invited] they would have joined, because it's in a very easy position.
>
> Among the Catalans, Santaló, Sbert and Abdreu's group has left a very bad impression of a far-too-easy cooperation and the Comunidades de América, Estat Catalá, part of Esquerra Catalana, part of Acció Catalana, and all the Catalan members of the Cortes and the Catalan parliament have publicly criticized this stance.[29]

Ultimately, without the Basque nationalists, on November 25, Diego Martínez Barrio was appointed JEL's president and Prieto secretary.[30] Irujo defended the decision of the Mexican delegates to leave the JEL talks, as well as boycotting of the Supreme Council for National Unity, an initiative of the PCE. For Irujo, Jauregi, Monzon, and most members of the EBB, the Spanish Republicans' positions went against the spirit of the Atlantic Charter and its stated right of self-determination. Moreover, in 1944 the political situation had changed a lot since 1931 to keep the same Spanish constitution of 1931 and the Junta was just a body for different republican factions to argue among one another.[31] Indeed, the National Alliance of Democratic Forces (ANFD) was created—without Basque nationalists—in Toulouse in September 1944, and within a month it joined the JEL. Thereafter, in January 1945, the JEL called for a meeting of the exiled Spanish Parliament members to decide on how to form the Spanish government-in-exile.

---

29. Julio Jauregi to Francisco Arregi, Mexico, December 15, 1943, AA/AN FSAE, AN-GE-467-1.

30. Diego Martínez Barrio (1883–1962), member of the Republican Union, had been minister and president of the Spanish Republic from 1931 to 1939; he was again named president in exile on August 17, 1945, a post he held until his death on January 1, 1962. José Antonio Agirre to Carles Pi i Sunyer, New York, February 14, 1944, AA/AN FSAE, AN-GE-467-2.

31. Manuel Irujo, "Política de avestruz," *Euzko Deya* (Buenos Aires), May 2, 1944.

In practice, this was a struggle among different exiled groups and forces to control the Spanish Republican government-in-exile in Mexico.

This was undoubtedly a difficult situation for the Basque government. On the one hand, Agirre foresaw the need to establish a unified Spanish Republican government before the UN meeting; on the other hand, most members of the government he led were calling for Basque self-determination and so opposed joined the Spanish Republican government-in-exile. It was in this context and with these goals in mind that Galeuzca was born. Neither Agirre personally nor the Basque government ever intervened in the disputes between the Spanish Socialists and the Communists, so the *lehendakari* was an appropriate arbiter for all sides.[32] Subsequently, Agirre took a middle course: maintaining his declaration in favor of Basque self-determination, the *lehendakari* agreed to leave to one side debate on the subject until after the government of the Spanish Republic-in-exile had been formed in Mexico. Generally speaking, the Basque government's political objectives, in terms of international politics, coincided with those of the Spanish Republican government-in-exile. The restoration of the Spanish Republic would require four steps in the postwar environment: (1) overthrowing Franco, as stipulated at the San Francisco Conference (a UN meeting of Allied delegates, held April–June 1945 in San Francisco, California, United States), (2) breaking off diplomatic relations between the Franco regime and the participating countries at the San Francisco Conference, (3) strengthening a definitive Spanish Republican government chosen by the Republican parliament, and (4) gaining UN recognition of the Spanish Republican government-in-exile.

The president of the Spanish Parliament-in-exile, Diego Martínez Barrio, issued a call for Parliament to meet on November 13, 1944, and on January 10, 1945, it met in Mexico. Seventy-two members attended the meeting, and a further forty-nine sent representatives in their place. Taking advantage of the climate of instability, the pro-Prieto members left the meeting, declaring that there was no quorum and that a Spanish government-in-exile could not be formed. Subsequently, delegates of the Spanish Republic went to the San Francisco Conference without having formed a government. At the level of international politics this indicated failure, because it demonstrated a lack of unity among the different factions.

Given this obvious strategic failure, Agirre realized how important it was to achieve unity among all Basque political forces in exile, a sine qua non to overthrow Franco and to gain credibility at the San Francisco Conference. As strategic unity was the main political objective, Agirre thought that the Basque nationalists should temporarily leave aside the demand for self-determination to push an urgent political and strategic agreement to ratify the union of political forces around the action of the Basque government-in-exile. In April 1945, Agirre met in Paris with Juan Ajuriagerra (who had illegally crossed the

32. Jose Antonio Agirre to Telesforo de Monzon, New York, January 31, 1944, AA/AN FSAE, AN-GE-467-1.

border), who supported the ideas of the *lehendakari*. That led to a conflict with Manuel Irujo, who resigned as head of the Basque minority in the Republican Parliament.

In early March 1945, all Basque political forces representing the various Basque nationalist and Basque Republican or Socialist political parties and trade unions reached agreement on most of the issues. A final document was agreed to on March 17, although the official signing did not occur until March 31. The Pact of Baiona was the starting point for consolidation of Basque unity of action before the meeting of the UNs' General Assembly in 1945, and its five points marked a program for future action that would last almost until 1975. The pact involved, first, that all signatory forces regarded the Basque government-in-exile headed by Agirre as the only legitimate representative body of the Basque people. Therefore, all Basque anti-Francoist forces would act in concert and under the guidelines of the Basque government to overthrow the dictatorial regime of General Franco and to reestablish republican legality, thus opposing any attempt to restore the Spanish monarchy that could arise in the heat of the European historical juncture. Although the document avoided mentioning the right of self-determination, the third point of the pact clearly stated that all signatories should respect and defend the democratic will of the Basque peoples freely expressed once democracy was restored in the Basque Country. In fact, the Pact of Baiona prioritized the recovery of democratic freedoms and the fight against the Franco regime in Spain over any resolution on the Basque national question.

During the meetings that preceded the signing of the Pact of Baiona, the Socialists called for the establishment of the Advisory Commission of the Basque government, which after the signing of the pact became the Basque Advisory Council. The pact was signed on March 31, 1945, by trade unions and political organizations in exile that had been based in Hegoalde since before the war. The signatories were Gregorio Ruiz de Ercilla (EAJ-PNV), Gabriel Goitia (EAE-ANV), Cándido Arregi (Mendigoxale Batza),[33] Ascensio Lasa (ELA-STV),[34] Francisco Méndez (PCE), José Campos and Ángel Jiménez (UGT), Ambrosio Garbisu, Ignacio Campoamor and Rufino García Larrache (IR), Ángel Jiménez, Fermín Zarza and Paulino Gómez Beltrán (Comité Central Socialista), Fernando Sasiain (Partido Republicano Federal), and Cándido Armesto and Félix Liquiniano (CNT).[35]

In total, 282 official representatives, accompanied by 1,444 delegates representing fifty countries, met in San Francisco between April 25 and June 26, 1945. Of the fifty governments represented by delegates in San Francisco, twenty-six had signed the "United Nations Declaration" during the Arcadia Conference in January 1942. However, only four of those hosted the conference. In other words, the delegates of the Allied countries

33. Mendigoxale Batza (the Union of Mountaineers) was created in 1934 after a split in EAJ-PNV over Basque independence.

34. Basque Workers' Solidarity is a Basque labor union. Eusko Langileen Alkartasuna (ELA) in Basque and Solidaridad de Trabajadores Vascos (STV) in Spanish.

35. Confederación Nacional del Trabajo (CNT, National Confederation of Labour).

directed the activities: Edward Stettinius Jr., the US Secretary of State; Anthony Eden, the foreign secretary of Great Britain; Vyacheslav M. Molotov, foreign minister of the Soviet Union; and Soong Tzu-wen, the Chinese foreign secretary. In general terms, an agreement to create the UN had been reached at meetings in Dumbarton Oaks (August 1944) and Yalta (February 1945), and the agreement was signed in San Francisco. The postwar world political map fell into the hands of the five major powers that would make up the UN Security Council (the United States, Great Britain, France, the Soviet Union, and China). The Spanish case was not among the most pressing issues, but it was important enough to be discussed at the conference.

Focusing on the Basque government's own specific nature rather than the JEL and the other Spanish Republican groups, the message Agirre took to San Francisco revolved around four points: the war of 1936–1939 was a result of a Falangist uprising against the democratically elected Spanish government in 1936 and was successful only because of support from the totalitarian governments of Hitler, Mussolini, and Oliveira Salazar; General Franco's regime collaborated with the Axis forces throughout World War II; General Franco's Spanish government was based on the same antidemocratic political doctrine and principles that underpinned the totalitarian governments of Hitler, Mussolini, and Oliveira Salazar; and, finally, in accordance with article 2.6 of the UN Charter, the regime in Spain implied a threat to international peace and security; therefore, the UN should take measures against Franco.

In fact, as soon as the Basque government delegation arrived in San Francisco, it sent a letter with these four principles to both the four main delegates and the Spanish Republican representatives.[36] Indeed, between 1945 and 1955, the Franco regime was kept outside the UN, and during those years, there was a close relationship between the Basque and Spanish Republican governments. In fact, at the beginning of this period, the Basque government-in-exile was able to direct matters quite successfully. The San Francisco Conference did not recognize General Franco's government and began to impose sanctions on the regime.[37] Similarly, though, it did not recognize the Spanish government-in-exile because there was no elected government to recognize. In this context, following the San Francisco Conference, the Mexican government recognized José Giral's Spanish government-in-exile on August 31, 1945.[38] As Mexican president Manuel Ávila Camacho stated:

> My country considers that the Republican government of Spain has never ceased to exist. We will never accept the intervention of the fascist countries to deprive the

---

36. José Antonio Agirre to Manuel Irujo, New York, September 17, 1945, AA/AN FSAE, AN-GE-488-3.

37. *Note by the Government of Euzkadi to the Apostolic Delegate at the United States*, New York, August 24, 1945, AA/AN FSAE, AN-GE-488-3.

38. José Giral (1879–1962), member of the Republican Left, was prime minister of the Spanish Republic between July and September 1936, minister of state in exile between May 1937 and April 1938, and prime minister in exile from August 1945 until his resignation in February 1947.

> republican government of its power and jurisdiction and, therefore, Mexico has granted its hospitality to the only government that legally represents the Spanish people.[39]

Guatemala also recognized the Spanish Republican government on September 10; the Panamanian and Venezuelan governments did so on November 7 and 8, respectively. Although several other democratic Latin American governments, such as that of Uruguay, did not officially recognize the exiled Republican authorities, they did not acknowledge the Franco regime either.[40]

Juan Negrín, the former head of government of the Spanish Republic, went to Mexico in 1945. After meetings on August 7 and 8 with the president of the Spanish Parliament, Diego Martínez Barrio, a meeting of Parliament was called for that August to form, once and for all, a Spanish government-in-exile. In those meetings, it was decided to appoint Martínez Barrio president of the republic again, although the appointment of a government was postponed until a later convening of the parliament. However, appointing Martínez Barrio president implied appointing a new prime minister, and José Giral was the most logical candidate for the position. At the same time, the different republican groups wanted a member of the EAJ-PNV in the cabinet, and Manuel Irujo was the most logical candidate.

However, both Irujo and EAJ-PNV's EBB demanded recognition of the right of self-determination as a basic condition of having a minister in the Spanish Republican government. Telesforo Monzon, the Basque government's delegate in Mexico, agreed with Irujo, as did most members of EAJ-PNV's council in Mexico. Furthermore, the EBB wanted to consult its members and sympathizers on the issue, in both the Basque Country and in exile. Irujo gave five conditions for agreeing to become a minister: (1) the Republican government had to recognize religious freedom; (2) the Republican government had to recognize a statute of autonomy for Galicia that had already been democratically approved; (3) the Republican government had to recognize a statute confirming the "special transitory arrangement" with the governments of the Basque Country, Catalonia, and Galicia; (4) similar to the projected Basque statute of autonomy of 1932, the new statute had to include Nafarroa as part of Basque Country; and (5) the Republican government had to recognize the right of self-determination.[41]

From the moment Agirre arrived in Mexico on August 25, without rejecting the right of self-determination, the *lehendakari* continued to suggest a debate in Parliament or at a later roundtable.[42] According to Joseba Rezola*:

---

39. *El problema de España ante el mundo internacional: Resolución aprobada por la 1ª Asamblea General de Naciones Unidas; Texto y discusión de la misma* (London: República Española, Ministerio de Estado, 1946), 32.

40. *Informe de José Antonio Aguirre sobre la situación internacional en relación con los vascos* (Report by Jose Antonio Agirre on the international situation concerning the Basques), Paris, September 11, 1939, AA/AN FSAE, AN-GE-463-2.

41. Manuel Irujo to Jesús María Leizaola, London, November 29, 1944, AA/AN FSAE, AN-GE-468-1.

42. Telesforo Monzon to Doroteo Ziaurritz (telegram), Mexico City, August 21, 1945, AA/AN FSAE, AN-GE-488-3.

> There are a lot of people who cling to these institutions [that] I consider are directed against us. I think as regards the Spanish Socialists in France and Mexico, and I believe we shouldn't waste any opportunity to say so, because it's true, that the constitution and the statute are dead and it's impossible to resuscitate them. . . . We must take into account that our people have a false idea about the statute. Many think that the statute is what we enjoyed during the war and, without realizing that at the time we almost experienced independence, the deception they'll feel when they realize just how much will be lost in these matters according to what the statute proposes would be very harmful to us.[43]

Finally, the EAE-ANV shared EAJ-PNV's view in that it did not agree with forming a government on these terms either.

Following the election of Diego Martínez Barrio as president, on August 17 the makeup of the new government was announced, with José Giral (IR) named prime minister. Manuel Irujo was minister of trade, Lluís Nicolau D'Olwer (ACR) was minister without portfolio, and Miguel Santaló (ERC) was minister of education. However, the government did not respond to Irujo's conditions, and he did not take up the position. The appointment of an EAJ-PNV minister also resulted in criticism from within the party, because there had not been time to organize any consultation, and the decision had been made without considering party opinion. For Leizaola, "They were a little aggrieved because, having consulted figures within the party and people in [the Basque Country] in regard to forming a government in Mexico, its announcement came before they'd sent any cable to Mexico."[44] However, after the path was cleared to acknowledge Irujo's demands, the Nafarroan minister agreed to take up his position in the government. José Giral was prime minister of the republic from August 1945 to February 1947, and Diego Martínez Barrio was president from 1945 to 1962. Juan Negrín, meanwhile, was expelled from the PSOE on April 23, 1946, over differences with Martínez Barrio and Prieto.

On October 20, 1945, in Mexico, Miguel Amilibia (a former PSOE representative in the Spanish Parliament for Gipuzkoa) and Antonio Huertas (ex-secretary of the CCSE) criticized the PSOE member of the Basque government, Santiago Aznar, for agreeing with the Basque national idea. They also supported creating the Basque Socialist Workers' Party within the PSOE. Ultimately, these were the first steps in a PSOE crisis that led to the removal of the socialist minister Santiago Aznar from the Basque government.

---

43. Joseba Rezola to Jose Antonio Agirre, September 15, 1945, AA/AN FSAE, AN-GE-471-1.

44. Jesús María Leizaola to Jose Antonio Agirre, Paris, October 20, 1945, AA/AN FSAE, AN-GE-488-3.

8

Paris: 1946–1956, the United Nations Struggle

After the Spanish republican government was formed in Mexico with one EAJ-PNV member, the *lehendakari* returned to New York and from there traveled to Paris, arriving on February 9, 1946, a day later than José Giral, the president of the Spanish Republic. Within a year, from February to August 1947, Rodolfo Llopis Ferrandiz would be the new president of the republic and Irujo the minister of justice.[1] With a new phase in Basque exiled politics beginning, the Basque government headquarters would be located in Paris until 1975.

The Basque government's pro-Allied stance and the defeat of the Axis powers did not bring with them, contrary to hopes, the overthrow of the Franco regime. During World War II, the Basque government based these hopes on four documents signed by the Allies: the Atlantic Charter (1941), the declarations at the Tehran Conference (1943), and the agreements signed at the Yalta and Potsdam conferences (1945). By this time, the UN had replaced the League of Nations, and a wave of optimism was sweeping through international politics. In this new context, the Spanish Republican government and the Basque government would do everything in their power to secure the diplomatic isolation of Franco's dictatorial regime.

It was also essential in the struggle against the Franco regime's agents to establish institutional relations with the governments of countries with UN delegates. At the 1945 San Francisco Conference and thereafter, although the Allies demonstrated a firm stance with regard to the Spanish government, it was clear to Republican exiles that, at the first UN General Assembly meeting in London (1946), they would have to battle against the Franco regime to get the votes of different countries' governments to avoid the inclusion of the Spanish regime within the UN. While the regimes of General Juan Domingo Perón in Argentina (1946–1955) and Marcos Pérez Jiménez in Venezuela (1952–1958) were hostile, the Basque government delegations generally received important support in South American democracies like Chile, Uruguay, and Mexico. In such cases, the Basque government-in-exile was able to secure direct host-government involvement,

1. Rodolfo Llopis Ferrandiz (1895–1983), member of the PSOE, was undersecretary of the prime minister during the war, secretary general of the PSOE in 1944, and prime minister of the republic between February and August 1947. After Llopis's short period as prime minister, Álvaro de Albornoz became prime minister between August 1947 and July 1951.

generous help, and solidarity. In Uruguay, the Basque government delegation received help from the centrist Partido Colorado (Red Party), in power from the beginning of the century until 1959, and the Christian-Democrat Civil Union. As opposed to the secular position of the Red Party, several leading figures in more conservative parties, such as the National Party and the White Party, were sympathetic to the Spanish regime's Catholicism and, with the Cold War already intensifying, viewed the Spanish state as an ally against the so-called red peril.

That said, from 1941 onward, by means of the delegations in different countries of the Americas, the Basque government tried to have as great a presence and to gain as much power as possible. In keeping with this line, the Basque government created the Basque Press Office (OPE) in Paris in 1947, a press and information service directed by Joxe Mari Lasarte. The office had an enormous task: day after day, all the Basque delegations in Europe and the Americas, as well as the intelligence services operating in the Basque Country, were sending press clips from the most widely distributed American and European newspapers on the Basque political or cultural struggle to the headquarters of the Basque Press Office. The OPE processed the reports daily, published them in the biweekly *Euzko Izpar Banatzea* (*EIB*) bulletin, and sent the bulletin to the delegates, who published items of interest in their local presses. The OPE operated in this way from 1947 to 1978. Together with the journal *Euzko Deya* (published in Paris), *EIB* soon became the main source of news from the Basque Country and provided the most up-to-date information possible about their homeland to Basques in exile.

The *EIB* had two main objectives. First, it sought to find a place within the press of different Latin American countries to publicize the conflict and political struggle in the Basque Country. This task was a bigger endeavor than just writing—the aim was to shape public opinion in the Americas against the Franco regime and in favor of Basque historical and political rights. Second, by appointing correspondents throughout the Americas, the *EIB* would become the Basque government's de facto official foreign news service and journal.

For example, in Uruguay, Bingen Ametzaga wrote 208 articles between 1947 and 1955. In the span of twelve years, the Basque government delegation in Uruguay published more than six hundred articles in the Montevideo press, in other words, an average of one article per week for twelve years. Mainstream newspapers such as *El Plata*, *El País*, *El Bien Público*, and *Lealtad* in Montevideo repeatedly emphasized the justice of the Basque exiles' case and denounced the Franco regime's excesses and ruthlessness in *EIB*.[2] The support offered by newspapers such as *El Plata* and *El País* in Uruguay or *El Nacional* in Venezuela was truly important to the Basque exile community. Together with the many articles, the behind-the-scenes work was perhaps most notable. The Basque government delegations in the Americas and Europe had to win over the press to their own positions in all the different countries.

2. Bingen Ametzaga to Pedro Basaldua, January 9, 1951, IAA, GT-Basaldua.P.1951.

Between 1946 and 1949, the Basque government's activity regarding the UN involved promoting five general policies: to encourage, finance, and coordinate the resistance in the Basque Country; to synchronize initiatives among the Basque centers in the Americas; to develop the aforementioned *EIB* and OPE information and press service; to bolster institutional cooperation with the Spanish Republican government-in-exile at an international level; and to continue with an active presence in international politics, principally centered on the UN and the European Communities.

Basque exiles in the Americas obviously took part more in activity directed at the UN than in resistance within the Basque Country. They did send money and make great efforts to support strikes in the Basque Country in 1947 and 1951, and they carried out important work to aid those people affected by shortages in postwar Iparralde during the period 1945–1947. However, the Basque delegations organized around the different Basque centers in the Americas concentrated most of their efforts on the first ten years of UN activity (1945–1955).

Of the UN activity, there are different periods during which the UN organized different diplomatic challenges against the Franco regime. In the period 1945–1947, the Franco regime was subject to severe disapproval and diplomatic isolation. Following the San Francisco Conference, as already noted, several countries (Mexico, Guatemala, Panama, and Venezuela) recognized José Giral's Spanish Republican government, whereas others (e.g., Uruguay) did not officially recognize the government-in-exile but also refused to recognize Franco's fascist government. At its fifty-ninth meeting, on December 12, 1946, the UN General Assembly adopted resolution 39(I), in which it declared:

> (a) In origin, nature, structure and general conduct, the Franco regime is a fascist regime patterned on, and established largely as a result of aid received from, Hitler's Nazi Germany and Mussolini's Fascist Italy; (b) During the long struggle of the United Nations against Hitler and Mussolini, Franco, despite continued Allied protests, gave very substantial aid to the enemy Powers. First, for example, from 1941 to 1945, the Blue Infantry Division, the Spanish Legion of Volunteers and the Salvador Air Squadron fought against Soviet Russia on the Eastern front. Second, in the summer of 1940, Spain seized Tangier in breach of international statute, and as a result of Spain maintaining a large army in Spanish Morocco large numbers of Allied troops were immobilized in North Africa; (c) Incontrovertible documentary evidence establishes that Franco was a guilty party with Hitler and Mussolini in the conspiracy to wage war against those countries which eventually in the course of the world war became banded together as the United Nations. It was part of the conspiracy that Franco's full belligerency should be postponed until a time to be mutually agreed upon.[3]

As a consequence, the General Assembly recommended that Franco's government be debarred from membership in international agencies established by or brought into

---

3. Paul Preston, Michael Partridge, and Denis Smyth, eds., *British Documents on Foreign Affairs: Reports and Papers from the Foreign Office Confidential Print, from 1945 through 1950* (Bethesda, MD: University Publications of America, 2000), 1:330.

relationship with the UN, as well as from participation in conferences or other activities arranged by the UN or other international agencies, until a new and acceptable government was formed in Spain. It also recommended that all UN members immediately recall from Madrid their ambassadors and the ministers plenipotentiary accredited there.

The years 1948 and 1949 proved transition years for the case of Spain. Several UN member countries made up the "third way" bloc—following the Argentine Peronist authorities' example—and began calling for an end to the measures taken against the Franco regime.[4] Further, the diplomatic isolation imposed on the Franco regime was not obligatory but a recommendation by the UN General Assembly. During the 1950s, several dictatorships were UN members, and the Franco regime was just one more on that list. To gain control of the UN, the Western bloc (nor, for that matter, the Eastern bloc) was not bothered if the letter or spirit of the UN Charter was broken, so long as doing so was for "practical" reasons; in other words, admitting totalitarian states into the UN in exchange for their support against the opposite bloc constituted realpolitik and a common practice during the Cold War.

The Cold War brought extremely serious consequences for the Basque government's foreign policy. Holding onto its majority in the US Congress, from 1947 on the Republican Party was opposed to the links that the Truman administration, via the US intelligence services, maintained with the Basque intelligence services. According to the Drumbeat Report, of May 8, 1947, prepared by the US armed forces for President Truman, Franco was no longer a threat and should be considered a potential ally.[5] The report suggested for the first time the possibility of building US military bases in Spain. Truman replied, "I won't fight tyranny with tyranny"; that is, he rejected the findings of the report, for the time being. However, his rejection did not mean that the United States had an anti-Francoist policy. In January 1947, George F. Kennan, from the US embassy in Moscow, submitted the report "The Sources of Soviet Conduct," which drew the attention of Secretary of the Navy James Forrestal. At the suggestion of Kennan, the US administration changed its attitude toward the Spanish government from temperate animosity to unpleasant closeness in order to secure US geopolitical influence in the Mediterranean. The deteriorating situation of the Cold War reinforced the centralization of the US intelligence services, which had begun in 1941, and the CIA was created by the National Security Act in 1947. The CIA director was granted broader powers by the CIA Act of June 20, 1949. Along with administrative autonomy, classified funding allowed the CIA wide-ranging strategic freedom.

With the Korean War on the horizon and the Cold War beginning, the US government was not interested in neofascist parties or groups in the Americas and, as a

4. The Non-Aligned Movement (NAM), a group of states not aligned with any major blocs.

5. *The Soviet Threat against the Iberian Peninsula and the Means Required to Meet It,* NARA, College Park, J.W.P.C. 465/1, reference a. J.W.P.C. 432/7.

consequence, the cooperation agreement with the Basque government was superfluous. Around December 1948, the first serious problems had arisen between the US and Basque administrations with respect to intelligence activities in the Americas. Some Basque agents were told by their CIA partners to facilitate information on people (politicians, members of the military, and of the clergy) who they considered friends, so they refused to pass on that information. With World War II ended and the presumed threat to be from communist subversion, the CIA was no longer interested in fascist activity in the Americas.[6] The Basque president's office began to receive the first reports about the CIA from different countries, and by March 1950, official relations were broken off in most places.[7]

During the Cold War, in the period 1950–1955, Spain began to receive some international acceptance. Several US Republican senators, such as Joseph McCarthy, began seeking to improve relations with Franco's government to secure another solid anticommunist ally in Europe and to be able to build military bases on Spanish soil. With an ongoing political witch hunt and a Republican majority in Congress, several (mainly) Republicans in both the US Senate and the House of Representatives–including Pat McCarran of Nevada, Styles Bridges of New Hampshire, and Joseph McCarthy of Wisconsin–lobbied to overturn the international measures against Franco that had been adopted in 1946.

In a 1975 report written for the Congressional Research service, Edward Lampson and Pauline Mian attributed the change in attitude toward Spain not to a change in the Spanish state itself but from the onset of the Cold War. With the Cold War, there were fears of a new threat to peace in Europe, and the enemy was no longer fascism but communism.[8] On April 27, 1950, Senator McCarran proposed that Congress approve a $50 million payment to General Franco to include Spain officially in the anticommunist ranks. "If we are really serious in fighting communism," McCarran said, "let us take into our alliance the people who have put communism out of business in their own country."[9] However, the measure was rejected by a vote of forty-two to thirty-five.[10] Only three months later, after the beginning of the Korean War, McCarran proposed an amendment to the 1948 treaty of economic cooperation with the Spanish regime (the Economic Cooperation Act of 1948), which authorized a $100 million grant to Spain. Congress approved McCarran's second proposal by a vote of sixty-five to fifteen on August 1, 1950. Almost all members of the Senate's Democratic leadership supported

6. Bingen Ametzaga to Jose Antonio Agirre, Montevideo, February 18, 1949; Bingen Ametzaga to Joxe Mari Lasarte, January 18, 1949. IAA, GT-Lasarte.JM.1949.

7. Bingen Ametzaga to Pedro Basaldua, Montevideo, April 11, 1950, IAA, GT-Basaldua.P.1950.

8. Edward T. Lampson and Pauline Mian, "Current Spanish–US Negotiations," report for the Congressional Research Service, Foreign Affairs Division, Washington, D.C., October 15, 1975, in Frank Church Collection, Boise State University Library, MSS 56, box 43, f. 14.

9. "Spain Denied Marshall Aid," *Burlington Hawk Eye Gazette*, Burlington (Iowa), Friday, April 28, 1950.

10. "Las actividades pro franquistas en Washington", EIB-OPE, 803, Paris, July 11, 1950, p. 3.

the proposal. In addition, a hundred million dollars was added to the funds agreed on in the General Appropriation Bill for the third year of the European Cooperation Administration. The effect of the Korean War (which lasted from June 25, 1950 to July 27, 1953) on diplomatic relations between Spain and the United States was also significant.[11]

The heating of the Cold War led—on November 4, 1950—to the UN repealing part of its 1946 resolution condemning Spain. The resolution resolved to revoke the recommendation for the withdrawal of ambassadors and ministers from Madrid and to revoke the recommendation to debar Spain from membership in international agencies established by or brought into relationship with the UN. The proposal provoked criticism from President Truman, and the House later reduced the sum of the loan to $62.5 million. When the bill was signed on September 6, President Truman declared that he would consider the provision an authorization and not a directive, and that the loan would be made available to Spain "whenever such loans will serve the interests of the United States in its conduct of foreign relations."[12] However, the United States eventually extended credit to Franco. In January 1951, McCarthy had initially argued for sending American forces to Europe, and the Republicans forced Truman to appoint Stanton Griffiths as US ambassador in Madrid. Also in 1951, the Export-Import Bank of the United States extended four separate credits totaling $17.2 million, and the General Appropriations Act of 1951 provided for credit as well.

Other measures adopted by the Truman administration also affected the Basque diaspora. President Truman appointed Senator Howard McGrath as US attorney general on August 24, 1949, a post he held until April 3, 1952. McGrath suspected that the Basques might have fascist sympathies, ignoring the fact that they had fought a war against both fascism and Nazism. As a consequence, McGrath kept Basques from entering the United States, stating that they were aliens of political faiths that might endanger US security. McGrath had made his ruling under the Anticommunist Internal Security Act passed by the Congress in 1950. The Security Act of 1950, sponsored by Nevada Senator Pat McCarran, chair of the Judiciary Committee, was one of the most important pieces of anticommunist legislation passed during the Cold War.[13] In response to this legal action, in 1951, Pete T. Cenarrusa in the Idaho House of Representatives passed a memorial urging Congress to take necessary action to activate a law previously passed to allow the entry into the United States of 250 skilled Basque sheepherders and, in general, to allow Basque sheepherders to work in the United States.[14] Cenarrusa explained that, because of McGrath's ruling, the wool industry of the West had suffered: the price

11. Xabier Irujo Ametzaga, *On Basque Politics: Conversations with Pete T. Cenarrusa* (Brussels: EURI, 2009), 145–47.

12. Brookings Institution, *Current Developments in United States Foreign Policy* (Washington, DC: Brookings Institution, 1950), 4:44. See also Lous Henkin, *Foreign Affairs and the United States Constitution* (New York: Oxford University Press, 1996), 395.

13. Ellen Schrecker, *The Age of McCarthyism: A Brief History with Documents* (London: Macmillan, 2002), 217.

14. Irujo Ametzaga, *On Basque Politics*, 30.

of both wool and mutton had increased considerably for consumers, and there was a shortage of wool for military and civilian uses.[15]

When Dwight D. Eisenhower became the president in 1953, the new Republican administration took the measures that Truman had refused, against Congress's wishes. John Foster Dulles, US secretary of state, sought military and economic agreements with several right-wing and ultraconservative regimes, such as that of Franco. After the UN rescinded the measures it had passed against the Franco regime in 1946, US Republicans in Congress managed to include Spain in their defense strategy for Western Europe, which ultimately led to the signing of the Pact of Madrid on economic and military cooperation on September 26, 1953. The Vatican, another strong ally of the Francoist regime in the international arena, after having adopted a series of partial agreements with the Spanish regime (provision of episcopal sees in 1941, provision of the non-consistorial benefits in 1941, provision of seminars and ecclesiastical faculties in 1946, election of the military vicariate in 1950) signed the Concordat on April 27, 1953.[16] The treaty benefited both sides: the Vatican obtained great advantages with regard to the legal status of the Catholic Church in Spain and the Franco regime received its coveted international diplomatic recognition, which it had been denied since 1946.

As a consequence, on November 4, 1950, a day after China had invaded Korea, the fifth UN General Assembly ratified the special committee's proposal to overturn its own resolution of December 12, 1946 (thirty-eight votes in favor, ten votes against, and twelve abstentions), to withdraw diplomatic missions from Spain and to bar Franco from UN participation. On January 30, 1953, Francoist Spain became a member of the UN Educational, Scientific, and Cultural Organization (UNESCO) and, to the shame of the world's suffering people—while eating the caviar, smoked salmon, and roast chicken brought by the Soviet representative Vasily V. Kuznetsov—representatives of the Security Council's five great powers (United States, United Kingdom, France, Taiwan, and the Soviet Union) discussed the quotas that corresponded to each bloc in the UN at the meeting of November 23, 1955.[17] With seventeen no votes and eight votes in favor, and the United States, China (Taiwan), and Belgium abstaining, the Security Council approved the admission of the new members, "bearing in mind General Assembly Resolution 918 (X) A/RES/357, having considered separately the applications for membership of Albania, Jordan, Ireland, Portugal, Hungary, Italy, Austria, Romania, Bulgaria, Finland, Ceylon, Nepal, Libya, Cambodia, Laos and Spain, would recommend to the General Assembly the admission of those countries and amendment to add Japan to

---

15. Interview with Pete T. Cenarrusa (1917–), Boise, April 18, 2010.

16. A concordat is an international treaty between the Holy See of the Catholic Church and a national government on religious matters often including both recognition and privileges for the Catholic Church in that particular state.

17. The Mexican and Uruguayan UN representatives voted against the incorporation of General Franco's regime to UNESCO. Jesús Galíndez to Bingen Ametzaga, New York, May 27, 1952, IAA, GT-Galíndez.J.1952.

that list."[18] The Eastern bloc managed to score four new allies in the UN, whereas the Western bloc successfully introduced six new partners, and the third-way bloc another six, among them several Arab countries. The next day, along with fifteen other countries, with fifty-five votes in favor and two abstentions, the tenth UN General Assembly welcomed the regime of General Franco to the UN, with the support of both the United States and the Soviet Union.[19]

These occurrences at the UN brought an end to the roughly eight-year collaboration between the Basque and US intelligence services. In 1954 the Eisenhower administration intensified its efforts to maintain contact with the Basque government, but the policy was short lived. That same year, US intelligence advised against such measures. However, recalling the rupture of the collaboration agreement in the field of secret services activity in 1950, the Basque intelligence groups in the Americas were wary of their US counterparts. From the 1960s on, under the Kennedy administration, the two governments began to cooperate again, although the links were not as extensive as they had been during the 1942–1950 period.[20]

The most immediate consequence of Spain joining the UN was the end of its ten-year-old policy of autarky and therefore the economic stabilization and political strengthening of the Franco regime. Ultimately, these things extended the Basque exile from 1955 to 1975. Members of the Basque government realized that they were facing an extended period of exile; in other words, Franco would remain in power until he died. The oldest among them had to relinquish the idea of ever seeing the Basque Country again; and from the 1960s on, a new generation would take up the struggle. The Basque government increased the resources to the resistance within the Basque Country. International political activity lost ground to cultural activity within the Basque Country, although naturally both press and diplomatic efforts were maintained and encouraged in the Americas and Europe.

From 1950, then, the Basque government was increasingly forced into autarky. Politically, the first consequence of the US shift was that the UN lost its struggle to overthrow Franco. The US government's decision to stop funding the Basque intelligence network meant economic ruin to the Basque government. In Uruguay, beginning in September 1948, the Basque government had a series of disputes with the CIA, lasting a year and a half, and in April 1950, the Americans broke off their cooperation. According to Bingen Ametzaga, head of the Basque intelligence services in Uruguay, the CIA

---

18. UN Doc. 109 (1955), Resolution of December 14, 1955 (S/3509); see also "En el laberinto de la ONU," EIBOPE, December 15, 1955, 3.

19. "Draft resolution (A/L.208) submitted by forty-one countries providing that the General Assembly, having received the recommendation of the Council that Albania, Jordan, Ireland, Portugal, Hungary, Italy, Austria, Romania, Bulgaria, Finland, Ceylon, Nepal, Libya, Cambodia, Laos and Spain be admitted to membership, having considered the application for membership of each of those countries, would decide to admit those sixteen countries to membership in the United Nations." The General Assembly voted separately on the recommendation of each of those countries.

20. Interview with Pello Irujo, Altzuza, July 15, 2006.

liaison in Uruguay told him that he was "too good a person to be a spy."[21] In Montevideo the delegation was forced to stop its work for an entire year, from May 1951 until June 1952. However, until Bingen Ametzaga left for Venezuela in 1955, with several initiatives under way, there was still some political activity in the Basque exile community in Uruguay.

Between 1941 and 1949, the need to forge a new strategy led to a debate between pro-American and pro-European factions in the Basque government.[22] This was a strategic rather than an ideological debate. In Paris, *Euzko Deya* accused Anton Irala and Jesús Galíndez of not taking into account several commentators' points of view and, as a consequence, of not having foreseen the acceptance of the Francoist regime in the UN. Likewise, others saw this as a consequence of the paper not having signed a political agreement with US intelligence in May 1942. Although in 1955 Galíndez attempted to excuse the US government's geopolitical strategy and the Basque government delegates for not foreseeing Franco's survival in 1946, elsewhere, it was clear that US and British policy toward Franco had not changed in ten years. In other words, the two countries had been opposed to any economic boycott or diplomatic isolation of the Franco regime.

However, following the refusal of the UN General Assembly to adopt anti-Franco measures in 1950—together with the Franco regime's signing of a concordat with the Holy See, an economic agreement with the United States in 1953, and the US and Soviet approval of Spain's UN membership in 1955—the pro-Europeans strongly condemned several members of the Basque government for their excessive optimism. Lasarte and Irujo were clear on the matter in their correspondence with Ametzaga: the Basque government should make a strategic return to Europe.[23] Without any doubt, the 1950 crisis would have a great bearing on Basque government planning from then on. Until that time, the Basque government's main priority in terms of foreign relations had been the work undertaken in regard to the UN, but that priority would never be as important. The European Communities were the new main theater for Basque political activity. The European members of NATO, against the Eisenhower administration's wishes, impeded the Franco regime from entering the organization. They also denied the regime the right to attend the 1957 Rome meetings that led to the creation of the European Economic Community, as well as a place or a voice in the European Parliament, which was established in 1958.

21. Bingen Ametzaga to Jose Antonio Agirre, Montevideo, February 18, 1949, IAA, GT-Agirre.JA.1949. Bingen Ametzaga to Joxe Mari Lasarte, January 18, 1949, IAA, GT-Lasarte.JM.1949.

22. Pro-European means in this context that some Basque politicians preferred to make Basque politics in Europe rather than in the Americas, within the European Communities.

23. Manuel Irujo to Bingen Ametzaga, Paris, June 26, 1951.

9

The 1950 Political Crisis and the Redefinition of the Government-in-Exile

The crisis of the loss of US funding to finance intelligence operations began to affect the Basque government at the end of 1948, and by 1949, as we have seen, it was common knowledge that the collaboration with the US was coming to an end. Between November 1949 and April 1950, most of the contracts in the different delegations of the Basque government in the Americas ended. As a consequence, and because 1950 marks the beginning of the Korean War, I use the expression "1950 crisis" to describe a metamorphosis in the strategy, outlook, and capabilities of the Basque government-in-exile.

Since the capture of Bilbao in June 1937, several members of the Basque government had died from various causes. Because it was not possible to hold elections in exile, to fill the empty positions, each party designated successors who were approved by the president after a consensus of the Council of Ministers accepted the nomination. Thus, with virtually no variation, the proportionality of the popular vote in October 1936 was maintained throughout the exile. However, the personnel continually shifted: in 1946 Eliodoro de la Torre (EAJ-PNV), who had taken over the health ministry from Alfredo Espinosa, who was executed in 1937—died at the age of sixty-two, leaving vacant both the health and the finance ministries. Thereafter, the health ministry was disbanded and Jesus María Leizaola (EAJ-PNV) took over responsibility for the treasury of the Basque government-in-exile until 1979. Leizaola held the positions of both minister of finance and minister of justice, Telesforo Monzon (EAJ-PNV) was named minister of culture in 1946, and Joxe Mari Lasarte (EAJ-PNV), a head of the Basque intelligence services in exile, occupied the Department of Interior.

The PSOE's internal dissension caused many problems for the Basque government. At the request of both sectors of the PSOE, headed by Juan Negrín and Indalecio Prieto, the party forced Santiago Aznar to resign as minister of industry in 1946 on the grounds that his ideological principles were too close to those of Basque nationalism; they appointed Fermín Zarza as his successor. Zarza would remain at the head of the Ministry of Industry until 1952. After the death of Juan Gracia in Paris in 1941, Enrique Dueñas was appointed in 1947, and he remained in office until 1948; in 1950, Zarza replaced him. Paulino Gómez then replaced Zarza as minister of social assistance in 1952. The Spanish Communist Party (PCE) also decided to remove Minister of Public Works Juan Astigarrabia from office in 1937 on the grounds that his statements and thoughts regarding the need for a Basque statute of autonomy had placed him ideologically very close to the Basque nationalists, which they viewed as responsible for the fall of the Basque front in June 1937. After the Molotov-Ribbentrop Pact was signed on August 23, 1939, the Basque government decided not to include members of the Communist Party in the government; however, the invasion of the Soviet Union in 1941 and the subsequent involution of the Communist Party against the Axis forces enabled the Basque government to accept Leandro Carro (PCE) as a substitute for Astigarrabia as minister of public works. However, in the context of the Cold War and, under pressure from the PSOE sector led by Indalecio Prieto, Carro resigned in 1948. Thereafter the party did not have any representative in the Basque government-in-exile (table 9.1.)

Table 9.1. The Basque government-in-exile, 1936–1960.

Department	Minister in charge
Presidency	Jose Antonio Agirre (EAJ-PNV, 1936–1960), Jesús María de Leizaola (PNV, 1960–1979)
Defense	Jose Antonio Agirre (EAJ-PNV, 1936–1937)
Home Office	Telesforo Monzon (EAJ-PNV, 1936–1946), Joxe Mari Lasarte (EAJ-PNV, 1946–1952), Martín Ugalde (EAJ-PNV, 1972–1975)
Treasury	Eliodoro de la Torre (EAJ-PNV, 1936-1946), Jesús Mª Leizaola (1946–1979)
Labor	Juan de los Toyos (PSOE)
Industry	Santiago Aznar (PSOE, 1936-1946), Fermín Zarza (1947–1952)
Commerce & Supplies	Ramón Mª Aldasoro (IR, 1936–1952), Ambrosio Garbisu (1952–1965), Manuel Carabias (1966–), Jesús Ausín
Social Assistance	Juan Gracia (PSOE, 1936-1941), Enrique Dueñas (1947–1948?), Fermín Zarza (1950-1951), Paulino Gómez (1952–1959), Juan Iglesias (1970–)
Health	Alfredo Espinosa (UR, 1936-1937), Eliodoro de la Torre (1937–1946)
Public Works	Juan Domingo Astigarrabia (PCE, 1936-37), Leandro Carro (PCE, 1946–1948)
Culture	Jesús Mª Leizaola (1936–1946), Telesforo Monzon (EAJ-PNV, 1946–1952)
Justice	Jesús Mª Leizaola (EAJ-PNV, 1936–1960)
Agriculture	Gonzalo Nardiz (EAE-ANV, 1936–1975)

Source. Iñaki Goiogana, Basque Nationalist Archive at Artea, Bizkaia.

The reorganization of the Basque government in 1946 also affected the network of delegations abroad, mainly those of New York, Buenos Aires, and Mexico City. For example, Joxe Mari Lasarte's nomination as minister of the interior in 1946 left the delegation in Buenos Aires without one of its main intelligence coordinators in the Southern

Cone. Likewise, when Ramon María Aldasoro (IR) resumed his ministerial portfolio, Francisco Basterretxea* (EAJ-PNV) took control of the delegation of the Basque government in Buenos Aires. Jesus Galíndez had to abandon his responsibility as head of the delegation of the Dominican Republic and became responsible for the New York delegation, which was practically empty after Manuel Sota, Anton Irala, and the *lehendakari* himself moved to either Baiona or Paris. Similarly, the transfer of Telesforo Monzon to Baiona to take over the Ministry of Culture left Julio Jauregi at the head of the Basque delegation in Mexico City.

The rebels apprehended delegates at the Basque delegations in Spain (Madrid, Barcelona, and Valencia) and in Paris, which Spanish agents seized, in collaboration with the occupying forces in 1940. With respect to the delegations in France after the war, after the death of Eliodoro de la Torre in 1946, Xabier Gortazar became head of the delegation of Baiona, a key delegation regarding the organization of the resistance against the Spanish dictatorship. After the liberation of the southern areas of France in 1944, there was no longer any reason to maintain the offices of the Basque government in Pau, Bordeaux, Tarbes, and Toulouse, which had been created to organize resistance against the German occupation. The same can be said of the delegation at Manila in the Philippines, which was disbanded after the surrender of Japan.

The Cold War also affected the Basque government's delegations in Eastern Europe that had opened their doors during World War II to join forces with the Allies against the Axis forces. From 1945, the two blocs' confrontation precipitated the closure of the Basque delegations in Belgrade (1945), Budapest (1946), and Sofia (1950), led by Máximo Andonegi and Pellomari Irujo.* By contrast, the Basque government opened a delegation in Rome in 1948 headed by Teodoro Agirre (table 9.2).

Table 9.2. List of delegations and delegates of the Basque government in exile (1937–1960)

State	City	Delegate or Secretary	Years
Argentina	Buenos Aires	Ramón Mª Aldasoro	1938–46
		Francisco Basterretxea	1946–48
		Pedro Basaldua	1948–82
Belgium	Brussels	Martin Lasa	1938–40/1944–76
Bulgaria	Sofia	Pellomari Irujo	1947–1950
Chile	Santiago de Chile	Pedro Aretxabala	1941–82
Colombia	Bogotá	Francisco Abrisketa	1939–45
		Andrés Perea	1945–80
Cuba	Havana	Jose Luis Garai	1939–48
Czechoslovakia	Prague	Juan Manuel Epalza	c.1940

State	City	Delegate or Secretary	Years
Dominican Republic	Ciudad Trujillo	Eusebio Irujo	1939–40
		Jesús Galíndez	1940–46
		Manuel Martínez de Ubago	1947–48
French Republic	Paris	Rafael Pikabea	1936–39
	Baiona	Xabier Gortazar	1937–40/1946–59
		Eliodoro de la Torre	1940–46
	Bordeaux	Juan Zubiaga Julián Mateo	1941–45
	Pau	Ceferino Jemein	1944
	Tarbes	Jesús Aizarna	1944
	Toulouse	Aurelio Kareaga	1944
Great Britain	London	Jose Ignacio Lizaso	1937–46
		Jesus Hickman	1946–
Hungary	Budapest	Pellomari Irujo	1940–46
Italy	Rome	Teodoro Agirre	1948–53
Philippines	Manila	Ricardo Larrabeti	1945
Spanish Republic	Barcelona	Luis Areitioaurtena	1937
		Manuel Irujo	1937
		Julio Jauregi	1938–39
	Madrid	Jose Sosa	1936–37
	Valencia	Juan Maidagan	1937
United States	New York	Anton Irala	1938–39/1942–46
		Manuel Sota	1939–42
		Jesús Galíndez	1946–56
		Pedro Beitia	1956–66
	Boise	Jon Bilbao	1939–40
Mexico	Mexico City	Francisco Belaustegigoitia	1939–42
		Telesforo Monzon	1942–46
		Julio Jauregi	1947–48
		Antonio Orbe	1948–57
		Jose Luis Irisarri	1957–60
		Antonio Zugadi	1960–66
		Manual Carabias	1966–80
Panama	Panama City	Juan G. de Mendoza	1937–49

State	City	Delegate or Secretary	Years
Peru	Lima	Rafael Orbegozo	1940–42
		German Ortiz	1942–50
		Jose Luis Orbegozo	1950
Uruguay	Montevideo	Ricardo Gisasola	1940–43
		Bingen Ametzaga	1943–55
		Pedro Artetxe	1955–#
Venezuela	Caracas	Jose Mª Garate	1940–48
		Luis Bilbao	1948–51
		Ricardo Maguregi	1951–55
		Lucio Aretxabaleta	1955–67
		Fernando Carranza	1967–80
Yugoslavia	Belgrade	Máximo Andonegi	1941–45

However, the closing of delegations was not the worst problem that the Basque administration faced in exile. As a consequence of the political breakdown of 1950, the Basque government had to undertake a serious financial restructuring. That restructuring resulted in profound administrative reorganization, which led to an emerging era for the Basque exile community.

The end of the collaboration with the US government forced Agirre's government to restructure its finances. Indeed, the 1950 budgetary collapse left the Basque government in dire financial straits. From 1937 on, because of the dependence of the Basque government on external sources, leaders had to examine the possibilities of new independent sources of financing until they could find an appropriate system of self-financing and administration. As Manuel Irujo explained to Bingen Ametzaga in a letter from October 1950, without counting on US or Spanish Republican aid, Basque capital would have to keep the Basque government going autonomously.[1] The Basque government was in desperate need of a safe financial source, a balanced budget that would offer financial survival and stability in the future.

Only two months after the rupture with US intelligence servies in the spring of 1950, the Basque government came up with an idea through a secret directive aimed at delegations in the Americas: in the form of an association, with the help of the delegations and Basque centers, sympathizers would make financial donations, and the interest or earnings made off those donations in ten years would be enough to maintain the Basque government-in-exile. Money would therefore be collected every year in different places around the Americas, with the center of operations in Caracas, where the richest Basque colony of the time was centered. This was, though, a very atypical type of

1. Manuel Irujo to Bingen Ametzaga, Paris, October 23, 1950, IAA, GT-Irujo.M.1950.

financing. As a rule, in a loan, the borrower (in this case the Basque government-in-exile) initially receives an amount of money, the principal, from the lender and is obligated to reimburse an equal amount of money to the lender at a later time. Typically, the borrower pays back the money yearly or monthly in regular installments. In the case of the Basque government, the lenders agreed that the government would not repay them within ten years, so the interest of the capital was entirely for the borrower. At the end of the ten-year period, many of the lenders gave the capital that they had initially deposited to the government. And this was the financial mechanism of the Basque government abroad until 1979. *Lehendakari* Agirre was pleased with the measures taken:

> The loan is granted on the basis of creating a capital that grows in volume and importance as time passes and we will face the cost of our organization with its interests. This means that lenders do not lose their capital, it is theirs. They only yield it temporarily and for a fixed interest. . . . With this system we aim to achieve a more stable and robust solution than the one of the non-repayable funds that, due to its nature tires the donors out. However, this way it is an investment of money that can be located in one place or in another, and the lenders are only asked the interests of the fraction of money invested. The idea has been welcomed everywhere and we are now arranging things so that it can provide a secure and stable base for our work from now on. . . . If we get all countries to respond in proportion to what the lenders in Venezuela have achieved, our cause will be economically solidified for the years of exile to come and, furthermore, it will allow us to return to our country and to start some works that require such acts of solidarity among the Basques around the world such as the creation of a Basque university and others to be built on such a collective spirit. . . . So far we have faced all sorts of difficulties so we should not be wary that, having seen the worst, new methods and perspectives could bring better days.[2]

The *lehendakari* had reasons to be optimistic. The reaction of the Basques in Venezuela had exceeded all expectations, not only in pure economic or political terms but also because of the willingness to cooperate that the collective showed. The Basques in Caracas gave the Basque government a donation of twenty-five thousand dollars in 1950 and the acceptance of the idea of the financial endowment, that is, their contribution of a capital whose interests would cover the needs of the Basque government-in-exile for the years to come.[3] The government had originally thought of a conventional type of loan, that is, to collect and manage the capital and to reimburse in regular installments some reduced interest to the lenders. But the Basque colony in Caracas thought it was more convenient for the government and more suited to the economic conditions of the country to relieve the government of the responsibility for the administration and payment of the interest and, instead, to renounce the interest for the years 1950, 1951,

---

2. Jose Antonio Agirre to Bingen Ametzaga, Paris, May 27, 1950, IAA, GT-Agirre.JA.1950.

3. Jose Mari Lasarte, "La última reunión del Gobierno Vasco," enclosed in a letter to Bingen Ametzaga, May 15, 1950, IAA, GT-Lasarte.JM.1950.

and 1952.[4] The Basques in Caracas proposed to fund-raise a principal of 1 million bolivars, of which they had already raised 600,000 in 1950. As President Agirre expressed in a report titled *Empréstito de Reconstrucción de Euzkadi* (Loan for the Reconstruction of Euskadi), on May 15, 1950, the Basque government-in-exile would try to push similar actions in the Basque centers in Cuba, Mexico, and the United States. In Uruguay, lenders could make loans in lots of five hundred pesos, and as in the case of Caracas, they would remain owners of their capital.[5]

The end of cooperation with the US intelligence services in 1950 led to a new migration in 1949. Members of the Basque government's intelligence services lost their jobs overnight, and without recourse to the Basque government's important role as a source of funding. Under these conditions, and without any degree of stability, several figures—such as Lasarte, Ametzaga, and Galíndez—were forced to seek a new line of work in a particular country or to journey from country to country in the Americas and Europe in search of work. At the same time, together with this interior migration of political origins, nature, and consequences, Basques experienced an apolitical economic migration from their homes to the Americas, beginning around 1947 and lasting twenty years, until the mid-1960s. Fleeing by ship, many young Basques held onto the dream of escaping the economic and political misery of the Franco regime and starting a new life in the Americas. Meanwhile, Basque migrants were also attracted by the political support and economic aid that many countries in the Americas offered. For example, the ship *Tacoma* arrived in Uruguay on December 20, 1949. Sixty-two Basques arrived in Montevideo on this ship to take up jobs with the National Association of Milk Producers, the result of an agreement between the cattleman Rafael Zabaleta and Minister of the Interior Alberto Zubiria, both of Basque origin. After spending two years in the country, the arrivals were offered the chance to stay with fixed work contracts and full Uruguayan citizenship. Many others were not so lucky, however. For example, month after month, hundreds of young people fled the Franco regime on cargo ships destined for the Americas, and they arrived in the new continent without papers or jobs.

The financial or budgetary crisis of the Basque government also led to administrative restructuring, which required a major reduction in staff. The number of employees of the Basque government reached its lowest level under Agirre's leadership in 1950. From 1937 on, the Basque government was organized according to a diagram endorsed in a memorandum that Joxe Mari Lasarte sent to each Basque delegation worldwide (figure 9.1).

The Ministries of the Interior and Home Office were directly linked to the president and to the New International Task Forces of the Federal European Union. The Council of Nafarroa, created in 1945 under Secretary Vicente Navarro, was dissolved in 1953, largely because of the budgetary crisis. The same applies to the Advisory Council, a

---

4. Jose Antonio Agirre to Bingen Ametzaga, Paris, May 27, 1950, IAA, GT-Agirre.JA.1950.

5. Ibid.

Figure 9.1. Diagram of Basque administration in the world, as sent to Basque delegations worldwide.

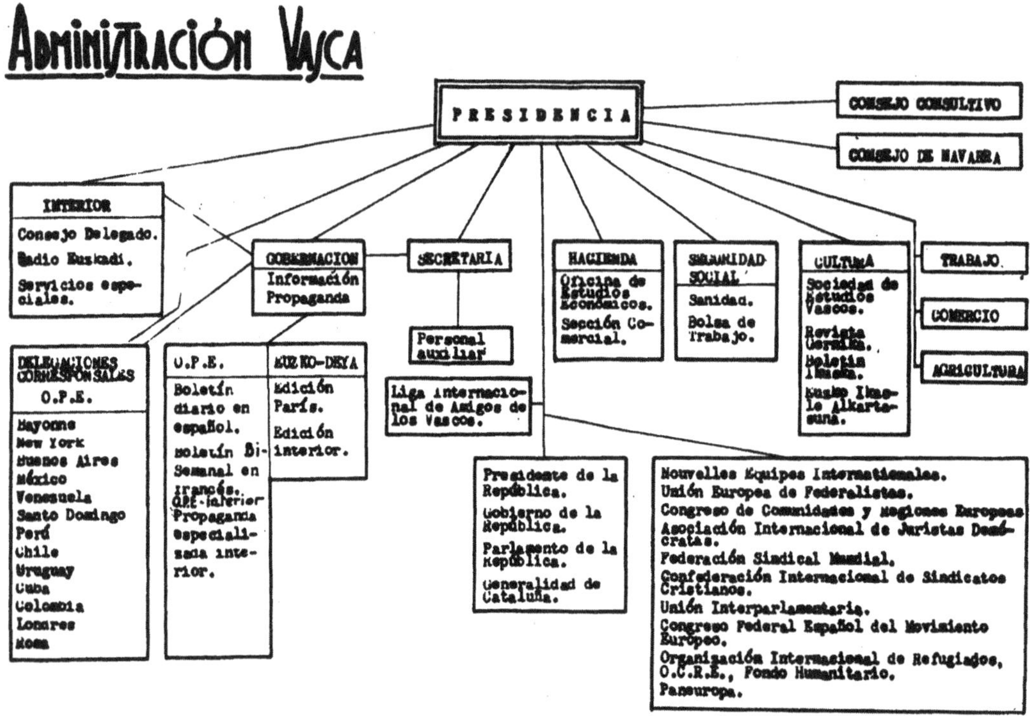

Source: *La última reunión del Gobierno Vasco*, enclosed in a letter to Bingen Ametzaga, May 15, 1950. (IAA).

re-creation of the Basque parliament-in-exile that could not meet as often as desirable because of budgetary limits.

The working conditions were appalling. No working schedule, no free weekends, and—for the most part—no vacations. President Agirre and Lasarte shared the same secretary for all the paperwork of the Ministries of the Interior and Home Office. These stressful conditions drove more than one counselor, and even the president himself, to exhaustion.[6] Salaries were extremely low and varied according to the number of family members of each government member: The president and higher ministers earned fifty thousand francs a month in 1949 (approximately $150 in 1949 dollars), lower-ranking officials with more than three children earned thirty-three thousand francs a month ($94 in 1949 dollars), twenty-three thousand francs a year for a general secretary with no children ($66), and eighteen thousand for the rest ($51). By way of comparison, the average US family of the time earned three hundred dollars a month.

6. Bingen Ametzaga to Jose Antonio Agirre, February 18, 1949.

Figure 9.2. Basque administration, personnel.

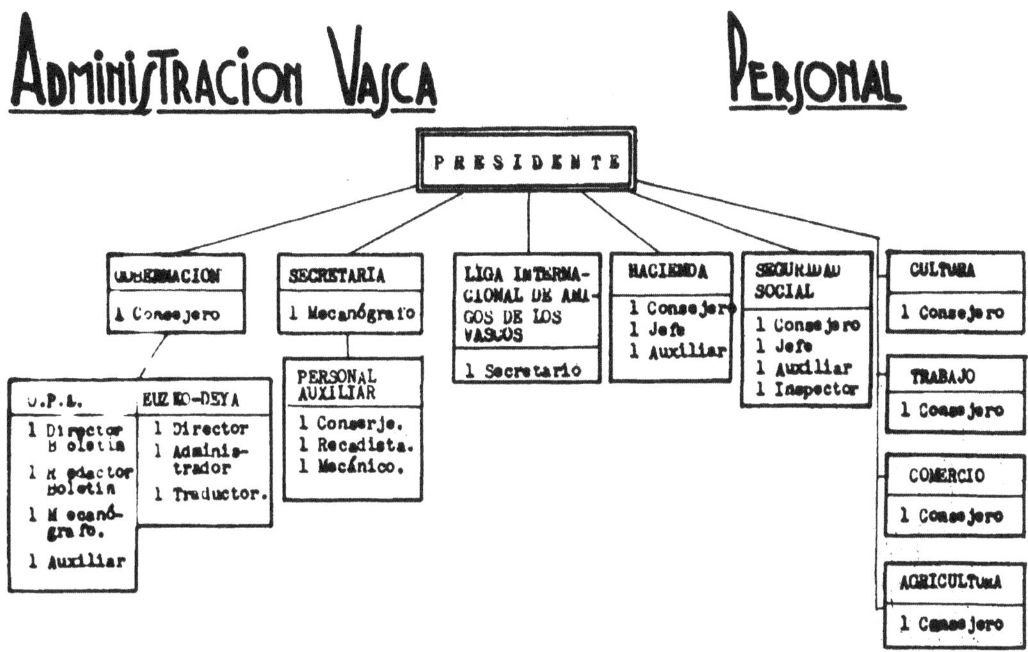

Source: *La última reunión del Gobierno Vasco*, enclosed in a letter to Bingen Ametzaga, May 15, 1950. (IAA).

According to the Lasarte Memorandum of 1949, the government-in-exile comprised twenty wage-earning officials, including the ministers and the president. In Lasarte's own words:

> All work is done with a minimum of staff. It has already reached such a limit that the desired performance is only reachable with the maximum personal effort. The understanding of the various services and the rational use of the working capacity of each staff member is also satisfactory. For example, the intense work of propaganda can only be done using the best sections of the Basque Press Office, *Euzko Deya* and auxiliary staff, and the contributions from other sections such as Treasury and the Secretary of the League of Friends of the Basques. In short, the work and performance is based only on personal sacrifice.[7]

The situation at the delegations was even worse. Most delegates did not earn a salary, and all delegation officials were volunteers. The Uruguayan delegation, headed by Ametzaga, from 1949 had a working team of ten to fourteen people. Most team members were also donors. The budgetary crisis forced the government to reduce the Baiona delegation to three officials in 1949.[8]

---

7. Jose Mari Lasarte to Bingen Ametzaga, May 1949, IAA, GT-Lasarte.JM.1949.

8. Ibid.

From 1949, the financial limitations also drastically limited both political and cultural activity. Events such as the general strike of 1947 in the Basque Country (which is discussed in chapter 10) were no longer possible; the government required absolute voluntarism and external contributions to carry out the 1948 and 1956 world congresses. The deceleration of international political and cultural activity after 1950 was largely due to a lack of funds. Accordingly, the amendment of the strategic guidelines for political and cultural action for the next decade and the administrative reconstruction of the Basque government-in-exile occurred before General Franco's regime joined the UN.

A symbol of this change in geopolitical strategy is the story of Jesús Galíndez, a main political commentator of the Basque government-in-exile and an active element of the Basque intelligence services. After the war's end in 1939, Galíndez went into exile to Bordeaux. Shortly before the German occupation, he was sent to work in the Basque government delegation in the Dominican Republic, at that time led by Eusebio Irujo. Irujo, critical of the dictatorship of Rafael L. Trujillo, tried to convince the *lehendakari* to act against the Trujillo regime at the international level. Agirre advised against this because of the precarious situation of Basque refugees on the island. After Irujo left for Venezuela, Galíndez led the delegation, endorsing Irujo's ideas about the regime. Galíndez was also secretary of the American Comparative Law Institute at the University of Santo Domingo; legal adviser to the Department of Labor and Economy; and professor of law in the School of Diplomatic and Consular Law, where he taught Ramfis Trujillo, son of the dictator.

In 1946, Galíndez moved to New York to work as an aid to the city's Basque delegation, especially as a political commentator and in the intelligence services. Galíndez also worked as a professor of Latin American public law and Hispanic cultural history at Columbia University while completing an advanced degree.[9] On February 27, 1956, the university accepted his voluminous dissertation, "The Age of Trujillo: A Case Study of Latin American Dictatorship," which severely criticized the Trujillo regime.[10] Although it has never been proven, it is widely recognized that Trujillo ordered the kidnapping of Galíndez and his transfer to Santo Domingo. On March 12, 1956, Galíndez was forcibly removed from his apartment in New York, transferred to Santo Domingo, tortured, and murdered. His body was thrown from an airplane into the Caribbean and has never appeared. He is considered to have "officially" died on August 30, 1963.[11] Galíndez's death shocked the Basque exile community and funeral masses were celebrated in Basque centers all over the Americas. From 1956, a Mass was dedicated each March to his memory. The World Basque Congress, held in Paris at the end of September 1956, dedicated a special session to the memory of Galíndez. The Basque political

9. Jesús Galíndez to Bingen Ametzaga, New York, March 29, 1954, IAA, GT-Galíndez.J.1954.

10. Jesús Galíndez to Bingen Ametzaga, New York, May 13, 1955, IAA, GT- Galíndez.J.1954.

11. Inaki Bernardo and Inaki Goiogana, *Galíndez: La tumba abierta; Guerra, exilio y frustración* (Bilbao: Sabino Arana Fundazioa, 2006).

literature of exile dedicated numerous articles, book chapters, and dissertations to his life and death.[12]

Galíndez's death was not the only sign of the changing geopolitical game. In 1951, the Basque government had to abandon its Paris headquarters, at 11 Avenue Marceau, because of a court decision. In 1937, Rafael Pikabea, Basque delegate in Paris, had rented the house from its owner, Hélène Brawn, a US national, for the installation of the Basque government's delegation. The EAJ-PNV gave orders, however, to Marino Ganboa, a Basque industrialist of American citizenship, to buy the property at a price of 1.46 million francs, which would come from the economic contributions of the Basques in the Americas. To avoid attracting the attention of authorities, both the EAJ-PNV and the Basque government formed corporations to take charge of the public goods of both institutions to avoid seizure. And so in February 1939, Finances et Entreprises purchased the building at 11 Avenue Marceau from Marino Ganboa, with Robert Letulle as public notary, for 1.6 million francs (1.4 million for the building and the rest for the furnishings therein). The company also acquired two buildings to house Basque refugees, in Noyon (Oise) and Compans (Seine-et-Oise). On December 18, Finances et Entreprises rented the building to LIAB, which in turn leased it without charge to the Basque delegation.

On January 30, 1940, the Spanish government passed a law according to which the Spanish state was the legal proprietor of all assets of the Spanish Republic, including those of the Catalan and Basque governments in France. Spain created the Asset Recovery Commission to give legal channel to the seizure of any movable or immovable property of institutions in exile. After the occupation of Paris by German forces, Spanish police officers, aided by Gestapo agents, forcibly occupied and looted the offices of Finances et Entreprises. The building was used as headquarters for the Casa España, the Spanish Cultural Institute, and the Spanish Falange in Paris.[13]

In June 1941, the Spanish embassy easily obtained an order to seize all Finances et Entreprises assets from the Civil Court of the Seine. After a month, the First Hall of the Civil Court of the Seine ruled that all assets of Finances et Entreprises were property of the Spanish government. On January 13, 1944, the assets were recorded in the Land Registry as belonging to the Spanish regime.

On August 20, 1944, a few days before the liberation of Paris, the Spanish officers abandoned the building at Avenue Marceau, leaving behind their files and documents, as well as the archive of the Basque delegation, which they had seized years earlier. After liberation, a group of Basques accompanied by French soldiers recovered the building, and Javier Landaburu, secretary-general of the LIAB, and Agustin Alberro, a member of the Basque delegation, reinstalled the Basque government delegation. Later that month, the Spanish consul in Paris advised French authorities, thus submitting the LIAB, as tenant, and Finances et Entreprises, as property owner, to various legal processes against

12. Bingen Ametzaga, "Jesús de Galíndez, hombre de la libertad," *Euzko Deya* (Mexico City), February 1959.

13. Javier Landaburu, "11, Avenue Marceau," *Euzkadi*, January 22, 1981.

Spain from 1945 to 1951. On June 6, 1951, the president of the Civil Court of the Seine ordered an emergency procedure and the immediate expulsion of the LIAB from the building due to pressure from the Spanish delegation in Paris. On June 28, 1951, the LIAB and the Basque government were expelled again from their headquarters. They moved to a new building on Rue Singer in Paris, where they remained until the end of the dictatorship in 1975.

Lehendakari Agirre noted:

> We left this building expelled by the police in execution of a sentence that describes the Basque government as a *gang of burglars*, a sentence obtained during the German occupation, under the protection of the enemy. I protest against this violence and declare that our honor, our conduct and our tradition, deserved a very different treatment. Our cause has been linked to yours, our blood has been shed next to yours in the struggle against the common enemy and we are now being expelled from this house to deliver it into the hands of those who, during the last war, have been supportive of our Axis opponents. I protest in the name of our people, to which this decision has caused one of the deepest pains suffered in exile, especially since the decision was made by friends with whom we share common grief and sacrifices for the cause of freedom and democracy, cause to which we remain, though, unalterably faithful.[14]

The Cold War forced the Basque government to put several strategies on the back burner. Once again, much like in the period before 1941, the government looked toward Europe and intensified resistance efforts in the Basque Country, and exiled cultural activity grew in importance. Indeed, Basque politics in exile entered a new phase after 1949, with different dreams and objectives. After the transition years of 1955 to 1960, maintaining the general principles it had agreed to in Paris, the Basque government started the 1960s with a different administrative organization, different institutional relations, and an altered international political framework. After eighteen years, the crisis had ended the first phase of the Basque exile in the Americas.

As related by Jon Bilbao, the Basque Country in 1954 was totally different from the one in 1951. In just three years the country had changed. A new generation, then in their thirties, began to seriously question the political tactics followed both by the EAJ-PNV in the interior, and by the Basque government-in-exile abroad. Many members of this young generation had attended training courses organized clandestinely by Euzko Gaztedi (Basque Youth), the youth wing of the Basque Nationalist Party. The instructors spoke of the history of the Basque Country, its old political and legal institutions, the nationalist political movement and the nationalist ideology and of freedom and independence for the Basque Country, but they did not teach these young people how all this would be achieved. Until 1951 both the structure of the Basque resistance as the Basque Government and the political parties composing it were in the hands of

14. Bingen Ametzaga, "El despojo de la Avenue Marceau," EIB-OPE, July 24, 1951, 3.

the former army officers or the former Basque politicians, who by self-sacrifice were kept in the designated jobs. Following the agreements of 1953 and the admission of Spanish state into the United Nations in 1955, it was clear to all that the Basque political exile was to extend and that therefore it was necessary to promote the mentioned formation workshops for preparing the new generation to face the struggle against the dictatorship. Juan Ajuriaguerra and Luis Mari Retolaza were among the organizers of these workshops. The strategy they wanted to promote among the young people--or so it was perceived by the new generation—was to wait and be ready by the time Franco died or any internal or external pressure forced a regime change. This prospect was not encouraging for these youth who believed they had to do something else, to force the change of regime and the achievement of freedom and independence. Nor did they believe that general strikes at home and political and economic pressure on the outside could cause a change of regime. These workshops for youth organized by the Basque Nationalist Party had great significance, not only for what who attended learned but especially because it allowed them to know each other and discuss more about strategies for the future than about the past. At these meetings it was born among several Basque young students the impression of stagnation of the previous generation, and the need to break it in some way and jump right in politics. And these young Basque nationalists created Ekin in 1954 and, later, ETA in 1958. Ten years after, in 1968, ETA became a terrorist organization.

10

The 1950 Political Crisis, Christian Democracy, and a Federation of European Nations

The rupture of the agreements on secret services with the Americans and the entrance of the Spanish regime in UNESCO in 1953 and in the UN in 1955 ended any possible action of the Basque government in exile within the UN or in collaboration with the US government. As a consequence of this political crisis, the Basque government shifted its struggle to the political fight against Franco in Europe. Even if Basque nationalism in general and the EAJ-PNV in particular had embraced markedly federalist and Europeanist projects since at least the 1920s, during the period 1937–1960, the first contacts between the EAJ-PNV and French Christian democracy were made during the war (1936–1937) and fundamentally after the collapse of Bilbao, motivated to a large extent by the creation of the LIAB. Among the prominent figures with the closest ties to Basque exile politics were Jacques Maritain; George Bidault, who became president of the Conseil National de la Resistance (National Council of the Resistance) in May 1943 following the capture and shooting of Jean Moulin; and Ernest Pezet.[1] In virtue of the Basque government's ideology, as well as its position against the occupation and the activities of its intelligence services and the Gernika Battalion, EAJ-PNV leaders were present at the national congresses of the Popular Republican Movement (MRP) in 1947–1949, 1951–1952, 1954, and 1959. The EAJ-PNV also maintained contacts with the Italian Christian Democracy Party through Alcide De Gasperi and Giovanni Gronchi, and it sent a representative to the congress held in Rome in 1946.[2]

1. Jacques Maritain (1882–1973), the author of more than seventy works between 1914 and 1973 and one of Christian democracy's leading thinkers, taught at various universities in Europe, the United States, and Canada (Columbia University, University of Chicago, Princeton University). George Bidault (1899–1983), founder of the Mouvement Républicain Populaire (MRP), in 1944 was elected prime minister of the republic in 1946; in 1949–1950, he served as defense minister (1951–1952) and minister of foreign affairs (1953–1954), and he became prime minister again in 1958 for the MRP. Ernst Pezet (1887–1966) was elected councilor of the Republic, senator, and French representative abroad between 1948 and 1959 for the MRP.

2. Alcide De Gasperi (1881–1954), founder of the Christian Democracy Party, was, together with Konrad Adenauer, Jean Monnet, and Robert Schuman, an architect of the European Community. He served as minister of foreign affairs and president of the Italian Council of Ministers. Giovanni Gronchi (1887–1966) served as trade and industry minister (1944–1946), president of the Chamber of Deputies (1948–1955), and president of Italy (1955–1962).

Beginning in June 1940, following the creation of the Basque National Council, the Basque delegation in London played a leading role in several initiatives related to the project of a European federation. In June 1941, the Basque delegation in London submitted a memorandum on European federation to the Foreign Office, the French Empire Defense Council, and the US embassy.[3] In September 1942, on the initiative of the Basque National Council, the Cultural Union of the Countries of Western Europe (UCPEO) was created, with the participation of Spanish (Salvador de Madariaga and Luis Portillo), Catalan (Carlos Pi Sunyer, Josep Maria Batista i Roca, Ramón Perera, and Ramon Ordeig i Mata), and Basque (José Ignacio Lizaso, Ángel Gondra, and Manuel Irujo) representatives.[4]

As Irujo noted in his report on the EAJ-PNV's talks with republican forces, the Spanish, Catalan, and Basque groups joined the UCPEO's National Council "specifying the distinctly national character of our framework and aspirations, in both the political and the cultural spheres, without our relationship with the Spanish group being of a different organic character than the one that links us to the French or the Belgian group."[5] Following Agirre's reappearance in October 1941 and in line with the actions of the Basque National Council, the Council of Europe in America was created in New York in March 1943, directed by Count Richard Nikolaus von Coudenhove-Kalergi, founder of the International Pan-European Union and author of the manifesto *Pan-Europa* (1923), in defense of a European federal state.

At the end of World War II, debates multiplied at all levels about the future of Europe, and numerous leagues, platforms, and unions sprang into being, with a variety of opinions on the political, economic, social, and cultural future of Europe. The subject was very confused and highly problematic, as orbiting around the central issue—the political form that such a European federation might adopt—were other problems to resolve: Europe's economic and social reconstruction and the thorny subject of the penalties to be imposed on and the political future of the former Axis powers and their allies. In addition, there was the increasingly open confrontation between the two blocs (East and West). In this context, the Basque government-in-exile had to enforce its position on the Basque political issue. It was a complicated task.

With the aim of coordinating the efforts of bodies such as the European League of Economic Cooperation (1946), the European Union of Federalists (UEF, 1946), the Parliamentary European Union (1947), and the Anglo-French United European Movements, the Committee for the Coordination of the European Movements held a congress in Paris in July and November 1947 and adopted the name of the Joint International

---

3. Memorandum by the National Council of Euzkadi to the Foreign Office, London, June 13, 1941, AA/AN FSAE, AN-GE-465-1.

4. Minutes of the meeting of Spaniards, Catalans, and Basques held in the Casal Catalá in London, October 7, 1942, AA/AN FSAE, AN-GE-466-1.

5. Report by Manuel Irujo on talks held in Mexico by the PNV with Spanish republican parties, London, December 31, 1942, AA/AN FSAE, AN-GE-466-1.

Committee for European Unity. At the urging of this organization, eight hundred European delegates met at The Hague in May 1948 in the Congress of Europe, presided over by Winston Churchill. The most prominent figures on the European political scene at the time, of various ideologies, came together to freely discuss the future of Europe. In October 1948, the European Movement was created. Duncan Sandys was elected president, and Léon Blum, Winston Churchill, Alcide De Gasperi, and Paul-Henri Spaak were named honorary presidents. In May 1949, the European Movement gave rise to the creation of the Council of Europe, which provided impetus for the Schuman Declaration of May 9, 1950, intended to create a new supranational community of European states.

The political moment experienced between 1945 and 1950 was, therefore, favorable to the Basque government and the political forces that constituted it, as Europe was not yet institutionally structured and thus was open to the participation of those parties and entities that had openly collaborated with the Allies and the resistance or that had politically and militarily opposed the Axis powers. Institutions such as the LIAB; the Basque National Council in London; the Basque delegations in Paris, New York, Buenos Aires, Santiago de Chile, and Montevideo; and the most prominent Basque political exiles enjoyed great prestige on the European stage and among foreign ministries (French, British, and US) because of their distinctly democratic attitudes and the unambiguous positions they had taken in the course of World War II.

All this is reflected in the Basque government's activities in relation to European politics during the period. Javier Landaburu (EAJ-PNV) and Juan Carlos Basterra (EAE-ANV) were invited to represent the Basque political groups in exile at the World Federalist Congress in Luxembourg in 1946. In 1947, the Basque Federalist Movement was created with the support of all the parties that constituted the Basque government—except the communists—and was subsequently admitted into the UEF, participating in the UEF congress held in the Palazzo Venezia in Rome in November 1948.[6] In their capacity as UEF members, the Basque delegation of Jose Antonio Agirre (in his capacity as president of the Basque government), Javier Landaburu (EAJ-PNV), Juan Carlos Basterra (EAE-ANV), and Lezo Urreztieta (Jagi-jagi, an EAJ-PNV splinter group led by Elias Gallastegi and in favor of Basque independence) attended the Hague Congress in May 1948.[7] Indalecio Prieto also attended, but as a representative of the PSOE, not of the Basque Socialist Central Committee.

In any event, this budding Europe was not the Europe of the Peoples that the Basque nationalists, the authors of the *Pan-Europa* manifesto, or all those who hoped for a European federation aspired to; it was a Europe of the States, an economic association

---

6. In fact, before its official foundation in 1947, Basterra and Landaburu had signed the documents of the World Federalist Congress in Luxembourg as representatives of the Basque Federalist Movement.

7. "La representación vasca en el Congreso Europeo de La Haya," EIB-OPE, May 5, 1948, 15; see also "Congreso de Europa: La Haya, 7 al 10 de mayo de 1948; Razones de nuestra presencia en el Congreso," May 1948, AA/AN FSAE, 125-18.

hobbled by political conflicts among its members and to which the United Kingdom, the Benelux countries, the Scandinavian countries, Switzerland, and the Eastern bloc as a whole would at first remain outsiders. It was, nevertheless, a significant step, insofar as it was a new member of a group of peaceful and democratic institutions, and one that left out the remaining dictatorships of Western Europe: Spain and Portugal. It would be in this context of democratic and federalist aspirations that Basque politics in Europe would play out in 1946.

In June 1947, a variety of Christian-Democratic groups created the New International Teams (NEI), an organization in support of European integration. Among its founders were Georges Bidault, Alcide De Gasperi, Robert Schuman, and Konrad Adenauer. Alongside them, Jose Antonio Agirre and Javier Landaburu attended the founding congress as representatives of the Basque Group (also known as the Basque Team or the Paris Group), which was consequently enrolled as a founding member of the NEI at the congress held in Chaudfontaine between May 31 and June 3, 1947. *Lehendakari* Agirre was elected a member of the Honorary Committee, and Javier Landaburu was elected a member of the Executive Committee, reflecting once again the prestige of Agirre in particular and the Basque government in general, given their attitudes in the course of the war. Fully in accordance with the ideals of the EAJ-PNV, the NEI considered European integration the best way to defend the Christian values of Western Europe against the Soviet bloc, which, in response, created the Information Bureau of the Communist and Workers' Parties (Cominform) to replace the Comintern in September 1947, by order of Stalin, not popular initiative. The Basque Group would actively participate in the NEI's second congress, held in Luxembourg (1948); in its third congress, held at The Hague (1949); and in its fourth congress, held in Sorrento (March 1950).

Noteworthy on the international level was Bingen Ametzaga's participation as the Basque government's delegate in Uruguay in the creation of the American Christian-Democratic Organization (ODCA) in the course of the congress held in Montevideo between April 18 and 23, 1947, on the urging of Dardo Regules.[8] Among the participants were Eduardo Frei Montalva and Alceu Amoroso Lima.[9] That first assembly of the organization composed the Montevideo Declaration, establishing the ODCA's five principles:

---

8. Bingen Ametzaga to Santiago Zarrantz, Montevideo, January 23, 1948. Dardo Regules (1887–1960), an activist in the Civic Union, a Christian-democratic party, was elected senator of the Republic in 1946 and served as interior minister in the administration of Luis Batlle Berres (1950–1951), of the Red Party. The author of numerous works, Ametzaga was among the most determined promoters of Christian democracy in Uruguay and across the Southern Cone. A determined collaborator with the Basque delegation, he maintained contact with the delegation until his death, collaborating against Franco and his supporters both inside Uruguay and at the United Nations.

9. Eduardo Frei Montalva (1911–1982) was elected senator of the Republic between 1949 and 1959 and served as president of Chile between 1964 and 1970. Alceu Amoroso Lima (1893–1983), a literary critic and professor of Brazilian literature at the University of Brazil and the Catholic University and subsequently rector of the University of the Federal District and president of the Centro D. Vital (1928–1968), was a prolific Brazilian Christian-Democratic writer and among the chief promoters of Christian democracy in the Americas.

1. To agree on political-strategic guidelines for international action based on the principles of Christian humanism, subject to democratic methods, and oriented toward achieving national and international social justice.
2. To formulate a political project that can sustain Latin American integration.
3. To strengthen and defend the values and rights of the human person and to promote the process of change and modernization of society.
4. To stimulate and coordinate cooperation among members.
5. To promote and develop a just relationship between man and his environment.[10]

The ODCA became one of the most influential organizations in the South American political sphere, bringing together a total of thirty-five political parties and movements from twenty-five countries across the continent, with an electoral backing equivalent to more than a third of the Latin American electorate. Nevertheless, 1949 was a turning point. With the financial crisis that broke out in November of that year and that would give rise to the breaking off of agreements with the US intelligence services, there were negative repercussions for the Basque government's political strategy. With no more US contacts, the government would focus all its attention on European politics, economic and administrative limitations would become clear, and only with heavy personal sacrifices would the government be able to maintain its political activity until 1975.

The outbreak of the Korean War on June 25, 1950, notably accelerated the process of union in Europe and the institutionalization of power sources, which severely limited the possibilities of bodies like the NEI and the UEF. Even if those organizations continued to have a certain weight, their field of action was limited to the strictly extrainstitutional, a field that had not existed before 1948. In March 1948, the Treaty of Brussels was signed, thus constituting the Western European Union. Several treaties and agreements followed: in April was the treaty creating the Organization for European Economic Cooperation; in May 1949, the Council of Europe was created; and in April 1951, the treaty constituting the European Coal and Steel Community was signed. At the Congress of Europe at The Hague (May 7–10, 1948), state teams were mandatory for participation in the Committee for the Coordination of the European Movements, which meant that the Basque group could not act independently, only in coordination with the Spanish and Catalan groups.

These circumstances would give rise to a bitter debate over the strategy of the Basque government. On the one hand, both the EBB and the majority of the Basque government's nationalist leaders were open supporters of independence and therefore reluctant to enter into joint lines of action with Spanish Republican forces. On the other hand, the circumstances demanded joint action. In this context, Juan Ajuriaguerra initiated contact

---

10. *Estatutos de la Organización Demócrata Cristiana de América, aprobados por el XIII Congreso, celebrado en Caracas, el 30 de noviembre de 1991*, reference in Pedro Basaldua to Bingen Ametzaga, Montevideo, April 12, 1947.

with the National Alliance of Democratic Forces,[11] and the EBB approved the political declaration of March 5, 1949, which opened the door to negotiation with the Spanish groups but without abandoning the basic positions of Europeanism, Christian-Democratic federalism, and Basque nationalism. The Basque government's dynamism and its capacity for effective action abroad would enable the Basque group to act with the necessary autonomy within the group of exiled Spaniards, Catalans, and Basques, and even to become the prime mover of that group. This option, chiefly promoted by *Lehendakari* Agirre and Ajuriaguerra, was broadly supported by Landaburu and Leizaola, but it provoked, if not rejection, at least misgivings from Irujo and Monzon.

When the first Congress of European Communities and Regions (CECR) was held on the UEF's initiative in April 1949, the EBB was in favor of attending, but without losing sight of the fact that this was an organization that had the objective of studying Europe's "regions" problem "apart from any separatist spirit."[12] The EBB insisted that the Basque delegates who attended the meeting be nationalists, affiliated with the EAJ-PNV or the EAE-ANV, and that they defend at the congress the propositions that Euskadi was a nation and that forming part of this organization did not mean renouncing the national character of the Basque delegation. Moreover, as Leyre Arrieta indicates, the welcoming reception for the delegates was held at the Basque government's headquarters in Paris.[13] This approach was common to all the stateless minorities, like those represented by the Scottish National Party and Plaid Cymru, which took an identical position.[14] In fact, in addition to the Scots, Welsh, and Basques, the national minorities of Bavaria, Brittany, Catalonia, Cornwall, Frisia, Friuli, South Tyrol, Val d'Aosta, Wallonia, and the Celtic Congress were represented at the congress.

On the initiative of the Federalists Union of Brittany, a CECR congress was held on October 9 and 10, 1949, in the Palais de Chaillot in Paris. Agirre attended as a representative of the Basque nation, presiding over the podium with the Breton nationalist Joseph Martray, who was elected the first general secretary, and the Walloon Charles Plisnier, who was elected the organization's first president. Pressure from the nationalist delegates led to an agreement in September 1949 establishing that the organization's official name would be the Congress of European Nations and Regions (CENR).[15] Basterra (EAE-ANV) was elected a member of the Central Committee, and the *lehendakari* was subsequently named a member of the CENR Patrons' Commission.

---

11. Organization created in Toulouse in September 1944 by former members of the defunct Popular Front, the coalition of leftist republican parties that won the February 1936 elections.

12. Julio Jauregi to Javier Landaburu, Baiona, April 7, 1949, AA/AN FSAE, Fondo EBB, 120-3.

13. Leyre Arrieta, *Estación Europa: La política europeísta del PNV en el exilio (1945–1977)* (Madrid: Tecnos, 2007), 152–54; see also Leyre Arrieta, "Red de relaciones europeas del PNV (1945–1977)," *Cuadernos de Historia Contemporánea* 30 (2008): 325.

14. Michael Keating and John McGarry, *Minority Nationalism and the Changing International Order* (Oxford: Oxford University Press, 2001), 253.

15. Peter Lynch, *Minority Nationalism and European Integration* (Cardiff: University of Wales Press, 1996), 136.

At the second congress, held in Versailles in November 1949 and attended by prominent leaders of the EAJ-PNV, the organization was restructured, giving rise to the birth of two new organizations in July 1949: the Federal Council of Minorities and Regions and the Federalist Union of European Minorities and Regions,[16] which would subsequently change its name to the Federalist Union of European National Minorities and Ethnic Communities.[17]

The CECR gave decided momentum to federalism in Europe by petitioning the governing powers for the creation of a European assembly or parliament that would facilitate authentic national representation and, as a consequence, the participation of the stateless nations in the political construction of Europe. The principles of autonomy and decentralization, as well as the historical, political (self-determination), linguistic, and cultural rights of Europe's stateless nations, were debated and brought to the attention of Europe's decision-making forums.

Nevertheless, beginning in 1950, and in virtue of the mentioned decision of the Hague Congress of May 1948 that state participation was required for participation in the Committee for the Coordination of the European Movements, the Basque government started down the path toward the creation of the Spanish Federal Council of the European Movement (CFEME), officially constituted in February 1951 in virtue of the agreement between Agirre and Salvador de Madariaga, an exiled Republican and the president of the European Movement's cultural section.[18] As Alexander Ugalde notes, the participation of Basque representatives in this organization provoked an intense debate within the EAJ-PNV and resulted in the decision to create the Basque Council for the European Federation (CVFE), later renamed the Europako Mugimenduaren Euskal Kontseilua, or Basque Council of the European Movement (EMEK/CVME) and officially constituted on February 1, 1951, at the Basque government's headquarters in Paris.[19] Gonzalo Nardiz (EAE-ANV) was elected president; Jesús María Leizaola (EAJ-PNV), José María Lasarte (EAJ-PNV), and Laureano Lasa (Socialist Movement), vice presidents; Javier Landaburu (EAJ-PNV), secretary; Ramón María Aldasoro (IR), delegate to the CFEME; Manuel Irujo (EAJ-PNV), in charge of propaganda; and Ramón Agesta, Iñaki Agirre, Víctor Gómez, Julio Jauregi, and Iñaki Renteria, voting members.[20]

---

16. *Yearbook of International Organizations, 2008–2009* (Brussels: Union of International Associations, 1972), 163.

17. *The Europa Year Book* (London: Europa Publications, 1968), 1:364.

18. "Acta de constitución del Consejo Vasco por la Federación Europea," Paris, February 1, 1951, AA/AN FSAE, Fondo EBB, 76–78; see also "Constitución del Consejo Vasco por la Federación Europea," *Alderdi*, February 1951, 5.

19. Alexander Ugalde Zubiri, *La aportación vasca al federalismo europeo/Europako Mugimenduaren Euskal Kontseilua (1951–2001): Europako federalismoari euskaldunek egindako ekarpena* (Gasteiz: Europako Mugimenduaren Euskal Kontseilua, 2001).

20. EMEK/CVME brought together a series of Basque organizations such as the Basque Federalist Movement and the Basque Groups of the Federal Council of Minorities and Regions, the New International Teams and their youth section, the Union of European Federalists, the Liberal International, the Young European Federalists, the Christian Workers' Movement for Europe, and the Basque Socialist Movement for the European Federation.

In any event, and despite the creation of the EMEK/CVME as a member of the CFEME, the growing institutionalization of the European Community organizations left ever less room to maneuver for institutions that, like the Basque government or other various political parties, represented stateless nations.[21] And this fact affected not only the nationalist parties but at times also resulted in the division or even disintegration of these organizations and civil platforms. This was the case of the UEF, which split into two separate bodies at the Luxembourg congress in March 1956, one led by Altiero Spinelli and the other by Hendrik Brugmans. Spinelli's majority faction aligned itself at the Paris congress of 1959 with the European Federalist Movement (MFE) created around the Italian leader in 1943 in Milan,[22] and Brugmans created and led (1956–1973) the European Federalist Action (AEF).[23] In addition to the activities already mentioned, the Basque government's representatives participated in forums such as the Westminster economic conference in April 1949, the European Cultural Conference in Lausanne in December 1949, and the Social Conference of the European Movement in Rome in July 1950.

One of the few political channels providing access to European Community institutions after 1950 was the Parliamentary Assembly of the Council of Europe, created as a result of article 22 of the statute of the Council of Europe signed in London on May 5, 1949. The Basque Group had access to the meetings of the assembly, the deliberative body of the Council of Europe, as part of the Spanish Republican Interparliamentary Group. Manuel Irujo represented the Basque parliamentary group at the first session of the European Parliamentary Assembly, held in Strasbourg in August 1949. This was a response to the strategic necessity of collaborating with other exiled republican groups within the framework of European Community institutions, but it did not entail allegiance to republican policy, much less the renunciation of ideological principles, such as the right of self-determination. In fact, practical politics had awarded the Basque government and its representatives, whether in the field of South American national politics, at the UN, or within the institutions of the European Community, a prominent role in the context of the anti-Franco struggle abroad. However, the strike of 1947 reinforced that leading role inside the Basque Country as well.

The Basque government's leadership in the context of international anti-Franco politics was taken for granted, such that in 1946, the leaders of the Republican government offered *Lehendakari* Agirre the presidency of the Spanish Republic's government-in-exile. Moreover, the offer was not exclusively the fruit of an internal debate among Spanish Republican officials; it also had support from the British authorities. As Jose Ignacio Lizaso, the Basque government's delegate in London, reported to the *lehendakari*,

21. As Leyre Arrieta notes, the Basque representatives were unable to intervene in the debates of the UEF's Strasbourg Congress in 1950; see Arrieta, "Red de relaciones europeas del PNV (1945–1977)," 324.

22. Altiero Spinelli, *Towards the European Union* (Florence: European University Institute, 1983), 6.

23. Hendrik Brugmans and Pierre Duclos, *Le fédéralisme contemporain* (Leiden: A. W. Sythoff, 1963), 143.

republican Prime Minister José Giral's government did not offer the guarantees requisite for a government in its circumstances, that is, a government-in-exile, weak by nature and therefore prone to being absorbed by socialist forces of the extreme left or even by communist forces. In the context of the Cold War in Europe, the British government would give credence and—should the occasion arise—political support as an alternative to Franco's regime only to a moderate, stable republican government headed by a strong executive and an undisputed leader who, like Agirre, "could offer the guarantees that [the British government] judged indispensable."[24]

This was a proposal that Prime Minister Giral had been floating since at least the spring of 1946 and that from the beginning received a negative response from the Basque government's nationalist leaders. Likewise, the EBB showed itself firm in this regard in considering the *lehendakari*'s presence in the Republic's government "unacceptable," not just as president but also as a minister or in any other form of institutional representation that was not in direct representation of the Basque people and in defense of Basque interests.[25]

It was not only the British who saw Agirre as a natural leader and the Basque government-in-exile as a model of functionality. When in 1947 Giral refused to continue at the head of the Republican government-in-exile, the president of the Republic in exile, Diego Martínez Barrio, arranged a meeting with Manuel Irujo and Julio Jauregi, in his capacity as a representative of the EBB. Because Agirre would not head the Republican government, Martínez Barrio asked the two Basque leaders to press the ERC to name a Catalan as prime minister. Nevertheless, Martínez Barrio announced to Jauregi and Irujo that, in the event that the Catalans refused, he would offer that post to a Basque nationalist leader, specifically to Agirre. For the same or similar reasons, however, neither the Catalan nationalist Carles Pi i Sunyer nor Jose Antonio Agirre accepted the leadership of the Republican government.

In the end, Rodolfo Llopis was named prime minister in February 1947. Nevertheless, in the midst of a severe internal crisis of Spanish socialism in exile and of the institutions of the Spanish republican government themselves, Llopis resigned his office six months later, in August 1947, reviving the crisis at a key moment on the international stage and doing the anti-Franco struggle little good. He would be replaced by Álvaro Albornoz, who would remain at the head of the Republican executive somewhat longer than his predecessor, until 1951, when he, too, resigned at an inopportune moment.[26]

The crisis of Spanish Republicanism and the ascent of Josep Tarradellas to the head of the Catalan government-in-exile likewise affected the Galeuzca Pact that Catalans, Galicians, and Basques had signed in 1944 to consolidate the three nations' political

---

24. Jose Ignacio Lizaso to Jose Antonio Agirre, London, August 1, 1946, AA/AN FSAE, AN-GE-651-7.

25. EBB to Jose Antonio Agirre, Baiona, May 11, 1946, AA/AN FSAE, Fondo EBB, 213-1.

26. Álvaro de Albornoz (1879–1954) was member of the Izquierda Republicana (IR, Republican Left), president of the Republic between May 1940 and June 1945, and prime minister of the Republic's government-in-exile between August 1947 and 1951.

Table 10.1. Heads of government of the Spanish Republican government-in-exile.

Período	Jefe de gobierno
1939–1945	Juan Negrín (PSOE)
1945–1947	José Giral (IR)
1947–1947	Rodolfo Llopis (PSOE)
1947–1951	Álvaro de Albornoz (IR)
1951–1960	Félix Gordón (UR)
1960–1962	Emilio Herrera
1962–1971	Claudio Sánchez-Albornoz
1971–1977	Fernando Valera (UR)

demands in relation to the Spanish republican government, especially the demand for the right of self-determination. Following the detention of the president of the Catalan government (the Generalitat), Lluís Companys, by the Gestapo and his subsequent murder by the Spanish regime on October 15, 1940, Josep Irla,[27] the president of the Catalan Parliament, took on the office of president of the Generalitat-in-exile on an interim basis. The Galeuzca Pact was signed at a meeting of the parliament of the Republic in Mexico City in 1945 and in close collaboration with the Basque government. At that moment, Irla formed a government including individuals of great prestige and deep Catalan nationalism, such as Carles Pi i Sunyer, Antoni Rovira, and Manuel Serra.[28] In line with the Galeuzca Pact, the EAJ-PNV and ERC agreed in 1947 to sign the Pact of Montpellier at a party congress attended by Julio Jauregi, Joxe Mari Lasarte, and Manuel Irujo as representatives of the Basque party.

After Irla resigned in 1954 because of his advanced age, a group of former deputies of the Catalan Parliament, meeting in the Spanish embassy in Mexico City, elected Francesc Farreras i Duran as president of the Catalan Parliament and Josep Tarradellas, then secretary of the ERC, a moderate nationalist and an enemy of the Galeuzca Pact and of any institutional ties with Basques and Galicians, as president of the Generalitat

27. Josep Irla i Bosch (1874–1958) was member of the ERC, deputy in the Catalan Parlament and Madrid Congress in 1932, president of the Catalan Parlament between August 1938 and October 1940, and president of the Generalitat in exile between October 15, 1940, and August 7, 1954.

28. Carles Pi i Sunyer (1888–1971) was member of the ERC, deputy in Spain's Parliament in 1931, deputy in the Catalan Parlament in 1931, economy minister in the Generalitat headed by Francesc Macià, mayor of Barcelona in 1934 and 1936–1937, president of the ERC between 1934 and 1936, culture minister of the Generalitat between 1937 and 1939, and president of the National Council of Catalonia between 1941 and 1945 in exile in London. As president of the National Council, he was among the most enthusiastic promoters of the Galeuzca Pact and a firm defender of the historical, political, social, and cultural rights of the Catalan nation. Antoni Rovira i Virgili (1882–1949) was member of the ERC and president of the Catalan Parlament in exile. Manuel Serra i Moret (1884–1963) was member of the Socialist Union of Catalonia, deputy of the Provisional Standing Commission of the Generalitat in 1931, economy and labor minister of the Generalitat government headed by Francesc Macià, deputy in the Catalan Parlament, second vice president of Parlament in 1938, and president of the Parlament in exile until 1954.

(Catalan government).[29] Tarradelas remained in that position from August 7, 1954, until April 24, 1980, which posed an obstacle to, and at times even made impossible, joint action by Basques and Catalans in exile.

Despite these obstacles, the decisive action of the EAJ-PNV representatives in European institutions, following a markedly Europeanist, federalist, republican, and Christian-Democratic line, enabled the participation of the Basques in private platforms and organizations, such as the European Movement, and to a lesser extent, in European institutions. This made it possible for the Basque government to express its opinions on and collaborate in the rebuilding of Europe. This made an extraordinary contribution to spreading knowledge and debate about the political and cultural conflict of the Basque people, a conflict that for the first time in Euskadi's modern history acquired an international dimension, not just in in the framework of the activities of delegations in the Americas (1938–1975), but also in the European sphere (1940–1975), and the UN (1946–1955).

The most noteworthy achievements of the Basque government-in-exile's political activities relating to the process of rebuilding Europe are two. First, its work in conjunction with groups from other stateless European nations, such as the Scots, Welsh, Tyrolese, Flemish, and Bretons, among many others, generated a broad debate about the protection of the historical, political, cultural, and linguistic rights of European nations without states and therefore without direct political representation in European Community institutions. This led to the otherwise improbable formation of organizations such as the Committee of the Regions, the immediate antecedent of which was the Consultative Committee of Local and Regional Authorities. Second, the coordinated work of the Catalan, Spanish, and Basque groups, most often led by the Basques, helped prevent the Spanish regime from taking root in Europe and thus becoming a member of the European Communities or even NATO.

---

29. Francesc Farreras i Duran (1900–1985) was a member of the ERC, deputy of the Provisional Standing Commission of the Generalitat, general director of the Ministry of Agriculture, Forests, Hunting, and Fishing (1931–1933), delegate of the Catalan government to the Caixa d'Estalvis of the Generalitat (Savings Bank), and exiled in Mexico, where he took part in cultural activities aimed at promoting Catalan language and culture in exile. Josep Tarradellas (1899–1988) was general secretary of ERC (1931–1932 and 1938–1957) and a deputy in the Spanish Parliament, health minister in Francesc Macià's government, and prime minister of the Generalitat and minister of economy and culture during the war.

11

Strikes and Academic Conferences: Cultural Action and Political Resistance, 1943–1954

The general strikes of 1947 and 1951 and the mounting of international cultural events like Uruguay's Gran Semana Vasca (Basque Cultural Week) in 1943 and the Basque Studies Congresses of 1948 and 1954 made up the two faces of the Basque government-in-exile's activity: on the one hand, the political struggle, both within the country and on the international stage, to overthrow General Franco's military dictatorship, and on the other hand, the parallel effort to channel from exile the academic and cultural efforts that it was impossible to carry out in Euskadi because of the proscriptions and limitations of the Spanish regime in the area of cultural activity.

All these actions formed part of a single political strategy intended to undermine and ultimately bring down Franco's regime.

In 1943, with the German defeat on the Russian front, the Allied invasion of southern Italy, and the US victories over the Japanese empire in the Pacific, the Axis forces definitively lost their strategic initiative. For the first time, Allied victory was, for many, including for many prominent German commanders, only a matter of time. In this context, Basque Cultural Week was an event of overwhelming significance in the life of the Basque exiles in the Americas. For the exiles, conscious of the critical situation in which General Franco's regime found itself with regard to international politics, the cultural week was an effort to carry to an audience in the Western Hemisphere a message of alliance with the league of pan-American countries against the Axis forces. It was also the Basque community's greeting to Uruguay, and by extension, to the Americas as a whole, as an integral part of the cultural, political, intellectual, and social life of the new continent. For the first time, a folklore and cultural festival of this magnitude, sponsored by the Basque government-in-exile's delegation in Buenos Aires, was held in full view of an American audience. Representative figures of intellectual, artistic, and political life in the Americas were invited to participate in the celebrations.[1] The festival was a demonstration of profound gratitude to figures such as Argentine President Roberto M. Ortiz, to whom the Basque exiles owed so much; Uruguayan President Juan José Amezaga,

1. Aratzazu Amezaga, "La Gran Semana Vasca del Uruguay," *Kultura* 5 (1983): 49–63.

and other prominent figures in South American political life who not only permitted, but also favored, facilitated, and even financed the adoption into their own homes of this population exiled from its homeland.[2]

With the aim of giving impetus to the cultural, diplomatic, and political work of the Basque government in Uruguay, Ramón María Aldasoro, the Basque government's delegate in Argentina, traveled to Montevideo on May 9, 1943, the day on which the thirty-first anniversary of the capital's Basque center Euskal Erria was celebrated. At a meeting on May 25, 1943, Euskal Erria's president informed the center's other members that Aldasoro had visited him, accompanied by Juan Domingo Uriarte and Ricardo Gisasola, to inform him that they were planning to hold a variety of cultural events in Montevideo.[3] After those first contacts, and doubtless after receiving the support of the members of the Basque center's governing committee, the event was publicized in *Euzko Deya* of Buenos Aires on May 30, under the title "Están en desarrollo importantes iniciativas de extraordinario interés para nuestra colectividad" (Important Initiatives of Extraordinary Interest to Our Community Are Being Developed).[4]

Bingen Ametzaga, the Basque government's delegate in Uruguay, was charged with contacting prominent political figures and the Uruguayan press and with promoting the publication, months in advance of Basque Cultural Week, of an entire cycle of articles on the nature, history, and life of the Basques in the Americas, as well as information about the the nature and complexity of the Basque political conflict, which was not well known at the time. The former task turned out to be easier than it first appeared. The president of Uruguay, Amezaga, was the descendant of Basque emigrants from Algorta and linked to Ametzaga by blood ties going two generations back. One meeting between Amezaga and Ametzaga would be sufficient to win the Uruguayan government's institutional support for the cultural week. Nor was it difficult to establish ties with the country's press, including *El Plata*, *El Día*, *El País*, *La Mañana*, and others, for which Ametzaga would later write numerous articles.[5]

Following almost a month of contacts between the Basque delegation and the representatives of Euskal Erria, on June 20, *Euzko Deya* announced the celebration of Basque Cultural Week in Montevideo and the inauguration of the Plaza Gernika, which would

2. Son of Nafarroan emigrants and married to a daughter of Basque emigrants, Luisa Iribarren, the president of Uruguay was, like Bingen Ametzaga, a descendant of Juan Bautista Ametzaga Elordi (born in 1780) and Maria Manuela Piñaga Leuro (born in 1779). As the grandson of Basque immigrants, Juan José Amezaga was a member of the Basque center Euskal Erria in Montevideo. Bingen Ametzaga to Inocencio Iribarren, 1950, IAA, GT-Iribarren.I.1950.

3. "La iniciativa de exhibir diversos valores artísticos y folklóricos vascos cuenta con la simpatía y la adhesión unánime de todo el pueblo uruguayo," *Euzko Deya* (Buenos Aires), September 30, 1943, 8–9.

4. "Están en desarrollo importantes iniciativas de extraordinario interés para nuestra colectividad," *Euzko Deya* (Buenos Aires), May 30, 1943.

5. Arantzazu Ametzaga, Bingen Ametzaga's daughter, has collected and placed in chronological order fifty of these articles, most of which appeared in *El Plata* from 1943 to 1955; see Arantzazu Ametzaga Iribarren, *Nostalgia*, 2 vols. (Donostia-San Sebastián: J. A. Ascunce, 1993).

eventually be inaugurated in Montevideo in 1944.[6] The Buenos Aires newspaper *La Nación* also published the news of the celebration of Uruguay's Basque Cultural Week in its June 22 issue. In August, the first three working groups for the cultural week were organized—the executive commission, the finance commission, and the art commission—and new commissions and subcommissions were created throughout the month in accordance with the new needs and requirements of the program, which was constantly evolving and expanding. For example, later the press commission and honorary commission were created. Julio Garra was elected president of the executive commission; Rodolfo Gorriti and Juan Ibarra Aguerrebere, vice presidents; Aitor Hormaeche, secretary; Enrique Berahu, deputy secretary; and José Manuel Iguain, treasurer. Women's commissions were also organized within each area. María Ana Bidegarai Janssen was elected president of the executive commission, and Blanca Hormaeche and Concepción Iturbey, vice presidents.

One of Ametzaga's chief tasks as a new member of the Montevideo delegation was to put together the honorary commission, made up entirely of prominent political and intellectual figures of Uruguayan society. In this, he could always rely on the invaluable help of María Luisa Iribarne, a member and president for many years of Euskal Erria's ladies' auxiliary; wife of Duncan Batlle Berres, a senator from the Red Party; and sister-in-law of Luis Batlle Berres, the man who would be the nation's president in 1947 and 1955, the second time as a member of the country's presidential collegium.[7] A member of a prestigious and politically important family in Uruguay in the first half of the twentieth century, Luis Batlle Berres was also the director of Radio Ariel. It was no coincidence, therefore, that Radio Ariel was responsible for the daily broadcast of events related to Basque Cultural Week and that it carried *Lehendakari* Agirre's statements after his reappearance in Montevideo in October 1941. All the prominent members of the Batlle family formed part of the honorary commissions, including those already mentioned, as well as César, Lorenzo, and Rafael Batlle Pacheco, also members of the Red Party.

In the end, there were 75 men and 101 women on the Men's honorary commission and the Women's Honorary Commission, respectively. In addition to President Amezaga, Amezaga's eight cabinet ministers also accepted the invitation to join the commission: José Serrato, foreign minister; Juan José Carbajal Victorica, interior minister; Tomás Berreta, minister of public works; Adolfo Follé Joanicó, education minister; Ricardo Cosio, treasury minister; Alfredo R. Campos, minister of national management; Arturo González Bidart, minister of ranching and agriculture; and Luis Mattianuda, health minister. The president's wife, Celia Álvarez Mouliá, and their three daughters, Ana María, Margarita, and María Asunción, all members of Euskal Erria, like their parents, formed part of the Women's honorary commission. In addition, the mayor of Montevideo, Juan

6. "Ante la Gran Semana Vasca de Montevideo," *Euzko Deya* (Buenos Aires), June 20, 1943.

7. Bingen Ametzaga to Joxe Mari Lasarte, Montevideo, November 17, 1943, IAA, GT-Lasarte.JM.1943.

P. Fabini, and the director of the city's metropolitan police department, Juan C. Gómez Follé, also agreed to participate in the events and to join the honorary commission.[8] As has already been mentioned, in view of the support and willingness to participate demonstrated from the beginning, the Basque government delegation decided early on to open the festivities with a ceremony recognizing and thanking the Uruguayan government, which had received *Lehendakari* Agirre in 1941 and 1942 and was welcoming the events of the cultural week with enthusiasm and selflessness.

In parallel to this collaboration of members of the government, most of whom belonged to the Red Party, the country's leading political force throughout the first half of the century, representatives of practically all the other political forces in the country provided help and expressed their willingness to participate in the events. Among many others were Dardo Regules, president of the Christian-Democratic Civic Union and subsequently senator and minister for that party; Tomás Brena, a deputy from the same party; Emilio Frugoni, president of the Socialist Party; Juan Andrés Ramírez, director of the daily newspaper *El Plata*; Eduardo Rodríguez Larreta, director of the daily newspaper *El País*;[9] Justino Zabala Muniz, director of the Official Service for Diffusion, Radio and Television, and Events (SODRE), the state communications service; Raúl Montero Bustamante, director of the Academy of Fine Arts; Ignacio Zorrilla de San Martín, a highly renowned poet and writer; Monsignor Antonio María Barbieri, archbishop and subsequently cardinal of Montevideo; José Iruretagoyena Anza, professor of law at the University of the Republic and president of the Banco Comercial and the prestigious Rural Association and Rural Federation, among many other organizations; Eduardo J. Couture Etcheverry, dean of the law school; and Adolfo Berro García and Justino Jiménez de Aretxaga, director of the department of phonetics and experimental phonology and professor of constitutional law at the University of the Republic, respectively. All would play a decisive role in the development of the Montevideo delegation's political and cultural activities following the events of Basque Cultural Week.[10]

October 30, 1943, a date evoking the memory of the abolition of the fueros in the Basque Country in 1876, was chosen as an appropriate day to inaugurate the festivities that would take place in the Uruguayan capital over the following two weeks. Montevideo's Basque Cultural Week had as a prelude a lecture by Bingen Ametzaga in the auditorium of the University of the Republic on October 15, in which he discussed the popular Basque poet Pedro de Enbeita, some of whose verses he sang. He highlighted the way in which Enbeita, while being an inspired artist, was also one of the most effective spokespeople for the Basque national movement. A large audience attended the lecture, as well as the cocktail reception and dance held on October 17 in the reception rooms

8. "La Gran Semana Vasca de Montevideo," *Euzko Deya* (Buenos Aires), August 20, 1943, 1.

9. Bingen Ametzaga to Joxe Mari Lasarte, Montevideo, July 16, 1945, IAA, GT-Lasarte.JM.1945.

10. "Con gran actividad y entusiasmo prosiguen los preparativos para la Gran Semana Vasca de Montevideo," *Euzko Deya* (Buenos Aires), September 20, 1943, 1.

of the Parque Hotel.[11] After these preparatory events and a series of daily radio chats, in which the Basque scholars Aldasoro and Ametzaga and their Basque-Uruguayan counterparts Rodolfo Gorriti, Juan Zorrilla de San Martín, Enrique J. Mochó, and Pedro Zubillaga participated, along with Manuel Iguain, María Ana Bidegaray de Janssen, María Luisa Iribarne de Batlle Berres, and Dionisio Garmendia, Basque Cultural Week began, though it would really last a fortnight, from October 30 to November 13.

Events began at 6:30 p.m. on October 30 with the opening of an exhibit of Basque art in the galleries of the Museum of Fine Arts. President Amezaga attended the opening ceremony, as did the president of the High Court of Justice and president of the Basque Week Honorary Commission, Julio Guani, and other distinguished Uruguayans. The president of the men's commission, Julio Garra, read some topical remarks, as did the president of the women's ccommission, María Ana Bidegaray de Janssen. The final speaker was Almeida Pintos, general director of public education, who spoke in place of Education Minister Folle Joanicó, who was unable to attend. That night at 9:45 p.m., a gala honoring President Amezaga took place at the SODRE headquarters.[12] The president attended the event from beginning to end, although it extended into the early morning hours. He gave constant signs of approval that resulted in the repetition of some musical numbers due to the appreciation he showed. The Basque delegate Aldasoro, a former minister in the Basque government, sat on President Amezaga's right in the presidential box, also occupied by Guani, Joanicó, Interior Minister Carbajal Victorica, and several other prominent members of the government. The theater was completely filled with spectators, who fervently applauded the popular songs and dances of the various regions of Euskadi, performed by a company of around 220 artists, the vast majority of them political refugees.[13]

Before the folklore spectacular, two lectures were held at the theater. One was by the engineer Urbano de Aguirre, president of the Pro-Basque Immigration Committee of Argentina and a prominent political figure in that country, and the other by Uruguay's greatest orator, José Iruretagoyena. Both speakers were descendants of Basques. Iruretagoyena's lecture was later published in full in the evening newspaper *El Plata* on November 2.

On Sunday, October 31, events began with a High Mass at the cathedral, at which the Basque priests Emilio Agirrezabal, Ignacio Ariztimuño, and Pedro Goikoetxea, all political refugees, officiated. The choir Lagun Onak provided music. After mass, the attendees, preceded by the *txistularis*[14] and by a group of young people who danced their way through the streets of the city (a spectacle never before seen in Uruguay and received by the public with unmixed appreciation), moved to the Plaza de la Independencia,

11. Bingen Ametzaga to Joxe Mari Lasarte, Montevideo, November 25, 1943, IAA, GT-Lasarte.JM.1943.

12. José Urbano Agirre, "Del fondo de la historia," *Euskal Erria* (Montevideo), March 1, 1944, 35.

13. "Danzas y coros," *La Mañana* (Montevideo), October 31, 1943.

14. The "txistu" is a traditional Basque fipple flute and "txistulari" is the txistu player.

where an event in honor of the national hero of Uruguay José Gervasio Artigas took place. The choirs—around 150 voices—performed the Uruguayan and Basque national anthems, accompanied by the Montevideo municipal band. Subsequently, Dr. Rodolfo spoke on the meaning of the event, which was presided over by the municipal intendant Juan Fabini. In the afternoon, the previous night's Basque folklore spectacular was repeated at SODRE, attended by Fabini and prominent figures.

On November 1, at 11 a.m., an event took place in honor of Bruno Mauricio Zabala, a Basque-origin founder of Montevideo. Dr. Juana Amestoy de Mochó, Bingen Ametzaga, and Rémulo Botto spoke, with Botto representing the mayor of Montevideo, who was unable to attend. After the speeches, some Basque dances were performed in the Plaza de Zabala. In the afternoon, at SODRE and in front of a full house, the Basque choir Lagun Onak gave a concert of sacred music, performing Schubert's Mass in A flat to great critical acclaim.

Two days later, on November 3, at the Museum of Fine Arts, where the exhibit of modern Basque painting was on display, a series of lectures opened with one by Bingen Ametzaga on Gernika and Basque liberties. The lecture was a study of individual, socioeconomic, religious, and political liberties as found in Basque legal codes and various historical events. At the end, Ametzaga highlighted the fact that October 1943 marked the 104th anniversary of the abolition of those liberties by Spanish government authorities,[15] liberties that Ametzaga expressed hope would be restored when, in the upcoming triumph of the democracies, a regime of justice and liberty would be established on the earth. The hall was filled with an audience that demonstrated, with its repeated applause, its identification with the lecturer. In the same location on November 4, at 6:30 p.m., the Uruguayan scholar Pedro Zubillaga spoke about the meaning of Basque Cultural Week. He returned to several of the themes touched on the previous day by Ametzaga, especially the loss of Basque liberties and the inextinguishable longing for their recovery, which was cherished among the Basques. He ended by declaring that when the day of justice, close at hand, should arrive, Uruguay's voice would be heard, friendly and strong in favor. He received much applause.

On November 8, the Basque musician and refugee priest Francisco Madina gave a lecture on Basque music accompanied by his own performances on the piano, as well as by the singer Sr. Torcida and a choir directed by Mújica. On November 11, the president of Euzkal Erria, Dr. Enrique Mochó, presented a lecture on education in the Basque Country, and on November 15, the lecture series came to an end with the art critic José España, who examined classical and modern Basque pictorial values, represented in the

15. At the end of the First Carlist War (1833–1839), the fueros were dramatically modified by the Ley de 25 de octubre de 1839 de confirmación y modificación de los Fueros (October 25, 1839 law on the confirmation and modification of the Fueros). In short, while retaining the fueros, the law made them subject to Spanish constitutional law. See Joseba Aguirreazkuenaga, *The Making of the Basque Question: Experiencing Self-Government, 1793–1877* (Reno: Center for Basque Studies, 2011), esp. 177–180.

exhibit of Basque art. Afterward, the president of the Gentlemen's Commission, Julio Garra, officially concluded Basque Cultual Week.[16]

The local press covered Basque Cultural Week with much praise and many illustrated reports throughout the fortnight. The support of the Uruguayan people was evident: the three ticketed performances were all sold out, the the Basque *dantzaris*[17]and singers were applauded as they passed through the streets, and people filled the galleries of the painting exhibit every afternoon (almost all the artists on display were exiles). Fundamentally, however, the Basque community of Uruguay obtained from official spheres an atmosphere not merely of courtesy but also of open emotional warmth, cooperation, and institutional support, all of which translated into a significant impact on the public stage in favor of the Basque people's cause and in opposition to the Spanish military regime. Starting with President Amezaga and Julio Guani, the ministers of education, interior, war, and others attended practically all the events, thereby highlighting the week's political undertones.[18]

In effect, Basque Cultural Week decisively promoted the influence of the recently created Basque delegation in the country. Following a series of contacts arising from the week, Ametzaga made plans with Adolfo Berro García, a philologist and director of the department of phonetics and experimental phonology at the Institute of Higher Studies of the University of the Republic of Uruguay, for the creation of a Basque studies cultural society, which would ultimately become the Department of Basque Studies attached to the Universidad de la República, the first of its kind in the world and a predecessor of the Center for Basque Studies at the University of Nevada, Reno.[19] In pursuit of this initiative, Ametzaga organized with Professors Carlos Vaz Ferreira, Leopoldo Agorio Etcheverry, and José Pedro Varela Acevedo, a program of study in Basque language and literature, attached from then on to the Department of Basque Studies.[20] Both parts of the curriculum would remain Ametzaga's responsibility throughout his exile in Uruguay, from 1943 to 1955.[21] This was the first experiment of this kind in the Americas and the first university chair in the Basque language since the closure in 1937

---

16. "La Gran Semana Vasca," *El Plata* (Montevideo), November 19, 1943.

17. A "dantzari" is a Basque folk dancer.

18. "Finalización de las actividades de los Comités de la Semana Cultural Vasca," *Euskal Erria* (Montevideo), January 1, 1944, 3.

19. Bingen Ametzaga to Jose Antonio Agirre, Montevideo, October 4, 1945, IAA, GT-Agirre.JA.1945.

20. Carlos Vaz Ferreira (1873–1958), professor of the philosophy of secondary education and, starting in 1913, responsible for the course Lectures at the University, was dean of the University of the Republic's School of Humanities between 1945 and 1953 and was rector of the university between 1928 and 1930 and between 1935 and 1941. Leopoldo C. Agorio Etcheverry (1891–1972) was a professor of urban planning, dean of the School of Architecture, and rector of the university between 1948 and 1952 and between 1952 and 1956. José Pedro Varela Acevedo (1874–1950), professor of international private law, Uruguayan history, and history of the Americas, was dean of the law school and rector of the university between 1941 and 1948.

21. Bingen Ametzaga to Joxe Mari Lasarte, Montevideo, July 7, 1945. IAA, GT-Lasarte.JM.1945.

of the chair created in Bilbao and held by Resurrección María Azkue.[22] Years later, in 1951, with the full support of the rector of the School of Humanities of the university, Justino Jiménez de Aretxaga, a professor of constitutional law, Ametzaga created a second chair in Basque culture.[23]

In this way, Ametzaga fulfilled one of his lifelong dreams. As director of primary education in the Basque government, in 1936, he had promoted the use of Euskara in the early grades, and in 1943, he saw Euskara taught at the university level in Uruguay.[24] Euskara was definitively winning the respect it deserved among all the other languages on the other side of the ocean from the Basque Country, respect that was denied and would continue to be denied to it and to its people in their homeland.

Two years later, on Basque soil, a group of political exiles and collaborators with the network of Basque political exiles created the Gernika Institute in Donibane Lohitzune on April 26, 1945, the eighth anniversary of the Basque town's bombardment by German airplanes.[25] The institute's chief promoters were Joxe Migel Barandiaran, Rafael Picavea, Iñaki Azpiazu, Policarpo Larrañaga, Julio Huici, and José Eizagirre. The Gernika Institute was established to organize, after the liberation of Iparralde in the summer of 1944 and during 1945, a series of lectures on Basque subjects, as well as classes in Euskara, and beginning in 1946, its roster of collaborators expanded to include the participation of prominent Basque exiles such as Joxe Mari Lasarte, Manu Sota, Juan Antonio Careaga, Javier Landaburu, Doroteo Ziaurritz, Vicente Navarro, Telesforo Monzon, and Nikolas "Orixe" Ormaetxea. The institute likewise began to publish the journal *Gernika-Eusko Jakintza*, which aimed to revive the academic efforts that had been impeded in Euskadi between 1936 and 1945 by the two wars.

Around 1946, the institute's members embraced the idea of creating a series of Basque cultural institutes throughout the Americas, to be named Eusko Jakin Billerak (Basque Scholars Committees), a plan that was put into practice in 1947. Drawing on the contributions of these committees and of the seminars that had been offered to that point, the institute began to publish the journal *Eusko Jakintza* (Review of Basque Studies).[26] In parallel, the Ikuska Basque Research Institute was born, created in 1946 by Joxe Migel Barandiaran, with the collaboration of Jon Bilbao and Marta Saralegi. René Lafon, Pierre Lafitte, Eugène Goyheneche, Philippe Veyrin, and Julio Caro Baroja were active collaborators in Ikuska.

With the aim of addressing financial and administrative problems, former members of the Gernika Institute and of Ikuska created the Gernika International Society of

22. "Nicolás Ormaetxea, *Orixe*," in Vicente Amezaga Aresti, *El hombre vasco* (Buenos Aires: Ekin, 1967), 304.

23. Bingen Ametzaga to Jose Antonio Agirre, Montevideo, May 25, 1951, IAA, GT-Agirre.JA.1951.

24. Telephone interviews with Carlos G. Mendilaharzu, member of the University of the Republic's Department of Basque Studies, August–September 2003.

25. Joxe Migel Barandiaran to Bingen Ametzaga, Baiona, June 23, 1947, IAA, GT-Barandiaran.JM.1947.

26. Bingen Ametzaga to Joxe Migel Barandiaran, Montevideo, August 8, 1947, IAA, GT-Barandiaran.JM.1947.

Basque Studies in Baiona (Bayonne in French) on February 12, 1948. Monsignor Jean Saint-Pierre was named honorary president of the new institution; Joxe Migel Barandiaran, president; Louis Dassance,* Telesforo Monzon, and Pierre Lafitte, vice presidents; and Manu Sota, general secretary. Philippe Ohyamburu, Ángel Lasarte, Jose Eizaguirre, Domingo Epalza, Teodoro Ernandorena, Manuel Intxausti, Michel Labeguerie, Javier Landaburu, Adolfo Larrañaga, and Pierre Lhande also participated, among others. Jon Bilbao was put in charge of the society's journal, which inherited its predecessor's name, *Eusko Jakintza*; eleven issues would be published between 1948 and 1957.[27]

Members of the Gernika Institute and of Ikuska decided between September 1947 and February 1948 to hold a world congress of Basque studies to bring together research on a full range of topics in Basque learning and culture carried out in the dark period of war and exile from 1936 to 1948. The last Basque studies congress organized by the Eusko Ikaskuntza Society for Basque Studies was dedicated to medicine and the natural sciences and was held in Bilbao in 1934.[28] The members of the Gernika International Society of Basque Studies decided to hold the seventh Basque studies conference in 1948 (previous conferences had been held in Oñati, 1918; Iruñea, 1920; Gernika, 1922; Gasteiz, 1926; Bergara, 1930).[29]

Three committees were created—an honorary committee, a sponsorship committee, and an executive or organizing committee—and it was decided to divide the congress into fifteen sections, each one the responsibility of an active member or collaborator of the organizing body. The organizing committee included the honorary president, Monsignor Jean Saint-Pierre; the executive president, Joxe Migel Barandiaran; and two secretaries, Manu Sota and Philippe Oyhamburu. The congress's honorary committee included, among others, Édouard Hériot, president of the National Assembly of the French Republic; Yvon Delbos, minister of education; Jean Sarrailh, rector of the Paris Academy; François Mauriac, member of the French Academy and president of the LIAB; and Ernest Pezet, councilor of the French Republic and an active member of the LIAB. In addition, more than one hundred well-known individuals and prominent cultural and political figures from more than fifteen countries in Europe and the Americas collaborated in the congress, such as the Colombian minister of national education, Germán Arciniegas; the Uruguayan minister of education, Oscar Secco Ellauri, and the president of the Scientific-Literary University of the Philippines, Bienvenido María González. Among the section presidents there were many people who were important to the Basque exile, such as Jon Bilbao, Louis Dassance, Domingo Epalza, Javier Gortazar,

27. Sebero Altube to Bingen Ametzaga, Pau, November 22, 1951, IAA, GT-Altube.S.1951.

28. Société Internationale des Etudes Basques Gernika, Programme Officiel, VIIème Congrès d'Etudes Basques, Biarritz, September 12–19, 1948, IAA, GT-Barandiaran.JM.1948.

29. Manuel Intxausti to Bingen Ametzaga, Uztaritze, June 29, 1948, IAA, GT-Intxausti.M.1948.

Manuel Intxausti, Jean Jauréguiberry, Michel Labèguerie, Pierre Lafitte, Telesforo Monzon, Pierre Narbaitz, and Philippe Veyrin.[30]

In total, there were around two hundred participants in the congress who presented 260 papers divided into three large groups and fifteen panels or sections, organized as follows—(1) the earth: geography, geology, paleontology, and speleology, under the direction of Domingo Epalza; oceanography, under the direction of Paul Arné; agriculture and livestock, under the direction of Louis Dassance; sailing, fishing, and related industries, under the direction of Marc Legasse; industry, commerce, and communications, under the direction of José Camiña; (2) man: anthropology and medicine, under the direction of Jean Jauréguiberry and Michel Labèguerie; ethnology and prehistory, under the direction of Joxe Migel Barandiaran; museum studies, under the direction of William Boissel; history, under the direction of Father Etcheverry; the Basques in the world and Basque emigration, under the direction of Manuel Intxausti; and (3) culture: law, under the direction of Jean Etcheverry-Ainchart and Javier Landaburu; language, under the direction of Jean Saint-Pierre and Pierre Lafitte; education, under the direction of Jon Bilbao; art, under the direction of Ramiro Arrue, Manu Sota, and Philippe Veyrin; religion, under the direction of Pierre Narbaitz.[31]

The congress sessions took place over the course of a week, between September 12 and 19, 1948, at the Lycée and the Musée de la Mer in Biarritz and the Musée Basque in Baiona.[32] Events began on Sunday, September 12, with a High Mass at 10:00 a.m. in the parish church of Donibane Lohitzune, officiated by Monsignor Jean Saint-Pierre, with the participation of the Schola Cantorum choir and *txistularis* who played the "Agur Jaunak."[33] Following Mass, there was a game of *rebote*, a traditional Basque ball game, at the town's municipal fronton court, between the Hazparne and Baigorri teams. After lunch, the opening session took place at 5:00 p.m. in the theater of the Biarritz Municipal Casino.[34] Monsignor Léon Terrier, the bishop of Baiona; *Lehendakari* Agirre, along with two of his cabinet ministers, Telesforo Monzon and Joxe Mari Lasarte; William Boissel, director of the Musée Basque; Paul Arné, director of the Musée de la Mer; and Pierre Narbaitz participated briefly. Joxe Migel Barandiaran, president of the International Society for Basque Studies (SIEB) and of the congress, Louis Dassance, president of Eskualzaleen Biltzarra and mayor of Uztaritze, and the Marquis of Arcangues, president of the Syndicat d'Initiatives of Biarritz (Board of Initiatives of Biarritz) and of the welcoming committee, also spoke. The day ended with a Fête Populaire Basque (Popular Basque Festival) put on by the municipality of Biarritz.

---

30. Joxe Mari Lasarte to Bingen Ametzaga, Paris, June 19, 1948, IAA, GT-Lasarte.JM.1948.

31. EIB-OPE, July 15, 1948.

32. Bingen Ametzaga, "VII Congreso de Estudios Vascos. Tendrá lugar en Biarritz del 12 al 19 de septiembre," *El Bien Público* (Montevideo), August 24, 1948.

33. "Agur Jaunak' is a Basque song sung or played with *txistu* at the opening of certain ceremonies to welcome or honor a person.

34. EIB-OPE, June 18, 1948.

Sessions began on Monday, September 13, held simultaneously at the Lycée and the Musée de la Mer in Biarritz and the Musée Basque in Baiona. Until September 18, sessions were held from 10:00 a.m. until 9:00 p.m., except for Thursday, when those attending the congress had the opportunity to participate in a trip to the town of Baigorri to attend the annual meeting of the Society of Friends of the Basque Language, an event that included the participation of *dantzaris*, *txistularis*, and *bertsolaris* from the town.[35] The presentations at the congress were organized around the fifteen sections, held from 10:00 a.m. to 1:00 p.m., and a series of four plenary lectures, for which those attending the congress came together as a group on Monday, Tuesday, Wednesday, and Friday, starting at 6:30 p.m.[36] On September 17, the academic sessions concluded with the theatrical debut of *Ramuntxo* by Toribio Alzaga at the Biarritz municipal theater. On Saturday, September 18, the congress's closing session took place at 4:00 p.m., and a formal dinner was held at 9:00 p.m. in the Biarritz municipal theater, with the participation of the Oldarra choir, the orchestral group Les Compagnons de Labourd, and the Orchestre de la Côte Basque, which played the Basque composer Pierre d'Arcangues's piece titled *Sorlekua*. September 19 was dedicated to a high mass with a homily by the bishop of Aire and Dax, Clément Mathieu. After mass, the *aurresku* of honor was performed in front of the authorities of the congress and the city of Biarritz, and the Grand Festival de la Danse Basque began at 4:00 p.m.

The congress was a resounding success on both academic and cultural levels, more than achieving the objective of bringing the leading researchers in the various spheres of Basque culture together around the same table.[37] Unfortunately, financial problems prevented the publication of the congress proceedings, which saw the light of day only years later thanks to the colossal labor of Jean-Claude Larronde and the Eusko Ikaskuntza society. Leaving aside its merits in the academic and cultural spheres, however, the congress was likewise a notable political success, as it entailed the effective realization in exile of actions directed toward promoting, organizing, and carrying out cultural activities that, because of their pro-Basque nature, were prohibited and even persecuted in Hegoalde. The Basque government's participation in the congress, both financially and—fundamentally—by putting its network of delegations throughout the Americas at the disposal of the event organizers, likewise entailed an affirmation that the network of Basque delegations and organizations around the world functioned in a coordinated way and with a view toward the cultural and political objectives established by *Lehendakari* Agirre's administration.

Another of the congress's great successes was that it provided a stimulus for embracing the idea, a few years later, of organizing a second international Basque studies

---

35. Société Internationale des Etudes Basques Gernika, Programme Officiel, VIIème Congrès d'Etudes Basques, Biarritz, September 12–19, 1948, IAA, GT-Intxausti.JM.1948.

36. Bingen Ametzaga to Manuel Intxausti, Montevideo, August 14, 1948, IAA, GT-Intxausti.JM.1948.

37. Bingen Ametzaga, "Congreso de estudios vascos," *El Plata* (Montevideo), August 9, 1948.

congress in exile. Sponsored by a group of Basque-studies experts from a variety of organizations, such as Euskaltzaleen Biltzarra and the International Society for Basque Studies, the Eighth Basque Studies Congress took place over the course of two summer months, between July 11 and September 12, 1954, in Iparralde, fundamentally in the towns of Baiona and Uztaritze.[38] Unlike the seventh congress, which was general in nature and consequently covered a wide spectrum of topics, the organizers of the 1954 congress sought to focus discussions and seminars on a specific topic, the critical situation of the Basque language as a result of the persecution it was suffering at the hands of the Spanish authorities.

Among the promoters of the idea of organizing a new congress were, with a few new faces, those who were involved in organizing the 1948 congress, namely Manuel Intxausti, Telesforo Monzon, Manuel Intxausti, Pierre Lafitte, Louis Dassance, Manu Sota, Joxe Migel Barandiaran, and Georges Hahn, director of the Université Internationale d'Eté de Uztaritze.[39] Bishop Mathieu was named president of the organizing committee, and Guillaume Eppherre, Louis Dassance, William Boissel, and Georges Hahn served as vice presidents. As at the previous congress, different sections were organized (in this case, fourteen), giving priority to the topic of the preservation of the Basque language. Around 140 participants from a variety of countries in Europe and the Americas presented around 172 papers.[40]

Even if it was somewhat more modest than the 1948 congress, fundamentally because of the financial crisis with which the Basque government-in-exile had been struggling since 1949, the 1954 congress was likewise a notable academic and political success and a new event of international significance that promoted Basque exile politics in the area of cultural policy.

The success of both congresses would have been impossible without a dense network of Basque delegations and centers that coordinated and communicated with one another throughout the Americas. This network, as we have seen, functioned on both political and cultural levels, and gave rise to a long series of cultural initiatives in different countries. This is the case, for example, of the Basque Cultural Commission created in Mexico City at the end of 1942. Its objective, according to its bylaws, was the study of Basques in Mexico from the first days of colonization to the twentieth century. The Basque Cultural Commission counted among its members prominent Basque exiles such as Telesforo Monzon, Santiago Aznar, Julio Jauregi, Joxe Mari Lasarte, Tomás Bilbao, Antonio Ruiz de Azua, Germán Iñurrategui, and Ramón Belasteguigoitia. The first executive committee was made up of Telesforo Monzon (president), Vicenta Lascurain (secretary), and José Luis Longa (deputy secretary). Following the structure of the Society for Basque Studies, the Basque Cultural Commission of Mexico was divided into

38. "Programme du VIIIe Congrès d'Etudes Basques," *Euzko Deya* (Paris), July 1, 1954, 1.

39. Manuel Intxausti to Bingen Ametzaga, Uztaritze, March 24, 1954, IAA, GT-Intxausti.JM.1954.

40. Jesús María Leizaola to Bingen Ametzaga, Paris, May 18, 1954, IAA, GT-Leizaola.JM.1954.

sections: Euskara and literature in Basque, history and literature in other languages, law, economic and social affairs, fine arts, and physical culture.[41]

A similar initiative came about in Buenos Aires on July 20, 1943: the Instituto Americano de Estudios Vascos (American Institute of Basque Studies). Its objectives—similar to those of the Mexican commission—were "to unite lovers of the Basque Country, specialized in some aspect of its prehistory, history, anthropology, folklore, language, law, economy, art, or other field of study, and to intensify these studies, pursuing them in greater depth and publicizing them."[42] The institute had a total of forty-two full voting members. The first executive committee was made up of Monsignor Nicolás Esandi (president), who would retain the office of president until his death in 1948; Elpidio R. Lasarte (first vice president); Justo Gárate (second vice president); Santiago Cunchillos (general secretary); Andrés Irujo (recording secretary); and Carlos Cucullo (treasurer). Some of the members, political exiles, had been active members of the Society for Basque Studies, Eusko Ikaskuntza, in Euskadi. Among this group were Cunchillos, Irujo, and Gárate. Beginning in August 1945, the institute would have its headquarters at the Gure Etxea Basque center in Buenos Aires.

Seven years after its creation, in April 1950, the institute began to publish the *Boletín del Instituto Americano de Estudios Vascos* (Bulletin of the American Institute of Basque Studies) in Buenos Aires. Its first director was the priest Gabino Garriga. In June 1950, the first issue of the bulletin, headquartered at the Ekin publishing house at 175 Calle Perú in Buenos Aires, came off the press. With a press run of five hundred copies, it was distributed in Argentina, Chile, Colombia, Mexico, the United States, Uruguay, and Venezuela. The bulletin would likewise be distributed in Baiona, Bilbao, Donostia, Gasteiz, Urruñe, "and wherever else."[43] The bulletin was published quarterly without interruption between 1950 and 1993, until the death of Andrés Irujo. There was also a period in 1978 when the bulletin was not published because of Irujo's marriage to María Elena Etxeberri. Even if the journal went through at least five different printers, for economic reasons, it maintained the same format and general characteristics during its forty-three years of existence. By 1993, it had published 174 issues under the direction of Andrés Irujo, who had likewise been its chief promoter from the beginning.

Alongside the *Boletín del Instituto Americano de Estudios Vascos*, the Western Hemisphere saw at least 130 Basque periodicals published in thirteen countries across three continents between 1877 and 1977, or an approximate total of eighty thousand pages of the periodical press published outside Euskadi. Some of these periodicals were highly remarkable for their frequency and longevity, practically reaching their hundredth anniversaries, as in the case of *Laurac Bat* of Buenos Aires (1878–1975) or the magazine of the Basque-Nafarroan Beneficent Association of Havana (1890–1972). We have already

41. *Euzko Deya* (Mexico City), March 1, 1943.

42. Interviews with Andrés Irujo, Buenos Aires, October 23–November 20, 1991.

43. Ibid.

mentioned *Euzko Deya* in Paris and *Euzko Izpar Banatzea*, the *Boletín de la Oficina de Prensa de Euzkadi* (Bulletin of the Euzkadi Press Office, EIB-OPE), which was undoubtedly one of the most widely distributed and voluminous periodicals in the history of the Basque exile: over its thirty-year life (May 2, 1947–July 22, 1977), it appeared three times a week, for a total of 7,001 issues and 35,085 printed pages on current Basque political affairs in the Americas and Europe. There were likewise other journals that turned out to be especially significant for their impact on the Basque community in exile, whether because of their political focus or their cultural contribution, which in most cases went together. Among these, and within the chronological span covered by this work, 1937 to 1960, it is appropriate to highlight *Euzko Deya* in Buenos Aires (the first series was published between 1939 and 1949, and then the second series began in 1950 and continued until 1987), the *Boletín del Instituto Americano de Estudios Vascos* in Buenos Aires (1950–1993), *Tierra Vasca-Euzko Lur* (*Basque Land*) in Buenos Aires (1956–1975), *Eusko Gaztedi* in Caracas (1948–1977), *Euskal Erria* in Montevideo (1912–1985), and *Euzko Gogoa* in Guatemala (1950–1959); the last journal undoubtedly deserves special mention.[44]

Euzko Gogoa was published entirely in Basque, in Guatemala, by the priest Jokin Zaitegi. Zaitegi arrived in the Americas from Belgium as an exile in 1937. He initially settled in Panama and subsequently traveled to El Salvador before definitively establishing himself in 1944 in Guatemala, where he worked as a professor at the University of San Carlos and at the American Institute. Zaitegi had participated in several literary competitions in Euskadi in the 1930s, for which reason he embraced the idea of promoting a literary journal dedicated fundamentally to poetic compositions and to the translation into Basque, in the Americas, of classics of world literature. In this way, the first volume of *Euzko Gogoa* appeared in 1950, printed at the Imprenta Hispania. The journal had its legal headquarters at Avenida Norte 11 in the Guatemalan capital, and the price of an annual subscription was ten dollars. Needless to say, because of the prohibition that weighed on the Basque language in Euskadi and the lack of means and resources among the Basque community in exile, *Euzko Gogoa* would quickly become the point of reference for literary creation in Basque around the world. Zaitegi was always the journal's director, although during its first six months he had the invaluable aid of Nikolas Ormaetxea, or Orixe, one of the twentieth century's great writers in Euskara, and beginning in 1954, of Andima Ibinagabeitia, an active and distinguished translator into Euskara.

Zaitegi remained in Guatemala until 1955. Between 1950 and 1955, twenty-seven issues of *Euzko Gogoa* were published: seven in 1950, six in 1951, six in 1952, five in 1954, and three in 1955. In 1955, Zaitegi decided to return to Euskadi and to publish *Euzko Gogoa* in Biarritz, where the journal's second epoch began, with a smaller format

44. *Euzko Deya: La voz de los vascos en América* was a periodical published by the Basque government's delegation in Buenos Aires, for which reason its directors were the Euzkadi government's delegates in the Argentine capital, Ramón María Aldasoro, Francisco Basterretxea, and Pedro Basaldua.

to cut costs and facilitate its transport in Hegoalde. Produced under the patronage of Manuel Intxausti, the seventeen issues that would emerge in the following five years, until the appearance of the final issue in 1959, would be printed at the Darracq press in Baiona. Six issues appeared in 1956, five in 1957, four in 1958, and two in 1959. In total, forty-four issues saw the light of day, or a total of 3,658 pages in Basque published in exile between 1950 and 1960.

During all this time, and despite the severe financial problems Zaitegi had to confront, the most distinguished pens of Basque literature in those days collaborated with the journal: Sebero Altube, José Luis "Txillardegi" Álvarez Emparanza, Bingen Ametzaga, Gabriel Aresti, Jon Etxaide, Nemesio Etxaniz, Frantzisko Etxeberria, Andima Ibinagabeitia, Jesus Insausti, Jaime Kerexeta, Federiko Krutwig, Antonio María Labaien, Bedita Larrakoetxea, Jesus María Leizaola, Manuel Lekuona, Jon Mirande, Salbatore Mitxelena, Santiago Onaindia, Nikolas "Orixe" Ormaetxea, Txomin Peillen, Étienne Salaberry, Juan San Martín, Sorne Unzueta, Andoni Urrestarazu, Agustin Zarrantz (known as "Polikarpo Iraizozkoa"), and Jokin Zaitegi himself, among many others.

Another essential contribution to the dissemination of Basque culture was made by the Ekin publishing house in Buenos Aires. Ixaka López Mendizabal and Andrés Irujo, both Basque exiles, first proposed the idea of creating a publishing house exclusively dedicated to publishing books on Basque subjects to Ramón María Aldasoro, the Basque government's delegate in Buenos Aires, in 1941.[45] The idea was favorably received, but the delegation lacked funds to tackle such an enterprise, so that Irujo turned to Sebastián Amorrortu, a Basque exile who had arrived in Argentina in 1910, who provided the necessary funds to set up the publishing house. In this way, the Editorial Vasca Ekin, a partnership with an initial capital of 1,500 pesos, was born in December 1941. That private contract would be transformed in January 1944, after the first publishing successes, into a limited-liability company with a corporate capital of fifteen thousand pesos. And that capital would be increased to fifty thousand pesos in 1951.

Initially, the idea was to found a publishing house dedicated exclusively to works on Basque culture, for which reason the first collection was called the Library of Basque Culture. In 1942 alone, the house would publish six titles. Its first book appeared in January 1942, *El genio de Nabarra* (The Genius of Navarre), by Arturo Campion, with a press run of one thousand copies that would soon sell out, for which reason Ekin would issue a second printing in July 1944 with another thousand copies. The publishing house's second production would be a work by Enrique Gandia titled *Primitivos Navegantes Extranjeros en Vasconia* (Early Foreign Travelers in the Basque Country), which appeared in March 1942 with a press run of 1,750 copies and sold out soon afterward. In July 1942, Ekin published *Viajeros extranjeros en Vasconia* (Foreign Travelers in the Basque Country), by Justo Garate, a political exile, in an edition of two thousand copies. In view

45. José Ramón Zabala, "Ekin: Una luz en el túnel," in *La cultura del exilio vasco*, vol. 2, edited by José Ángel Ascunce (Donostia-San Sebastián: Ascunce, 1994).

of its success, that work was followed in July 1942 by *Pinceladas Vascas* (Basque Sketches), a compilation of works by Arturo Campion, Juan Iturralde y Suit, and Pierre Loti, of which 2,500 copies were printed. In November 1942 there appeared *La aportación vasca al derecho internacional* (The Basque Contribution to International Law) by Jesús Galíndez, a political exile, of whose work 2,500 copies were produced. Finally, also in 1942, *La democracia en Euzkadi* (Democracy in Euzkadi), by Jose Ariztimuno, a Basque priest shot in 1937, was published in 2,500 copies.

The press runs of Ekin's publications were always, starting in 1942, between 1,500 and 2,500 copies, save for exceptions such as *La lengua vasca* (The Basque Language) by López Mendizabal, of which 3,000 copies were issued in the first printing in 1943 and 2,530 in the second in 1949. Along the same lines, *Lehendakari* Agirre's work *De Gernika a New York pasando por Berlín* (*From Guernica to New York by Way of Berlin*), in which the president recounted the odyssey of his escape from the Gestapo across Europe, was published in 1943 with an initial press run of 5,000 copies that would soon sell out; a second printing followed in 1944 with 3,020 copies, and a third in the same year, a pocket-sized photostatic reproduction with a press run of 15,000 copies.

Starting in 1943, Ekin's catalog would include—in addition to the publication and reprinting of books on Basque culture in the Library of Basque Culture collection, for which López Mendizabal would be responsible—other books of a marked political and doctrinal character included in the collections Aberri ta Azkatasuna (Basque Homeland and Freedom) and Euskal Idazleak (Basque Writers), directed by Andrés Irujo, such as *Los vascos en el Madrid sitiado* (The Basques in Besieged Madrid), by Jesús de Galíndez, and *Los vascos y la República española* (The Basques and the Spanish Republic), by Andrés de Lizarra.[46] By 1954, the year of the Eighth Basque Studies Congress in Baiona, Ekin had published the works of forty Basque exile authors in a total of 151,200 copies, 82,180 of which corresponded to the Library of Basque Culture, which had published 42 titles by that year. Books written in Basque accounted for a total of four thousand copies. Ekin would publish in Euskara Jose Eizagirre's novel *Ekaitzpean* (Under the Storm) in 1948 and Juan Andoni Irazusta's works *Joañixio* (Little John) in 1946 and *Bizitza garratza da* (Life is Hard) in 1950, both bitter chronicles of Basque emigration and exile in the Americas, as well as Francisco Abrisketa's poetic anthology of Colombian authors, *Kolonbiar olerki-txorta euzkeraz* (Anthology of Colombian Poems in Basque) in 1967. As Irujo remarked, the work in Euskara that had the greatest impact was the translation of William Shakespeare's *Hamlet* by Bingen Ametzaga (1952), of which one thousand copies were printed and that reached numerous universities, philologists, and scholars around the world—the distribution of Ekin's books covered all of the Western Hemisphere, fifteen countries in Europe, three in Africa, two in Oceania, and one in Asia. Undoubtedly, alongside the journal *Euzko Gogoa* published in Guatemala by the exiled

46. Arantzazu Ametzaga Iribarren, "Andrés Irujo Ollo: El documentalista vasco del exilio," in *Sesenta años después: Euskal Erbestearen Kultura* (Astigarraga: Fundación Hamaika Bide and Saturraran Argitaletxea, 2000), 259–84.

Basque priest Jokin Zaitegi, Ekin's work in Basque occupies a prominent place in the cultural endeavors of Basque political exiles in the Americas.

Despite its thriving sales, however, Ekin confronted numerous financial problems in its fifty-year existence. As Irujo informed Ametzaga by letter in 1954, Ekin had suffered one of the worst financial crises in its history between 1953 and 1954,[47] and the editor was of the opinion that the house could not take on a new edition in Euskara, and scarcely even one in Spanish, because it was hopelessly in debt to its printer.[48] Nevertheless, once it had overcome the financial crisis, along with a health crisis suffered by Irujo, Ekin issued beginning in 1955 a series of strongly ideological works for free, clandestine distribution in Euskadi.[49] The idea was to use the income from works with high sales to pay for the publication of works of very small format, such that they were easy to transport and hide, on political subjects and intended for distribution inside the country through the EAJ-PNV's resistance network. The first of the works was *Ami vasco* (Basque friend) in 1957 by Father Evangelista de Ibero.[50] The press run was 2,500 copies, which were distributed inside the country fundamentally by priests.[51] *Ami vasco* was followed by two works written in Euskara, Ibero's work translated into Basque under the title *Euzko ami* (1958) and subsequently Txomin Jakakortexarena's pamphlet "Tu hermano de la clandestinidad" (Your Brother in the Underground, 1961), which was likewise published in Basque with the title *Zure anaia ixilkari* (Your Silent Friend) in 1961; all were widely distributed and had a significant impact in the country.[52]

In any event, problems were inseparable from Ekin's history. The years 1959 and 1960 were complicated. The press acquired new machinery and found that the building's foundation was insufficient to support it, which resulted in a doubling or even tripling of production costs, but Ekin maintained the prices of its recent publications. In consequence, it became difficult to meet the costs of printing.[53] And finances were not the only problem Irujo faced. Publishing works in Euskara in the Americas was not an easy task. The galleys of the works in Euskara were prepared by professionals who, obviously, did not speak Euskara, for which reason the type was set letter by letter, notably increasing production time and hence costs. To mention one example, the translation of *Hamlet* was printed at Talleres Gráficos A. Domínguez[54] in La Plata, and in the final proofs, after two years of corrections, the author found seventy-four transcription errors.[55]

---

47. Andrés Irujo to Bingen Ametzaga, Buenos Aires, August 21, 1954, IAA, GT-Irujo.A.1954.

48. Andrés Irujo to Bingen Ametzaga, Buenos Aires, January 15, 1954, IAA, GT-Irujo.A.1954.

49. Interviews with Andrés Irujo, Buenos Aires, October 23–November 20, 1991.

50. Andrés Irujo to Bingen Ametzaga, Buenos Aires, December 6, 1955, IAA, GT-Irujo.A.1955.

51. Andrés Irujo to Bingen Ametzaga, Buenos Aires, July 1, 1957, IAA, GT-Irujo.A.1957.

52. Andrés Irujo to Bingen Ametzaga, Buenos Aires, January 29, 1958, IAA, GT-Irujo.A.1958.

53. Andrés Irujo to Bingen Ametzaga, Buenos Aires, July 31, 1961, IAA, GT-Irujo.A.1961.

54. Bingen Ametzaga to Ramón Ametzaga, Montevideo, February 17, 1953, IAA, GT-Ametzaga.R.1953.

55. Andrés Irujo to Bingen Ametzaga, Buenos Aires, January 28, 1953, IAA, GT-Irujo.A.1953.

Beginning in 1965, the situation became increasingly difficult, as López Mendizabal's departure left Irujo alone and thus responsible for everything. In 1967, the publishing house's roof was in imminent danger of collapse, which raised the possibility that the entire enterprise might even have to be closed. So carpenters came, removed the roof, and installed another kind of roof. It was impossible to do more than cover the books with paper and take out the desks.[56] But although Argentina's economic situation was growing increasingly worse and it seemed impossible to survive the economic crisis, the house kept publishing, even though at times Irujo saw closing as the only solution.[57] In addition, a number of government regulations had a major impact on the publishing house, which found itself unable either to receive packages from abroad or to send them, as the government decided that only publishing houses with a capital of three hundred thousand pesos could do so (and Ekin had fifty thousand pesos).[58]

Nevertheless, despite all the troubles, all the prohibitions imposed on Ekin's books by the Argentinean government, the various financial crises, and the administrative limitations, Ekin survived the exile and even published several titles during the 1980s. In total, Ekin published more than one hundred titles between 1942 and 1985, many of them of high quality and of great interest for the study of this period of Basque history. This is demonstrated by the fact that a number of them have recently been reprinted, as is the case of *Inglaterra y los vascos* (England and the Basques, 2004) and *Instituciones jurídicas vascas* (Basque Legal Institutions, 2006), by Manuel Irujo; *Los vascos y la república española* (The Basques and the Spanish Republic, 2005), by Andrés Irujo; and *Los vascos en el Madrid sitiado* (The Basques in Besieged Madrid, 2005), by Jesús Galíndez.

Strikes and Political Actions

The Basque government was a decided promoter of political activities directed toward overthrowing the Spanish military regime. Many of these actions took place abroad, on the international stage, in forums such as the UN and the evolving European Community, but both the Basque government and the parties that constituted it likewise decisively promoted actions by the resistance inside Euskal Herria. This was the case of the general strikes of 1947 and 1951 and of those that would follow throughout the coming two decades.

The celebration of May Day, or Labor Day, during the four decades of military dictatorship came to acquire an openly subversive character, not only of social protest, but of political and cultural protest as well. At the same time, the suppression of all basic human rights and liberties made the attempt to convert them, de facto, into a criminal act, thereby giving rise to harsh police reactions and repression in relation to May Day celebrations. Nevertheless, during the first ten years of the dictatorship, between 1936

56. Andrés Irujo to Bingen Ametzaga, Buenos Aires, February 20, 1967, IAA, GT-Irujo.A.1967.

57. Andrés Irujo to Bingen Ametzaga, Buenos Aires, August 11, 1965, IAA, GT-Irujo.A.1965.

58. Andrés Irujo to Bingen Ametzaga, Buenos Aires, November 12, 1967, IAA, GT-Irujo.A.1967.

and 1946, the celebration of May Day did not have much of an international impact, as the two wars, for obvious reasons, eclipsed the activities of the Basque government and the Basque political parties and labor unions in exile.

The end of the worldwide conflict and the Spanish regime's open collaboration with the Axis forces led the victorious governments to issue, on March 5, 1946, a joint declaration, subsequently known as the Tripartite Declaration, condemning the origins of Franco's regime and noting, in consequence, the impossibility of maintaining normalized diplomatic relations with it—all this, nonetheless, without infringing on the right of noninterference in the Spanish state's internal affairs. This declaration was followed on December 15, 1946, by the UN General Assembly's declaration in which it criticized the Spanish regime's fascist character, recommended its exclusion from all international organizations and the withdrawal of ambassadors from Madrid, and encouraged the prompt restoration of liberties and the Spanish state's return to the international community.[59]

Nevertheless, once the war was over and the Spanish regime had been publicly condemned at the UN, and in view of the upcoming decision on the applicability of the European Recovery Program or Marshall Plan to Western Europe as a whole, for which the participating European states would gather at a summit on July 12, 1947, the call for a general strike on May 1 of that year was hoped to destabilize the regime and damage its already-tarnished international reputation.[60] In fact, by means of the call for a general strike, the Basque political forces hostile to the dictatorship aimed to demonstrate that, in contrast to the division and inaction of the Spanish political groups, the Basque people were mobilized in a coordinated way around the Basque government-in-exile, its legitimate political authority. Therefore, a democratic government, in which all the Basque political forces opposed to the dictatorship (except for the communists) were represented, had massive popular support and consequently constituted a guarantee of success for the transition to democracy.

In this way, on April 31, 1947, in Bilbao, the delegated council and the resistance committee, the Basque government's main arms responsible for the labor mobilization, in agreement with the country's three strongest labor unions, the ELA-STV, the UGT, and the CNT, issued a call for a general strike in Bizkaia.[61] The call turned out to be a resounding success. Major industrial plants such as La Naval and Euskalduna practically had to close their doors; around 20 percent of the workers at Altos Hornos de Vizcaya heeded the call and approximately 15 percent of the employees at Basconia and Babcok Wilcox. In any event, the strike affected a large number of firms, including Astilleros del Nervión, Aurrera, Campsa de Santurce, Echevarria, Eléctrica del Cadagua, Fábrica de Dinamita de Galdacano, Firestone, Forjas de Amorebieta, General Eléctrica Española,

---

59. Álvaro de Albornoz, *El gobierno de la República española se dirige a las Naciones Unidas*, Paris, November 15, 1948, 1.

60. Jesús Galíndez, "La Asamblea General de Naciones Unidas," *Euzko Deya* (Paris), October 15, 1947, 5.

61. Páginas de la Resistencia Vasca, *La huelga en Bizkaya y Gipuzkoa* (leaflet), Montevideo, June 1947.

Mutiozabal, Material Industrial, Talleres Castrejana, Talleres Cortazar, Talleres Erandio, Talleres Omega, Talleres de Zorroza, and in general, the majority of the factories in the industrial belt of greater Bilbao.[62] The number of strikers, the majority belonging to the metallurgical sector, was approximately twenty-five thousand.

On Friday, May 2, Genaro Riestra, the civilian governor of Bizkaia, ordered the police and the Civil Guard to take control of the streets and the factories for the purpose of preventing labor-union actions, and he published an official statement in the press in which he ordered employers to immediately expel from their factories and workshops all those workers who had heeded the call to strike on May 1. He did allow a one-week period in which those dismissed could apply for reinstatement at the same firm to which they had provided their services up to that point. Riestra added that such applications should be sent by the factories involved to the civilian government to be examined and approved on a case-by-case basis, noting that those reinstated in this way would lose all rights of seniority they might have had.[63]

On Saturday, May 3, Riestra issued a warning by radio that all workers on parole should present themselves to the authorities to prove that they had reported to work that day, at the time ordered by their employers, who were to submit lists of the workers who had supported the May 1 mobilization.[64] Riestra's measures, which affected around twenty-five thousand workers and the overwhelming majority of Bilbao's industry, were not well received, either by the workers or by the international media. Even if the labor minister, José Antonio Girón de Velasco, demanded greater rigor, some employers decided not to comply with the governor's demands, to avoid losing their most skilled workers.[65] This obliged Riestra to issue a new press statement on Sunday, May 4, in which he announced that, having failed to comply with the order of May 3, the industrialists José Álvarez Ormiluge, managing director of Gráficas Álvarez, and Alberto Wicke, director of Imprenta Industrial, had been jailed that very morning and assessed, in addition, a fine of ten thousand pesetas each.[66]

Despite the repression, however, the strike continued on May 3 and 4, and Riestra saw himself obliged to mobilize the regular army and the Legion, which occupied Bilbao. The six hundred agents of the national police normally stationed in the city were reinforced with 2,500 agents from various locations across Spain. To prevent workers from fleeing across the border, Civil Guard detachments were deployed in the passes of the Pyrenees. On May 5, the police detained Agustín "Xabale" Unzurrunzaga, a former *gudari* and member of the ELA-STV Local Committee in Bergara accused of having

62. "Les basques ont lance le premier cri de révolte contre la tyrannie franquiste," *Euzko Deya* (Paris), May 3, 1947, 1–7.

63. *El correo español: El pueblo vasco* (Bilbao), May 2, 1947.

64. Páginas de la Resistencia Vasca, *La huelga en Bizkaya y Gipuzkoa* (leaflet), Montevideo, June 1947.

65. "Les basques ont lance le premier cri de révolte contre la tyrannie franquiste," *Euzko Deya* (Paris), May 3, 1947, 1–7.

66. *Gaceta del Norte* (Bilbao), May 4, 1947.

hung an *ikurriña* (the Basque national flag). Having been tortured, Unzurrunzaga died at the hands of the police that same day. The media, which security forces operated, reported that he had committed suicide by throwing himself in the path of a streetcar. His family succeeded in having the body brought to Bergara, where a large crowd gathered in an expression of mourning and protest, for which reason the police ordered that the body be returned to the commissary in Donostia.[67] This led to the workers of Bergara joining the strike, which, contrary to all predictions, grew in strength on May 5, spreading to the construction sector and to workers at the port. Workers at firms such as Echevarria de Begoña, Firestone, La Basconia de Dos Caminos, Sociedad Española de Oxígeno, and Unión Química del Norte, which had not previously been affected, now joined the strike. With these new signs of support, the workers decided to remain on strike until Riestra's dispositions were annulled.

Parallel to this, the delegated Council and the resistance committee sent a message to the UN demanding solidarity from the press and international institutions and demanding condemnation of the Spanish regime. At the same time, a resistance fund was set up to collect funds to aid the families of workers who suffered reprisals.[68] The news was, in effect, widely publicized in the European and American press. Unzurrunzaga's murder and the reaction of the strikers in Gipuzkoa fed the publication of articles about the Basque strike.

On May 7, Jose Antonio Agirre sent a message to the strikers, congratulating them for the strike's success and encouraging them to continue with the same attitude until they saw their rights and those of their people fully respected. At a packed press conference held at the Basque government's delegation in Paris, the Basque government took responsibility in front of the international press for the strike movement and for coordinating the organizations operating underground, which took direction from the Basque government-in-exile.[69] Acting in coordination, the ELA-STV, the UGT, and the CNT appealed to the World Federation of Trade Unions and the International Federation of Christian Trade Unions for aid and solidarity, and on the following day, the former group released a manifesto signed by its general secretary, Louis Saillant, in solidarity with the Basque people. On that same day, Agirre and Irujo met with high-ranking officials in the French Ministry of Foreign Affairs.

After a week of mobilization, however, the conflict's energy began to fade, starting on May 9. Conscious of the pressure exercised on the workers as a group, the three Basque unions announced the end of the strike on Radio Euzkadi, congratulating the workers for their action and encouraging them to continue the struggle against the dic-

67. Páginas de la Resistencia Vasca, *La huelga en Bizkaya y Gipuzkoa*, Montevideo, June 1947.

68. "Les basques ont lance le premier cri de révolte contre la tyrannie franquiste," *Euzko Deya* (Paris), May 35, 1947, 1–7.

69. "Ce que fut la grève dans la zone de Bilbao," *Euzko Deya* (Paris), May 31, 1947, 1–8.

tatorship.[70] The government of the Republic, which for political reasons had remained on the sidelines of the organization of the strike and had not made a statement about it, hurriedly issued a note supporting the Basque workers on May 10, and the civilian governor of Gipuzkoa put out a press statement on May 11 declaring that the strike had ended.[71] For his part, *Lehendakari* Agirre in a radio message referred to the strike as the greatest victory popular forces had obtained against Franco's regime up to 1947 and stressed the Basque government's effective and coordinated control of the anti-Franco forces within the country and the peaceful nature of the strike.[72]

One of the keys to the strike was the solidarity of the Basque working class, which turned out to be stronger than the best predictions had supposed. None of the organizers thought that the strike would be maintained for nine days or that the international impact would be so great. The reaction of numerous employers, who viewed the measures adopted by Riestra and by the state's labor minister with distaste, generated a current of opposition to the Franco regime's repression within the Basque business community. And as far as international opinion was concerned, on November 12, 1947, the UN political committee adopted, with twenty-nine votes in favor, five against, and twenty abstentions, the proposal put forward by a sizable group of Latin American democracies in support of the resolution adopted on December 12, 1946, in opposition to the Spanish government.[73]

Perhaps the most noteworthy consequence, however, was that, despite their cost, strikes were a good strategy in the anti-Franco struggle. Hence, the 1947 strike in Bizkaia and Gipuzkoa was followed by numerous labor mobilizations in the 1950s and 1960s, such that it is possible to speak of a Basque strike "tradition." Following the model established in Euskadi in 1947, large-scale labor mobilizations materialized during the 1950s in Spain as a whole. This is the case of the 1951 strike in Catalunya, provoked by the Spanish government's move at the end of 1950 to raise streetcar fares in Barcelona while maintaining them in Madrid. This discriminatory policy led to a streetcar boycott starting on March 1, 1951, which was followed by other significant manifestations of protest in Euskadi that spring.[74] Along these lines, the mobilization of 1951 had a significant echo in Iruñea, where a significant general strike took place, completely paralyzing the city for four days and generating serious disturbances, in the course of which harsh confrontations took place between demonstrators and the forces of public order.[75] Two years later, when on November 30, 1953, the managers of Astilleros Euzkalduna in Bil-

70. "Primero de mayo de 1947, una fecha y una advertencia," *Euzkadi*, May 1948, 1.

71. "Ce que fut la grève dans la zone de Bilbao," *Euzko Deya* (Paris), May 31, 1947, 1–8.

72. Páginas de la Resistencia Vasca, *La huelga en Bizkaya y Gipuzkoa*, Montevideo, June 1947.

73. "El problema español en el Comité Político de la Asamblea General de la ONU," *Euzko Deya* (Paris), November 15, 1947, 10; see also "Documents de l'ONU: Les Basques et le problème franquiste," *Euzko Deya* (Paris), November 30, 1947, 3.

74. Jose Antonio Agirre to Bingen Ametzaga, Paris, May 9, 1951, IAA, GT-Agirre.JA.1951.

75. José Luis Díaz Monreal, "La huelga general de 1951 en Pamplona," *Estudios de Ciencias Sociales* 10 (1997): 101–21.

bao announced the suspension of piecework and overtime, a new strike began, which ended a few days later when the firm accepted an increase in wages, even if it went on to dismiss those workers most implicated in the protests. The year 1962 was characterized by an increase in strikes, which began in the Asturian mining industry and immediately spread to Euskadi, where the government declared a state of emergency.

Between 1963 and 1975, the number of strikes multiplied fivefold–one movement smothered by the brutal repression in Gasteiz on March 3, 1976, which left five dead. As can be seen, the labor struggles against Francoist repression did not end until after the dictator's death and resulted in what became a culture of organized resistance to the totalitarian regime.

12

Rethinking Resistance after the Collapse of a Political Project: 1956–1960

In the midst of the political and financial crisis produced by the entry of Franco's dictatorship to the United Nations in 1955, and facing a necessary and urgent change of strategy, *Lehendakari* Agirre's government organized one of its last major events, the World Basque Congress, held September 23–30, 1956, at the Hotel Quay D'Orsay in Paris. The most obvious goal and task of the meeting was to hit on a new course for political and cultural activity in the midst of the Cold War and to discover fresh new directions in general to overcome the 1950–1955 crisis. In this context, in view of the 1947 and 1951 general strikes, two of the main objectives were for the Basque government to bring its political struggle back to Europe, as had been the case in the period 1936–1941, and to encourage cultural activity and political resistance within the Basque Country itself.

Jose Antonio Agirre announced the plans for the World Basque Congress in his Christmas message of 1954. The Basque government drew up a questionnaire with the aim of collecting information and opinions on economic, social, political, and cultural issues from Basques inside and outside the Basque Country. This questionnaire, twenty pages in length, would serve as a guide for developing the congress's overall program and had as its chief objective determination of the Basque government's lines of action starting in 1956.[1] As the questionnaire itself stated, acquiring adequate knowledge of the country's situation after twenty years of Franco's dictatorship demanded in-depth study of the country's current state from a variety of perspectives, including those of people living within the country and of the exiles, as well as of those who experienced the war and of the younger generation born in the postwar years.

In contrast to the enthusiasm of the Basque nationalist political groups that made up the Basque government-in-exile, the EAJ-PNV and the ANV, the PSOE was opposed in principle to the idea of holding a political event independent of the republican government's policy. Indalecio Prieto made this known, as he observed with misgivings the holding of Basque and Catalan political events outside the control of the government of the Republic. Nevertheless, the PSOE participated—at least nominally—in the congress,

1. *Congreso Mundial Vasco: Cuestionario*, 4.714. AA/AN FSAE, DP.1036.3.

through the CCSE, the meetings of which were attended by its general secretary, Paulino Gómez Beltrán. In the Cold War context, the PCE was excluded from the congress, and the two remaining parties, the IR and the UR, were in decline, for which reason their participation in the congress was merely nominal.

According to the congress's bylaws, attending the congress as full members would be the president of the government of Euzkadi and his ministers; the president and members of the Delegated Council and the Basque Resistance Committee; the president and members of the Basque Consultative Council; the former counselors of the Basque government; the Basque Country's representatives in the Spanish Parliament and those who had served in that capacity previously; the former deputies of Araba, Gipuzkoa, Navarra, and Bizkaia; the elected mayors; the representatives of Basque political parties and labor unions; the delegates of the government of Euzkadi abroad; the delegates of the International League of Friends of the Basques and of the Basque communities and associations of all countries; and Basque citizens registered for the congress on an individual basis. The executive committee was composed as follows: Jesús Solaun* (EAJ-PNV), Gabriel Goitia (ANV), De Pablo (Socialist Central Committee of Euzkadi in France), Herrán (ELA-STV), José Campos (Central Committee of the UGT of Euzkadi), Aransaez (CNT), Alberto Buj (UR), and J. López Angulo (IR). Pedro Basaldua represented Federación de Entidades Vasco Argentinas - Eusko Argentinar Bazkun Alkartasuna (FEVA-EABA, Federation of Basque-Argentine Associations); Pedro Aretxabala and Santiago Zarranz, the Basque organizations in Chile; and Juan Bautista Lasarte, the Basque center Euskal Erria of Montevideo and the Basque delegation in Uruguay. In total, 366 people attended the congress from more than twenty countries in Europe and the Americas, 45 of them from within the country. Of the 366 attendees, 363 were full voting participants, of whom 217 attended the congress as individuals, 38 as representatives of the Basque government, 58 as representatives of political parties and associations of various kinds (mainly Basque diaspora communities or labor unions), and 5 as observers.[2]

After the welcoming ceremony for the participants and a lunch at the Basque delegation in Paris, located at 50 Rue Singer, the inaugural plenary session of the World Basque Congress took place on September 24 at 9:30 in the morning, with a greeting from President Agirre, who spoke for five hours, summarizing the labor and efforts of the Basque government's twenty years in exile (1936–1956).[3] The executive committee was formally constituted, and the bylaws were read. On the following day, at 9:30 a.m., the congress's Political Section opened discussions with the presentation of papers and the reading or explication of the communications received, followed by a general discussion that extended into the evening. The following day, September 26, the Socioeconomic Section's discussion took place, with the presentation of papers and a general discussion.

---

2. *Euzko Deya* (Paris), September 1, 1956, 12.

3. *Exposición de la obra y gestión del gobierno vasco (1936–1956)*, AA/AN FSAE, DP.1036.6.

On September 27, the Cultural Section's discussion was held, and on September 28, it was the turn of the special section "The Basques in the World." On September 29, at 11 a.m., the congress concluded with a reading of the conclusions and recommendations arising from the four days of discussion. The events ended with a folklore festival held at the Paris Fronton on September 30, and on October 1, a ceremony was held at the headquarters of the Basque delegation in Paris commemorating the twentieth anniversary of the proclamation of the Basque Country Statute of Autonomy in October 1936.[4] In total, 144 communications were presented, of which 66 corresponded to the Socioeconomic Section, 24 to the Political Section, and 44 to the Cultural Section.[5]

As far as the Political Section was concerned, the congress reached four general conclusions. First, the attendees agreed to express their gratitude to the governments of those states, both in Europe and in the Americas and Asia, that had taken in and welcomed the Basque exiles, underlining the fact that in countries such as Argentina, Chile, Mexico, Uruguay, and Venezuela, Basques obtained advantageous treatment that in many cases translated into the grant of citizenship to all exiled Basque citizens who arrived on their coasts. They also thanked the governments of the British, Belgian, and French states for having taken in thousands of child refugees in the spring and summer of 1937.

Second, the congress issued a call for peace. In the congress's opinion, the principal pillars of world peace would be effective acknowledgment of the right of popular self-determination, respect for the fundamental rights of the human person and for human dignity, observance of international conventions and treaties, the integration of states and stateless nations within organizations of an international character both in Europe and in the Americas, improvement of living conditions for workers in all countries, and substantive and disinterested aid for culturally and economically less-developed peoples.

The congress likewise made evident its complete rejection of General Franco's dictatorial regime, and in view of the scope that movements of opinion opposed to the totalitarian regime were attaining in the country, visibly expressed in workers' strikes, student protests, manifestos of intellectuals, military attitudes, and the attitudes of various social strata, the congress expressed its solidarity and sympathy and recommended that the Basque government-in-exile, the political parties that constituted it, and Basque public opinion in general support and cooperate with the movements, with the aim of promoting the fall of the regime and the reestablishment of a democratic government on foundations of reconciliation and harmony.

With regard to the political status of the Basque Country, the congress recognized the government of Euzkadi headed by Jose Antonio Agirre, born of the democratically expressed popular will of the Basque citizenry, as the Basque people's legitimate authority, and the congress proclaimed that government to be an appropriate instrument to

4. *Euzko Deya* (Paris), September 1, 1956, 1.

5. EIB-OPE, September 28, 1956, 6.

continue directing labors conducive to the country's liberation. All this without mentioning the government of the Republic in exile. Likewise, the congress stated that the 1936 statute of autonomy was the expression of the will of all the Basques and proclaimed that it constituted the symbol of Basque union in the fight for liberty. With a view toward unity of action among all groups opposed to the Spanish military regime, the congress stated that the Pact of Bayonne, signed March 31, 1945, which prioritized the fall of Franco's regime over claims for the right of self-determination or the independence of Euskadi, constituted a guarantee of union and heartfelt solidarity in the enterprise of reestablishing liberty and democracy on firm foundations. The congress likewise emphasized that the Nafarroan people could decide whether to join an autonomous Basque Country, as was established in the additional provision of the 1936 statute of autonomy.

In any event, the congress declared that the autonomous regime put forward did not imply in any way the Basques' renunciation of their historical rights, the comprehensive restoration of their age-old legal system, or their right of self-determination and even to independence.[6] In summary, the conclusions of the Basque World Congress's Political Section constituted a minimum common denominator of agreement among socialists and republicans on one side and Basque nationalists on the other. In this way, unity of action and the search for common strategies for overthrowing General Franco's regime became the congress's real political objective, and that unavoidably entailed giving up any real possibility of preparing a political program, as it obliged the congress to settle for reaffirming the political postulates put forward in the statute of autonomy in October 1936 and the Pact of Bayonne in 1945.

With the aim of bringing the government of Euzkadi closer to the Basque people, reinforcing as much as possible the citizenry's organic and ongoing participation and allowing it to effectively intervene in the life and activities of the Basque government-in-exile, the congress recommended to the government that its consultative council include those individuals who had served in popularly elected offices in Euzkadi or had held positions in the Basque government or army or in the resistance, as well as delegates of the Basques in the Americas. Expanded in this way, the consultative council would thus serve as an advisory body to the Basque government, meeting once a year for the purpose of advising on general and budgetary policy as it saw fit. Nevertheless, as the delegates of the council itself stated on December 1, 1956, financial issues prevented both that expansion and annual meetings of the council.

The socioeconomic section was likewise extremely interesting because of the abundance of papers presented and the subsequent general discussion. Among other things, the participants concluded that Basque industry was in urgent need of restructuring and focused their attention on the quality of employment contracts and the lack of protection for workers under the dictatorial regime. Along these lines, the congress stated the

6. *Euzko Deya* (Paris), October 1, 1956, 7–9.

need to raise and fix minimum wages, establish a maximum workday of eight hours, and promote the creation of cooperatives in which workers would have a share of profits as a means to stop the decline in quality of life that was taking place as the result of a poorly managed mining and steel industry and the massive immigration of workers.

The cultural section was extremely interesting both for its content and for the participants who came together in Paris of 1956. The Basque World Congress was the culmination of the efforts made at the Seventh and Eighth World Basque Studies Congresses of 1948 and 1954, held respectively in Biarritz and in Baiona.

Discussion in the cultural section centered from the beginning on the situation of persecution and open decline suffered by the Basque language in Euskal Herria. In the opinion of the congress participants, one of the country's most serious problems in 1956 was the policy of "de-Basquification" promoted by the dictatorship, which affected the Basque language in an especially tragic way through the prohibitions and punishments imposed on speakers of Euskara. As a consequence of this repressive cultural policy, the Basque language was suffering one of the most severe processes of decay in its long history. Specifically, the congress focused its attention on studying the prohibitions on writing or speaking in Euskara, both in public and in private, and the imposition of monolingual education in Spanish, all of which entailed the nonexistence of a press or literature written in Euskara, and in general, a sharp reduction in the Basque-speaking population among the younger generations and a drastic decrease in the use of Euskara in public.[7]

Following an evaluation of these circumstances, the congress proposed the creation of a commission that would work to promote and foster the Basque language, both with regard to its diffusion, use (literary and conversational), and teaching and with regard to developing its internal study and to promoting linguistic normalization through, for example, encouraging the translation of classic works into Basque. This would give rise to the establishment of Euskal Kulturaren Alde (EKA), a platform that, in line with the creation of the commission to promote Euskara Day in 1949, following the Seventh Basque Studies Congress in 1948, would have the objective of encouraging young people to use and learn Euskara and collecting funds to sponsor activities conducive to the spread of the language and its linguistic study. The cultural section ended by congratulating the Basque government-in-exile for its efforts to promote Basque cultural heritage and by applauding initiatives that could intensify the defense and development of Basque culture in general and Euskara in particular.[8]

The fourth and final section of the World Basque Congress was "The Basques in the World." The deliberations were attended by Pedro de Basaldua and Miguel Cristóbal, representing Argentina; Jon Bilbao, representing Cuba and the United States;

---

7. *Crónica del Congreso Mundial Vasco: París, 23 de septiembre al 1 de octubre de 1956*, 46–51, AA/AN FSAE, DP.1036.6.

8. *Congreso Mundial Vasco, C: Sección Cultural. Distribución de las comunicaciones recibidas según las disciplinas a las que se refieren*, AA/AN FSAE, DP.1036.3.

Pedro Aretxabala and Santiago Zarranz, representing Chile; Alfredo Ruiz del Castaño, representing Mexico; Juan Bautista Lasarte, representing Uruguay; and Joxe Mari Lasarte, Juan Olazabal, and Fernando Carranza, representing Venezuela. The delegates, on behalf of the Federation of Basque Organizations of Chile, the Basque center Euskal Erria of Montevideo (Uruguay), the Federation of Basque-Argentine Organizations, and the Basque Center of Caracas (Venezuela), agreed to establish the Confederation of Basque Organizations of the Americas (CEVA), with headquarters in the Basque center of Caracas, in accordance with the proposed bylaws and declaration of principles submitted by the Federation of Basque-Argentine Organizations and ratified at the congress.[9]

Eight months later, on May 18, 1957, at the Basque Center of Caracas, in accordance with article 6 of CEVA's bylaws, José María Etxezarreta was named president of the organization, and Joxe Mari Lasarte and Ramón Arozarena were named secretaries. On November 5, 1960, at the Laurak Bat Basque center in Buenos Aires, the first CEVA congress was held, attended by the new *lehendakari*, Jesús María Leizaola. The organization's new president, Lucio Aretxabaleta, presided over the congress's deliberations, assisted by its new secretaries, Andrés Irujo and Andoni Astigarraga, and delegates from the Basque organizations of Argentina, Brazil, Chile, Uruguay, and Venezuela attended.

The Basque World Congress of 1956 had the primary objective of seeking new strategic channels for anti-Franco action and consolidating the trust of all Basques in the Basque government, after twenty years of struggle in exile, as a legitimate representative of Basque sovereignty. It fulfilled its objectives, and the event met with a strong echo in the world press, both in Europe and in the Americas, which emphasized that, despite the repression of the dictatorship during these twenty years, the Basque people had known how to maintain and organize their struggle for liberty and democracy on their own soil and in exile, conducive to the overthrow of the Spanish military regime and the defense of their right as a nation to independence.

Although it is not often emphasized, the 1956 Paris meeting was timely, because Western societies—including the Basque Country—would soon begin a profound transformation, around 1958 and throughout the 1960s. For example, in calling the Second Vatican Council (1962–1965), Pope John XXIII gave a new impulse to the church; the Cuban missile crisis (1962), during John F. Kennedy's presidency, transformed international relations between the United States and the Soviet Union and resulted in an intensification of the Cold War; and social and economic transformations within Western society as a whole brought with them profound changes within the Basque Country as well.

Together with these transformations, a generational change also occurred in the Basque exile community: new political objectives; a surge in cultural activity on the part of the EKA organization and other similar cultural groups; the creation of the Eusko Gaztedi Indarra Caracas group and, more generally, the activity promoted by the

---

9. *Crónica del Congreso Mundial Vasco: París, 23 de septiembre al 1 de octubre de 1956*, 52, AA/AN FSAE, DP.1036.6.

Basque center in the Venezuelan capital throughout the 1960s and up to Franco's death; the first Aberri Eguna (Day of the Homeland) celebrations; the creation of Euskadi ta Askatasuna (ETA, Basque Homeland and Freedom); and so on. In short, all these developments reflected the beginnings of a new Basque exile community.

Whatever the case, the political equation began to founder during World War II, when the British government signed the first financial cooperation agreements with General Franco's regime and, still farther back, at the time of the timid international arbitration of the Non-Intervention Committee, before and after the bombardments of Durango and Gernika. The struggle against totalitarianism did not envisage in the long run—a position fueled by a utilitarian and even a commercial view of the conflict—a struggle in favor of democracy in Europe. From a perspective based on ideological criteria, it was quite difficult to foresee that the British government would cover up and later proscribe agreements between de Gaulle's Free France and the Basque National Council or that, thereafter, the Spanish regime would be admitted to the heart of the UN in exchange for the inclusion of a handful of satellite states.[10]

---

10. Iñaki Goiogana, Xabier Irujo, and Josu Legarreta, *Un nuevo 31: Ideología y estrategia del gobierno de Euzkadi durante la Segunda Guerra Mundial a través de la correspondencia de José Antonio Aguirre y Manuel Irujo* (Bilbao: Sabino Arana, 2007), 14.

13

Lehendakari Jose Antonio Agirre's Death in Exile

On Friday, March 18, 1960, in his office at the Paris delegation, the *lehendakari* confessed to Father Iñaki Azpiazu that he felt ill and that he was going to take the day off to rest over the weekend. But on March 19, he showed up at the delegation again, for which he was scolded by both Azpiazu himself and Alberro, Javier Landaburu, and Manuel Irujo, who were working that day. He assured them that he felt better and even told Irujo that, as usual, the two of them would have dinner that Saturday with Alberto Onaindia at his house in Paris, where they visited until 11:30 p.m., the time at which Irujo needed to catch the bus that would take him home.[1]

On Sunday, March 20, he spent all day in bed with a mild fever, but he attended a six p.m. Mass and received communion in his parish of Saint Pierre du Gros Caillou. On Monday, March 21, Mari Zabala, the *lehendakari*'s wife, called the delegation to say that her husband would be unable to come in to work because of a bad cold. Immediately, Azpiazu called Dr. Lasa to ask him to visit him, and he found Agirre with his bronchial passages very congested, for which reason he recommended that he rest in bed for at least a couple of days. On Tuesday, Zabala called the delegation again and told Azpiazu that her husband had gotten worse and felt severe pain in his chest, extending into his left arm, for which reason both Azpiazu and Lasa went in person to the president's residence. Lasa diagnosed angina, prescribed an anticoagulant, and ordered that he remain absolutely quiet and receive no visitors. But the *lehendakari* appeared to improve and even joked with Lasa, whom he asked to bring him the newspaper along with the medicine.

At 5:30 p.m. on March 22, Agirre asked his wife to bring him tea and pastries and the newspaper. She served him the refreshments and brought him a copy of *Le Monde*. Upon leaving the room, she heard him breathing with difficulty, and when she entered, she found her husband in the throes of death. He died minutes later. Friends and family began to arrive around 6:30 p.m., including Jesús María Leizaola, Alberto Onaindia, Javier Landaburu, Dr. Lasa, and Manuel Irujo. Zabala closed her husband's eyes, and the parochial coadjutor of Saint Pierre du Gros Caillou administered last rites.

---

1. Manuel Irujo, "Los últimos momentos de Jose Antonio, el primer presidente de Euzkadi," *Alderdi* 14, nos. 157–158 (May 1960): 7–8.

The *lehendakari*'s death deeply moved the Basque exiles. José Ignacio Lizaso, the Basque government delegate in London, noted that the position taken by the Allies (principally the United States and Great Britain) toward the Franco regime in 1955 had led to Agirre's sad premature death on March 22, 1960, at the age of fifty-six, after a lifetime of defending a political and cultural project for the Basque Country.

The wake was held in the first instance in his residence, where prominent figures of French, Spanish, Catalan, Galician, and Basque political and cultural life arrived. Late on March 24, Father Onaindia led a recital of the rosary in Euskara, and on the following day, the *lehendakari*'s body was transferred to the Basque government's delegation, where it remained throughout the day.[2] The funeral, officiated by Onaindia, was held in the parish church of Saint Pierre du Gros Caillou on Saturday morning, March 26. Larralde played the "Eusko Gudariak" and the Basque national anthem on the organ, and a Basque choir sang *Libera me* by Lorenzo Perosi.[3] The Mass was attended by the members of the family, accompanied by the leaders of the governments of Euskadi, Catalonia, and the Spanish republic in exile. Also present were prominent Frenchmen such as Georges Bidault, Francisque Gay, François Mauriac, Ernest Pezet, Jean Letourneau, and Paul Coste-Floret, and the ministers of the French republic Paul Bacon (labor), Edmond Michelet (veteran's affairs), and Robert Buron (public works) sent representatives. In addition, representatives of the Basque, Catalan, Galician, French, and Spanish political parties attended, as did the ambassadors of Chile and Venezuela.[4]

Once the funeral ceremonies ended at 12:30 p.m., the cortege departed for Donibane Lohitzune, where the body would be buried. After arriving in Poitiers around 6:45 p.m., the body was deposited in the church of Saint Hilare le Grand, and Father Azpiazu recited a prayer there. As Javier Landaburu recounted, it was an emotional moment because of the contrast between the intimacy of the ceremony and the magnificence of the church, at that hour practically empty.[5] The following morning, Sunday, March 27, the cortege departed for Burdeos, where it arrived at 1:15 p.m. and, after a ceremony in honor of the deceased, was received by a colony of Basques in Le Souquet, around ninety kilometers north of Donibane Lohitzune. The cortege finally reached Donibane at 5:00 p.m., where the group was awaited by a reception committee led by Telesforo Monzon, joined by several thousand people from various locations in Euskadi, who had arrived only after successfully overcoming the numerous limitations and obstacles imposed by the Spanish police, who practically closed the border to prevent the passage of sympathizers.[6]

---

2. EIB-OPE, March 23, 1960, 4.
3. "Le président Aguirre est mort," *Euzko Deya* (Paris), April 1, 1960, 1–4.
4. EIB-OPE, March 28, 1960, 3.
5. Javier Landaburu, "Después de la muerte del Lehendakari," *Alderdi* 14 (May 1960): 8–11.
6. "Les obsèques à Saint-Jean-de-Luz," *Euzko Deya* (Paris), April 1, 1960, 5–6.

From early afternoon that day until early morning on Monday, March 28, thousands stood in line to pay their respects to the deceased president at Monzon's house, where the body lay in repose. The flag of one of the companies of the Saseta Battalion was draped over the coffin. Around 9:30 a.m., the coffin was transferred to the local parish church, where Agirre's cousin Florentino Lekube said a funeral Mass, accompanied by a sizable group of sixty priests, including Monsignor Clément Mathieu, the bishop of Aire and Dax; Monsignor Larralt, a bishop expelled from China who was representing the bishop of Baiona; the abbot of the Benedictines of Belloc; and the prior of the Benedictines of Lazkao. At the end of Mass, Mathieu gave an eloquent eulogy, and at 11:30 a.m., the large crowd departed for the cemetery.[7]

At an emergency meeting held at the Basque government minister Arbizu's residence in Baiona, the ministers and other authorities and representatives of political parties, labor unions, and institutions of the Basque government-in-exile there agreed that Vice President Leizaola should immediately—in accordance with the law—assume the responsibilities of *lehendakari* of the Basque executive power. In consequence, when the coffin was set down in front of the cemetery gate in Donibane Lohitzune, Jesús María Leizaola stepped forward and took the oath of office as president of the government of Euzkadi,[8] a responsibility he would exercise until after the fall of Franco's regime in 1975. Subsequently, the coffin was deposited in the cemetery chapel, and visitation began that same day, in consideration of those who had not been able to cross the border over the weekend. On April 15, a Friday, during a private ceremony attended by around three hundred people, the coffin was finally interred in a tomb that the government of Euzkadi had had constructed in the cemetery.

Memorial services in memory of the *lehendakari* were held in practically all the Basque colonies of the Americas. The Basques of Argentina, Australia, Brazil, Chile, Colombia, Guatemala, Mexico, Uruguay, and Venezuela organized no fewer than a hundred funeral Masses, religious services, and memorial services in memory of the president.[9] Innumerable prominent figures in public life of the Americas sent their condolences to the *lehendakari*'s family, as well as to the members of the government-in-exile. This was the case, for example, of the Venezuelan House of Representatives, which published in the March 25 issue of the *Gaceta Oficial* a memorial to the death of Jose Antonio Agirre, "a representative figure of the Basque people and a worthy defender of liberty, democracy, and social justice."[10]

Likewise, and despite repression, religious services in memory of Agirre were organized in around one hundred localities in the Basque Country. Especially moving ceremonies took place, such as that of the political prisoners in Larrinaga prison who

7. Telesforo Monzon, "Agirre Lehendakariaren gauilla," *Alderdi* 14 (May 1960): 11–17.

8. "Acuerdos del Gobierno de Euzkadi y del Consejo Consultivo Vasco," *Euzko Deya* (Paris), April 1, 1960, 7.

9. EIB-OPE, April 1, 1960, 3.

10. *Alderdi* 14 (May 1960): 31.

prayed the rosary together on their knees and refused that day's food. And the memorial services and ceremonies in honor of the *lehendakari* held in the last days of March continued into April, when the Basque government decided to dedicate the Aberri Eguna, celebrated on Sunday, April 17, 1960, to the memory of Jose Antonio Agirre, with a Mass in the parish church of Donibane Lohitzune officiated by Jokin Zaitegi.[11] Likewise, the regular Easter Sunday Masses in practically all the Basque centers in the Americas were also celebrated in memory of the *lehendakari*.

Jose Antonio Agirre's death was followed by a second presidential administration of the Basque government-in-exile, headed by Jesus María Leizaola, which would extend until four years after the fall of Franco's regime in November 1975. On Saturday, December 15, 1979, after forty-three years in exile, Leizaola returned to Euskadi, where he was received by more than forty thousand people packed into the San Mamés soccer stadium, who, singing the "Eusko Gudariak," said their final farewells to a government that had fought in exile since June 1937. The following day, in a formal ceremony held in Gernika, Leizaola symbolically transferred the office of *lehendakari* to Carlos Garaikoetxea, whom the Basque people had democratically elected as president of the Basque Council. So began a new stage in the history of Euskadi.

11. EIB-OPE, March 31, 1960, 1.

14

Final Considerations

In July 1936, Mola's revolt against the Republic in Nafarroa set in motion a wave of exiles who fled the wave of war and Francoist repression to the nearest available safety: the remaining, and dwindling, territory of the legitimately elected Basque government. Among the many terrible stories of exile, the exile of thirty-two thousand children younger than sixteen years in 1936 and 1937 stands out. Many of these children never returned home, and many others never saw their parents again.

From the summer of 1937—when the coup forces took Bilbao—a second phase of exile began and until the fall of Barcelona in the spring of 1939 the epicenter of this tsunami of exile shifted to Barcelona, as the Basque government struggled to administer an exile that initially affected nearly two hundred thousand Basque citizens. During this time, the Basque government organized colonies (schools) for evacuated children, sought to repatriate as many families as requested it, and created hospitals and a placement service for working-age men and women who found themselves refugees without the possibility of returning to their homes in Hegoalde. Finally, the Basque government organized its Paris headquarters, where the guiding principles were developed for what would become its national and international policies during at least the first decade of its history, from 1939 to 1955.

The fall of Barcelona meant the beginning of a third phase of exile, lasting from the fall of 1938 to the fall of 1940. Attacks by groups and parties of the French extreme right in the spring of 1939 and the German occupation that came about in the brief space of a month, between May and June of that year, forced numerous Basques to flee Europe. These events, together with the already-strong Basque tradition of emigration to the Americas, were some of the decisive factors that led to the first wave of exiles to the Americas. Unlike the first two phases of the Basque political exile, caused by Franco's insurrection, in this third phase of exile, the Basques were escaping from German troops and police, who were persecuting them in collaboration with the Spanish secret police and the Vichy regime's forces. Hence, it was an exile caused by the German occupation, not directly by the Spanish dictatorship. In fact, on November 30, 1940, Heinrich Müller, head of the Gestapo, ordered that "Spanish Reds" up to fifty-five years of age who had worked for the French army be sent to German concentration camps. This measure, agreed to with the Spanish police, had already begun to be implemented in August

1940 and had as a consequence the detention, torture, and death of numerous Basque, Catalan, and Spanish exiles. As a result, between February and September 1939, around ten ships carried Basque exiles who, departing from the ports of Iparralde, Burdeos, or Marseilles, escaped the horror under which Europe was suffering and headed for the Americas.

The fourth phase of the Basque exile lasted from May 1940 to October 1941. As a consequence of the disappearance of *Lehendakari* Agirre following the events at Dunkirk in May 1940, the Basque National Council, led by Manuel Irujo, was formed in London; it was an institution that would represent the Basques until Agirre's reappearance a year and a half later. In line with the Basque national platform approved in Meudon in the spring of 1939, the London National Council negotiated active Basque participation in World War II directly with the British government and with the French Empire Defense Council, led by Charles de Gaulle, in exchange for recognition of an independent Basque state after the war. During this fourth phase of exile, between 1940 and 1942, a second great wave of Basque emigration to the Americas took place. On July 26, 1940, the ship *St. Dominique* left Burdeos for Mexico. On January 15, 1941, the *Alsina* left from Marseilles to Senegal, and on November 4, 1941, the *Quanza* headed for Mexico. The *Río de la Plata* left Cuba for Argentina on March 12, 1942. The Portuguese-flagged *Nyassa* carried the last large group of Basque exiles escaping from occupied Europe, departing for the Americas on May 22, 1942.

Lehendakari Agirre's reappearance in October 1941 marked the beginning of the fifth phase of the Basque exile, lasting until the end of World War II. In line with the political principles of Meudon, the Basque government concluded agreements with the Roosevelt administration under which the Basque intelligence services would collaborate with US intelligence until 1949. The agreements led to *Lehendakari* Agirre's trip to various South American countries between August and October 1942 and helped strengthen the network of Basque delegations in South America.

This hopeful fifth period gave way at the beginning of October 1945 to a sixth period of uncertainty that lasted from the end of World War II until 1950. Once the war was over, and in response to the Basque government's clear commitment to the Allied cause and the open collaboration of Franco's government with Axis forces, the UN sentenced the Spanish government to international isolation and vetoed its entry into the organization. Between 1945 and 1950, the chief challenge of the Basque government-in-exile's international policy would be to maintain the Spanish regime's international isolation, for the purpose of causing General Franco's fall. The years 1947 and 1948 were ones of transition in this regard. The Franco-Perón protocol signed in 1948 was the first rupture in the Spanish regime's isolation, notably easing UN pressure on Franco's regime in the Cold War context.

After the years of transition came the crisis of the interval from 1950 to 1955. Between the winter of 1949 and 1953, the Basque government began to suffer the financial consequences from the cancelation of the agreements reached with the US administration on intelligence matters. Together with this, on November 4, 1950, the day after the Chinese intervention in the Korean War, with thirty-eight votes in favor, twelve abstentions, and only ten votes in opposition, and after just two hours of debate, the Fifth Session of the UN General Assembly accepted the Special Political Commission's proposal to withdraw the punitive measures imposed on the Spanish regime. From January 30, 1953, the Spanish dictatorship would be a member of UNESCO, and in that same year, Franco's regime signed a concordat with the Vatican and an economic-strategic accord with Eisenhower's Republican administration. Finally, and certainly shamefully, the representatives of the powers on the UN Security Council negotiated the entry of several countries into the UN community while snacking on the caviar, smoked salmon, and roast chicken brought to their meeting by Soviet representative Vasily V. Kuznetsov on November 23, 1955. After several rounds of voting, in which a total of seventeen vetoes were cast in a single day, with eight votes in favor and the abstention of the United States, China, and Belgium, the Security Council agreed on the Spanish state's entry into the UN.[1] In this way, the Eastern Bloc added four new members to the UN, and the West, for its part, added six. Finally, the third-way bloc succeeded in including another six new members on the list, including two Arab countries. On the following day, together with fifteen other countries and with fifty-five votes in favor, Franco was admitted into the UN community by the tenth session of the General Assembly.

The Spanish regime's admission to the UN community led to the final period of the Basque political exile, a period of profound crisis that would mark the last five years of *Lehendakari* Agirre's government-in-exile, until his death in 1960.

The Basque government did not achieve—not in 1937 or during the prewar first exile or in 1946 during the postwar era—its principal objective: to undermine General Franco's neofascist regime until it could be ousted. Instead, from 1937 on, the Basque government managed to establish a durable political network and a structure, by intensifying its resistance efforts year by year. Indeed, this structure grew and expanded right up to 1975. Elsewhere, from 1937 on, it also managed to publicize and promote the historical and political rights of the Basque Country at the international level, both in the Americas and in Europe. Finally, the Basque government-in-exile also managed to encourage, create, and stimulate a network of Basque institutions in the Americas that united around the political struggle of the Basque Country, as well as international organizations that brought together the Basque delegations and centers and other Basque organizations. Together with these three main political goals, the Basque government's political trajectory facilitated a debate of Spain's new 1978 constitution by presenting a stable, lasting, and progressive program it had defended and maintained for four decades. When *Lehendakari* Jesús María Leizaola made way for Carlos Garaikoetxea in 1979, the Basque government, which had for so long maintained the ideals of human

1. UN doc. 109 (1955), Resolution of December 14, 1955 (S/3509); see also "En el laberinto de la ONU," EIB-OPE, December 15, 1955, 3.

rights, the political right of self-determination for the Basque people, and the principle of the historical and cultural singularity of the Basques, was the only legitimate Basque republican organization that remained active in international politics.

The study of the Basque government that Agirre led in exile between 1937 and 1960 poses a fundamental question: what factors explain the survival of the Basque government-in-exile for thirty-eight years? The response is to be found in three decisive factors: first, the markedly democratic practices of the Basque government-in-exile attracted the interest, sympathy, and solidarity of democratic political parties, governments, and institutions, both in the Americas and in Europe, to the Basque cause; second, the development of institutionalized networks of Basque communities and centers in the Americas, the Philippines, and certain European regions helped maintain the government's vitality and facilitated its administrative work in exile; third, the authority of the leaders in the Basque government and the assimilation by Basque communities in the Americas of the political program they defended facilitated to a significant extent the Basque diaspora's support and popular backing for the political project represented by the Basque government-in-exile.

With regard to the first factor, the attitude of the Basque government and of the nationalist parties and forces that formed that government-in-exile (e.g., EAJ-PNV, EAE-ANV, Jagi-jagi, ELA-STV) always were decidedly on the side of democracy, human rights, the republican political system, and a federalist and pan-European conception of the European Community. This fact explains the attitude of Christian-Democratic writers such as Jacques Maritain, François Mauriac, and Georges Bernanos toward the Basque government. They were not the only ones: writers, thinkers, and humanists of evident democratic stamp such as Germaine Malaterre-Sellier, Louis Martin Chauffier, Emmanuel Mounier, Marc Sangnier, Yves Simon, Paul Vignaux, Claude Bourdet, Jacques Maudale, Maurice Merleau-Ponty, Stanislas Foumet, Francisque Gay, and Georges Bidault always showed themselves ready to collaborate with the Basque government-in-exile and to take an active part in the International League of Friends of the Basques (LIAB).

And the support shown by certain political forces and leaders of the European democracies in 1939 and 1940 would be repeated in the Americas. On October 9, 1941, coming from Brazil, *Lehendakari* Agirre arrived in Uruguay, where with the mediation of Alberto Guani, foreign minister in the Uruguayan government, the Congress of Deputies held a session in honor of the *lehendakari* on October 15, giving him the opportunity to set out his political project and demonstrating the acceptance of the Uruguayan people and their government to the Basque nationalist ideal. This attitude did not cease in subsequent years. All the presidents of Uruguay between 1941 and 1955—Alfredo Baldomir, Juan José Amezaga, Tomás Berreta, and Luis Batlle Berres—collaborated actively with the Basque government's delegation in that country; the annual meetings held between the Basque government's delegate and the Uruguayan president during the period are a clear example and reflection of this collaboration. The support provided was institutional and political, but also social. In addition to the presidents' support, the Basque delegation during these years could rely on that of the most renowned members of Uruguayan literature's so-called generation of serene masters (Raul Montero Bustamante, Carlos and María Eugenia Vaz Ferreira, Juan Zorrilla de San Martín, Juana Ibarbourou, Eduardo Acevedo, José Pedro Varela Acevedo, Carlos Sabat Ercasty, Emilio Oribe); of Christian democrats and members of the Catholic Church (Dardo Regules, Antonio María Barbieri, and Juan Andrés Ramírez); that of prominent figures in university life (Eduardo J. Couture Etcheverry, Leopoldo Agorio Etcheverry, Eduardo Berro García); and that of other influential individuals in the political, diplomatic, academic, and cultural worlds of Uruguay at that time.

A good example of this collaboration is that of Justino Zabala Muniz, an essayist, writer, congressional deputy, senator, member of the Uruguayan National Council of Government, minister of education (named in 1952), and communications director of the Official Radio Broadcasting Service, who was himself a descendent of Basque emigrants and was exiled in Brazil during the dictatorship of Gabriel Terra. After Spain was admitted to UNESCO in 1953, Zabala, a radical democrat, in 1954 named Bingen Ametzaga a press representative for the eighth UNESCO General Assembly, to be held in Montevideo, and at the urging of that Basque delegate, he invited Javier Landaburu and Alberto Onaindia to the assembly as representatives of the Basque government. When the General Assembly met, the invitees read the reports of Jose Antonio Agirre and Manuel Irujo in a plenary session, and Zabala himself read out the long list of teachers whom the Spanish regime had shot or dismissed, one by one, in the presence of Joaquín Ruiz Jiménez, the Spanish dictatorship's representative at the assembly.[2] This event can be explained only from a perspective of profound collaboration fostered by a shared vision of democratic values and comprehensive respect for human rights.

Nor was Uruguay in any way an isolated case, as the Basque government-in-exile's delegations carried out an impressive diplomatic labor throughout the length and breadth of the Americas. What has been said about the presidents of Uruguay also applies to Argentine President Mario Ortiz; Chilean President Pedro Aguirre Cerdá; and the Venezuelan presidents Rómulo Betancourt, Raul Leoni, Rafael Caldera, and Carlos Andrés Pérez. In this regard, as far as the Basque government's propaganda activities are concerned, it is necessary to highlight the efforts made, starting in 1947, to enable the publication and distribution of the *Boletín de la Oficina de Prensa de Euskadi*, issued by the press service of the Basque government in Paris. The press delegation in Montevideo alone saw to the publication of more than six hundred articles in the Uruguayan press between 1943 and 1955, an article a week.

The legitimacy and social acceptance enjoyed by the Basque centers in the Americas likewise enabled to a large extent the diplomatic work of the Basque delegations and facilitated the support of various Western Hemisphere governments in the context of the UN policy of isolating the Spanish regime between 1946 and 1955. In general,

2. Bingen Ametzaga to Jose Antonio Agirre, Montevideo, October 20, 1954.

the Basque centers enjoyed a great deal of influence in the governments of the countries of the Americas, to the point that in the case of Uruguay, Juan José Amezaga, president and descendant of Basques, was a member of the Euskalerria Basque center in Montevideo. This fact likewise explains why in many countries the influence of the Basque government between 1942 and 1955 was more decisive than that of the Republican government-in-exile or even, in the most extreme cases, such as those of Uruguay and Venezuela, than that of the Spanish government itself. In general terms, the Basque government logically obtained the support of democratic governments, whereas Franco's regime was able to benefit from the support of the Latin American dictatorships. In this regard, the Basque government-in-exile's delegations proved especially active in Argentina between 1940 and 1942, in Chile during and after World War II, in Mexico (working through the Republican government-in-exile) between 1940 and 1955, in Uruguay between 1941 and 1955, and in Venezuela between 1940 and 1942 and subsequent to the arrival of democracy in the late 1950s.

However, the triumphs of the Basque government within the democracies of the Americas had their other side when significant diplomatic clashes occurred between Western Hemisphere totalitarianism and the Basque political class in exile. In the case of the Dominican Republic, starting in 1950 and according to Trujillo's wishes, the Basque exiles were moved from Santo Domingo to Venezuela or Mexico, even if, due fundamentally to the harsh criticisms levied against Trujillo's dictatorial government by Jesús Galíndez in his doctoral dissertation, the execution of the former took place in 1956. The decrees that Argentina's President Ortiz approved in 1940 to facilitate Basque emigration to that country were annulled by Colonel Perón in 1947 at the request of Spanish ambassador José María Areilza. Following Ekin's publication of *Para qué . . . ?* (For what . . . ?) by Juan A. Ansaldo on June 13, 1951, and with Areilza's intervention, the publishing house closed on November 8 and 9 and its director Andrés Irujo was brought in to the police station.[3] In the same way, following the coup d'état against President Rómulo Gallegos in 1948 and the subsequent dictatorship of Marcos Pérez Jiménez between 1952 and 1958, the Venezuelan government voted in favor of the Spanish regime's admission to the UN community. Once a democratic regime had been reestablished in Venezuela under President Rómulo Betancourt in 1958, the door to institutional collaboration between the Basque government-in-exile and the Venezuelan government was opened once again.

In addition to its ideological firmness, the Basque government was capable of maintaining a united and centralized organization in the Americas and Europe during the years of exile thanks to a communications system rooted in both hemispheres. Unlike what happened during the Basque exiles of the nineteenth century, the political struggle that the Basque government pursued from 1937 onward succeeded in uniting the whole of the Basque diaspora in Latin America around a single ideal, with unprecedented

3. "Por qué se prohibió el libro de Alsaldo en la Argentina," EIB-OPE, July 9, 1953, 4.

strength. In this regard, the Basque centers were the central point of encounter for the Basque exiles. This fact can be explained taking into account that the three chief functions of these institutions in the Americas coincided to a large extent with the work of the Basque government-in-exile. On the one hand, the centers sought to bring Basque citizens together and to maintain living and dynamic Basque societies in the Americas. This was linked to high rates of endogamy and to the fact that, after a century and a half of migration, the new generations of Basques arriving in the Americas turned fundamentally to these meeting places. Second, the organization of sports and cultural events to keep Basque traditions alive in these centers across the generations was among the associations' chief objectives. Finally, receiving, welcoming, and aiding recently arrived Basque immigrants in starting a new life in a foreign country was also one of the Basque centers' fundamental functions.

All these objectives complemented the Basque government-in-exile's activities, and that organization of a political struggle succeeded in uniting the aspirations and labors of the Basques of Europe and the Americas for four decades. The Basque government's first delegation was that of Buenos Aires, created on November 15, 1938, and made up of Ramón María Aldasoro, Santiago Cuchillos, Ixaka Lopez Mendizabal, and Pablo Artxanko. The Venezuelan delegation was created on February 23, 1940, with José Mara Garate at its head; the Boise subdelegation was created on March 11, 1940, the work of Jon Bilbao; and that of the Dominican Republic was created on the same day, under the leadership of Eusebio Irujo. The Panama delegation was set up on July 22, 1941, with Juan González Mendoza at the head, and Pedro Aretxabala was charged with leading the Chilean delegation beginning on October 9, 1941. Although the Montevideo delegation was created earlier, it was Agirre himself who organized it around Ricardo Gisasola in November 1941, then around Bingen Ametzaga starting in August 1943.

In substance, the delegations were embassies of the Basque government that worked to strengthen Euskal Herria's political, commercial, and cultural relations abroad. From this perspective, the Basque national platform that Agirre proposed was no mere ideological option but a material necessity. Beginning in 1939, when the government of the Republic was in a state of complete disintegration and relations with the Basque government had sharply deteriorated, both the Basque National Council and the Basque government itself, following Agirre's reappearance, reaffirmed the necessity of collaborating with the republican government-in-exile, but also the imperative necessity of exercising their functions autonomously and independently in forums such as the UN and the European Community, as well as in diplomatic relations with governments in the Americas and Europe. Moreover, even if the Republican government assisted the Basque government financially during the first years in exile, there is no doubt that from 1945 onward the Basque government-in-exile was entirely independent of the government of the Republic.

The Basque national platform that the *lehendakari* proposed in Meudon was not simply the program of one nationalist party; rather, it responded to economic needs and to an extremely delicate political situation in which it would have been impossible to move forward in any other way. The Basque government's administrative independence made it possible to manage the exile of thirty-two thousand minors, as well as the schools and health and infirmary services they required; it also made it possible to provide assistance to prisoners, victims of reprisals, and exiles. It was only in virtue of this administrative independence that the Basque government was able to negotiate with the French government in 1939 and 1940 for the release of Basque refugees interned in concentration camps and to see that the necessary material and spiritual aid reached them. An exemplary case was that of Iñaki Azpiazu, a chaplain with the Catholic Refugee Aid Committee; another was that of Victoriano Gambra, better known as Aita Patxi. According to the historian Hilari Raguer, as a consequence of his dedication to the Basque prisoners and refugees, those who were at his side could be heard to say, "I'm an agnostic, but I believe in the God of Aita Patxi."[4]

After the Basque government's health minister Alfredo Espinosa was shot in 1937, it was Eliodoro de la Torre who took responsibility for the Basque government-in-exile's Ministry of Health beginning in 1937. In the course of this work, de la Torre created the La Roseraie hospital in Bidart, the Osasuna infirmary for pulmonary illnesses in Kanbo, and the Berck-Plage sanatorium for 350 refugee children from Gorlitz. Minister de la Torre remained in Marseilles until 1941, organizing and administering from there the exiles' journey to American shores, and once they arrived in Argentina, Chile, Cuba, the Dominican Republic, Uruguay, or Venezuela, the Basque exiles found delegations made up of members of the Basque centers and of the Basque government's various delegations waiting for them in their ports of arrival, thus enabling them to avoid the quarantines that other groups of exiles were forced to endure.

Moreover, in virtue of the Political Responsibilities Act, many of the exiles were deprived of their rights of citizenship, such that, made stateless and hence citizens without rights or documents, it was extremely difficult for them to obtain documents that would allow them to enter Latin American countries. With the intention of providing a solution to this problem, the Basque Relief Committee and the General Interests of Euskadi Committee were created on December 16, 1938. These institutions gave rise to the creation of the LIAB in France in April 1939. In the same way, the Refugee Relief Committee was created in France on August 29, 1939, through the mediation of the EAJ-PNV, and finally, the Pro-Basque Immigration Committee was created through the mediation of the Basque government's delegation in Buenos Aires. Thanks to the intervention of this last committee, on January 18 and 20, 1940, Argentine President Ortiz approved a decree granting citizenship and all civil and political rights inherent therein to all those recommended by the Pro-Basque Immigration Committee, chaired by José Urbano Agirre, without any bureaucratic procedures and within fifteen days.

4. Interview with Hilari Raguer, Monastery of Montserrat, July 23, 2010. See also, Raguer i Suñer, Hilari, *Aita Patxi: Prisioneros con los Gudaris* (Barcelona: Claret, 2006).

My own grandparents thus obtained passports and paid employment in Buenos Aires within fifteen days after their arrival in the port, where they were received with full honors after having been exiled, interned in a concentration camp, and sentenced to death in Europe. Perhaps it was because of all this that Pierre Dumas wrote that "few human groups throughout history have offered more beautiful examples of solidarity and of the spirit of organization than the Basques. It might be said that a 'better-organized exile' was never seen."[5]

Thanks to the ideological and strategic decisions taken in Meudon, many lives were saved, and many Basque refugees were fed, educated, and cared for. This line of action enabled the Basque government to ensure the safety of many prisoners scattered across French territory who would otherwise have been transported to German death camps. The Basque national platform formulated at Meudon was in the last analysis a decision based on responsibility. Moreover, the correspondence of the Dominican Republic and Montevideo delegations demonstrate that numerous Catalans and Spaniards were able to enter American countries thanks to the work of the Basque delegations, as the Republican government lacked services in those countries. Such was the case, for example, of Pilar Escosura, who, having arrived in Santo Domingo, Dominican Republic, as a widow on her own with her young son, turned to the local Basque delegation as the only institution that had some success in helping refugees who arrived there escaping from the war, without money, in many cases lacking the papers necessary to enter another country, and without knowing anyone who might be able to help them. After she obtained an interview with the Basque delegate and confessed to him that she was not Basque, he gave her the necessary papers to enter Venezuela as a Basque—perhaps by fortune, many years later, the delegate's daughter married the son who was accompanying her.[6] Pilar Escosura's case was not an exception. Hundreds of Spaniards and Catalans entered Venezuela as Basques through the offices of the delegation in Santo Domingo alone.

The possession of a shared political objective generated a very high level of political awareness and participation or volunteerism, both among the exiles and among the Basques of the centers that received them. This was fundamentally a political exile, similar to other exiles suffered by the Basques during Alfonso XIII's dictatorship (1923–1931) and earlier, following the wars of the nineteenth century, between 1833 and 1876. In virtue of the political background of the 1936 exile, the level of political involvement was comparable and proportional to the repression exercised by the Spanish, French, and German regimes against the Basque exiles as a group. The *lehendakari*, the ministers of the EAJ-PNV, and the members of the EBB who took part in the Meudon meetings in 1939 all did so with the independence of Euskal Herria in mind, an ideological posi-

5. Pierre Dumas, *Euzkadi: Les Basques devant la guerre d'Espagne* (Paris: Éditions de l'Aube, 1938), 47.

6. Interview with Pilar Escosura, Caracas, Venezuela, November 1991.

tion that won generalized favor among the Basques of the Americas for the first time in virtue of the reality of the dictatorship on Basque soil.

The exiles of 1936 were ideological militants who as a group had a very prolific bibliographic production. There was a constant demand for bulletins, periodicals, and books by the Basques, exiles or not, living in the Basque centers of the Americas. The cultural activity of the exiles as a group between 1937 and 1955 was abundant, both in the political sphere and in literature, history, philosophy, anthropology, and other areas of human knowledge, to such an extent that practically all the exile institutions and societies had their own newspapers or periodicals. Basque centers, political parties, delegations, and the Basque government itself were able to produce publications like those of the Ekin publishing house, the Buenos Aires *Boletín del Instituto Americano de Estudios Vascos*, *Euzko Izpar Banatzea*, *Euzko Deya*, *Gernika*, *Ikuska*, and *Los Vascos en Venezuela*. Bibliographic production in the Basque language was also abundant.

The two Basque nationalist parties and the labor unions and groups that made up the Basque government also published periodicals or newspapers, and this entire system was maintained through a subscription system, as a kind of cooperative, until 1975. As an example, members of the EAJ-PNV in Caracas, in addition to their donations for the construction and maintenance of the local Basque center and the Basque government, might also pay subscriptions as a member of the ELA-STV and for the periodicals *Alderdi*, *Euzkadi*, *Gudari*, the Paris *Euzko Deya*, and *Tierra Vasca—Eusko Lur*, in addition to annual fees to receive *Euzko Izpar Banatzea—Boletín de la Oficina de Prensa de Euskadi*, the bulletin published by the Basque government's press office. In addition, there were also collaborations dedicated to promoting literary and cultural production in Basque, developed by the Societies of Friends of the Basque Language, such as the periodical *Euzko Gogoa*. In all these cases, the periodicals survived thanks to the subscriptions or donations of Basques in the diaspora; it must be noted that exile generally did not favor economic prosperity and that most Basque exile families enjoyed an adequate standard of living but one that was austere and lacking in luxuries.

The bibliographic production was likewise extremely abundant. Going through Bingen Ametzaga's library in Caracas, I found some 69 books written between 1936 and 1956 in the area of politics or political commentary; 66 books dedicated to legal history; 140 on Basque linguistics; around 100 translations, not counting the translations included in ten years of *Euzko Gogoa*; another 100 dramatic and poetic works written in Euskara; 182 devotional books in Euskara; 53 literary works and republished classics; 15 literary works in Spanish; 32 books in the area of literary criticism; 37 on the history of Euskal Herria; and 114 on Basque ethnology, art, and culture. In total, this was a bibliographic production of more than nine hundred titles related to Basque language, history, culture, or politics.

Between 1877 and 1977, the Basque diaspora published more than 130 newspapers and periodicals spread across thirteen countries on three continents, that is, some eighty thousand pages published outside Euskal Herria over the course of a century, or around eight hundred pages a year. *Laurac Bat*, a periodical published by the Laurac Bat Basque center in Buenos Aires (1878–1975), and the periodicals of the Basque-Nafarroan Beneficent Association of Havana (1890–1972) came close to completing a century of existence. *Euzko Izpar Banatzea—Boletín de la Oficina de Prensa de Euskadi*, the Basque government's bulletin, came out three times a week for thirty years (1947–1977), for a total of 7,001 issues, or 35,085 pages.

A fundamental factor in explaining the persistence of a government-in-exile for forty years is the authority of the political leaders who made up the Basque government. These political leaders had to confront the economic difficulties associated with being away from home, had to give up seeing their homeland ever again, and had to suffer from a distance the deaths of parents or loved ones whom the majority would never see again. To all this must be added the anguish, torture, and torment suffered by many of the Basque government's leaders as a result of the political persecution to which they were subject or to their work in the resistance. In this regard, the example of numerous Basque priests who, like Aita Patxi, risked or gave their lives for their congregants on numerous occasions, Leizaola's personal decision to remain in Bilbao until only hours before the city's fall to personally turn over the prisoners and so guarantee their lives, Agirre's odyssey through German-controlled territory in 1940 and 1941, the decision by Ajuriagerra and Rezola to return to Euskadi and voluntarily surrender as prisoners to face a certain death sentence after the Italian and Spanish violation of the Pact of Santoña, and other similar actions helped propagate the respect for the authorities of the Basque government-in-exile. Prominent Basques of a variety of creeds and ideologies, such as Aita Patxi and the Communist leader Dolores Ibárruri "La Pasionaria," were known far beyond their own cultural and political borders and became iconic figures of exile and of the struggle for human rights, both in Europe and in the Americas. Finally, the violent deaths of well-known individuals, such as the minister Alfredo Espinosa, Jose "Aitzol" Ariztimuño, and Esteban "Lauaxeta" Urkiaga, in addition to the thousands of Basques shot, tortured, imprisoned, or exiled, undoubtedly favored the adhesion of Basques in diaspora communities to the Basque government and the institutional support of foreign governments for it, all of which helps explain this government's survival and continued activity in exile for four decades.

Within the government-in-exile there were no known cases of corruption, and offices that did receive salaries—the great majority of the most active members of the Basque government-in-exile never received a salary—received very low salaries. It is a remarkable fact that salaries were calculated on the basis of the number of the incumbent's dependent children rather than the work performed. In addition, Agirre knew how to overcome the difficulties of conflicting ideological perspectives, thereby forging a homogeneous and united group at the heart of the Basque government. The democratic political program and respect for human rights in the face of the horror of the Western dictatorships likewise helped the political delegates who defended the Basque government-in-exile's policies to enjoy popularity among the Basque communities, at the same time that it based their mandate on the political authority and dignity that come with the defense of human rights in the face of despotic governments.

The Basque exile of 1936 also has distinctive characteristics from earlier Basque exiles. First, unlike the exiles of the nineteenth century and the 1920s, it affected people of all ages. Often, entire families arrived in the Americas: husbands and wives with children and even grandparents. From 1936 onward, thousands of children experienced exile and long years of separation from their families. In contrast, the exile affected individuals and families from all social classes. Families with little or no property escaped together with families with some capital, and as a consequence, the social ties generated in the Basque centers also varied. On the one hand, the majority had lost all their possessions; on the other hand, some exiles succeeded in making large amounts of money in the Americas; and finally, Basques who had succeeded in making large fortunes in the Americas as exiles or emigrants before 1936 collaborated with exile networks, so that there continued to be a wide range of variation among the families who gathered at the Basque centers between 1937 and 1960.

It was also an extraordinarily long exile, affecting two entire generations between 1936 and 1975. Although return was the main focus of the Basque political exile, only the second generation of Basque exiles, most of them born in the Americas after 1940, would be able to return, and it would be to this generation, fundamentally after 1960, coinciding with *Lehendakari* Agirre's death, that the task of bearing witness to the political struggle during the last fifteen years of exile would fall. These exiles always evinced a greater intention of returning to Euskal Herria than the exiles or emigrants of the nineteenth century. If in the eyes of many Basque emigrants the Americas were a land of hard and generally ill-paid work, for the exiles, the Americas were the land of liberty that had taken them in when they were in flight and persecuted by a military government. As Andrés Irujo said, "The Americas were the umbilical cord that linked us to Euskadi, so that, being Basques and hence Europeans, all of us children of exile are also Americans at heart."[7]

Although return was the dream of many Basque emigrants and exiles, when the former returned to their native land after several decades in the Americas, they found another reality, one to some degree alien to them. Thus, during the nineteenth and twentieth centuries, some of those emigrants who returned to Euskadi after making money in the Americas decided after a year or two on Basque soil to return to the Americas, as they were unable to adapt to the new reality they found after years of absence. This was not the case of the exiles, who knew that they would find a situation different from the one they left, and for whom it was precisely the challenge posed by the overthrow of Franco's regime and the restoration of democracy or the defense of the Basque people's historical rights that increased their desire to return and mitigated the pain of returning after long years of absence. The exiles of 1936 possessed a political project for Euskal

7. Interviews with Andrés Irujo, Buenos Aires, October 23–November 20, 1991.

Herria, a desire to bring to fruition the dream that proved impossible in 1936, and the intention to return democracy to Euskadi some day—this belief in a political project is another factor that explains the persistence of the Basque government-in-exile.

Ignorant of what the future would bring them, many exiles embarked in Marseilles without even knowing at what port the ship departing from Europe would leave them. Uncertainty was one of the exiles' greatest concerns. In unfamiliar countries, amid strange societies, without knowing for certain when they would reunite with their families or even whether they would see their relatives and friends again, separated from all that they had known and loved for decades, many literary authors of the Basque exile took refuge in nostalgia, and the old life and the old ways were the topic of conversation around countless dinner tables. In many Basque exiles' homes, it was not unusual to see the suitcase with which they had arrived in the Americas above the lintel of the front door. They kept it there as a sign that they would indeed one day pack it once more and make the return trip to see their native soil again and witness the fulfillment of their political project. "Chesterton tells the story that one day, as he was in his cozy retreat in Battersea packing for a vacation trip, a friend came in and asked him where he was going. Chesterton then had to explain to him, in his inimitable paradoxical style, that his destination was precisely Battersea. Certainly, he was heading off to Paris, Belfast, Heidelberg, Frankfurt, but this pilgrimage through various parts of Europe had ultimately no other object than that of finding an island named England and within it, a pleasant place by the name of Battersea, at the sight of whose marvels his eyes, renewed by that pilgrimage, would rejoice as never before."[8]

---

8. Bingen Ametzaga Aresti, "La comarca y el mundo," *El Plata* (Montevideo), 1953.

Biographical Appendix

I have included in this appendix biographical sketches of forty distinguished individuals associated with the Basque government-in-exile who were especially active in the political and cultural spheres between 1937 and 1960. Place and year of birth and death follow each name.

Francisco Abrisketa Irakulis, Bilbao, 1913–Bilbao, 1983. After obtaining degrees in economics and law from the University of Deusto, Abrisketa found work in the Economic Studies Section of Banco de Vizcaya. Following the outbreak of the war and the formation of the Basque government, he was named adviser to the Ministry of Industry, as a consequence of which, following the occupation of Bilbao in 1937, he went into exile in Baiona, where he continued collaborating with the Basque government until late 1937. From there, he moved to Bogotá, where he worked at the Centro de Estudios de la Dirección Nacional de Estadística (National Statistics Board's Studies Center), part of the Office of the Comptroller General of the Republic (1937–1940). In 1938, he was named the Basque government's delegate in Bogotá, an office he held until 1946. Together with Alberto Ricaurte, he established the firm Industrias Ricaute y Abrisqueta Ltd. and was an adviser to the Bank of the Republic and the National Accounting Office (1941–1945). He was professor of economics and statistics at the National University and the Xavierian Pontifical University (1938–1945), which earned him an appointment as head of the Statistics Section of the Pan-American Union, the precursor to the Organization of American States, for which he moved to Washington, D.C. (1946–1949). In 1946, the Colombian government awarded him the Cruz de Boyacá for his services to the republic. He served as general secretary of the Second Inter-American Statistics Congress in Bogotá in 1950, and in 1969 he was named director of Icollantas, a company that manufactured tires and other rubber products. A prolific writer, he published numerous studies in the Bogotá *Anales de Economía y Estadística.* Among his most noteworthy works is *Parnaso Colombiano en Euzkera: Kolonbiar Olerki-Txorta Euzkeraz* (Colombian Parnassus in Euskara) (1967), which won the 1967 José Antonio Agirre Prize.

Jose Antonio Agirre Lekube, Bilbao, 1904–Paris, 1960. In 1926, Agirre obtained a degree in law. In 1931, he was elected mayor of Getxo for the EAJ-PNV. On June 28, 1932, after the proclamation of the Second Republic, he was elected deputy to the constitutional convention. At the convention, he was secretary of the Basque-Nafarroan minority, chaired by Joaquín Beunza. In the elections of 1932 and 1936, Agirre was again elected a parliamentary deputy. Once the statute for autonomy was approved, the Gernika assembly of mayors elected Agirre *lehendakari* of the autonomous Basque state on October 7. His exile began with the fall of Bilbao on June 19, 1937. That summer, he moved to Barcelona; in January 1939, he left for Paris, where he framed the Basque national platform in the course of the 1939 Meudon meetings: collaboration with the Spanish republican government but maintaining of complete financial and administrative autonomy and diplomatic independence. World War II surprised Agirre in Dunkirk, where he lost a sister to German bombing. Persecuted by the Gestapo, he went into hiding in Berlin, and following a year and a half of vicissitudes, he escaped from occupied Europe thanks to the help of the Panamanian embassy, which provided him with a false identity: José Andrés Álvarez Lastra. In October 1941, he arrived in Uruguay, where he was received with the honor due to a head of government. In November 1941, he moved to New York, where he negotiated the collaboration agreements with the OSS in May 1942 and taught modern history at Columbia University. For the purpose of organizing the government's administrative and counterespionage network, in August 1942, Agirre began a two-month trip to South America, where he gave twenty-three lectures and attended more than one hundred events in ten different countries. In 1945, he returned to Paris, where he continued at the head of the Basque government, concluding the Pact of Bayonne with the republican parties to reinforce the unity of action of all the anti-Franco forces ahead of the 1945 San Francisco conference. He never renounced the Meudon principles: the Basque government's freedom of action was constant from 1940 to 1975. Beginning in 1950, in the context of the Cold War, the collapse of the agreements led to a change of direction in his government's policy, and the Europeanist and federalist platform was strengthened by the creation of the Basque Council for the European Federation in 1951. Following the liberation, Agirre likewise promoted the activities of the resistance within Spain with the strikes of 1947 and 1951, as well as cultural activities (the Basque studies conferences of 1948 and 1954). The World Basque Congress held in Paris in 1956 united these strategies and marked out the line to follow in the world's new geopolitical context. Agirre died on March 22, 1960; he is buried in the cemetery of Donibane Lohitzune.

Juan Ajuriagerra Otxandiano, Bilbao, 1903–Aiegi, 1978. Ajuriagerra obtained a degree as an industrial engineer in 1927 and worked for the firm Babcock and Wilcox until 1936. Between 1934 and 1937, he was a member of the Bizkai Buru Batzar, the EAJ-PNV's executive body in Bizkaia. Ajuriagerra was among those chiefly responsible for the Pact of Santoña (August 1937), by which the Basque army, defeated and unable to retreat, surrendered to Italian forces on a series of conditions that the latter failed to fulfill. Because all the soldiers were held as prisoners, Ajuriagerra decided to surrender himself and face the same fate as his men. Between 1937 and 1944, he was transferred from one prison to another on various occasions and suffered numerous punishments. From prison, he organized a resistance network in conjunction with the Allied secret services. The death sentence he had received in 1937 was commuted to life imprisonment, and he remained in prison until 1944, when he escaped and moved to Paris. From 1945 onward, he continued his resistance work, collaborating in the Aberri Eguna celebrations and the strikes in Bilbao and Iruñea in 1947 and 1951. In 1951, he was named president of the EAJ-PNV, an office he held until 1977. He was imprisoned during the mobilizations related to the Burgos trial in December 1970.[1] Following Franco's death, Ajuriagerra was a member of the Assembly of Basque Parliamentarians and the Basque General Council and president of the Basque General Council-Government's Mixed Commission. He died in 1978.

Ramón Maria Aldasoro Galarza, Tolosa, 1897–Havana, 1952. The holder of a bachelor's degree in law from the Central University of Madrid, Aldasoro was vice president of the Academy of Law and Social Sciences and a lawyer for the Bizkaia Delegation. A member of the Republican Left, he was a parliamentary deputy for Bizkaia and a civilian governor of Gipuzkoa. Following the coup d'état, he was named minister of commerce and supply. He headed the delegation that Agirre sent to South America in 1938. As the Basque government's delegate in Buenos Aires, Aldasoro collaborated with José Urbano Agirre and other members of the Argentine capital's Basque colony to create the Pro-Basque Immigration Committee, which enabled numerous Basque refugees to enter the country and have access to citizenship. He also served as director of the Buenos Aires periodical *Euzko Deya*. He was a member of the first executive committee of the Basque Council for the European Federation and served as its delegate to the Spanish Federal Council of the European Movement.

Bingen Ametzaga Aresti, Algorta, 1901–Caracas, 1969. The holder of a bachelor's degree in law and commercial technical engineering and a member of the EAJ-PNV, Ametzaga began to write at a very young age, winning awards in several literary competitions in 1933 and 1934. In 1936, he was named the Basque government's general director of primary education. He directed the creation of the first *ikastolas* (Basque schools), and in response to the Luftwaffe bombing campaign, he collaborated on the children's evacuation. He later became director of the Donibane Garazi children's refugee colony in 1937. Subsequently, in Barcelona, he was named secretary of the Department of Justice and inspector of the colonies of Basque children in England. Following the fall of Paris, he sailed for Buenos Aires on the *Alsina*. In 1942, he was among the founders of the American Institute of Basque Studies, and in 1943, he formed part of the organizing committee of Basque Week in Uruguay and created the Department of Basque Studies

1. At the end of October 1970 a court martial against sixteen Basque nationalists took place at Burgos, Spain. It was very soon known as "The Burgos Trials." Thirty-two men and women were to be tried by a Spanish court martial, including sixteen who escaped to other countries in absentia. Among the defendants there were three women and two Roman Catholic priests. According to the indictments, they were all accused of collaborating in the assassination of Melitón Manzanas. The prosecutor had demanded death sentences against six of the sixteen defendants, three of them being given double sentences, and faced death by garroting if found guilty on charges of military rebellion or terrorism. The prosecutor was demanding jail sentences totaling more than seven hundred years for the rest with prison terms ranging from six to seventy years. However, the trial was expected to last only a few hours.

at the University of the Republic School of Humanities and Sciences, which would be responsible for courses in Basque language and culture between 1943 and 1955. Between 1943 and 1950, he directed Basque intelligence in Uruguay, and in 1944, he was named president of Galeuzca Uruguay. In 1955, Ametzaga moved to Caracas and was named cultural secretary of the Basque Center. He began to work at the General Archive of the Nation in 1957 and at the Fundación Boulton in 1960. The author of seven books, numerous translations, and hundreds of newspaper articles, Ametzaga was named a corresponding member of Euskaltzaindia, the Academy of the Basque Language, in 1957. His most noteworthy works included the translation of *Hamlet* into Euskara (1952) and the collection of lectures *El hombre vasco* (The Basque man, 1967).

Santiago Aznar Sarachaga, Bilbao, 1903–Caracas, 1979. A member of the UGT Spanish labor union since at least 1920, Aznar joined the Socialist Youth and went into exile during Alfonso XIII's dictatorship, in 1923 and 1926. He was elected secretary of the UGT's textile union in 1930 and of the Bilbao Socialist Group and the Basque-Nafarroan Socialist Youth Federation between 1930 and 1933. He was elected a city councilor in Bilbao for the PSOE in 1931 and general secretary of the UGT in Bizkaia in 1934. He was an active participant in the revolution of 1934, for which he was detained and sentenced to prison. He was named a member of the Bizkaia Defense Committee for the UGT in 1936 and was subsequently appointed minister of industry in the Basque government. In June 1937 he was a member of the Bilbao Defense Committee, created by Leizaola to prevent excesses before the city's fall to the coup forces. He continued his government work in exile in Barcelona, and following the occupation, he went into exile in Mexico in 1942. Acceptance of the Basque national platform proposed by Agirre in Meudon in 1939 brought Aznar into conflict with members of his own party, forcing him to resign his post as minister in 1945, although he continued to engage in activity on behalf of the Basque government. He died in exile in Caracas.

Joxe Migel Barandiaran Aierbe, Ataun, 1889–Ataun, 1991. Ordained a priest in 1914, Barandiaran received a bachelor's degree in theology from the Ecclesiastical University of Burgos in 1915. While serving as a teacher at the Vitoria Normal School, together with Telesforo Aranzadi and Enrique Eguren, he carried out the first scientific excavations at Aralar in 1917 and began the exploration of the Santimamiñe Caves in 1918. He participated in the Oñate Basque Studies Congress, at which Eusko Ikaskuntza, the Society for Basque Studies, was founded. In 1920, he was named vice rector of the Vitoria Conciliar Seminary, and a year later, he founded the Eusko Folklore Society and its journal, *Anuario de la Sociedad de Eusko Folklore* (1921–1925). Rector of the Aguirre Minor Seminary (1926–1930), Barandiaran became a member of the academies of the Basque and Spanish languages in 1927 and 1929, respectively. Following the outbreak of World War II, he went into exile, residing in Sara between 1940 and 1953. During those years, he gathered around him well-known members of the Basque exile, such as Intxausti, Monzon, Lasarte, Sota, Bilbao, Epalza, and Mathieu and prominent figures of Basque exile culture such as Dassance, Lafitte, Llhande, and Saint Pierre. Together with them, he created the Gernika Institute in 1945, the Ikuska Basque Research Institute in 1946, the Basque Scholars Committees in 1947, the Gernika International Society of Basque Studies in 1948, and the periodical *Eusko Jakintza.* In 1953, he returned to Euskadi, where he conducted numerous excavations and, between 1964 and 1980, held the chair of Basque ethnology at the University of Nafarroa. He was a prolific author, and his complete works were edited in twenty-two volumes by La Gran Enciclopedia Vasca between 1973 and 1984.

Pedro Basaldua Ibarmia, Barakaldo, 1906–Buenos Aires, 1985. A member of the EAJ-PNV, in 1936, Basaldua was named Agirre's personal secretary, a post he held until 1949. Following the war, he went into exile in Paris, where he was director of the periodical *Euzko Deya.* After Francisco Basterretxea's departure, Basaldua was named the Basque government's delegate to Argentina, where he stood out for his work with the intelligence services and his collaboration in the development of Christian-Democratic networks in South America. As delegate, he collaborated with the Argentine Federation of Basque Organizations and served as director of the Buenos Aires periodical *Euzko Deya.* He was the author of six books.

Francisco Basterretxea Zaldibar, Bermeo, 1886–Madrid, 1975. Basterretxea studied law at the University of Valladolid and found work in the Bermeo branch of the Banco de Vizcaya. Together with Jose Antonio Agirre, he was elected deputy for Bizkaia on the Pro-Basque Statute in the 1931 elections. He was a member of the Autonomy Commission, which drafted the Basque statute, and of the Court of Constitutional Guarantees. A member of Eusko Ikaskuntza since in 1921, he was put in charge of maritime problems in 1922, a position he filled until 1936. Together with Policarpo Larrañaga, he founded the fishermen's union Eusto Kostarteko Bazkuna. A member of the Autonomy Commission since 1930, he participated in drafting the proposed General Statute of the Basque State and the Basque-Nafarroan Statute. A parliamentary deputy in 1931 for the EAJ-PNV, he was a member of the Court of Constitutional Guarantees. In 1937, he fled to Paris. Basterretxea collaborated with the government delegation as an accountant until June 1940. In January 1941, he sailed for Argentina on the *Alsina.* He was a founding member of the American Institute of Basque Studies in 1942 and helped form Galeuzca in Buenos Aires in 1945. There he was designated a member of the editorial board of the periodical *Galeuzca,* where he would publish several articles in 1945 and 1946. Between 1946 and 1952, he was the Basque government's delegate to Buenos Aires.

Jon Bilbao Azkarreta, Cayey, 1914–Bilbao, 1994. In 1936, when Bilbao was studying history in Madrid, he joined the Basque army. After the rebel troops took Bilbao in June 1937, he fled to exile in Baiona, and in 1938, he moved to New York. In 1939, he was named a subdelegate of the Basque government and sent to Boise, Idaho, where he created a subdelegation to collect funds and obtain support for the Basque government. He got the bachelor's degree at Columbia University in 1939 and, in September 1940, he enrolled in the University of California, Berkeley, where he would remain until 1942, where he got the master's degree in history. In 1944, he returned to New York, where he collaborated on the periodical *Basques* and with the Belgian Office for Ibero-America, working as associate editor of *La Revista Belga* (1944) and *Ambos Mundos* (1945–1946), service for which he was decorated in 1945. From 1947 to 1950, he was editor of *Eusko-Jakintza*, collaborating on the organization of the Society for Basque Studies' Congress in 1948. He was a professor at Georgetown University in 1964 and 1965 and at the US Naval Academy in Annapolis between 1966 and 1968. In 1968, he moved to the University of Nevada, Reno, at the invitation of the director of the Basque Studies Program (later renamed Center for Basque Studies), William A. Douglass. He would remain there until 1980. His time in Reno was noteworthy for the creation of the Center for Basque Studies library, the largest in the Basque diaspora, and for the publication of his work *Eusko Bibliographia*, a ten-volume catalog, published between 1970 and 1977, of works published in Euskadi, with a total of four hundred thousand entries. In 1981, Bilbao returned to Euskadi, where he created the Bibliographic Institute of Basque Studies, the Basque Diaspora Studies Institute, and the International Basque Bibliography Association. The author of numerous books and articles, he coauthored *Amerikanuak: Basques in the New World* (1975) with Douglass.

Louis Dassance, Uztaritze, 1888–Uztaritze, 1976. Having obtained a degree in agronomy in Paris, Dassance he was awarded the Croix d'Guerre for service in World War I. Between 1919 and 1939, he was elected lieutenant mayor of Uztaritze, and between 1939 and 1959, he served as mayor. He was honorary president of the Agricultural Mutual-Aid Society of the Lower Pyrenees and vice president of the Agriculturalists' Federation of the Lower Pyrenees and the Regional Agricultural Credit Union. He was a founding member of the periodical *Gure Herria* in 1921, becoming its administrator in 1928. He was president of Eskualtzaleen-Biltzarra between 1926 and 1959, and of Ikas beginning in 1957. Following the liberation, he collaborated actively with Barandiaran, Monzon, Intxausti, Lasarte, Lafitte, Sota, Bilbao, and others in the creation of Ikuska, the Gernika Institute, and the International Society for Basque Studies. Active in the periodicals published in Iparralde, he collaborated in the organization of the seventh and eighth Basque Studies Congresses in 1948 and 1954. In 1960, he was named vice president of the Conseil National de Défense des Langues et Cultures Régionales (National Council for the Defence of Regional Languages and Cultures) in Paris and honorary president of Eskualtzaleen-Biltzarra (Council for the Defense of the Basque Language). He was the author of numerous articles in periodicals such as *Eskualduna*, *Eusko Jakintza—Revue d'Études Basques*, *Herria*, *Gure-Herria*, *Gure-Almanaka*, and *Bulletin du Musée Basque*. In 1948, he was named a knight of the Legion of Honor, and in 1955, he was named Officier d'Académie and awarded the Ordre du Mérite Agricole. In 1949, he became a member of the Academy of the Basque Language.

Jesús Galíndez Suárez, Amurrio, 1915–Santo Domingo, Dominican Republic (?), 1956. In 1936, Galíndez obtained a law degree from the Central University of Madrid, where he was trapped by the war and would form part of the EAJ-PNV delegation in the capital. In February 1939, he went into temporary exile in Burdeos, and in November 1939, he moved to the Dominican Republic, working in the Basque government's delegation led by Eusebio Irujo. Following Irujo's departure for Venezuela, Galíndez headed the delegation from 1940 to February 1946. He then moved to New York, where he collaborated with the delegation led by Anton Irala on all matters related to the counterespionage operations of the Basque secret services. He likewise collaborated with numerous periodicals and newspapers in the Americas (e.g., *El Plata, El País, El Nacional*) and with the Basque exile press (e.g., *Euzko Deya, Alderdi, OPE-EIB*). In 1951, he became professor of Spanish American public law and the history of Ibero-American civilization at Columbia University in New York. In February 1956, Colombia accepted his dissertation "The Trujillo Era: A Casuistic Study of Spanish American Dictatorship," provoking the wrath of the dictator, who ordered his kidnapping and subsequent murder in March 1956. A prolific writer, Galíndez was the author of nine books on civil and public law and numerous journalistic articles on current political events, fundamentally in relation to the so-called Spanish case at the UN.

Justo Garate Arriola, Bergara, 1900–Mendoza, 1994. Garate obtained a bachelor's degree in medicine from the Central University of Madrid and the University of La Plata in Argentina and pursued specialized study in Freiburg (1924), Paris (1925), Berlin (1926), and Heidelberg (1927). He was a member of the standing committee of the Society for Basque Studies from 1932, when he was chosen as a voting member for the medicine section. In 1931, he was a candidate for EAE-ANV. During the war, he worked as a doctor at the Bilbao Civil Hospital and was a founder of the Basque university's School of Medicine. Following the war, he went into exile in Argentina, where he was a professor of pathology at the University of Mendoza School of Medicine from 1954 and director of the medical school's Institute of Clinical Medicine beginning in 1955. In 1957, he served as vice dean and counselor of the School of Medicine. A founding member of the American Institute of Basque Studies in 1942, Garate was president of the Mendoza Group of the Argentine Goethe Society and a corresponding member of the Academy of the Basque Language. He was a prolific author, whose most notable works included *Ensayos euskarianos* (Basque Essays, 1935), *Viajeros extranjeros en Vasconia* (Foreign Travelers in Gascony, 1942), *Cultura biológica y arte de traducir* (*Biological Culture and the Art of Translation*, 1943), and *El carlismo de los vascos* (The Carlism of the Basques, 1980). In 1982, he was awarded an honorary doctorate by the University of the Basque Country.

Paulino Gómez de Segura Beltrán de Heredia, Bilbao, 1891–Toulouse, 1963. At the age of sixteen, Gómez joined the Socialist Youth and began to work in the bakers' union, taking part in various strikes and mobilizations. He was elected secretary of the Society of Bakery Workers and created the Center of Workers' Societies. A member of the UGT, he was elected to the union's Industrial Court, Parity Committee, and Mixed Jury. In 1931, he was elected city councilor in Bilbao, and he subsequently worked on the staff of the Bizkaia Delegation and participated actively in the mobilizations of 1934.

Following the outbreak of the war and until the formation of the Basque government, he was a commissioner on the Bizkaia Defense Committee. After the war, he went into exile in Toulouse and was elected to the PSOE Executive Committee at its 1944 congress. He also served as vice president of the UGT and president of the Socialist Central Committee of Euskadi (CCSE), the Euskadi Central Committee of the UGT, and Spanish Democratic Solidarity. Following Fermín Zarza's 1951 resignation, he was named minister of social assistance in the Basque government-in-exile in 1952, an office he held until 1959.

Juan Gracia Colás, Bilbao, 1888–Paris, 1941. After studying accounting and commerce, Gracia obtained a post as tax inspector in the Bilbao municipal government. A member of the PSOE from a very young age, he organized the Second Congress of Iberian Esperantists in 1924 and was president of the Bilbao Esperanto Group from 1925 to 1926. Elected city councilor and first and third lieutenant mayor in the Bilbao municipal government between 1920 and 1923, he was named a member of the Bizkaia Defense Committee after the outbreak of the war and was subsequently named minister of social assistance in the Basque government. His chief occupations during the war were organizing assistance to the Basque refugees in Bilbao, arranging the children's exodus between May and August 1937, and obtaining assistance for the Basque refugees in Catalonia and France following the fall of Bilbao. In 1939, he showed himself favorable, though with hesitations, to accepting the Basque platform proposed by Agirre in Meudon and was a decided supporter of the creation of the Socialist Central Committee of Euskadi, for the purpose of stressing the Basque socialists' independence with regard to the PSOE's central executive body. Shortly before the German invasion, he fled Paris on foot, but two hundred kilometers south of the French capital, German troops overtook him, leading him to return to the city, where he died in hiding in the spring of 1941.

Andima Ibinagabeitia Idoiaga, Elantxobe, 1906–Caracas, 1967. Between 1921 and 1935, Ibinagabeitia studied humanities, philosophy, and theology in Loiola, Oña, and Marneffe. In Loiola, he met Jokin Zaitegi, Esteban "Lauaxeta" Urkiaga, and Plazido Muxika, with whom he would collaborate for many years. He moved to Bogotá (1929–1930) and subsequently to Bucaramanga (1930–1933), where he directed the Natural History Museum. In April 1935, however, on the eve of his ordination, he decided to leave the Society of Jesus and found work in Portugal. In 1943, he returned to Euskadi, collaborating with the Basque government's secret services in favor of the Allies, but in 1947, he fled to Paris, where he collaborated with the Basque government's delegation. In 1954, he moved to Guatemala to collaborate with Zaitegi on *Euzko Gogoa*, and in 1956, he moved to Caracas, where he was named secretary of the Basque center's Cultural Commission beginning in 1959. He was the author of two systems for teaching Basque and of numerous translations of literary works into Euskara.

Manuel Intxausti Romero, Manila, 1900–Uztaritze, 1961. Intxausti was born into a wealthy family of Basque merchants who had settled in the Philippines. In 1920, he obtained a law degree from the Central University of Madrid, and in 1933, he established himself in Donostia, where he remained until 1936. At the start of the war, Intxausti moved to Uztaritze, where together with Bishop Clément Mathieu, he created the International League of Friends of the Basques (LIAB), which would serve as a liaison between the French and Basque governments, fundamentally on matters concerning refugees and the children's exodus. In August 1939, Intxausti moved to New York, where beginning in November 1941, he assisted *Lehendakari* Agirre by facilitating political contacts with the US government and raising funds. On returning to Uztaritze in 1947, Intxausti was among the chief promoters of the seventh and eighth Eusko Ikaskuntza congresses in 1948 and 1954. Intxausti was one of the great patrons of Basque exile culture, contributing large sums of money for medical assistance to refugees and for Basque cultural activities in Iparralde between 1947 and 1960.

Anton Irala Irala, Bilbao, 1909–Donibane Lohitzune, 1996. The general secretary of the Federation of Basque Schools, Irala was detained in 1936. Having succeeded in escaping, he was named secretary of the presidential ministry of the Basque government by *Lehendakari* Agirre. Together with Monzon and de la Torre, Irala was in charge of organizing the purchase of weapons and provisions to supply the Basque army, as well as transporting these items to Bilbao. In 1937, he moved to the Basque government's delegation in Paris, where he collaborated closely with Intxausti to create the International League of Friends of the Basques (LIAB). In August 1938, he traveled to the United States to organize the Basque government's press and propaganda activity for the purpose of obtaining diplomatic and financial assistance from that country; he remained there until January 1939. Subsequently, having been named the Basque government's delegate in New York, Irala worked together with Lasarte, Galíndez, and Sota to organize the Basque secret services that would function until 1950. Irala wrote numerous articles, some of them published under the title *Escritos políticos sobre la situación vasca* (Political Writings on the Basque Situation, 1997), and the books *Bat bitan banatzen da* (1975), translated into Spanish in 1976 under the title *Uno se divide en dos* (One Is Divided into Two), *Revolución-represión o Burujabetza: El combate del pueblo vasco por su identidad* (Revolution-Repression or Burujabetza: The Basque People's Fight for Their Identity, 1981), and *Violencia y negociación política: Confusión y engaño en el País Vasco* (Violence and Political Negotiation: Confusion and Deception in the Basque Country, 1998).

Andrés Irujo Ollo, Lizarra, 1907–Buenos Aires, 1993. Earning a bachelor's degree in law in 1930, Irujo was active in the EAJ-PNV from the age of sixteen, collaborating in its publications from early on. He belonged to the Basque Students Group and signed the republican Manifesto of the Madrid Athenaeum, headed by Manuel Azaña. The military uprising surprised Irujo in Gipuzkoa, where he would be named president of the Defense Committee, charged with guaranteeing public order and preventing lynchings until the creation of the Basque government. Following the fall of Gipuzkoa, he moved with his brother Manuel to Madrid and subsequently to Valencia and Barcelona. In 1939, he took refuge in Cap Breton, working as the secretary of the Basque Section of the Friends of the French Republic. Following the occupation, he went into exile in Buenos Aires, where he worked together with Ixaka López Mendizabal to promote the creation of the Ekin publishing house, which would ultimately publish more than one hundred works between 1942 and 1977. In 1943, he created the American Institute of Basque Studies, which would publish a bulletin, first appearing in 1950, that would attain significant cultural prestige beyond the Basque communities. He was the author of numerous articles and two books, *Los vascos y la República española: Contribución a la historia de la guerra civil, 1936–1939* (The Basques and the Spanish Republic: Contribution to the History of the Civil War, 1936–1939, 1944) and *Los vascos y las cruzadas* (The Basques and the Crusades, 1946).

Manuel Irujo Ollo, Lizarra, 1891–Iruñea, 1981. In 1912, Irujo obtained a degree in law. He was elected deputy for Nafarroa in 1919 (results annulled) and 1921. He decisively promoted the creation of the Caja de Ahorros de Navarra in 1921. In 1923, he was elected again, but the results were annulled following the inauguration of Alfonso XIII. After the dictatorship fell, he returned to the office of deputy for Nafarroa in 1930 and was elected parliamentary deputy for Gipuzkoa in the elections of 1931 and 1933. As a member of Eusko Ikaskuntza, he was named to its standing committee as a voting member for general administration beginning in 1932, and he organized the Basque Cultural Week in 1933. Together with Agirre and Landaburu, he was invited to meet with the Vatican secretary of state in January 1936, although no agreement was reached with the Holy See with regard to the 1936 elections. In February 1936, he was again elected deputy for the EAJ-PNV. Following the outbreak of the war, he accepted a position as minister without portfolio in Francisco Largo Caballero's government between September 1936 and May 1937, in exchange for the approval of the statute of autonomy. He stood out for his efforts to humanize the war, and he continued this work—agreements with the International Red Cross, prisoner exchanges, reorganization of the prisons, and management of the courts—as justice minister in Juan Negrín's government, an office he held until December 1937. He gave up that post for reasons of conscience but continued to serve as minister without portfolio until August 1938, when he definitively resigned. In exile, he created and chaired the National Council of Euskadi in June 1940, the body in which the Basque government's functions were vested until the *lehendakari*'s reappearance in October 1941. In this role, he promoted the intelligence collaboration agreements with the British government and the French Empire Defense Council, in exchange for a political agreement on the establishment of an independent Basque state. A decided promoter of Galeuzca, he was among the founders of the Cultural Union of the Countries of Western Europe and the Federal Union with Portugal and Catalonia, successfully arranging Basque entry into the Union of European Federalists. A member of the Pro-Iberian Community of Nations Committee in London, he backed the Federation of European Nations from the 1930s onward. Following Agirre's reappearance, Irujo showed himself little inclined to signing collaboration agreements without a prior political agreement regarding Basque sovereignty. He was a minister in the republican government-in-exile between 1945 and 1947. He promoted the creation of the Spanish Federal Council of the European Movement, which he would chair, and the Basque Council for the European Federation. For his work in the political construction of Europe, he was named honorary president of the Peninsular Federal Council of the European Movement in 1972. He returned from exile in 1977 and was elected senator for Nafarroa for the Autonomy Front. In 1979, he was elected to the Nafarroan parliament at the head of the Basque nationalists' coalition list. A prolific writer, he was the author of seven books and hundreds of articles and speeches, an anthology of which was published in seven volumes between 1982 and 1984.

Pellomari Irujo Ollo, Lizarra, 1910–Iruñea, 1983. Having obtained a degree in law, Irujo joined EAE-ANV in 1930. He worked together with Father Hilario Olazaran to recover traditional dances like the Lizarra *baile de la era* (dance of the age) and was a member of the editorial board of *La Merindad de Estella*, a newspaper with wide circulation in the region that coup authorities would embargo in 1936. Following the outbreak of the war, he became a legal adviser to the commissariat of the Gipuzkoa Defense Committee. In the course of this work, he was detained while trying to evacuate from the country several supporters of the coup d'état whom republican militias had threatened. Although those individuals initially prevented him from being shot, a military court subsequently sentenced him to death. He remained in prison for seven years. There he met the painter Javier Ziga, who introduced him to the world of painting. Once released, he was exiled to the province of Cuenca, but on Ajuriagerra's suggestion, he moved to Madrid, joining the Basque resistance network. Wanted by the police, in 1946, Irujo fled to Baiona, where he was named cultural attaché to the Basque government's delegations in Sofia and Budapest. After the end of World War II, he moved to Buenos Aires, where together with Tellagorri he directed the periodical *Tierra Vasca—Eusko Lur*, an ANV publication distributed in the Americas and Europe. Along with his journalism, he was noteworthy for his art, exhibited on several occasions. After the fall of the dictatorship, he resided in Iruñea, where he died.

Julio Jauregi Lasanta, Bilbao, 1910–Madrid, 1981. A graduate of the University of Deusto with a bachelor's degree in law, a lawyer for the ELA-STV labor union, and a member of Catholic Action, Jauregi was elected parliamentary deputy in 1936. Following the uprising, he was named an industrial commissioner for the Bizkaia Defense Committee, and in 1937, he was appointed legal adviser to the president's office and the Justice Department of the Basque government. In 1937, he moved to Barcelona, where he was named the Basque government's secretary in Catalonia. In 1939, he fled to Paris, and following the occupation, he took refuge in the town of Ardèche. He succeeded in fleeing to Mexico, where he was named the Basque government's delegate, a responsibility he carried out until his return to Biarritz in 1946. In 1974, he moved to Madrid. In 1979, he was elected senator for the EAJ-PNV.

Francisco Javier Landaburu Fernández de Betoño, Gasteiz, 1907–Paris, 1963. In 1926, Landaburu obtained a degree in law. In 1927, he was elected secretary of the Baraibar

Group, dedicated to promoting Euskara in the city of Gasteiz, and beginning in 1930, he was a legal adviser to the Araba Chamber of Commerce and Industry. As a member of the Society for Basque Studies, he was commissioned to draft the proposed statute of autonomy for the Basque Country. In 1933, he was elected a parliamentary deputy for Araba. Following the military coup, Landaburu was arrested, and as a member of the EBB, he was forced to make a public declaration against the Popular Front. In hiding for more than a year, Landaburu succeeded in escaping into exile in September 1937. In Paris, he was elected secretary of the International League of Friends of the Basques. During the occupation, Landaburu lived clandestinely in Paris, collaborating with the resistance. Beginning in 1944, he was the Basque government's delegate in Paris, and as a convinced Europeanist, he participated in founding several international organizations, such as the Union of European Federalists, the Federalist Union of European Ethnic Communities, and the New International Teams. Following Jose Antonio Agirre's death, Landaburu was chosen as vice president of the Basque government, but he died three years later, in 1963. A prolific writer, he was the author of *La causa del pueblo vasco* (The Cause of the Basque People, 1956); his complete works were edited by Idatz Ekintza in 1983, in five volumes.

Joxe Mari Lasarte Arana, Donostia, 1912–Donostia, 1974. The holder of a bachelor's degree in law, Lasarte was a parliamentary deputy for the EAJ-PNV in 1936. On the morning of July 19, 1936, hours after the uprising, Lasarte and Manuel Irujo declared the EAJ-PNV's absolute rejection of the military rebels' acts. Following the formation of the Basque government, Lasarte was assigned responsibility for setting up its information services. In exile in Paris, he forged ties between the Basque government's secret services and those of France. He traveled to the Americas to set up the Basque secret services in Chile, Argentina, and Uruguay and was one of the promoters of the Basque Cultural Week in Montevideo in 1943. Once World War II was over, he moved to Paris, and in 1946, he succeeded Eliodoro de la Torre as a Basque government minister, following the latter's death. From Paris, he created and directed the *Boletín de la Oficina de Prensa de Euskadi* in 1947 and represented the EAJ-PNV in the New International Teams, being among those responsible for maintaining relations with the international Christian-Democratic movement. Following the death of his wife, Lasarte moved to Caracas in 1952, where together with his brother he led the company Lasarte and Lasarte. On returning from exile, he dedicated himself to the internal organization of the EAJ-PNV and to the consolidation of the Liceo de Santo Tomás in his native city.

Jesús Maria Leizaola Sánchez, Donostia, 1896–Donostia, 1989. In 1915, Leizaola obtained a degree in law. He worked as a legal adviser for the Gipuzkoa Legal Delegation. He was elected a parliamentary deputy for the EAJ-PNV in 1931 and 1933, and he represented the Basque minority on the Constitution Commission of the Constitutional Convention, but he resigned in protest of the central government's refusal to grant the Basque people the statute of autonomy. He was secretary of the Gipuzkoa Deputation until 1936, and following the outbreak of the war, he was named justice and culture minister in the government of Euskadi. When Bilbao fell in June 1937, he escorted the prisoners of war to the enemy lines to guarantee their safety. He moved to Barcelona and subsequently to Paris. During the occupation, Leizaola took refuge in Betharram, and once the war ended, he was named finance minister in the Basque government-in-exile in 1946 and vice president in 1948. In March 1960, upon Jose Antonio Agirre's death, Leizaola was named *lehendakari*, an office he held until the fall of the dictatorship. On the occasion of the 1974 Aberri Eguna, he traveled clandestinely to Gernika. He returned from exile in 1977, and in 1979, he symbolically turned over leadership of the new Basque government to Carlos Garaikoetxea, elected *lehendakari* of the Basque government in 1981. He was the author of numerous works about Basque literature and of numerous articles, which are collected in his complete works, published by Sendoa in four volumes between 1981 and 1985.

Ixaka López Mendizabal, Tolosa, 1879–Tolosa, 1977. Born into a family of printers established in Tolosa since the seventeenth century, López continued the tradition of his elders. He obtained a doctorate in law in 1903 and was one of the founding members of Eskualtzaleen Biltzarra. In 1916, together with Luis Eleizalde and José Eizagirre, he represented Basque nationalism at the Third Conference of Nationalities held in Lausanne. He was one of the founders of the Academy of the Basque Language in 1918. He was a member of the city council of Tolosa in 1931 and president of the EBB. After the fall of Tolosa to the coup forces, his press's books were publicly burned. Exiled, he established himself in Buenos Aires, where he collaborated actively with the Basque government's delegation. A promoter of the Argentine Section of the International League of Friends of the Basques and a founding member of the Basque Institute of Basque Studies, he founded the Editorial Vasca Ekin together with Andrés Irujo. In 1965, he returned from exile and established himself in Tolosa, setting up a press once again. He was the author of numerous works, among the most notable of which were textbooks for teaching Euskara to children, such as *Xabiertxo* (1925), the *Diccionario vasco-castellano* (Basque-Spanish Dictionary, 1916), and *Etimologías de apellidos vascos* (Etymologies of Basque Surnames, 1958).

Telesforo Monzon Ortiz de Urruela, Bergara, 1904–Baiona, 1981. A law student in Madrid, Monzon abandoned his studies and in 1931 was elected town councilor in the municipal government of Bergara. He was elected president of the EAJ-PNV in Gipuzkoa in 1932 and parliamentary deputy in 1933. Following the military coup, Monzon became a member of the Gipuzkoa Defense Committee, from which he resigned because of the deaths that the committee could not prevent. Named minister of the interior and of citizen safety in the Basque government, he created the Ertzaina, a body of motorized police that guaranteed public order in the area controlled by the Basque government. Nonetheless, following bombing by German aircraft on January 4, 1937, there was an assault on various prisons in Bilbao, which Monzon, together with the ministers Juan Astigarrabia and Juan Gracia, were able to halt only after 224 prisoners had been murdered. In 1937, he went into exile, and following the occupation, he fled to Mexico, where he resided until 1945. In 1946, he returned to Paris, where he remained as culture minister and minister without portfolio until resigning in 1953, opposed to the policy of alliances with Spanish Republican forces. In 1969, he founded and chaired the Anai Artea association, with the goal of welcoming and assisting Basque refugees in Iparralde. He returned from exile in 1977 and was a promoter of Herri Batasuna beginning in 1979, being elected a deputy to the Basque parliament in 1980. He was a prolific author of literary works in Basque, and his complete works were published by Jaizkibel in 1986 in six volumes.

Mateo Mújica Urrestarazu, Idiazábal, 1870–Zarautz, 1968. Mújica studied at the University of Oñate and earned a doctorate in theology at the University of Salamanca. He was a professor at the Vitoria-Gasteiz Conciliar Seminary, and in October 1903, he was named canon lector of that city's cathedral chapter. He was named bishop of El Burgo de Osma in 1918, of Iruñea in 1924, and of Gasteiz in 1928. As bishop, he inaugurated the city's major seminary in 1930. He showed himself opposed to the establishment of the Second Republic, for which reason he was expelled in 1931, residing in Poitiers until his sentence was commuted in 1933. Following the uprising, Mújica had problems with the rebel commanders, as he had defended Basque language and culture in numerous sermons, even translating his pastoral letters and sermons, as well as a chapter of *Don Quijote*. Fearing for his life, the bishop of Valencia intervened with the coup authorities to prevent Mújica's death, but in October 1936, he was sentenced to exile on the orders of General Miguel Cabanellas, president of the National Defense Committee. Together with the cardinals Francisco Vidal i Barraquer and Pedro Segura, Mújica refused to sign the "Collective Letter of the Spanish Bishops to the Bishops of the World" of July 1, 1937, in which eight archbishops, thirty-five bishops, and five capitular vicars requested support for Franco's cause. Exiled in Iparralde, he was authorized to return in 1947, establishing himself in Zarautz, where he died. At Barandiaran's urging, he wrote *Imperativos de mi conciencia* (Imperatives of My Conscience, 1945) in exile.

Gonzalo Nardiz Bengoetxea, Bermeo, 1905–Bilbao, 2003. Active in EAE-ANV since its founding in 1930, Nardiz had previously been a town councilor in Bermejo and a deputy for the antimonarchy block. A member of the commission in favor of the autonomy plebiscite, he was on the staff of the Bizkaia Deputation. Following the outbreak of the war, he was named a supply, armament, and lodging commissioner for the troops of the Bizkaia Defense Committee for the EAE-ANV. Subsequently, he was named agriculture minister in the Basque government in 1936, standing out for his activity at the head of the supply and armament directorates of the Euskadi army. Exiled in Paris, Mexico City, and Baiona, he continued to serve as agriculture minister until 1952 and as minister without portfolio in the Euskadi government-in-exile until 1979.

José Olivares Larrondo, Algorta, 1892–Buenos Aires, 1960. A writer and journalist known by the pseudonym "Tellagorri," Olivares collaborated from a very young age on periodicals and newspapers such as *Gobela*, *Euzkadi*, and *Excelsior*, the first of which he directed with Bingen Ametzaga. As a forward on the league-champion Arenas soccer team and on the 1913 Euskadi team, he was a sports reporter and ultimately became director of the mentioned sports newspaper *Excelsior.* In 1930, he joined EAE-ANV, and between 1930 and 1933, he directed the party's daily newspaper *Tierra Vasca—Eusko Lur.* Following the fall of Bilbao, he went into exile in Baiona and subsequently moved to Paris to work for the Basque government's delegation, where he collaborated on organizing the information agency responsible for editing the *Cahiers de documentation basque.* In 1941, he left Marseilles for exile on the *Alsina*, arriving in Buenos Aires in April 1942, where he directed the daily newspaper *Tierra Vasca—Eusko Lur* with Pellomari Irujo. He was a member of the editorial committees of the Buenos Aires periodicals *Euzko Deya* and *Galeuzca*, and he collaborated with numerous Basque exile periodicals, as well as with others such as *A Nosa Terra*, *Anti Nazi*, *Argentina Libre*, *Crítica*, *La Revista Belga*, and *Ambos Mundos.* He was the author of numerous works, three of which were published, *París abandonada* (Abandoned Paris, 1942), *Horas joviales* (Merry Hours, 1950), and *Antón Sukalde* (1978).

Alberto Onaindia Zuloaga, Markina, 1902–Donibane Lohitzune, 1988. Onaindia studied theology at the Gasteiz seminary and earned a doctorate in Rome. He was named professor at the Saturraran seminary and, in 1929, canon of the Valladolid cathedral. He collaborated on the formation of the Basque Christian Social Action Association (AVASC) for the organization of labor relations. Together with José Ariztimuño and Policarpo Larrañaga, he was one of the great thinkers of cooperativist Basque labor unionism. In 1936, he was named an adviser to the presidential ministry, and in September of that year, he collaborated on the first meetings between representatives of the Basque government and the coup forces to consider peace terms. He was one of those most responsible for the negotiations leading to the surrender of the Basque government's troops in Santoña in August 1937. He was likewise charged with justifying to the Vatican the pro-republican attitude of the Basque government and the EAJ-PNV and denouncing the shooting of Basque priests (including his brother) and the policy of indiscriminate bombing, as in Bilbao, Durango, Otxandio, and Gernika. In 1940, he moved to London, and between 1941 and 1956, he was responsible for Basque radio broadcasts on the BBC under the pseudonym James Masterton; after the liberation, he began a weekly program in Spanish under the pseudonym Dr. Olaso, with an audience that reached 4 million listeners. Because of pressure from the Spanish government, his broadcasts were banned in November 1957. He continued collaborating with the Basque resistance until the end of the dictatorship.

Nikolas Ormaetxea Pellejero, Orexa, 1888–Añorga, 1961. Ormaetxea studied the humanities, philosophy, and theology in several Jesuit seminaries between 1905 and 1922. After leaving the Society of Jesus, he moved to Bilbao in 1924 to work for the Academy of the Basque Language together with Resurrección María Azkue, soon becoming one of the leading figures of the Eusko Pizkundea literary movement. In 1929, he took charge of the Euzkel Atala section (the section written in Euskara) of the nationalist daily newspaper *Euzkadi.* In those years, he wrote a twelve-article series under the title

"Euskal Literaturaren Atze edo Edesti Laburra" (Brief History of Basque Literature), published in *Euskal Esnalea* in 1927, and he translated the anonymous sixteenth-century Spanish novel *Lazarillo de Tormes* into Euskara as *Tormes'ko Itsu-mutilla* (1929). Between 1931 and 1936, he lived in Orexa, where he wrote what may be his masterworks, *Euskaldunak* (1950) and *Barne Muinetan* (1934), under the pseudonym "Orixe." Following the outbreak of the war, he was detained and interned in the prison of San Cristóbal, where he remained for six months. After his release, harassed by the Spanish police, he fled to Donibane Lohitzune. He was detained by Vichy security services in 1940, however, and interned in the Gurs concentration camp, where he remained for four months. Thanks to the income he received from the translation of the Lefèvre missal into Euskara, *Urte guziko Meza-Bezperak* (1949), in 1950, he moved to Guatemala, where he spent six months collaborating with Jokin Zaitegi on the periodical *Euzko Gogoa*. From there he moved to Zaragoza (El Salvador), where he wrote four books and numerous religious poems. He spent his last years in Euskadi and was named a member of Euskaltzaindia in 1959. Orixe is considered one of the leading exile writers and one of the most noteworthy figures of all of Basque literature.

Rafael Pikabea Legia, Oihartzun, 1867–Paris, 1946. Having obtained a degree in business and possessing a large fortune, Pikabea was elected as an independent Catholic deputy for Donostia in 1901 and 1903 and subsequently as a senator in 1907 and 1910. In 1902, he collaborated in the release of Sabino Arana. He founded numerous businesses: the Papelera Española, the Cooperativa Eléctrica Donostiarra, Saltos de Agua de Valcarlos, and the Sociedad General de Obras de Saneamiento. In 1903, he founded the newspaper *El Pueblo Vasco*, which quickly became very successful. In 1923 and 1927, he would again be elected senator, and following the fall of Alfonso XIII's dictatorship, he began collaborating with the EAJ-PNV. Following the 1936 military uprising, he contributed with Manuel Irujo to the submission of the rebel military personnel of the Loiola garrison in Donostia. He was the Basque government's delegate in Paris beginning in 1936 and organized the Paris press office together with Felipe Urkola and Eugène Goyhenetche. Following the occupation, he fled to Marseilles, but the Vichy police detained him as he was preparing to sail to the Americas on the *Alsina*. Once released, he resided first in Tardets and subsequently in Donibane Loitzune. Pikabea was one of the founders of the Gernika Institute in 1943 and of the periodical *Gernika*, published by the Basque Cultural Extension Institute in 1945.

Joseba Rezola Arratibel, Ordizia, 1900–Donibane Lohitzune, 1971. The holder of a bachelor's degree in law, Rezola was a member of the EAJ-PNV's Gipuzkoa committee. Starting in October 1936, as the Basque government's defense secretary, he collaborated with Kandido Saseta to create and organize the Euzko Gudarostea, the Basque regular army. Following the violation of the Pact of Santoña by the Italian commanders, the EAJ-PNV leaders Juan Ajuriagerra and Joseba Rezola decided to stay and share the fate of the imprisoned *gudaris*. Following a council of war, the coup authorities sentenced him to death, a penalty subsequently commuted to life imprisonment. Released in 1943, he moved to Madrid to head Basque resistance activities in the area. Following the signing of the Pact of Baiona in 1945, he was named president of the Delegated Council and the Resistance Committee. However, having been detained several times, he had to escape to Iparralde. In exile, he continued to be one of those most responsible for the Basque resistance forces, and together with Joxe Mari Lasarte, he was one of those chiefly responsible for Radio Euzkadi's broadcasts in Iparralde between 1946 and 1954, until it was closed because of pressure from the Spanish embassy in Paris. Following Javier Landaburu's death in 1963, he was chosen as vice president of the Basque government-in-exile. He died in exile in 1971.

Jesús Solaun Gorostizaga, Arrankudiaga, 1903–Bilbao, 1979. A graduate of the University of Valladolid with a bachelor's degree in law, in 1935, Solaun was named a member of the Bizkai Buru Batzar (the EAJ-PNV executive body in Bizkaia) and of the EBB, offices he held until 1977. After the war, he was transferred to the prison of Puerto de Santa María, where he remained until 1940. Once released, he moved to Bilbao and subsequently to Donostia, where he collaborated actively with the resistance. In this work, his activity in relation with the 1947 and 1951 strikes stands out. Wanted by the Spanish police, he succeeded in fleeing to Baiona after four months in hiding and resided there until 1952, collaborating with the local Basque delegation. In 1952, he moved to Biarritz, and following the dictator's death, he returned to Bilbao in 1976 and was named president of the EAJ-PNV tribunal in 1977.

Manuel Sota Aburto, Getxo, 1897–Bilbao, 1979. A graduate of the universities of Salamanca and Cambridge, with a bachelor's degree in law, he taught at the latter after completing his studies. Back in Euskadi, he participated in the Euzko Pizkundea literary movement, writing literary pieces in both Euskara and Spanish, the most noteworthy of which included *Negarrez igaro zen atsoa* (1932), translated into Euskara by the poet Lauaxeta; *Iru gudari* (1933); and *Libe* (1934), a play begun by Sabino Arana and completed by Sota. He collaborated with periodicals such as *La Gaceta Literaria*, *Revista de Occidente*, *Litoral*, and *Pyrenaica*, of which he was director between 1928 and 1930. President of the Bilbao Athletic Club (1926–1929), he was named to the standing committee of the Society for Basque Studies as a voting member for sports in 1932, a post he held until 1936. In exile, Sota worked for the Basque government's delegation in New York, doing significant work on matters relating to the espionage agreements reached with the US government. Once World War II was over, he returned to Euskadi, pursuing intensive activity in Iparralde together with prominent figures of Basque exile culture such as Manuel Intxausti, Joxe Miguel Barandiaran, Louis Dassance, Telesforo Monzon, and Pierre Lafitte. He actively participated in the organization of the Basque studies congresses of 1948 and 1954 and was a member of the Gernika Institute and Ikuska. Sota likewise collaborated on the organization of the first Euskara Eguna, or International Basque Language Days, beginning in 1949.

Eliodoro de la Torre Larrinaga, Barakaldo, 1884–Baiona, 1946. De la Torre chaired the Deusto consumers' cooperative and participated in creating the Modern Dispensary of the Basque Doctors Group. In 1930, he collaborated on creating Basque Employees' Solidarity (SEV), which he would come to chair. He was likewise one of the directors of the Federation of Cooperatives, and in 1933, he was elected vice president of the National Confederation Council of the ELA-STV labor union. He was elected a town councilor in the municipal government of Deusto (EAJ-PNV) in 1931 and a parliamentary deputy for Bizkaia in 1933 and 1936. Upon the formation of the Basque government, he was named treasury minister. He was an effective manager of currency controls, promoted the introduction of paper money popularly known as "Eliodoros," and he administered the acquisition of war matériel. After Basque minister Alfredo Espinosa was shot in 1937, de la Torre became health minister. In this role, he created the Gernika, Euzkadi, and Otxandiano hospitals in Catalonia, the La Roseraie hospital in Bidarte, and the Kanbo tuberculosis sanitarium. In exile, the collapse of republican institutions and the clashes between Prieto and Negrín forced de la Torre to develop an autonomous financial policy, one that would guarantee the continued operation of the Basque government at the same time that it saved the lives of thousands of refugees interned in concentration camps. He remained in Marseilles until 1941, facilitating the departure to the Americas of numerous Basque refugees. Persecuted by the Vichy police, he collaborated with the French Resistance. A promoter of the Gernika Battalion in 1944, he died in exile in 1946.

Juan de los Toyos González, Barakaldo, 1890–Mexico City, 1965. A member of the UGT and of the PSOE, de los Toyos was permanent secretary of the UGT's metallurgical section in Bizkaia in 1917 and in Gipuzkoa in 1930. He was elected a town councilor in the municipal government of the industrial locality of Eibar in 1931 and participated in the protest movements of 1934, for which he was imprisoned. A manager of the socialist production cooperative ALFA, he was named minister of labor, social security, and communications following the formation of the Basque government in October 1936, standing out for his work on the development of daily wages and subsidies for the unemployed, war pensions, and the reorganization of the postal system. A member of the Socialist Central Committee of Euskadi, he opposed *Lehendakari* Agirre's Basque national platform, as a result of which he came into conflict with his fellow socialist Santiago Aznar, leading to the latter's resignation from the Basque government. In 1942, he went into exile in Mexico City, where he was named administrator of the Colegio Madrid, created by the republican government. Pressured by Indalecio Prieto, de los Toyos resigned as a Basque government minister. He died in exile in 1965.

Martin Ugalde Orradre, Andoain, 1921–Donostia, 2004. After the fall of Villa in 1937, he went into exile in Iparralde, completing high school at the student colonies of Donibane Garazi and Donibane Lohitzune established by the Basque government-in-exile. In 1940, he was interned in the Gurs concentration camp, and following the occupation, he fled to Andoain. In October 1947, he moved to Caracas, where he worked as a correspondent for the daily newspaper *Elite*. He joined the EAJ-PNV and the ELA-STV labor union, and in 1948, he was among the founders of Eusko Gaztedi, being elected president of the Basque center in 1950 and director of the periodical *Euzkadi*. He worked for the Creole Petroleum Corporation's periodicals *El Farol* and *Nosotros* and wrote articles for numerous Basque exile periodicals, such as *Alderdi*, *Eusko Deya*, *Euzko Gaztedi*, *Tierra Vasca—Eusko Lur*, and *Zeruko Argia*. In recognition of his work, he received the Basque center's literary prize in 1950, the prize for narrative given by the daily newspaper *El Nacional* in 1955, and the Basque government's gold medal in 1959. In 1961, he published *Iltzalleak* (Murderers) in Caracas, and in 1962, he obtained a degree in journalism from Northwestern University in Evanston. In 1969, he moved to Hondarribia, but in 1973, he was exiled once again. He wrote *Síntesis de la historia del País Vasco* (Synthesis of the History of the Basque Country) in 1974, and in 1976, he returned from exile. In 1977, he edited *El libro blanco del Euskera* (The White Book of Euskara), and in 1989, he became president of the executive council of *Euskaldunon Egunkaria*, the only periodical written entirely in Euskara, a post he held until 1998, when he was named an honorary director. In 1993, he became an honorary member of Euskaltzaindia.

Jokin Zaitegi Plazaola, Arrasate, 1906–Donostia, 1979. He entered the Jesuit order in 1920, completing his theological studies at the seminaries of Comillas, Oña, Loiola, and Marneffe. In Loiola he met Esteban "Lauaxeta" Urkiaga, Plazido Mujika, and Andima Ibiñagabeitia, with whom he would collaborate on literary matters, soon becoming one of the leading figures of the Eusko Pizkundea literary movement. Together with other Basque priests, he would create the Basque Poets Association, and he would soon become prominent for his poetry and his translations into Euskara, winning several literary prizes. Upon the outbreak of the war, he fled into exile in El Salvador and Panama. In 1944, in Guatemala, he left the Society of Jesus and began to teach at the University of San Carlos. In 1950, with the collaboration of Nikolas "Orixe" Ormaetxea and Andima Ibiñagabeitia, he created the periodical *Euzko Gogoa*, written entirely in Euskara. A year later, in 1951, he created the Liceo Landibar and the Santa Mónica Residence, the future Basque center of the Guatemalan capital. In 1953, the Academy of the Basque Language named Zaitegi a corresponding member. Between 1955 and 1960, he directed *Euzko Gogoa* from Miarritze, and he returned to Guatemala in 1962 without having been able to create the Basque Writers Center, intended to promote literary work in Basque. In 1972, he returned to Euskadi, and in 1976, he was named an honorary member of Euskaltzaindia.

Santiago Zarranz Etxeberria, Basauri, ????–Donostia, ????. A *gudari* during the war, he went into exile in Santiago de Chile, where he arrived in April 1939 on board the steamer *Oropesa*. In November 1942, while Pedro Aretxabala was delegate, he was named secretary of the Basque government's delegation in Chile and was consequently one of those most responsible for the Basque secret services in Chile. In July 1943, the delegation, prompted by Zarranz and Aretxabala, began to collect signatures for a testimonial in honor of US President Franklin D. Roosevelt by the Basques of the Americas, as a symbol of the Euskadi government's alignment with the Allies and in opposition to the forces of the Axis, and in November 1943, he represented the Chilean Basque communities at Basque Cultural Week in Uruguay. Together with Aretxabala, he obtained from President Pedro Aguirre Cerdá the promise that all Basque emigrants arriving in Chile would be guaranteed entry into the country. Zarranz calculated that the number of Basque exiles in Chile oscillated between seven hundred and eight hundred. He was among the founders of Euzko Etxea in Santiago de Chile in 1949, and together with Pedro Aretxabala, he represented the Chilean Basque organizations at the World Basque Congress held in Paris in 1956. Zarranz collaborated on the publication of the Chilean periodical *Euzkadi* from its foundation in 1943, and in 1983, he directed a special edition of the Chilean periodical *Euzko Deya* in which he published the lengthy article "Presencia vasca en Chile" (Basque Presence in Chile).

Doroteo Ziaurritz Aginaga, Tolosa, 1883–Donibane Lohitzune, 1951. Having graduated from the University of Zaragoza with a degree in medicine, he earned a doctorate at the Central University of Madrid and completed a specialty course in Paris. He was elected mayor of Tolosa in the 1931 elections, and following the outbreak of the war, he was elected president of the EBB, an office he held until his death in exile in 1951. In his role as mayor of Tolosa, he participated in the assembly held in Gernika on October 7, 1936, to name Jose Antonio Agirre *lehendakari* of the government of Euskadi. As president of the EBB, he had a prominent role in Agirre's decision to adopt the Basque national platform at the 1939 Meudon meetings. During the period of the Basque National Council in London, he threw all the EBB's support behind Manuel Irujo and José Ignacio Lizaso, and he played a critical role in matters surrounding the signing of the 1945 Pact of Bayonne, which the EAJ-PNV considered a strategic accord for the sake of unity of action against Franco. He actively participated in the development of the 1947 general strike and in the organization of the 1948 Basque Studies Congress.

Note on Sources

This book is mainly based on primary sources and archival documentation, as the notes reveal. These are contemporary documents by people involved in the events discussed, and most of the documents are registered as diplomatic or political files. In addition, the author interviewed several Basque political exiles.

Apart from these primary sources, the author conducted several interviews with figures of the Basque exile, such as Maria Teresa Agirre Lekube, sister of *Lehendakari* Agirre; José Elizalde Arzua, a Basque soldier during the campaign in the Basque Country (1936–1937), member of the French resistance, and member of the Gernika Battalion in 1945; Mari Carmen Hendaia, one of the children who went into exile in the colonies for refugee children organized by the Basque government; Andrés Irujo, founder and editor of Editorial Vasca Ekin and the Instituto Americano de Estudios Vascos; Maritxu Aranzadi, member of the secret services operating in the Spanish prisons; and Carlos G. Mendilaharzu, member of the Department of Basque Studies at the Universidad de la República in Montevideo.

Also, I have had the honor of personally shaking hands with some of the figures of the Basque exile such as Jesús María Leizaola, Juan Ajuriagerra, Julio Jauregi, Joxe Mari Lasarte, Telesforo Monzon, Manuel, Andrés and Pellomari Irujo, Martin Ugalde, Francisco Abrisketa, Jon Bilbao, Justo Garate, Joxe Migel Barandiaran, Miguel Pelay Orozko, Txomin and Juan Manuel Epalza, Txomin Jakakortexarena, Joseba Elosegi, Timoteo Plaza, Frank Church, and Josep Tarradellas, among others.

I also had access to the primary bibliography generated during the years of expatriation (1937–1975) by the key figures of the Basque political exile. Most of them were published by Ekin in Buenos Aires.

I visited and consulted four main archives in researching this book, the Archive of Basque Nationalism; the National Archives and Records Administration at College Park, Maryland; the Center for Basque Studies Archive at the University of Nevada, Reno; and the Irujo-Ametzaga family archive. I want to thank all of them for the warm welcome they gave me.

The Euskal Abertzaletasunaren Agiritegia (Archive of Basque Nationalism) is part of the Sabino Arana Foundation and is the main source of archival documentation on the War of 1936 and the subsequent Basque exile (1936–1975). The archive houses nearly thirty thousand monographs on Basque topics. The archive also contains more than five thousand periodical publications—or more than 130,000 issues—and more than 1 million documents on the history of Basque nationalism from the archives of the EAJ-PNV (1894–2008). It has more than 1,200 private donations (documents, photographs, and various objects). Apart from the abundant documentation (e.g., letters, governmental administrative documentation, photographs), the archive has a rich library containing hundreds of pamphlets, magazines, books, other documents, and videos, as well as a museum. The categories of classification and the type of inventory—Word or PDF format—available in the archive are fully described at the web site of the Sabino Arana Foundation (http://www.sabinoarana.org).

The files at the National Archive are organized according to the nature of the documents housed. Information regarding the war in the Basque Country (1936–1937) is almost entirely covered by funds from US Department of State, deposited in the headquarters of the National Archives in College Park, Maryland. The National Archive is the largest archive in the world, featuring various documents, as well as photographs, posters, maps, drawings, and other material of interest. The National Archives keeps significant documentation of the US embassy to the Spanish Republic generated by the US ambassador Claude G. Bowers and the US consul at Bilbao, William E. Chapman. All the documentation is on microfilm and easily accessible.[1] The assistants are extremely efficient and friendly. The archive also has a good Web page information service (see http://www.archives.gov/dc-metro/college-park).

The Center for Basque Studies' archive and library at the University of Nevada, Reno, is the largest library on Basque issues outside of the Basque Country. The library has a vast archive, with documents dating to the eighteenth century, and houses a good collection of documents related to the War of 1936, and other files donated by Basques from all over the Americas, especially the United States. Further information may be found at the library's Web page (www.library.unr.edu/basquelibrary/).

The Irujo-Ametzaga archive is a private collection of documents generated by both the Irujo and Ametzaga families in exile (1936–1975). The archive houses about five thousand documents of diverse nature, among them letters, political documents, manuscripts, reports, and photographs. All the documents are being progressively published.[2]

In addition to these archives, I must highlight the work of the Susa Argitaletxea publishing house in Zarautz. Susa maintains a Web site titled Armiarma (http://www.armiarma.com/), which contains a large anthology of literary works written in Basque,

1. For a complete description of the documents regarding the war of 1936 in the Basque Country, see Xabier Irujo Ametzaga, "NARA of the United States (NARA)," in *Guía de fuentes documentales de la Guerra Civil en Euskadi*, edited by José Luis de la Granja and Santiago de Pablo (Donostia-San Sebastián: Eusko Ikaskuntza, 2010).

2. The first part of the documents to be published was an anthology of the articles by Bingen Ametzaga written in exile: *Nostalgia/Herrimina* (Donostia-San Sebastián: Eusko Jaurlaritzako Kultura Saila, 1993). The poems in Basque by Bingen Ametzaga were also published as *Itsaso aurrean* (Zarautz: Susa, 2006). The letters on cultural issues by Bingen Ametzaga in America (1940–1969) have been compiled by Xabier Irujo in two volumes published by Utrusque Vasconiae in 2009: *Bingen Ametzaga Aresti: Gutunak I (1941–1968)* and *Bingen Ametzaga Arestiri egindako gutunak II (1939–1969).*

among them the key works by the Basque writers in exile (1937–1975). The works have not been compiled, cataloged, and transcribed, but they are available for consultation and research. The site also features the Literatur Aldizkarien Gordailua, with four major journals on the history of the Basque Country, *Gernika* (1945–1953), *Egan* (1948–), *Euzko Gogoa* (1950–1959), and *Olerti* (1959–1995). It also features the Klasikoen Gordailua and the Literaturaren Zubitegia, rich anthologies of poetry works in the Basque language for the period studied in this book.

I also must remark on the vast work of searching, cataloging, digitizing, and editing of Alberto Irigoyen and Adriana Patrón between 2004 and 2007, which includes in twelve CD-ROMs all the Basque journals published outside the Basque Country between 1877 and 1977: totaling 130 publications in thirteen countries and more than thirty-two thousand digital pages. The collection was published under the title *Hemeroteca de la diáspora vasca: Prensa americana y de otros países* (Newspaper and Periodicals Library of the Basque Diaspora: Newspapers of the Americas and Other Countries), was published by the Central Publications Service of the Basque Government in Gasteiz in 2007.

Primary Sources

This bibliography aims to point readers toward the classics of the Basque exile, primarily those works of intense ideological or political nature, as well as the main literary works written in Basque. In any case, it is not an exhaustive list. The works listed here are based on those volumes in the library of Bingen Ametzaga Aresti in Montevideo.

Abrisqueta, Francisco. *Presencia vasca en Colombia.* Vitoria-Gasteiz: Eusko Jaurlaritzaren Argitalpen Zerbitzu Nagusia/Servicio Central de Publicaciones del Gobierno Vasco, 1983.

——, ed. *Presencia vasca en América: Recopilación de trabajos de Jesús Galíndez publicados en la prensa vasca del exilio.* Vitoria-Gasteiz: Eusko Jaurlaritzaren Argitalpen Zerbitzu Nagusia/Servicio Central de Publicaciones del Gobierno Vasco, 1984.

Aguirre [Agirre], Jose Antonio. *Cinco conferencias pronunciadas en un viaje por América.* Buenos Aires: Ekin, 1944.

——. *De Gernika a Nueva York pasando por Berlín.* Buenos Aires: Ekin, 1944. Reprint, Madrid: Foca, 2004. Translated as *Escape via Berlin: Eluding Franco in Hitler's Europe.* Reno: University of Nevada Press, 1991.

——. *Diario de Agirre.* Tafalla: Txalaparta, 1998.

——. *Entre la libertad y la revolución, 1930–1935: La verdad de un lustro en el País Vasco.* Bilbao: Talleres Gráficos Emeterio Verdes Achirica, 1935.

——. *Guernica: Recuerdo de un crimen franquista.* Bogotá: Euzkadi'ko Ordezkaritza Colombia'n, 1944.

——. *El informe del Presidente Aguirre al gobierno de la República: Sobre los hechos que determinaron el derrumbamiento del frente del norte (1937).* Bilbao: La Gran Enciclopedia Vasca, 1978.

——. *Mensajes del Lendakari: 1940–1945.* Caracas: Gudari, 1976.

——. *Mensajes del Lendakari: 1936–1940.* Caracas: Gudari, 1975.

——. *Obras completas.* 2 vols. Donostia: Sendoa, 1981.

——. *Veinte años de política del Gobierno vasco (1936–1956).* Durango: Editorial Vizcaína, 1978.

Aldasoro, Ramón María. "El gobierno vasco y la República española." *Galeuzca* 2 (1945): 71–75.

——. "El gobierno vasco y la República española." *Galeuzca* 3 (1945): 118–24.

——. "El gobierno vasco y la República española." *Galeuzca* 4 (1945): 162–67.

Amezaga Aresti, Vicente. *El hombre vasco.* Buenos Aires: Ekin, 1967.

Ansaldo, Juan Antonio. *¿Para qué...? De Alfonso XIII a Juan XXIII.* Buenos Aires: Ekin, 1951.

Aralar, José de [Gabino Garriga]. *Los adversarios de la libertad vasca, 1794–1829.* Buenos Aires: Ekin, 1944.

——. *La rebelión militar española y el pueblo vasco.* Buenos Aires: Sebastián Amorrortu, 1937.

Astilarra [Andoni Astigarraga Larrañaga]. *Historia documental de la guerra de Euzkadi.* 3 vols. Mexico City: Editorial Vasca, [1941].

Azpiazu, Iñaki. *7 meses y 7 días en la España de Franco: El caso de los católicos vascos.* Caracas: Gudari, 1964.

——. *El caso del clero vasco: Conferencia pronunciada en el Centro Laurak-Bat, de Buenos Aires, el 18 de octubre de 1957.* Buenos Aires: Ekin, 1958.

——. *Examens de conscience pour les futurs prêtres: Avec préface de Mgr Clément Mathieu.* Imprimerie Catholique, 1942.

——. *Los vascos somos víctimas de un genocidio...: Conferencia pronunciada el día 6 de diciembre de 1958, con motivo de la celebración del Día Universal del Euskera.* N.p.: Argi eta Garbi, [1959].

Azpilikueta, Dr. [Jose Antonio Agirre]. *The Basque Problem as Seen by Cardinal Gomá and President Aguirre.* New York: Basque Archives, 1939.

Barandiaran, José Miguel. *Obras completas.* 22 vols. Bilbao: La Gran Enciclopedia Vasca, 1973–1984.

Basaldua, Pedro. *Con los alemanes en París.* Buenos Aires: Ekin, 1945.

——. *Crónicas de guerra y exilio.* Bilbao: Idatz-Ekintza, 1983.

——. *El dolor de Euzkadi.* Barcelona: Comisariat de Propaganda de la Generalitat de Catalunya, 1937.

——. *En España sale el sol.* Buenos Aires: Orden Cristiano, 1946.

——. *El Estatuto Vasco y la República Española.* Buenos Aires: Euzko-Deya, 1952.

——. *Jesús de Galíndez: El delegado vasco víctima de Trujillo.* Bilbao: Ereintza, 1981.

——. *Jesús de Galíndez: Víctima de la tiranía de América.* Buenos Aires: Macco, 1956.

——. *El libertador vasco Sabino de Arana y Goiri.* Buenos Aires: Ekin, 1953.

——. *Situación religiosa en España: Dolorosas realidades.* Santiago de Chile: Casa del Niño, 1947.

Bilbao, Jon. *América y los vascos*. Bilbao: Eusko Jaurlaritzaren Argitalpen Zerbitzu Nagusia/Servicio Central de Publicaciones del Gobierno Vasco, 1991.

——. *Eusko bibliographia: Diccionario de bibliografía vasca*. 10 vols. Donostia: Auñamendi, 1970–1981.

——. *Vascos en Cuba*. Buenos Aires: Ekin, 1958.

Biurrun Garmendia, Gabriel. *Rosas de Nínive*. Buenos Aires: Ekin, 1945.

Cortesao, Armando, Luis Araquistain, Manuel Irujo Ollo, and Carles Pi i Sunyer. *La comunidad ibérica de naciones*. Buenos Aires: Ekin, 1945.

Duhalde, Pierre [Policarpo Larrañaga]. *Le nationalisme basque et la guerre civile en Espagne*. Paris: n.p., 1937.

Dumas, Pierre. *Euzkadi: Les basques devant la guerre d'Espagne*. Paris: Éditions d'Aube, 1938.

Eguizalde, Ibon de. *Un homme, un clergé, un peuple: Euzkadi*. Paris: Peyre, 1938.

Eizagirre, José. *Ekaitzpean*. Buenos Aires: Ekin, 1948.

——. *Le probleme basque dans le panorame politique de l'Etat Espagnol: Rapport présenté a l'Union Universelle pour le Droit et la Paix*. Baiona: Société d'Edition et d'Imprimerie du Sud-Ouest, 1945.

Ertze Garamendi, Antonio. *Mis memorias*. Mexico: Garamendi, 1999.

Estornés Lasa, Bernardo. *Sabin euskalduna*. Zarautz: Eusko Argitaldaria, 1931.

Estornes Lasa, José. *Un gudari navarro en los frentes de Euzkadi-Asturias-Catalunya*. Donostia: Auñamendi, 1979.

Galíndez, Jesús. *Artículos políticos (1943–1956)*. Bilbao: Alderdi, 1985.

——. *Estampas de la guerra*. Buenos Aires: Ekin, 1951.

——. *Presencia vasca en América*. Vitoria-Gasteiz: Eusko Jaurlaritzaren Argitalpen Zerbitzu Nagusia/Servicio Central de Publicaciones del Gobierno Vasco, 1988.

——. *Principales conflictos de leyes en la América actual*. Buenos Aires: Ekin, 1945.

——. *Los vascos en el Madrid sitiado*. Tafalla: Txalaparta, 2005.

——. *Los vascos en el Madrid sitiado: Memorias del Partido Nacionalista Vasco y de la Delegación de Euzkadi en Madrid desde septiembre de 1936 a mayo de 1937*. Buenos Aires: Ekin, 1945.

Garate, Justo. *Un crítico en las quimbambas: Autobiografía y escritos*. Donostia: J. A. Ascunce, 1993.

Goicoechea Oroquieta, Ramón. *Ami vasco*. Buenos Aires: Ekin, 1957.

——. *Euzko ami*. Buenos Aires: Ekin, 1958.

Guaresti, Juan José. *País Vasco y estado español: La solución argentina*. Buenos Aires: Ekin, 1951.

Gudari [Elías Gallastegi Uriarte]. *Por la libertad vasca: En plena lucha*. Bilbao: Talleres Gráficos Emeterio Verdes Achirica, 1933.

Gurrutxaga, Ildefonso. *Reflexiones: Aprendamos nuestra historia.* Donostia: Saturraran, 2002.

——. *Reflexiones sobre mi país.* Donostia: Saturraran, 2002.

Irazusta, Jon Andoni. *Bizitza garratza da.* Buenos Aires: Ekin, 1950.

——. *Joañixio.* Buenos Aires: Ekin, 1946.

Irujo Ollo, Andrés. "Inventario Bibliográfico Vasco (1892–1950)." *Boletín del Instituto Americano de Estudios Vascos,* 1970–1973.

Irujo Ollo, Manuel. *Desde el Partido Nacionalista Vasco.* 7 vols. Bilbao: Ekin-Idatz Ekintza, 1982–1984.

——. *Escritos en Alderdi.* 2 vols. Bilbao: Eusko Alderdi Jeltzalea/Partido Nacionalista Vasco, 1981.

——. *La guerra civil en Euskadi antes del Estatuto.* Madrid: Gar, 1978–1979.

——. *Inglaterra y los vascos.* Buenos Aires: Ekin, 1945.

——. *Instituciones jurídicas vascas.* Buenos Aires: Ekin, 1945.

——. *La misión del nacionalismo.* Tolosa: López-Mendizabal, 1931.

——. *Navarra ante el Estatuto Vasco.* Lizarra: Imprenta Fray Diego de Estella, 1931.

——. *Navarra libre, dentro de Euzkadi libre.* Iruñea: n.p., 1931.

——. *Un vasco en el ministerio de justicia.* 3 vols. Buenos Aires: Ekin, 1978-1979.

Irujo Urra, Daniel. *Inocencia de un patriota.* Buenos Aires: Irrintzi, 1913.

Ispizua, Tiburcio. *Odisea del clero vasco exiliado.* Bilbao: Tiburcio Ispizua, 1986.

Iturralde, Juan [Juan José Usabiaga]. *El catolicismo y la cruzada de Franco.* 3 vols. Toulouse: EGI Indarra, 1965.

——. [Juan José Usabiaga]. *La guerra de Franco: Los vascos y la iglesia.* 2 vols. Donostia: Gráficas Izarra, 1978.

Jakakortexarena, Txomin. *Tu hermano de la clandestinidad.* Buenos Aires: Ekin, 1961.

——. *Zure anai ixilkari.* Buenos Aires: Ekin, 1961.

Jauregui, Julio. *Sobre la declaración del Gobierno Vasco en Nueva York: Acusaciones sin fundamento.* Mexico City: Eusko Deya, 1945.

Jemein, Ceferino. *18 de julio de 1936: El nacionalismo vasco y la sublevación militar en Euzkadi.* Bilbao: Alderdi, 1986.

——. *Euzkadi en guerra (1936–1937).* Bilbao: Alderdi, 1988.

——. *El primer gobierno vasco.* Bilbao: Alderdi, 1987.

Landaburu, Francisco Javier. *La causa del pueblo vasco.* Paris: Alderdi, 1956. Reprint, Bilbao: Editorial Geu Argitaldaria, 1977.

——. *Crónicas de política internacional.* Bilbao: Idatz Ekintza, 1982.

——. *Escritos en Alderdi, 1949–1962.* Bilbao: Eusko Alderdi Jeltzalea/Partido Nacionalista Vasco, 1980.

——. *Obras completas.* 5 vols. Bilbao: Idatz Ekintza, 1983.

——. *La question basque et la guerre civile en Espagne.* Brussels: Bureau Universel de Presse, n.d.

Leizaola, Jesús María. *Les Amis de l'Espagne Nouvelle: Le drame du Pays Basque.* Paris: SGIE, 1937.

——. *Les Basques et la construction européenne.* N.p.: Eusko Alderdi Jeltzalea/Partido Nacionalista Vasco, n.d.

——. *Contribución de los vascos a la formación y a la ciencia del derecho.* Bilbao: Minerva, 1937.

——. *Doroteo de Ziaurriz: Presidente del Euzkadi Buru Batzar 1935–1951.* Bilbao: Alderdi, 1985.

——. *Los facciosos son los culpables...* Bilbao: Eusko Jaurlaritza/Gobierno Vasco, 1937.

——. *La intervención de Alemania en favor de Franco en las operaciones del territorio vasco.* Bilbao: Eusko Jaurlaritza/Gobierno Vasco, 1937.

——. *Obras completas.* 4 vols. Donostia: Sendoa, 1981.

——. *El PNV en la vida práctica de dos tercios de siglo.* 2 vols. Caracas: Editorial Gudari, 1976.

Lizarra, Andrés de [Andrés Irujo Ollo]. *Los vascos y la República española.* Buenos Aires: Ekin, 1944.

Manning, Leah. *A Life for Education.* London: n.p., 1970.

Mendizabal, Alfredo. *Aux origines d'une tragédie.* Paris: Desclée de Brouwer, 1937.

Mitxelena, Koldo. *Historia de la literatura vasca.* Madrid: Minotauro, 1960.

Mitxelena, Salbatore. *Idazlan Guztiak.* 2 vols. Oñati: Editorial Franciscana Aranzazu, 1977.

Montserrat, Victor. *Le drame d'un peuple incompris: La guerre au Pays basque.* Paris: Peyre, 1937.

Monzon, Telesforo. *Hitzak eta Idazkiak.* 6 vols. Donostia: Jaizkibel, 1986.

——. *Urrundik.* Mexico City: Grafícas Cultura, 1945.

Múgica, Mateo. *Imperativos de mi conciencia: Carta abierta al Presbítero D. José Miguel de Barandiaran.* Cambo: n.p., 1945. Reprint, Buenos Aires: Liga de Amigos de los Vascos, 1946.

Muguerza, José María. *De Euskadi al campo de exterminio (memorias de un gudari).* Donostia: Haranburu, 1978.

Norbait [Andima Ibinagabeitia]. *Euskera Irudibidez (Nuevo método de euskera básico).* Paris: n.p., 1953.

Ojanguren, Ángel. *De procónsul británico en Bilbao a delegado vasco en Roma.* Bilbao: Fundación Sabino Arana. Sabino Arana Kultur Elkargoa, 1990.

Olarso [Miguel Pelay Orozco]. *Preludio sangriento.* La Plata: Calomino, 1943.

Oldargi [Manu Sota]. *La democracia vasca.* Santiago de Chile: Delegación de Euzkadi, 1944.

Onaindia, Alberto. *Experiencias del exilio: Capítulos de mi vida, II.* Buenos Aires: Ekin, 1974.

———. *Hombre de paz en la guerra: Capítulos de mi vida, I.* Buenos Aires: Ekin, 1973.

———. *Obras completas.* 4 vols. Bilbao: La Gran Enciclopedia Vasca, 1980.

———. *El Pacto de Santoña: Antecedentes y desenlace.* Bilbao: Laiz, 1983.

———. ed. *Hoy como ayer: Documentos del clero vasco.* Donibane Lohitzune: Axular, 1975.

Onaindia, Santiago, ed. *Milla euskal olerki eder.* Amorebieta: Itxaropena, 1954.

Ormaetxea, Nikolas. *Euskaldunak.* Bilbao: La Gran Enciclopedia Vasca, 1950.

———. *Euskaldunak poema eta olerki guziak.* Donostia: Auñamendi, 1972.

———. *Idazlan Guztiak.* 4 vols. Donostia: Etor, 1991.

———. *Urte guziko Meza-Bezperak.* Tours: Garikoitz'tar Laguntzailleak, 1949.

Tellagorri [José Olivares Larrondo]. *Comentarios a la doctrina de Acción Nacionalista Vasca.* Buenos Aires: Ediciones Tierra Vasca, 1957.

———. *París abandonada.* Havana: Ediciones La Verónica, 1942.

Trabudua, Polixene. *Crónicas de amama.* Bilbao: Fundación Sabino Arana/Sabino Arana Kultur Elkargoa–Emakunde, 1997.

Urarte, Agapito de. *En la patria vasca, justicia y libertad.* Bilbao: n.p., 1936.

Villasante, Luis. *Historia de la literatura vasca.* Bilbao: Sendoa, 1961.

Zaitegi, Jokin. *Berriz ere goldaketan, Berriz ere Goldaketan.* Guatemala City: Imprenta Hispania, 1962.

———. *Goldaketan.* Mexico City: Pizkunde Argitaletxea, 1946.

———, ed. *Euzko Gogoa.* Literatura Aldizkarien Gordegailua, Gipuzkoako Foru Aldundia, http://andima.armiarma.com/eugo/.

Zarranz, Santiago. *Presencia vasca en Chile.* Santiago de Chile: Eusko Jaurlaritzako Kultura Saila, Eusko Etxea, 1983.

General Bibliography

Abellán, José Luis, ed. *El exilio español de 1939*, 6 vols. Madrid: Taurus, 1976–1978.

Abellán, José Luis, and Emilio Palacios Fernández. *Memoria del exilio vasco: Cultura, pensamiento y literatura de los escritores transterrados en 1939*. Madrid: Biblioteca Nueva, 2000.

Abertzale bat, Epaltza'tar Txomin (1882–1956) (Nazien aurka). Donibane Lohitzune: Axular, 1978.

Aduriz, Iñaki, José Ángel Ascunce, and Jose Ramon Zabala. "América y los vascos: Introducción y estudio bibliográfico." *RIEV* 43, no. 1 (1998): 117–47.

Agirreazkuenaga, Joseba. *The Making of the Basque Question: Experiencing Self-Government, 1793–1877*. Reno: Center for Basque Studies, 2011.

Agirreazkuenaga, Joseba, and Jaume Sobrequés, eds. *Eusko Jaurlaritza eta Catalunyako Generalitatea: Erbestetik parlamentuen eraketara arte (1939–1980)*. Oñati: Herri Arduralaritzaren Euskal Erakundea/Instituto Vasco de Administración Pública, 2007.

Aguirre Zabala, Iñaki. "José Antonio Aguirre y Lecube: Político-historiador del pueblo vasco (1904–1960). *Notitia Vasconiae* 1 (2002): 579–606.

Ajuria, Peru, and Koldo San Sebastián. *El exilio vasco en Venezuela*. Vitoria-Gasteiz: Eusko Jaurlaritzaren Argitalpen Zerbitzu Nagusia/Servicio Central de Publicaciones del Gobierno Vasco, 1992.

Alday, Jesus Maria. *Crónicas: La voz del clero vasco en defensa de su pueblo*, 2 vols. Bilbao: Idatz-Ekintza, 1986.

Alonso Carballés, Jesús Javier. "Educación, cultura e identidad de los niños vascos en el exilio." In *Sesenta años después: Euskal Erbestearen Kultura*, edited by Xabier Apaolaza, José Ángel Ascunce, Iratxe Momoitio. Donostia: Hamaika Bide Elkartea, 2000.

———. *1937, los niños vascos evacuados a Francia y Bélgica: Historia y memoria de un éxodo infantil, 1936–1940*. Bilbao: Asociación de Niños Evacuados el 37/37an Atzerriraturiko Haurren Elkartea, 1998.

Álvarez Gila, Oscar. "Clero vasco y nacionalismo: Del exilio al liderazgo de la emigración (1900–1940)." *Studi Emigrazione/Migration Studies* 133 (1999): 103–17.

———. *Euskal Echea: La génesis de un sueño (1899-1950)*. Vitoria-Gasteiz: Eusko Jaurlaritzaren Argitalpen Zerbitzu Nagusia/Servicio Central de Publicaciones del Gobierno Vasco, 2003.

———. "Francoren garaiko Euskal Eliza eta Amerika: babeslekua eta arazoen iturburua." *Muga* 84 (1993): 44–51.

———. "La Guerra Civil en el País Vasco, el exilio y la opinión pública uruguaya (1936–1940)." *Vasconia: Cuadernos de Historia-Geografía* 31 (2001): 165–79.

Álvarez Gila, Oscar, Ronald Escobedo, and Ana Zabala, eds. *Emigración y redes sociales de los vascos en América*. Vitoria-Gasteiz: Euskal Herriko Unibertsitatea/Universidad del País Vasco, 1996.

Amezaga Iribarren, Arantzazu. *Crónicas del Alsina: Pasajeros de la libertad*. Bilbao: Idatz Ekintza, 1982.

———. "José María Lasarte: Un recuerdo personal." *Euzkadi*, April 13, 1978.

———. *Manuel Irujo, un hombre vasco*. Bilbao: Fundación Sabino Arana/Sabino Arana Kultur Elkargoa, 1999.

———. *Memorias de Montevideo*. Donostia: Saturraran, 2009.

———. *Nostalgia*, 2 vols. Donostia: J. A. Ascunce, 1993.

Amezaga Iribarren, Mirentxu. *Nere Aita*. Donostia: Txertoa, 1991.

Amezaga Urlezaga, Elías. "Diáspora del 36: Nómina de prensa y periodistas vascos en ultramar." In *Sesenta años después: Euskal Erbestearen Kultura*, edited by Xabier Apaolaza, José Ángel Ascunce, Iratxe Momoitio. Donostia: Hamaika Bide Elkartea, 2000.

———. *Lehendakari Aguirre: Una vida al servicio de su pueblo*. Vitoria-Gasteiz: Eusko Jaurlaritzaren Argitalpen Zerbitzu Nagusia/Servicio Central de Publicaciones del Gobierno Vasco, 1990.

———. *El primer Aguirre*, 4 vols. Bilbao: Idatz Ekintza, 1988.

———. *Tellagorri, 1892–1960: Estudio y selección de textos*. Getxo: Edigetxo, 1992.

Amezaga Urlezaga, Elías, and Arantzazu Amezaga. *Vicente de Amezaga (1901–1969)*. Getxo: Edigetxo, 2001.

Anasagasti, Iñaki, ed. *Conversaciones sobre José Antonio Aguirre*. Bilbao: Idatz Ekintza, 1983.

Anasagasti, Iñaki. "El exilio vasco 1936–1941." *Muga* 40 (February 1985): 26–39.

———. "La financiación del exilio." *Muga* 42 (April 1985): 48–63.

———. *Homenaje al Comité Pro-Inmigración Vasca en Argentina (1940): Fuentes documentales*. Donostia: Txertoa, 1988.

———. *Jesús María de Leizaola: Primer consejero de justicia y cultura del gobierno vasco*. Vitoria-Gasteiz: Eusko Jaurlaritzaren Argitalpen Zerbitzu Nagusia/Servicio Central de Publicaciones del Gobierno Vasco, 1986.

———. *Julio Jauregui, parlamentario y negociador vasco*. Bilbao: Alderdi, 1986.

Anasagasti, Iñaki, ed. *El primer gobierno vasco*, 2 vols. Vitoria-Gasteiz: Eusko Jaurlaritzaren Argitalpen Zerbitzu Nagusia/Servicio Central de Publicaciones del Gobierno Vasco, 1986.

Anasagasti, Iñaki, and Koldo San Sebastián. *Los años oscuros: El gobierno vasco—El exilio (1937–1941)*. Donostia: Txertoa, 1985.

Antoniutti, Ildebrando. *Memoria autobiografiche*. Udine: Ani Grafiche Friulane, 1975.

Apalategi, Jokin, and Xabier Palacios, eds. *Identidad vasca y nacionalidad: Pluralismo cultural y transnacionalización*. Vitoria-Gasteiz: Instituto de Estudios del Nacionalismo, 1995.

Apaolaza, Xabier, ed. *Herri bat bidegurutzean*. Donostia: Saturraran, 2003.

Arana Martija, José Antonio. *Elai-Alai, Euskalherriko lehenengo koreografi taldea, primer grupo coreográfico del País Vasco*. Gernika: Gernika Kultur Elkartea, 1977.

———. *Eresoinka: Embajada cultural vasca 1937–1939*. Vitoria-Gasteiz: Eusko Jaurlaritzaren Argitalpen Zerbitzu Nagusia/Servicio Central de Publicaciones del Gobierno Vasco, 1986.

Aranguren, Luis de. *Memorias de un exiliado vasco*. Mexico City: Editorial Vasca, 1958.

Areilza, José María. *Alcalá Zamora y Carlton Hayes opinan sobre España*. Madrid: Instituto de Estudios Políticos, 1945.

———. *Reivindicaciones de España*. Madrid: Instituto de Estudios Políticos, 1941.

Arrien, Gregorio. *La generación del exilio: Génesis de las escuelas vascas y colonias escolares (1932–1940)*. Bilbao: Onura, 1983.

———. *Niños evacuados en 1937: Álbum histórico*. Bilbao: Asociación de Niños Evacuados el 37/37an Atzerriraturiko Haurren Elkartea, 1988.

Arrien, Gregorio, and Iñaki Goiogana. *El primer exilio de los vascos: Cataluña, 1936–1939*. Barcelona: Fundación Sabino Arana/Sabino Arana Kultur Elkargoa, 2002.

Arrien, Gregorio, and Félix Zubiaga. *Niños evacuados a Gran Bretaña (1937–1940)*. Bilbao: Asociación de Niños Evacuados el 37/37an Atzerriraturiko Haurren Elkartea, 1991.

Arrieta Alberdi, Leyre. *Estación Europa: La política europeísta del PNV en el exilio (1945–1977)*. Madrid: Tecnos, 2007.

———. "Landaburu, el alavés europeísta." *Sancho el Sabio: Revista de Cultura e Investigación Vasca* 31 (2009): 199–220.

Arrieta Alberdi, Leyre, and José Antonio Rodríguez Ranz. *Radio Euzkadi, la voz de la libertad*. Bilbao: Euskal Irrati Telebista, 1998.

Arteche, José. *Un vasco en la postguerra: Diario 1939–1971*. Bilbao: La Gran Enciclopedia Vasca, 1977.

Artetxe, Lucio. *Diario de un abertzale: Prisión central de Burgos, 1940*. Bilbao: Fundación Sabino Arana/Sabino Arana Kultur Elkargoa, 1998.

Artis-Gener, Avelli. *La diáspora republicana.* Barcelona: Euros, 1976.

Ascunce, José Ángel, ed. *El exilio: Debate para la historia y la cultura.* Donostia: Saturraran, 2008.

Ascunce, José Ángel, María Luisa San Miguel, and Mónica Jato, eds. *Exilio y universidad (1936–1955)*, 2 vols. Donostia: Saturraran, 2008.

Ascunce, José Ángel, Xabier Apaolaza, and Marien Nieva, eds. *Encuentros con Martín de Ugalde: Martin Ugalde azterkisun.* Donostia: Saturraran, 2003.

Ascunce, José Ángel, Iratxe Momoitio, and Xabier Apaolaza, eds. *Sesenta años después: Euskal erbestearen kultura*, 2 vols. Donostia: Saturraran, 2001.

Ascunce, José Ángel, and María Luisa San Miguel, eds. *Los hijos del exilio vasco: Arraigo o desarraigo.* Donostia: Saturraran, 2004.

Ascunce, José Ángel, and José Ramón Zabala, eds. *Eugenio Ímaz: Asedio a un filósofo.* Donostia: Saturraran, 2002.

Astigarraga Larrañaga, Andoni de. *Abertzales en Argentina.* Bilbao: Alderdi, 1986.

———. *Breve historia de la FEVA.* Buenos Aires: Federacion de Entidades Vasco Argentinas, 1971.

Aulestia Txakartegi, Gorka. *Erbesteko euskal literaturaren antologia.* Donostia: J. A. Ascunce, 1992.

———. "Erbestetik barne minez." *Sancho el Sabio: Revista de Cultura e Investigación Vasca* 14 (2001): 250–251.

Ayuntamiento de Bilbao, ed. *José Antonio de Aguirre: Lehen Lehendakaria—Primer Lehendakari.* Bilbao: Bilboko Udala/Ayuntamiento de Bilbao, 2003.

Azcona Pastor, José Manuel, Inés García-Albi Gil de Biedma, and Fernando Muru Ronda. *Historia de la emigración a Argentina en el s. XX.* Vitoria-Gasteiz: Eusko Jaurlaritzaren Argitalpen Zerbitzu Nagusia/Servicio Central de Publicaciones del Gobierno Vasco, 1992.

Bandrés Unanue, Luis Mari. *El primer gobierno vasco.* Vitoria-Gasteiz: Eusko Jaurlaritzaren Argitalpen Zerbitzu Nagusia/Servicio Central de Publicaciones del Gobierno Vasco, 1986.

Barandiaran, Luis. *José Miguel de Barandiarán: Patriarca de la cultura vasca.* Donostia: Sociedad Guipuzcoana de Ediciones y Publicaciones, 1976.

Barruso, Pedro, Miguel Larrañaga, and José Ángel Lema. *Catálogo del Archivo Manuel de Irujo: Guerra y exilio (1936–1981)*, 2 vols. Donostia: Eusko Ikaskuntza, 1994.

Belaustegigoitia, Ramón de. *México de cerca.* Madrid: Sindicato de Publicidad, 1930.

Beltza [Emilio López Adán]. *El nacionalismo vasco en el exilio (1937–1960).* Donostia: Txertoa, 1977.

Benet, Josep. *Exili i mort del president Companys.* Barcelona: Editorial Empuries, 1990.

——. *La mort del president Companys.* Barcelona: Edicions 62, 1998.

Bernardo Urquijo, Iñaki, and Iñaki Goiogana Mendiguren. *Galíndez, la tumba abierta: Guerra, exilio y frustración.* Bilbao: Fundación Sabino Arana/Sabino Arana Kultur Elkargoa, 2006.

Bernoville, Gaëtan. *La farce de la main tendue: Du Frente Popular au Front Populaire.* Paris: Éditions Bernard Grasset, 1937.

Beti, Iñaki, and Mari Karmen Gil Fombellida, eds. *Arte eszenikoak erbestean: Las artes escénicas en el exilio.* Donostia: Saturraran, 2009.

Blasco Olaetxea, Carlos. *Conversaciones: Leizaola.* Bilbao: Idatz Ekintza, 1982.

Bodin, Louis, and Jean Touchard. *Front Populaire 1936.* Paris: Armand Colin, 1985.

Boothby, Robert J. G. *I Fight to Live.* London: Victor Gollancz, 1947.

——. *My Yesterday, Your Tomorrow.* London: Hutchinson, 1962.

Bowers, Claude G. *My Mission to Spain: Watching the Rehearsal for World War II.* New York: Simon and Schuster, 1952.

Cadogan, Alexander. *The Diaries of Sir Alexander Cadogan, O.M., 1938–1945.* London: Cassell, 1971.

Cassin, René. *Les hommes parties de rien: Le réveil de la France abattue, 1940–1941.* Paris: Plon, 1975.

Castelao, Alfonso R. *Obras*, 6 vols. Vigo: Editorial Galaxia, 2000.

Castresana, Luis. *El otro árbol de Guernica.* Bilbao: La Gran Enciclopedia Vasca, 1977.

——. *La verdad sobre "El otro árbol de Guernica."* Bilbao: La Gran Enciclopedia Vasca, 1972.

Cazaubon, Xavier. *L'Arrondissement de Bayonne et la Guerre Civile d'Espagne 1936–1939: Travail d'étude et de recherche.* Bordeaux: Université de Bordeaux III, Faculté des Lettres et Sciences Humaines, 1984–1985.

Centro de Información Católico Internacional. *El clero y los católicos vasco-separatistas y el Movimiento Nacional.* Madrid: Centro de Información Católico Internacional, 1940.

Chueca, Josu. "Erregimen frankistaren aurkako zenbait ekintza eta erakunderen berri." *Boletín Gerónimo de Uztariz* 4 (1990): 111–18.

Chueca Intxusta, Josu. *Gurs: El campo vasco.* Tafalla: Txalaparta, 2007.

Clark, Robert P. *The Basque Insurgents: ETA, 1952–1980.* Madison: University of Wisconsin Press, 1984.

——. *The Basques: The Franco Years and Beyond.* Reno: University of Nevada Press, 1979.

Clavijo, Julio. *La població refugiada a Olot durant la Guerra Civil (1936–1939): Estudi i fonts documentals.* Olot: Ediciones El Bassegoda, 1997.

Le clergé basque: Rapports présentés par des prêtes basques aux autoritiés ecclésiastiques. Paris: H. G. Peyre, 1938.

Cobb, Christopher H. *Los milicianos de la cultura.* Bilbao: Servicio Editorial Universidad del País Vasco, 1995.

Conductas diáfanas: Los socialistas vascos frente a la actitud del gobierno provisional de su región. Santiago: n.p., 1943.

Corcuera, Javier, and Yolanda Oribe, eds. *Historia del nacionalismo vasco en sus documentos*, 4 vols. Bilbao: Eguzki, 1991.

Correia, Magali. *Les basques espagnols refugiés en France pendant la Guerre Civile d'Espagne (1936–1939).* Paris: Université de Paris X, U.E.R. d'Histoire, 1985–1986.

Courougnon, Michel. *Les exilés des sept.* Hendaia: Mugalde, 1977.

Cuesta, Josefina, and Benito Bermejo, eds. *Emigración y exilio: Españoles en Francia (1936–1946).* Madrid: Eudema, 1996.

Dalloz, Jacques. *Georges Bidault: Biographie politique.* L'Harmattan: Chemins de la Mémoire, 1993.

Dean, Vera M. *The Four Cornerstones of Peace.* New York: McGraw Hill, 1946.

Diaz Esculies, Daniel. *El catalanisme politic a l'exili (1939–1959).* Barcelona: La Magrana, 1991.

Dios Unanue, Manuel. *El caso Galíndez: Los vascos en los servicios de inteligencia de EEUU.* Tafalla: Txalaparta, 1999.

Donovan, William J. *Fifth Column Lessons for America.* Washington, D.C.: American Council on Public Affairs, 1941.

——. *The Struggle to Create a United Europe.* New York: American Committee on United Europe, 1952.

Douglass, William A., and Jon Bilbao. *Amerikanuak: Basques in the New World.* Reno: University of Nevada Press, 1975.

Dreifort, John E. *Yvon Delbos at the Quai d'Orsay: French Foreign Policy during the Popular Front, 1936–1938.* Lawrence: University Press of Kansas, 1973.

Dreyfus-Armand, Genevieve. "Approche des minorités régionales dans l'exil: Eléments sur l'histoire des Basques et des Catalans en France (1939–1975)." *Exils et Migrations Ibériques au XX Siecle*, Centre d'Études et de Recherches sur les Exils et Migrations Ibériques, 1995, 23–40.

——. "El exilio vasco: La actividad cultural de los exiliados del 39 en Francia." In *Sesenta años después: Euskal Erbestearen Kultura*, 247–54. Donostia: Hamaika Bide Elkartea, 2000.

Duplá, Antonio. *Presencia vasca en América.* Donostia: Gakoa Liburuak, 1992.

Eliodoro de la Torre: Primer consejero de Hacienda del gobierno vasco. Vitoria-Gasteiz: Eusko Jaurlaritzaren Argitalpen Zerbitzu Nagusia/Servicio Central de Publicaciones del Gobierno Vasco, 1984.

Elosegi, Alberto. *El verdadero Galíndez.* Bilbao: A. Saldaña Ortega, 1990.

Esnaola, Serafín, and Emiliano Iturraran. *El clero vasco en la clandestinidad*, 2 vols. Elorrio: Jaime de Kerexeta, 1994.

Estévez, Xosé, ed. *Antología del Galeuzca en el exilio (1939–1960)*. Donostia: J. A. Ascunce, 1992.

Estornés Lasa, Mariano. *Gentes vascas en América.* Donostia: Auñamendi, 1961.

Euskal Batzar Orokorra–Congreso Mundial Vasco: 25 aniversario. Gasteiz: Eusko Jaurlaritza/ Gobierno Vasco, [1981].

Euzkadi Buru Batzar. *La democracia vasca en Londres: Confirmación doctrinal y de conducta.* Mexico: Euzkadi Buru Batzar, 1941.

Euzko Apaiz Talde. *Historia general de la Guerra Civil en Euskadi.* Donostia: Haranburu, 1981.

——. *Archivos del Clero Vasco I: Año 1936, En la persecución.* N.p.: E.A., 1978.

Fagan, Patricia Weiss. *Exiles and Citizens.* Austin: University of Texas Press, 1973.

Fernández, Marcial. *Trascendencia y hondura de Castelao.* Mexico City: Triskele, 1951.

Fernández de Pinedo, Emiliano. *La emigración vasca a América: Siglo XIX y XX.* Gijón: Jucar, 1993.

Fernández Fraga, Germán. *Contra-figura de José Antonio de Aguirre.* Montevideo: n.p. 1941.

Gachiteguy, Adrien. *Les basques dans l'Ouest Américain.* Bordele: Exkila, 1955.

García Sanz-Marcotegui, Ángel, ed. *El exilio republicano navarro de 1939.* Iruñea: Nafarroako Gobernuko Argitalpen Zerbitzua, 2001.

Garitaonaindia, Carmelo. *Jose Antonio Aguirre, primer lehendakari.* Bilbao: Herri Arduralaritzaren Euskal Erakundea/Instituto Vasco de Administración Pública, 1990.

Garmendia, José María, and Alberto Elordi. *La resistencia vasca.* Donostia: Haranburu, 1982.

Goiogana, Iñaki. "36ko Gerrari buruzko saio bibliografiko minimo bat." In *1936ko Gerra Euskal Herrian: Historia eta memoria.* Edited by Mikel Errazkin and Juantxo Agirre. Donostia: Udako Euskal Unibertsitatea, 2009.

——, ed. *José Antonio Agirre Lekube: Diario 1941–1942.* Bilbao: Fundación Sabino Arana/ Sabino Arana Kultur Elkargoa, 2010.

Goiogana, Iñaki, Xabier Irujo, and Josu Legarreta. *Un nuevo treinta y uno: Ideología y estrategia del Gobierno de Euzkadi durante la Segunda Guerra Mundial a través de la correspondencia de José Antonio Aguirre y Manuel Irujo.* Bilbao: Fundación Sabino Arana/Sabino Arana Kultur Elkargoa, 2007.

Goitia, Xabier. *Eusko umeak atzerrian.* Bilbao: Labayru Ikastegia-BBK, 1991.

Gordon Ordás, Félix. *Mi política fuera de España.* 4 vols. Mexico City: Talleres Gráficos Victoria, 1965–1970.

Gurruchaga, Ander. *El código nacionalista vasco durante el franquismo*. Barcelona: Anthropos, 1985.

Gutierrez Rave, José. *Las cortes errantes del Frente Popular*. Madrid: Editora Nacional, 1954.

Hayes, Carlton. *The United States and Spain: An Interpretation*. New York: Sheed and Ward, 1951.

——. *Wartime Mission in Spain, 1942–1945*. New York: Macmillan, 1945.

Heine, Hartmut. *La oposición política al Franquismo de 1939 a 1952*. Barcelona: Crítica, 1983.

Hernández, José Ángel. "El exilio nacionalista vasco en Colombia: El caso de Fernando Irusta." *Sancho el Sabio* 32 (2010): 85–93.

Hilderbrand, Robert C. *Dumbarton Oaks: The Origins of the United Nations and the Search for Postwar Security*. Chapel Hill: University of North Carolina Press, 1990.

Hull, Cordell. *The Memoirs of Cordell Hull*. New York: Macmillan, 1948.

——. *The Papers of Cordell Hull*. Washington, D.C.: Library of Congress Photoduplication Service, 1974.

Ibarzabal, Eugenio. *50 años de nacionalismo vasco (1928–1978)*. Bilbao: Ediciones Vascas, 1978.

Intxausti, Joseba. "Euzko-Gogoa-ren lankideak: Zaitegi eta Euzko-Gogoa (I)." *Jakin* 12 (1979): 120–37.

——. "Hamar urteko lana (1950–1959): Zaitegi eta Euzko-gogoa (eta II)." *Jakin* 13 (1980): 96–113.

Irigoyen Artetxe, Alberto, and Adriana Patrón, eds. *Hemeroteca de la diáspora vasca: Prensa americana y de otros países* [12 DVDs]. Vitoria-Gasteiz: Eusko Jaurlaritzaren Argitalpen Zerbitzu Nagusia/Servicio Central de Publicaciones del Gobierno Vasco, 2007.

Irujo Ametzaga, Xabier, ed. *Bingen Ametzaga Aresti: Gutunak I (1941–1968)*. Donostia: Utriusque Vasconiae, 2009.

Irujo Ametzaga, Xabier. *Bingen Ametzaga Aresti (1901–1969)*. Bidegileak No. 25. Vitoria-Gasteiz: Eusko Jaurlaritzako Kultura Saila, 2002.

——. *Bingen Ametzaga Arestiri egindako gutunak II (1939–1969)*. Donostia: Utriusque Vasconiae, 2009.

——. *Euskal erbeste politikoa Uruguain (1943–1955): Eusko jaurlaritzaren administrazioa eta kanpo ekintza atzerrian*. Oñati: Herri Arduralaritzaren Euskal Erakundea/Instituto Vasco de Administración Pública, 2005.

——. *Homo spelens*. Donostia: Utriusque Vasconiae, 2009.

——. *Itsaso aurrean*. Zarautz: Susa, 2006.

——. *Itzulpena erbestean*. Donostia: Utriusque Vasconiae, 2009.

———. *On Basque Politics: Conversations with Pete Cenarrusa.* Brussels: EURI, 2009.

Irujo Ametzaga, Xabier, and Alberto Irigoyen Artetxe. *La hora vasca del Uruguay: Génesis y desarrollo del nacionalismo vasco en Uruguay (1825–1960).* Montevideo: Sociedad de Confraternidad Vasca Euskal Erria, 2006.

———. *La sociedad de Confraternidad Vasca Euskal Erria de Montevideo.* Salamanca: Eusko Jaurlaritzaren Argitalpen Zerbitzu Nagusia/Servicio Central de Publicaciones del Gobierno Vasco, 2007.

Irujo Ollo, Manuel. "José María Lasarte." *Euzkadi,* March 22, 1978.

Izagirre, Koldo, ed. *Iokin Zaitegi.* Zarautz: Susa, 2000.

Iztueta, Paulo. *Erbesteko euskal pentsamendua.* Donostia: Utriusque Vasconiae, 2001.

Iztueta, Paulo. *Herbestean.* Donostia: Caja de Ahorros Provincial de Guipúzcoa, 1979.

Iztueta, Paulo, and Jon Diaz, eds. *Jokin Zaitegi gutunak.* 3 vols. Donostia: Utriusque Vasconiae, 2007.

Iztueta, Paulo, and Ibai Iztueta. *Orixe: Gutunak (1917–1961).* Donostia: Utriusque Vasconiae, 2006.

Jauregui, Julio. *Sobre la declaración del gobierno vasco en Nueva York: Acusaciones sin fundamento.* Mexico City: Eusko Deya, 1945.

Jauregi Beraza, Eduardo. *Joseba Rezola: Gudari de gudaris, Historia de la resistencia.* Bilbao: Fundación Sabino Arana/Sabino Arana Kultur Elkargoa, 1992.

Jimenez, Edorta. *Hemingway eta euskaldunak.* Zarautz: Susa, 2003.

Jiménez de Aberasturi, Juan Carlos, ed. *Los Çen la II Guerra Mundial: El Consejo Nacional Vasco de Londres (1940–1944).* Centro de Documentación de Historia Contemporánea del País Vasco 6. Gasteiz: Eusko Ikaskuntza, 1991.

———. *De la Guerra Civil a la Guerra Fría (1939–1947).* Donostia: Txertoa, 2001.

———. *De la derrota a la esperanza: Políticas vascas durante la segunda guerra mundial (1937–1944).* Oñati: Herri Arduralaritzaren Euskal Erakundea/Instituto Vasco de Administración Pública, 1999.

———. "La red Comète en el País Vasco (1941–1944)." *Oihenart: Cuadernos de Lengua y Literatura* 14 (1997): 121–31.

———. *Vascos en la Segunda Guerra Mundial: La red Comète en el País Vasco, 1941–1944.* Donostia: Txertoa, 1996.

———. "Los vascos en la II Guerra Mundial: Pasar el Bidasoa; El itinerario de la red "Comète" en el País Vasco." *Muga* 82 (1992): 36–55.

Jiménez de Aberasturi, Juan Carlos, and Rafael Moreno. *Al servicio del extranjero: Historia del Servicio Vasco de Información 1936–1943.* Madrid: Antonio Machado Libros, 2009.

Jiménez de Aberasturi, Juan Carlos, and Koldo San Sebastián, eds. *La huelga general del 1 de mayo de 1947: Artículos y documentos.* Donostia: Eusko Ikaskuntza, 1991.

Keppel, David. *FPK: An Intimate Biography of Fredrick Paul Keppel.* Washington, D.C.: Privately printed, 1951.

Laborde Duronea, Miguel. *Vascos en Santiago de Chile.* Santiago de Chile: Eusko Etxea, 1991.

Lachaise, Bernard. *Yvon Delbos, 1885–1956.* Périgueux: Fanlac, 1993.

Laharie, Claude. *Le camp de Gurs 1939–1945: Un aspect méconnu de l'histoire du Béarn.* Pau: Infocompo, 1985.

Landa, Carmelo. *Jesús María Leizaola: Vida, obra y acción política de un nacionalista vasco (1896–1977).* Bilbao: Fundación Sabino Arana/Sabino Arana Kultur Elkargoa, 1995.

Larrañaga, Policarpo. *Emakume Abertzale Batza: La mujer en el nacionalismo vasco.* Donostia: Auñamendi, 1978.

Larronde, Jean-Claude. *VIIème Congrès d'Études Basques: Eusko Ikaskuntzaren VII. Kongresua: VII Congreso de Estudios Vascos.* Donostia: Eusko Ikaskuntza, 2003.

——. *VIIIème Congrès d'Études Basques: Eusko Ikaskuntzaren VIII. Kongresua: VIII Congreso de Estudios Vascos.* Donostia: Eusko Ikaskuntza, 2003.

——. *El batallón Gernika: Gernika Batallun euskalduna, Los combates de la Pointe-de-Grave (Abril de 1945).* Baiona: Bidasoa, 1995.

——. *Eugene Goyheneche.* Donostia: Eusko Ikaskuntza, 1989.

——. *Exilio y solidaridad. La Liga Internacional de Amigos de los Vascos.* Milafranga: Bidasoa and Hegoa, 1998.

——. *Manuel de Ynchausti (1900-1961): Etorri handiko mezenas bat; Manuel de Ynchausti (1900-1961) Un mecenas de gran elocuencia.* Milafranga: Bidasoa, 1998.

——. *"La Roseraieko" ospitalea.* Milafranga: Bidasoa, 2002.

Legarreta, Dorothy. *The Guernica Generation: Basque Refugee Children of the Spanish Civil War.* Reno: University of Nevada Press, 1984.

Lorenzo, José María. *Rebelión en la ría: Vizcaya 1947: Obreros, empresarios y falangistas.* Bilbao: Universidad de Deusto, 1988.

Lormier, Dominique. *Bordeaux pendant l'occupation.* Bordeaux: Sud-Ouest, 1992.

Madariaga, Salvador de. *Memorias de un federalista.* Buenos Aires: Editorial Sudamericana, 1967.

Madarieta, Asier. "El último grito de unidad del exilio. El Congreso Mundial Vasco de 1956." In *Eusko Jaurlaritza eta Catalunyako Generalitatea: Erbestetik Parlamentuen eraketara arte (1939–1980).* Edited by Joseba Agirreazkuenaga and Jaume Sobrequés. Oñati: Herri Arduralaritzaren Euskal Erakundea/Instituto Vasco de Administración Pública, 2007.

Marquès, Pierre. *Les enfants espagnols réfugiés en France (1936–1939)*. Paris: P. Marquès, 1993.

Marquina, Antonio. "El Pacto Galeuzca: Planteamientos federales de Euzkadi y Cataluñya tras la Guerra Civil." *Historia 16* 46 (1980): 27–37.

Marquina Barrio, Antonio. "El servicio secreto vasco." *Historia 16* 9 (1984): 11–26.

Martínez, Joaquín G. *Influencia vasca en la conformación política, económica y social de la República Argentina*. Buenos Aires: n.p., 1977.

Martínez Gorrano, María Eugenia. "El exilio vasco de 1939 en Colombia: circunstancias y aportaciones mas destacables." In *Emigración y redes sociales de los vascos en América*. Edited by Óscar Álvarez Gila, Ronald Escobedo, and Ana Zabala, 215–228. Vitoria-Gasteiz: Euskal Herriko Unibertsitatea/Universidad del País Vasco, 1996.

Martínez Salazar, Ángel, and Koldo San Sebastián. *Los vascos en México: Estudio biográfico, histórico y bibliográfico*. Vitoria-Gasteiz: Eusko Jaurlaritzako Lehendakaritza/Presidencia del Gobierno Vasco, 1992.

Mayeur, Françoise. *L'Aube: Étude d'un journal d'opinion 1932–1940*. Paris: Cahiers de la Fondation Nationale des Sciences Politiques, Librairie Armand Colin, 1966.

Medina, Xavier. *Los otros vascos: Las migraciones vascas del siglo XX*. Madrid: Fundamentos, 1997.

Mees, Ludger. *El profeta pragmático: Aguirre, el primer Lehendakari (1939–1960)*. Irun: Alberdania, 2006.

——. "Manuel Irujo: La heterodoxia de un demócrata." *Vasconia* 32 (2002): 133–53.

Mees, Ludger, and Santiago de Pablo. "El gobierno vasco en el exilio." *Cuadernos de Alzate* 18 (1998): 41–56.

Milza, Pierre, and Denis Peschanski, eds. *Exils et migration: Italiens et Espagnols en France, 1938–1946*. Paris: L'Harmattan, 1994.

Mínguez, Alberto. *El pensamiento político de Castelao: Antología bilingüe*. Paris: Ruedo Ibérico, 1965.

Miralles, Ricardo. "La política exterior de la República española hacia Francia durante la Guerra Civil." *Historia Contemporánea* 10 (1993): 29–50.

Mugarza Mecolalde, Daniel. *El decenio crítico: La política y la guerra en el País Vasco entre 1930 y 1940*. Oñati: Gráficas Logroño, 1974.

Mújica, Gregorio. *Los titanes de la cultura vasca*. Donostia: Auñamendi, 1962.

Muñoz, Edurne, ed. *Jose Antonio Agirre: Proiektu kultural bat*. Donostia: Saturraran, 2007.

Naharro-Calderón, José María. *El exilio de las Españas de 1939 en las Américas*. Barcelona: Anthropos, 1991.

Ordaz, María Ángeles. "El FBI y los vascos del exilio de 1939 en Estados Unidos." In *Emigración y redes sociales de los vascos en América*. Edited by Óscar Álvarez Gila,

Ronald Escobedo, and Ana Zabala, 229–40. Vitoria-Gasteiz: Euskal Herriko Unibertsitatea/Universidad del País Vasco, 1996.

Ordaz, María de los Ángeles. "La delegación vasca en Nueva York, una década bajo el punto de mira del FBI." *Estudios de Historia Social y Económica de America* 12 (1995): 179–97.

Pablo, Santiago de, Ludger Mees, and José Antonio Rodríguez Ranz. *El péndulo patriótico: Historia del Partido Nacionalista Vasco II (1936–1979).* Barcelona: Crítica, 2001.

Pàmies, Teresa. *Los niños de la guerra.* Barcelona: Ediciones Bruguera, 1977.

Pastor, Robert. *Euskalerria en Venezuela.* Donostia: Ediciones Vascas, 1979.

Peillen, Txomin, ed. *Euskaldun etorkinak Ameriketan.* Donostia: Utriusque Vasconiae, 2003.

Pelay Orozco, Miguel. *Juan Ajurriaguerra: Su vida, su obra, su muerte.* Bilbao: Idatz Ekintza, 1987.

Pi i Sunyer, Carles. *Memories de l'exili.* 2 vols. Barcelona: Curial, 1978–1979.

Pike, David W. *Vae Victis! Los republicanos españoles refugiados en Francia 1939–1944.* Barcelona: Ruedo Ibérico, 1969.

Pons Prades, Eduardo. *Los derrotados y el exilio.* Barcelona: Ediciones Bruguera, 1977.

———. *Las guerras de los niños republicanos (1936–1995).* Madrid: Compañía Literaria, 1997.

Plata Parga, Gabriel. *La derecha vasca y la crisis de la democracia española (1931–1940).* Bilbao: Bizkaiko Foru Aldundia/Diputación Foral de Bizkaia, 1986.

Prieto, Indalecio. *Textos escogidos.* Oviedo: Junta General del Principado de Asturias, 1999.

Problema de España ante el mundo internacional: Resolución aprobada por la 1ª Asamblea General de Naciones Unidas; Texto y discusión de la misma. London: República Española, Ministerio de Estado, 1946.

Rafaneau-Boj, Marie-Claude. *Los campos de concentración de los refugiados españoles en Francia (1939–1945).* Barcelona: Editorial Omega, 1995.

Raguer, Hilari. *La espada y la cruz: la iglesia 1936-1939.* Barcelona: Bruguera, 1977.

———. *Divendres de Passio: Vida i mort de Manuel Carrasco i Formiguera.* Montserrat: Publicacions de l'Abadia de Montserrat, 1984.

———. "Paul Vignaux y Manuel de Irujo." *Cristianesimo nella Storia* 12 (1991): 381–90.

———. *La pólvora y el incienso: La iglesia y la Guerra Civil Española.* Barcelona: Península, 2008.

———. *Salvador Rial, vicari del cardenal de la Pau.* Montserrat: Publicaciones de l'Abadia de Montserrat, 1993.

———. *La Unio Democratica de Catalunya i el seu temps (1931–1939).* Montserrat: Publicacions de l'Abadia de Montserrat, 1976.

Rodríguez, Miguel José. "Los vascos en la Segunda Guerra Mundial: Contra Hitler, Franco y Stalin." *Historia 16* 291 (2000): 74–87.

——. "Los vascos en la Segunda Guerra Mundial: Memoria del Batallón Gernika." *Historia y Vida* 351 (1997): 78–87.

Romaña Arteaga, José Miguel. *La Segunda Guerra Mundial y los vascos.* Bilbao: Mensajero, 1988.

Rubio, Javier. "Las cifras del exilio." *Historia 16* 30 (1978): 15–32.

——. *La emigración de la Guerra Civil de 1936–1939.* 3 vols. Madrid: San Martín, 1977.

Ruiz de Gauna, Adolfo. *Catálogo de publicaciones periódicas vascas de los siglos XIX y XX.* Vitoria-Gasteiz: Eusko Jaurlaritzaren Kultura Saila, 1991.

Salazar González, Julene, and Roberto Hernández Ponce. *Cuatrocientos años de presencia vasca en Chile.* Santiago de Chile: Eusko Etxea, 1991.

Sallaberry, Francis. *Quand Hitler betonnait la Côte Basque.* Baiona: Harriet, 1988.

San Sebastián, Koldo. *The Basque Archives: Vascos en Estados Unidos (1938–1943).* Donostia: Txertoa, 1991.

——. *Crónicas de postguerra (1937–1951).* Bilbao: Idatz Ekintza, 1982.

——., dir. *El exilio en América* [videorecording]. ETB, 1992.

——. *El exilio vasco en América: 1936–1946, Acción del gobierno.* Donostia: Txertoa, 1988.

——., dir. *José Antonio Aguirre* [videorecording]. ETB, 1992.

——., ed. *Origen de la comunidad vasca en México.* Harriluze: Getxo-Gernika, 1993.

——. "Programa y organización del Gobierno Vasco (1936–1937)." *Muga* 60–61 (1987): 82–93.

——. "La reorganización del gobierno vasco (1943–1946)." *Muga* 70 (1989): 72–81.

Sancho de Beurco [Luis Ruiz de Aguirre]. *Vascos por el mundo.* Donibane Lohitzune: Askatasuna, 1975.

Sauret, Joan. *L'exili politic català.* Barcelona: Aymà, 1979.

Schlesinger, Stephen E. *Act of Creation, the Founding of the United Nations: A Story of Superpowers, Secret Agents, Wartime Allies and Enemies, and Their Quest for a Peaceful World.* Boulder, CO: Westview Press, 2003.

Schor, Ralph. *L'opinion française et les étrangers en France 1919–1939.* Paris: Publications de la Sorbonne, 1985.

——. "Les partis politiques français et le droit d'asile (1914–1939)." *Revue Historique* 540 (1981): 445–59.

Sebastian, Lorenzo, and Ana Gemma Mendaza. "Euzko Deya: La voz de Euskadi, la voix des Basques: Órgano de prensa del gobierno vasco en Francia (noviembre 1936-mayo 1940)." In *Españoles en Francia 1936–1946: Coloquio Internacional; trabajos presentados, Salamanca 2, 3 y 4 de mayo de 1991*, 345–56. Salamanca: Universidad de Salamanca, 1991.

Sebastián García, Lorenzo. *Entre el deseo y la realidad: La gestión del Departamento de Cultura del Gobierno Provisional de Euzkadi (1936–1937)*. Oñati: Herri Arduralaritzaren Euskal Erakundea/Instituto Vasco de Administración Pública, 1994.

Shain, Yossi, ed. *Governments in Exile in the Contemporary World of Politics*. London: Chapman and Hall, 1991.

Sierra Bustamante, Ramón. *Euzkadi: De Sabino Arana a José Antonio Aguirre; Notas para la historia del nacionalismo vasco*. Madrid: Editora Nacional, 1941.

Sodigné Loustau, Jeanine. "L'accueil des réfugiés civils de 1936 á 1940; un exemple: La région Centre." *Matériaux pour l'Histoire de Notre Temps* 44 (October–December 1996).

Southworth, Herbert R. *Guernica, Guernica: A Study of Journalism, Diplomacy, Propaganda and History*. Berkeley: University of California Press, 1977.

Steer, George L. *The Tree of Gernika: A Field Study of Modern War*. London: Hodder and Stoughton, 1938. Reprint, London: Faber and Faber, 2009.

Stein, Louis. *Más allá de la muerte y el exilio: Los republicanos españoles en Francia (1939–1955)*. Barcelona: Plaza y Janés, 1983.

Stephenson, William S., ed. *British Security Coordination: The Secret History of British Intelligence in the Americas, 1940–1945*. New York: Fromm International, 1998.

Stettinius, Edward R. *The Diaries of Edward R. Stettinius Jr., 1943–1946*. New York: New Viewpoints, 1975.

Thomas, Gordon. *Secret Wars: One Hundred Years of British Intelligence inside MI5 and MI6*. New York: Thomas Dunne Books, 2009.

Torres, Eugenio. *Ramón de la Sota, 1857–1936: Un empresario vasco*. Madrid: LID, 1998.

Totoricagüena, Gloria. *Diáspora vasca comparada: Etnicidad, cultura y política en las colectividades vascas*. Vitoria-Gasteiz: Eusko Jaurlaritzaren Argitalpen Zerbitzu Nagusia/Servicio Central de Publicaciones del Gobierno Vasco, 2003.

Tusell, Javier. *Las democracias cristianas europeas después de la Segunda Guerra Mundial*. Madrid: Fundación Humanismo y Democracia, 1984.

——. *Historia de la democracia cristiana española: Los nacionalismos vasco y catalán*. Vol. 2. Madrid: Sarpe, 1986.

Ugalde, Martín. *Biografía de tres figuras nacionales vascas: Arana-Goiri, Agirre y Leizaola*. Donostia: Sendoa Argitaldaria, 1984.

——. *Hablando con los vascos*. Madrid: Ariel, 1974.

Ugalde Zubiri, Alexander. *La acción exterior del nacionalismo vasco (1890–1939): Historia, pensamiento y relaciones internacionales*. Oñati: Herri Arduralaritzaren Euskal Erakundea/Instituto Vasco de Administración Pública, 1996.

———. "La actuación internacional del primer gobierno vasco durante la Guerra Civil (1936–1939)." *Sancho el Sabio* 6 (1996): 187–210.

———. *La haportación vasca al federalismo europeo: Europako Mugimenduaren Euskal Kontseilua (1951–2001); Europako federalismoari euskaldunek egindako ekarpena.* Gasteiz: Europako Mugimenduaren Euskal Kontseilua, 2001.

———. "La contribución del gobierno vasco a la acción de la República española ante Naciones Unidas en 1945–46." In *La política exterior de España en el siglo XX.* Edited by Javier Tusell et al., 327–37. Madrid: Universidad Nacional de Educación a Distancia, 1997.

———. "The International Relations of Basque Nationalism and the First Basque Autonomous Government (1890–1931)." In *Paradiplomacy* in *Action: The Foreign Relations of Subnational Governments.* Edited by Francisco Aldecoa and Michael Keating, 170–84. London: Frank Cass, 1999.

United Nations: Delegates and Officials of the United Nations Conference on International Organization, revised May 28. San Francisco: United Nations, 1945.

United States Delegation to the United Nations Conference on International Organization: Charter of the United Nations: Report to the President on the Results of the San Francisco Conference by the Chairman of the United States Delegation, the Secretary of State. Washington, D.C.: US Government Printing Office, 1945.

Uriarte, José R. *Los vascos en la nación argentina.* Buenos Aires: Ekin, 1897.

Urkizu, Patri, ed. *Andima Ibiñagabeitia: Erbestetik barne-minez; Gutunak 1935-1967.* Donostia: Susa, 2000.

———., ed. *Jon Miranderen Gutunak (1948-1972).* Donostia: Susa, 1995.

Urrutia, Txema. *El roble y el ombú: Viaje a la América de los vascos.* Vitoria-Gasteiz: Eusko Jaurlaritzaren Argitalpen Zerbitzu Nagusia/Servicio Central de Publicaciones del Gobierno Vasco, 1992.

Usabel, Gaizka. "Lo vasco en el mundo: Revistas, verdades y estereotipos; Selecciones de artículos." *Muga* 54–55 (May–June 1986).

Valle, José María del. *Las instituciones de la República española en el exilio.* Paris: Ruedo Ibérico, 1976.

Vascos en la construcción de Europa. Bilbao: Eusko Alderdi Jeltzalea/Partido Nacionalista Vasco, 1989.

Velez de Mendizabal, Joxe M. *Iokin Zaitegi.* Arrasate: Arrasateko Udala, 1981.

Viganux, Paul. *Manuel Irujo, Ministre de la République dans la Guerre d'Espagne (1936–1939).* Paris: Beauchesne, 1986.

Villanueva Edo, Antonio. *El sanatorio de Gorliz.* Bilbao: Bizkaiko Foru Aldundia/Diputación Foral de Bizkaia, 1991.

Villegas, Jean Claude, ed. *Plages d'exil: Les camps de réfugiés espagnols en France, 1939.* Paris: BDIC (Bibliothèque de Documentation Internationale Contemporaine), 1989.

Zabala, José Ramón, ed. *Non zeuden emakumeak? La mujer vasca en el exilio de 1936.* Donostia: Saturraran, 2007.

Zabala Allende, Federico. *El gobierno de Euzkadi y su labor legislativa 1936–1937.* Oñati: Herri Arduralaritzaren Euskal Erakundea/Instituto Vasco de Administración Pública, 1986.

Zafra, Enrique, Rosalia Grego, and Carmen Heredia. *Los niños españoles evacuados a la URSS (1937).* Madrid: Ediciones de la Torre, 1989.

Zuberogoitia, Aitor. *Jose Antonio Agirre.* Donostia: Elkar, 1997.

Zugazagoitia, Julián. *Guerra y vicisitudes de los españoles.* Barcelona: Editorial Crítica Grijalbo, 1977.

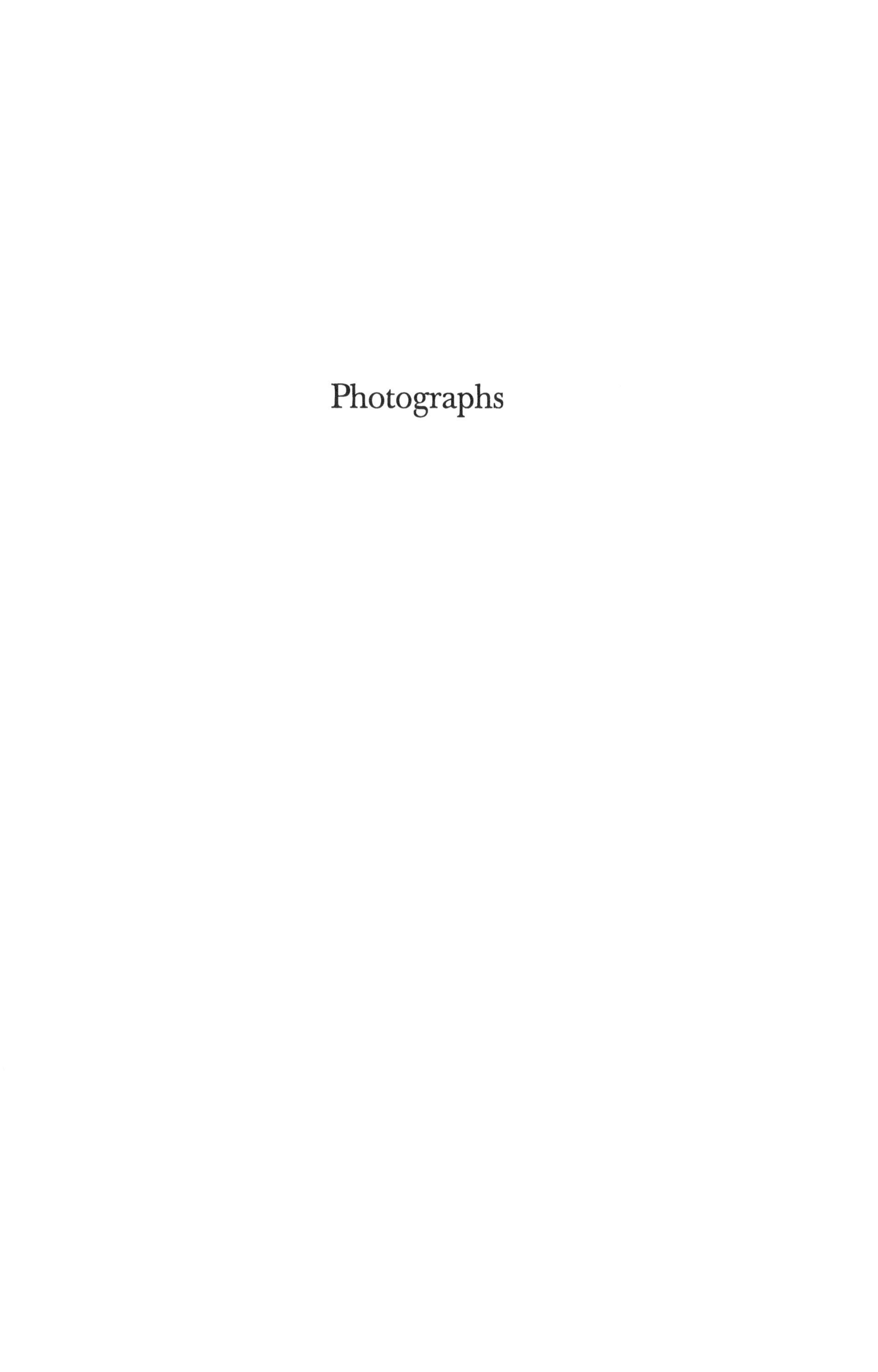

Photographs

Ministers of the new Basque Government on Bilbao's Gran Via the day after the election of Jose Antonio Agirre as Lehendakari (president) of the Basque autonomous state, in October 1937. From left to right: Telesforo Monzon, Gonzalo Nardiz (behind), Juan de los Toyos, Santiago Aznar, Alfredo Espinosa, Eliodoro de la Torre, Civil Governor of Bizkaia José Echevarría Novoa, Jose Antonio Agirre, President of the Gestora of the government of Bizkaia Rufino Laiseca, Jesús Ma. Leizaola and Ramón Ma. Aldasoro. Source: Anasagasti Archive.

José María Areilza, with the fascist uniform of the Falange, greeting the occupying troops in a ceremony that took place after the occupation of Bilbao before the Carlton hotel, former headquarters of the Basque government led by Jose Antonio Agirre. Bilbao, 1937.
Source: Anasagasti Archive.

Basque delegation in Rome. Source: Irujo-Ametzaga Archive.

Colony or school for Basque refugee children in exile in Donibane Garazi, in the Northern Basque Country, in 1937. The colony of Donibane Garazi was one of the largest and was home for nearly five hundred children. In the center, standing, Bingen Ametzaga, director of the school until 1938. Source: Irujo-Ametzaga Archive.

Basque exiles on the *Quanza* in their way to the Americas. Some of them landed in Veracruz (Mexico) and others continued their trip towards Caracas (Venezuela), Havana (Cuba), and finally, aboard the *Río de La Plata* to Buenos Aires (Argentina). It was an odyssey that lasted from January 15, 1941 until April 15, 1942. Source: Irujo-Ametzaga Archive.

Jesus Ma. Leizaola (1896–1989), member of the EAJ-PNV, vice president and minister of justice and culture of the Basque government-in-exile. After the death of Lehendakari Agirre in 1960, Leizaola became the new Lehendakari of the Basque government-in-exile until the fall of the Spanish dictatorial regime. Source: Anasagasti Archive.

Eliodoro de la Torre (1889–1946), member of the EAJ-PNV, minister of finance of the Basque government-in-exile and also minister of health after the capture and execution of minister Alfredo Espinosa in the summer of 1937.
Source: Anasagasti Archive.

Juan Gracia (1891–1941), member of the PSOE, minister of social welfare of the Basque government-in-exile until his death in occupied Paris. Source: Anasagasti Archive.

Doroteo Ziaurritz, chair of the Euzkadi Buru Batzar of the Basque Nationalist Party.

Gudari (Basque soldier) of the Gernika Battalion that took part in the fight for the liberation of Pointe-de-Grave in April 1945. Source: Center for Basque Studies Archive, University of Nevada, Reno.

Boise Ada County all Basque volunteer company in Boise (Idaho) in 1942. Source: Center for Basque Studies Archive, University of Nevada, Reno.

Jose Ignacio Lizaso, delegate of the Basque Government in London during World War Two with his family.

Andima Ibinagabeitia, Jokin Zaitegi, and Nikolas Ormaetxea, Orixe. Source: Center for Basque Studies Archive.

Lehendakari Jose Antonio Agirre in Río Grande do Sul (Brazil) in October 1941, after his escape from the occupied Europe. From left to right, standing:
Juan Domingo Uriarte and Julio Iturbide. From left to right, seated: Jose Antonio Agirre still with moustache (which he wore in his disguise as Dr. José Alvarez Lastra) and the Uruguayan consul to Brazil, Dr. Balbela. Source: Irujo-Ametzaga Archive.

Reception in honor to Lehendakari Jose Antonio Agirre at the House of Government of Uruguay in October 1941. From left to right: (third) Julio Iturbide, Minister Javier Mendivil, Jose Antonio Agirre, President of Uruguay Alfredo Baldomir, President of the Pro Basque Immigration Committee of Argentina José Urbano Agirre, Delegate of the Basque Government in Argentina Ramón Ma. Aldasoro. Source: Irujo-Ametzaga Archive.

Jose Antonio Aguirre speaking from one of the seats at the Parliament of the Republic of Uruguay. Montevideo, October 1941. Source: Irujo-Ametzaga Archive.

Jose Antonio Agirre and Eusebio Irujo in Caracas in 1955. Source: Irujo-Ametzaga Archive.

Seventh Congress of Basque Studies held in Biarritz on September 12–19, 1948. Source: Anasagasti Archive.

Celebration of the Aberri Eguna in Donibane Lohitzune, in the Northern Basque Country, in 1939. Dancing an Ingurutxo: Telesforo Monzon, Maria Josefa Ganuza, Manuel Epalza, Carmen Solano, Xabier Gortazar, Luisa Landecho, Jesús Ma. Leizaola. Source: Anasagasti Archive.

Lehendakari Jose Antonio Agirre (1904–1960).
Source: Irujo-Ametzaga Archive.

Jesús Galíndez (1915–1956). Source: Anasagasti Archive.

Dantzariak (basque dancers) on their arrival at the port of Montevideo, Uruguay, for the celebration of the Great Basque Week of Montevideo. October 30, 1943. Source: Irujo-Ametzaga Archive.

Bingen Ametzaga giving a speech during the inauguration of Gernika Square in Montevideo, Uruguay, on May 13, 1944. Source: Irujo-Ametzaga Archive.

Bishop Clement Mathieu with Jose Antonio Agirre during the celebration of the Seventh Congress of Basque Studies held in Biarritz in September 1948. Source: Anasagasti Archive.

Joseba Rezola during his visit to Caracas, Venezuela, in 1970. From left to right: the president of the Social Christian Party of Venezuela Pedro del Corral, Joseba Rezola, and the president of Venezuela, Rafael Caldera. Source: Anasagasti Archive.

Manuel Irujo and Canon Alberto Onaindia during the presentation of the book *La causa del pueblo vasco* by Xabier Landaburu on November 14, 1977 at the Teatro de la Florida in Gasteiz-Vitoria. It was the first public appearance of Canon Onaindia in the Basque Country in forty years since he went to exile in 1937. Source: Anasagasti Archive.

Jose Antonio Agirre in Montevideo, Uruguay, in 1941. Source: Irujo-Ametzaga Archive.

Ramón de la Sota Aburto (1897–1979), ca. 1977.
Source: Anasagasti Archive.

Department of Basque Studies at the University of the Republic of Uruguay. From left to right: Carlos G. Mendilaharzu, Gabriel Biurrun, Bingen Ametzaga, Héctor Tosar Errecart, Lauro Ayestarán, and Eduardo Berro. Montevideo, 1943

Francisco Abrisketa (1913–1983) at the Hotel Ercilla in Bilbao on October 27, 1983. Source: Anasagasti Archive.

Andrés Irujo (1907–1993). Source: María Elena Etcheverry.

Basque World Congress held in Paris in 1956. From left to right: Manuel Campomanes, Jesús Ma. Leizaola, Jose Antonio Agirre, Ambrosio Garbisu, Paulino Gómez, and Gonzalo Nardiz. Source: Anasagasti Archive.

Manuel Irujo (1891–1981).
Source: Irujo-Ametzaga Archive.

A Basque priest playing "pilota" or Basque handball in the Northern Basque Country, ca. 1955. The sign "Herriaren Indarra Batasuna" literally means, "The strength of a nation is in its unity." Source: Center for Basque Studies Archive, University of Nevada, Reno.

Cover of one of the recordings produced at the Basque Center of Caracas (Venezuela) by the local Choir Pizkunde. Source: Irujo-Ametzaga Archive.

Lehendakari Jose Antonio Agirre during the celebration of a mass on Aberri Eguna day at the Basque Center in Caracas, Venezuela, in 1955. Source: Irujo-Ametzaga Archive.

Visist of US senator Frank Church to the Basque Center of Caracas, Venezuela, in 1972. In the photograph the 110 students of the Euzkadi Ikastola (Basque school) of the Basque Center. Upstairs, in the center, Manuel Irujo, Bethine Church and Frank Church. In the third row from the bottom, eighth from the left, Xabier Irujo, author of this book. Source: Boise State University Frank Church Archive.

Two Basque dancers of the Basque Center of Caracas, Venezuela, in 1972. From left to right, Xabier Irujo and Jon Ander Escosura. Source: Irujo-Ametzaga Archive.

Lehendakari Jesús Ma. Leizaola (1896-1989). Source: Anasagasti Archive.

The end of the Spanish dictatorship and the Basque political exile. Manuel Irujo celebrating the Alderdi Eguna in Aralar on September 25, 1977. Source: Anasagasti Archive.

The end of the Spanish dictatorship and the Basque political exile. A young couple with a baby celebrating the Alderdi Eguna in Aralar on September 25, 1977. Source: Anasagasti Archive.

Talk on the figure of Sabino Arana in Bilbao, ca. 1977. From left to right: Martin Ugalde, Arantzazu Ametzaga, Miguel Pelay Orozko. Source: Irujo-Ametzaga Archive.

Andoni de Astigarraga, "Astilarra" (1920–). Source: Anasagasti Archive.

The end of the Spanish dictatorship and the Basque political exile. From left to right: Lehendakari Jesús Ma. Leizaola and his successor, Lehendakari Carlos Garaikoetxea during the Alderdi Eguna celebrated on September 6, 1982.
Source: Anasagasti Archive.

Ninth Congress of Basque Studies celebrated in Bilbao in October 1983. From left to right: José Ma. Retana, William Douglass, and Jon Bilbao. Source: Anasagasti Archive.

Index

www.ingramcontent.com/pod-product-compliance
Lightning Source LLC
Chambersburg PA
CBHW080228270326
41926CB00020B/4184
9781935709206